For Our

Common

Home

For Our Common Home

PROCESS-RELATIONAL RESPONSES TO *LAUDATO SI'*

JOHN B. COBB, JR.

IGNAIO CASTUERA

EDITORS

WITH AN INTRODUCTION BY BILL MCKIBBEN

PROCESS CENTURY PRESS
ANOKA, MINNESOTA 2015

For Our Common Home: Process-Relational Responses to Laudato Si'

© 2015 Process Century Press

Process Century Press books are published in association with the International Process Network

Process Century Press
RiverHouse LLC
802 River Lane
Anoka, MN 55303

Cover image: Ocean Biology Processing Group at NASA's Goddard Space Flight Center <https://www.nasa.gov/image-feature/goddard/a-sky-view-of-earth-from-suomi-npp>.

Section image: NASA "Earthrise," 24 December 1968 <http://www.nasa.gov/multimedia/imagegallery/image_feature_1249.html>

Toward Ecological Civilization Series
Jeanyne B. Slettom, Series Editor

ISBN 978-1-940447-08-7
Printed in the United States of America

Series Preface:
Toward Ecological Civilization

We live in the ending of an age. But the ending of the modern period differs from the ending of previous periods, such as the classical or the medieval. The amazing achievements of modernity make it possible, even likely, that its end will also be the end of civilization, of many species, or even of the human species. At the same time, we are living in an age of new beginnings that give promise of an ecological civilization. Its emergence is marked by a growing sense of urgency and deepening awareness that the changes must go to the roots of what has led to the current threat of catastrophe.

In June 2015, the 10th Whitehead International Conference was held in Claremont, CA. Called "Seizing an Alternative: Toward an Ecological Civilization," it claimed an organic, relational, integrated, nondual, and processive conceptuality is needed, and that Alfred North Whitehead provides this in a remarkably comprehensive and rigorous way. We proposed that he could be "the philosopher of ecological civilization." With the help of those who have come to an ecological vision in other ways, the conference explored this Whiteheadian alternative, showing how it can provide the shared vision so urgently needed.

The judgment underlying this effort is that contemporary research and scholarship is still enthralled by the 17th-century view of nature articulated by Descartes and reinforced by Kant. Without freeing our minds of this objectifying and reductive understanding of the world, we are not likely to direct our actions wisely in response to the crisis to which this tradition has led us. Given the ambitious goal of replacing now dominant patterns of thought with one that would redirect us toward ecological civilization, clearly more is needed than a single conference. Fortunately, a larger platform is developing that includes the conference and looks beyond it. It is named Pando Populus in honor of the world's largest and oldest organism, an aspen grove.

As a continuation of the conference, and in support of the larger initiative of Pando Populus, we are publishing this series, appropriately named "Toward Ecological Civilization."

~John B. Cobb, Jr.

Other books in this series

Dedication

On August 1, 1536, John Calvin wrote the preface to his *Institutes,* dedicating it to the French king, Francis I. He wrote at a time of "disturbances, tumults, and contentions"—referring to the Reformation that had upended church and society. He pleaded with the king for a fair hearing, that his fellow reformers not be "reduced to the last extremity" but escape persecution.

On August 1 of 2015, not quite 500 years later, we dedicate our book to another Francis I, His Holiness the Bishop of Rome, author of the encyclical letter *Laudate Si'—On Care for Our Common Home.* Now is also a time of "disturbances, tumults, and contentions," but this time the subject is climate change, and Earth itself is on the verge of being "reduced to the last extremity." Now it is Pope Francis who writes, not to an elite ruler but to "every living person on this planet," calling for an integral ecology of environment, economy, and equality. He asks for nothing short of a complete transformation in how we teach, how we govern, how we do business, how we think, and who we include. His moral leadership has given heart to thousands of people around the globe who have labored, sometimes in despair, for the future of this planet. In gratitude for his courage, for the thoroughgoing nature of his thought, and for his irenic inclusion of all creatures ("great amd small")—we dedicate this book to him.

Contents

PART FIVE: MULTI-FAITH, MULTI-CULTURAL RESPONSES

Acknowledgements

Getting this book published so soon after the appearance of the encyclical to which it responds has required a lot of cooperation and help from a lot of people. This generosity expresses the enthusiasm of so many and their eagerness to contribute to a project that, we hope, will enliven, deepen, and extend the discussion of *Laudato si'*.

Special thanks go to the publisher of Process Century Press, Jeanyne Slettom, who has given this task top priority and provided guidance in the whole process, and to John Sweeney who provided expeditious proofreading. We are grateful to all the contributors who responded to our request for comments quickly without sacrificing quality. Andrew Schwarz and Anthony Manousos helped the co-editors prepare the material to send to Slettom in manageable condition. Bonnie Tarwater assisted with author biographies.

Preface

John B. Cobb, Jr.

If there are historians thirty years from now, they may identify the summer of 2015 as a crucial turning point in human, perhaps even planetary, history. On July 20, James Hansen reported that sea levels are rising much faster than expected, ten feet in the next fifty years. Others noted that ocean ecosystems are also collapsing faster than expected. These two phenomena combined with storms of greatly increased ferocity could cause starvation, vast movements of populations, and wars. By themselves they could bring about the end of civilization.

During the same summer, the destructiveness of the Western financial system, which gives such power to the private banks, came to a head in the instance of Greece. For decades the Western financial institutions prevented many Third World countries from becoming sovereign nations, ensuring that they served the Western economies. This summer, because the resistance of Greece could not be hidden, it became clear that the same treatment was being used on European nations as well. Sadly, at the end, resistance changed to capitulation. Once more, hopes for the survival of sovereign nations in the context of global capitalism were dashed. Greece is now governed by foreign banks.

In this same summer, Puerto Rico missed a payment on its debts. The banks have already pounced. Will it be next? Perhaps the blatancy of financial dominance in the political world will stimulate resistance.

Perhaps not. Indeed, June may be remembered as the month when the American Congress unabashedly surrendered authority over the nation's business to the transnational corporate and financial worlds. Granting Fast Track to the Transpacific Partnership and other "trade agreements" may come to symbolize the end of sovereign nations, whose coming to dominance was symbolized by the Treaty of Westphalia (1648). That treaty ended the Thirty Years War by handing the decision about the religion of a people over to political authorities.

That transfer of authority marked the end of Christendom and the beginning of the nation state as the basic unit of power and object of loyalty in the West. In June 2015, the American Congress gave the president freedom to support corporations secretly negotiating "trade agreements" binding governments at all levels. Congress now denies itself and the people of the United States any role in these agreements except rubber-stamping them. They create new courts to deal with disputes between corporations and government. This new judiciary is controlled by the corporations. That many countries have not been able to stand against the power of the financial institutions has long been clear, but in most instances this could be interpreted as surrender to the American empire. For the American government officially to transfer to the corporate world its power to govern the United States is a unique event.

The transfer of power from governments to corporations and financial institutions is not good news for the environment. Corporations are required by law to put the profits of shareholders first. The economic theories to which they normally subscribe support this policy, as does the culture of business. Governments have a mixed record, but concern for the long-term interest of their subjects is, at least, a proper interest. The excessive influence of corporations on governments has been a major cause of irrational politics.

But there is another possibility. Thus far, the corporate and financial worlds have used their power to prevent nation states from taking actions to avoid destructive climate change. They have seen such action as a threat to their profits. But the social and cultural climate is changing, and corporate leaders are not unaffected. It is possible that, with their control of what happens secured, they will decide that opposing all efforts to mitigate climate change is not in their real interest. There is a chance that, despite the discouraging results of United Nations action so far, this action will advance dramatically at the climate summit in Paris in December 2015.

Corporate leaders are human beings with consciences and concern for their descendants—and sometimes for humanity as a whole. Some of them will not want to abandon New York City to rising sea levels and intensifying storms. Hence, some support for restricting greenhouse gases may come from human concerns. But there is another reason for support. More and more people have been blaming climate disasters and other ecological problems on capitalism itself. For corporate leaders to continue to support persons who reject the scientific consensus that greenhouse gases are a major factor in climate change adds fuel to the fire of anti-capitalism. It is in the interest of the financial elite to show the world that a response to this crisis, narrowly defined, can be consistent with capitalism. We will see at Paris what they come up with.

Prospects for Paris also brightened in August when Obama used the regulatory power of the administration to reduce carbon emissions from power plants. The actual effects in the United States remain uncertain, but his official act and accompanying statement signal that Obama is positioning himself, for the first time, to give constructive leadership at a United Nations conference.

While democratic nationalism gave way to corpocracy in the West and its people were generally feeling discouraged and depressed, the East moved with new energy and confidence. In this same summer, the global political scene changed dramatically, although the American public was kept ignorant. From July 8-10, 2015, in Ufa, Bashkortostan, the 7th BRIC (Brazil, Russia, India, China, and the Union of South Africa) Summit met with the Shanghai Cooperative Organization, the Eurasian Economic Union, and both national and international development banks to plan the economic future of the Eurasian continent.

The continent will be knit together by a complex system of superfast trains. These and many other infrastructure projects will be financed by public banks. They will not need the dollar and will bypass the Breton Woods Institutions (World Bank, International Monetary Fund, and World Trade Organization). The economic dynamism emerging in the

Eurasian heartland stands in stark contrast with the economic decay of much of Europe and the stagnation of the United States. Many observed the restoration of a bi-polar world with hope, while Western authorities villainized Putin and kept their own citizens ignorant.

Western leaders were desperate to prevent their loss of global hegemony. They sought regime change in Russia by economic sanctions and undercutting its export of oil, to no avail. In the summer of 2015 they shifted focus to military threats including the use of nuclear weapons. The danger of nuclear war rose to its highest point since the Cuban missile crisis. We can hope the knowledge that nuclear war is "Mutually Assured Destruction" will deter even the fanatics who now manage our international policies from this final outrage.

These are events of great importance. But it *may be* that what happened on June 18, 2015, was ultimately more important. Certainly it is more hopeful. That day may be remembered as the turning point away from the mad dash of humanity to destroy itself, toward an awakening to common sense. On that day Pope Francis published the encyclical *Laudato si'*, proposing radical change. He gave to the critique of the present form of global capitalism new respectability and spiritual passion. He rightly located our current economic system as an expression of a world-view that must be transformed.

Of course, the elite are doing what they can to discredit Francis' ideas, especially about the economy. Within the Catholic Church the encyclical and its author will have to struggle against all the entrenched elite who seek to maintain the status quo. In the general public, the elite who still care more about their wealth and power than the well-being of their grandchildren will work to undermine the influence of the encyclical. Their control of the media and the academy is so thorough that they may succeed. If they offer concessions on greenhouse gases and minor adjustments on taxes, they will hope to use these to marginalize the discussion of alternative economic systems. But they may not succeed. Because of Pope Francis, we are in a new ballpark. From now on it will be more difficult to persuade people that "there is no alternative" (TINA).

The pope's primary audience was not the elite in the church or in the wider world. He addressed the world's people. And millions have resonated with Francis' call. Before then, we had scores of leaders working for rational change, and therefore, effectively, no leader at all. Now the cause of LIFE has a champion who cannot be ignored. Perhaps historians will note that *Laudato si'* evoked hundreds of movements and energized the 99.9999% to install political leaders who care more for human flourishing than for the corporate "bottom line." If so, the financial takeover of Greece, the surrender of national sovereignty by the American Congress, and the shift of world leadership to Eurasia will be blips on the screen of history. The process of saving our common home will begin.

A few people may still remember that from June 4-7, 2015, shortly before *Laudato si'* was publicly presented, some sixteen hundred of us met in Claremont, California, to renew and deepen our commitment to our common home at a conference called "Seizing an Alternative." They may remember the joy we felt, soon after, when the pope spoke much as we had spoken. We resolved to merge our little movement into the great one that we hope Pope Francis will lead. Perhaps a few historians may view us as significantly contributing to the great movement.

At any rate that is now the hope that guides us. This book is our first public expression of that hope. All the contributors were connected with the event. We come from many countries, view the global situation from diverse spiritual and academic orientations, and focus on diverse issues. We are united by the hope of moving the world toward an "ecological civilization" or "integral ecology."

We know that however deeply felt were our convictions as our conference ended, its success depends on what we do in its aftermath. We rejoice that many positive things are happening, and we hope for many more. This book is just one. We hope that by sharing our multifarious responses to the encyclical, *Laudato si',* we can strengthen, enliven, broaden, and deepen the discussion.

We dare to think that if Francis wants to make a real difference, we have something important to offer. Francis is calling for a new worldview, one that emphasizes the interconnection of all things. He forcefully rejects the limitation of this connectedness to human beings. He really means "all things." Some of us found such a worldview years ago in the philosophy of Alfred North Whitehead. The alternative we asked conference attendees to seize was the perspective of interrelatedness, and we offered Whitehead as a rich expression of that vision.

Francis expresses a vivid sense of urgency about transforming thought as well as action. We would like to share the results of work we have been doing for decades. At the conference we featured ecological economics and ecological agriculture. We believe that, at the theoretical level, they are ready for inclusion in an integral ecology. We have worked on many other topics, and in this book one will find not only an essay on agriculture but also others on economics, finance, law, management, technology, education, and ecclesiology. No doubt Francis will want to gather his own people to work on these and many other topics. But he shows willingness to make use of the work of others. We gladly offer to share our proposals and to work with others on their modification and development.

Francis seems eager for Christians to work together with people of other faiths and no faith in responding to the global crises. He gave some emphasis to indigenous spirituality. For decades we Whiteheadians have been engaged in such efforts. Our conference included people from other parts of the world and of diverse faiths. In this book we have spokespersons for indigenous wisdom and African religion as well as Hinduism, Buddhism, Islam, and Eastern Orthodoxy. Although at least five of the contributors are Jewish and many are Protestant, none of them focused sufficiently on Judaism or Protestantism, for me to list those traditions here.

Perhaps our greatest potential contribution to implementing Francis' vision could be in relation to China. That is where the reception of Whiteheadian thinking has gone the farthest. This is partly because it is congenial to classical Chinese thought. Although from 1919 on Chinese leaders tried to suppress traditional Chinese thought, recently they have shifted their support. Meanwhile we have worked with Chinese thinkers to develop their idea of "ecological civilization." This seems to be synonymous with the pope's "integral ecology."

The Chinese Communist Party has written into its constitution the goal of becoming an "ecological civilization." Our June2015 conference was not only the Tenth International Whitehead Conference, but also the Ninth Ecological Civilization forum, held annually in Claremont for Chinese visitors. The subtitle of this conference was "Toward an Ecological Civilization." If we want to have a global movement toward integral ecology, we cannot ignore China. Two articles in this book will clarify the perspective that is now gaining ground there.

The contributions to which I have referred so far are to be found in Parts Four and Five 2of this book. The seven sections are preceded by a poem by Pat Patterson, the poet laureate of the conference, and by an essay by Bill McKibben, the conference's keynote speaker. Part One is a collection of commentaries on the encyclical, more and less critical. To a Protestant, it is interesting to see that some of the most critical responses come from Catholics who are disappointed that the pope did not go still further. It is obvious that one threat to accepting his leadership is that he retains aspects of the Catholic natural law tradition that many find oppressive. His dismissal of the negative consequences of population growth and remnants of an anthropocentric relation to other animals are noted. But most of those who are put off by the continuance of some traditional Catholic teaching on points of this sort are prepared to work with and for the encyclical as a whole.

Part Two consists of reflections on the likely reception of the encyclical. Is it too late to make any significant difference? Will changing the way people think make a difference in their actions? Given the great variety of audiences to which it is addressed, does the encyclical succeed in reaching those most important to a significant movement?

Part Three is composed of papers that focus on what is now happening and what needs to happen. Many of those who are working hardest toward the goals of Pope Francis' encyclical are ecofeminists. The pope is clearly ensconced in the traditional Catholic world of patriarchal thought and practice. Does this mean that ecofeminists must refuse to join the efforts to bring about the integral ecology the pope seeks? The first chapter in this section is Catherine Keller's recommendation to other ecofeminists to continue their emphases and work for reform while joining in the efforts to realize the pope's goals.

The second paper in this section is a brief consideration of the new relationship between the Center for Process Studies, which organized the conference, and Religion and Ecology, the institution founded by Mary Evelyn Tucker and John Grim, which is currently the most effective organization in the field. It is our hope that many organizations that have worked quite separately in the past will see that strength can come from closer interconnection. Indeed one major effort in the followup to our conference will be to encourage people working for reform in many areas to understand the underlying commitments they share and support one another in the task of attaining an integral ecology.

Other papers describe possibilities immediately at hand. One focuses on the international movement of Transition Towns, which is open to all. Working for progress on the United Nations road to Paris is an immediate task. Promoting the "ecological footprint indicator" is another ongoing possibility. The section concludes with two longer pieces that result from extended thinking over a period of time about where our situation is and what we should now be doing.

Part Five includes multi-faith and multi-cultural essays, and gives special attention to developments in China. Part Six discusses the philosophy of the encyclical and its relation to that of Whitehead. It explains why we Whiteheadians are so enthusiastic about the pope's call. This section includes contributions by the current executive director of the International Process Network (from Bulgaria) and his already-identified successor (from the Azores). The book concludes with a call to action.

The responses were not written with this structure in mind. Many of them could fit equally well in several sections. As a reader, feel free to dip in wherever an author or topic is of particular interest. Our hope is that your commitment to joining in the effort to achieve an integral ecology will be strengthened and that you will find stimulation to make your contribution in your own voice. The change for which Francis calls is enormous. May it begin with us!

John B. Cobb, Jr.
Claremont, CA
August 2015

Editor's Note: All citations from the encyclical refer to paragraph numbers; for example, "all things are connected" (16).

NEW WAVE

Pat Patterson

In dawning light
amidst threat and extinction
where we have bid farewell
to so many once-for-all species
millions vow to stand
in courageous company
to plead plot fight
hold on to a reclaimable world
even in drought hurricane flood

Giants inspire us
life defenders visionaries
leaders ordinary people
who will not acquiesce
to sacrifice of the earth to economy
who will not countenance
a throw-away world
with its countless broken people
and dwindling species

Dream of a new earth fills the air
from the Vatican to vacant lots
becoming fertile gardens
from struggling islands in the sea
clinging to their coral reefs
from slums to hillside shacks
from tender care of children
and growing things
to magnificent schemes for reclamation

A fresh wave of life rolls on our shores
lifting us to new levels of hope
The call of Pope Francis
movements of eco-civilization
songs assemblies actions
The grand outcry of stop halt enough
we have but one earth
one incredible creation
sacred for all that live to defend
to hold to treasure

Introduction: On Care for Our Common Home

Bill McKibben

On a sprawling, multi-cultural, fractious planet, no individual can be heard by everyone. But Pope Francis comes closer than anyone else. He heads the planet's largest religious denomination and so has 1.2 billion in his actual flock, but even (maybe especially) outside the precincts of Catholicism his talent for compelling gesture has earned him the respect and affection of huge numbers of people. From his seat in Rome he addresses the developed world, much of which descended from the Christendom he represents; but from his Argentine roots he speaks to the developing world, and with firsthand knowledge of the poverty that is the fate of most on our planet.

So no one could have weighed in more usefully on the first truly planetary question we've ever faced: the rapid heating of the earth from the consumption of fossil fuels. Scientists have done a remarkable job of getting the climate message out, reaching a workable consensus on the problem in relatively short order. But national political leaders, beholden to the fossil fuel industry, have been timid at best—Barack Obama, for instance, barely mentioned the question during the 2012 election campaign. Since Francis first announced plans for an encyclical on climate change, many have eagerly awaited his words.

1

And on those narrow grounds, *Laudato si'* does not disappoint. It does indeed accomplish all the things that the extensive news coverage highlighted: insist that climate change is the fault of man; call for rapid conversion of our economies off coal, oil, and gas to renewable energy; and remind us that the first victims of the environmental crisis are the poor. (It also does Americans the service of putting climate denier politicians—a fairly rare species in the rest of the world—in a difficult place. Jeb Bush, say, was reduced to saying that in the case of climate the pope should butt out, leaving the issue to politicians. "I think religion ought to be about making us better as people," he said,[1] in words that may come back to haunt him.) The pope's contribution to the climate debate builds on the words of his predecessors—in the first few pages he quotes from John XXIII, Paul VI, John Paul II, and Benedict—but clearly for those prelates ecological questions were secondary. He also cites the path-breaking work of Bartholomew, the Orthodox leader sometimes called the "green patriarch"; others, from the Dalai Lama to Anglican Archbishop Desmond Tutu, have spoken with resonance and power on this issue as well. Still, Francis' words fall as a rock in this pond, not a pebble; they help greatly to consolidate the current momentum towards some kind of agreement at the global conference in Paris in December. He has, in effect, said that all people of good conscience need to do as he has done and make this question a key priority. The power of celebrity is the power to set the agenda, and his timing has been impeccable. On those grounds alone, *Laudato si'* stands as one of the most influential documents of recent times.

It is, therefore, remarkable to actually read the whole document and realize it is far more important even than that. In fact, it is a different animal entirely from what the media reports might lead one to believe. Instead of a narrow and focused contribution to the climate debate, *Laudato si'* turns out to be nothing less than a sweeping, radical, and highly persuasive critique of how we inhabit this planet—an ecological critique, yes, but also a moral, social, economic, and spiritual critique. In scope and tone it reminded me instantly of E. F. Schumacher's *Small is Beautiful,* and of the essays of the great American writer Wendell Berry. As with those writers, it's no use trying to categorize it as liberal or conservative; there's some of each, but it goes far deeper than our political labels allow. It's both caustic and tender, and it should unsettle every non-poor reader who opens its pages.

The ecological problems we face are not, in their origin, technological, says Francis. Instead, "a certain way of understanding human life and activity has gone awry, to the serious detriment of the world around us" (101). He is no Luddite ("who can deny the beauty of an aircraft or a skyscraper?" [103]), but he insists that we have succumbed to a "technocratic paradigm," which leads us to believe that "every increase in power means an increase in progress itself . . . as if reality, goodness and truth automatically flow from technological and economic power as such" (105). This paradigm "exalts the concept of a subject who, using logical and rational procedures, approaches and gains control over an external object" (106). Men and women, Francis writes, have from the start "intervened in nature, but for a long time this meant being in tune with and respecting the possibilities offered by the things themselves. It was a matter of receiving what nature itself allowed, as if from its own hands." In our world, however, "human beings and material objects no longer extend a friendly hand to one another; the relationship has become confrontational." With the great power that technology has afforded us, it's become "easy to accept the idea of infinite or unlimited growth, which proves so attractive to economists, financiers, and experts in technology. It is based on the lie that there is an infinite supply of the earth's goods, and this leads to the planet being squeezed dry beyond every limit" (106). The deterioration of the environment, he says, is just one sign of this "reductionism which affects every aspect of human and social life" (107). And though "the idea of promoting a different cultural paradigm . . . is nowadays inconceivable" (108), the pope is determined to try exactly that, going beyond "urgent and partial responses to the immediate problems of pollution" (111) to imagine a world where technology has been liberated to serve the poor, the rest of creation, and indeed the rest of us who pay our own price even amid our temporary prosperity. The present ecological crisis is "one small sign of the ethical, cultural, and spiritual crisis of modernity," he says (119), dangerous to the dignity of us all.

Thus girded, the pope weighs in to a variety of contemporary debates. Automation versus work, for instance. As he notes, "the orientation of the economy has favored a kind of technological process in which the costs of production are reduced by laying off workers and replacing them with machines," which is a sadness since "work is a necessity, part of the meaning of life on this earth, a path to growth" (128). The example he cites demonstrates the subtlety of his argument. Genetic modification of crops is a way, in a sense, to automate or rationalize farming. There's no "conclusive proof" that GMOs may be helpful to our bodies; there's extensive proof, however, that "following the introduction of these crops, productive land is concentrated in the hands of a few owners" who can afford the new technologies (134). Given that half the world still works as peasant farmers, this accelerates the exodus off the farm and into cardboard boxes at the margins of overcrowded capital cities; there is a need instead to "promote an economy which favors productive diversity," including "small-scale food production systems . . . be it in small agricultural parcels, in orchards and gardens, hunting and wild harvesting or local fishing" (129). (And lest anyone think this is a romantic prescription for starvation, the United Nation's Food and Agriculture Organization has in the last few years published one study after another showing that small farms in fact produce more calories per acre. Not per dollar invested—if you want to grow rich, you need a spread. But if you want to feed the world, clever peasant farming will suffice).

It's not just small versus large. The pope insists on giving priority to diverse culture over the "leveling effect on cultures" encouraged by a "consumerist vision," which diminishes the "immense variety which is the heritage of all humanity" (144). In words that are somewhat remarkable coming from the head of an institution that first set out to universalize the world, "the disappearance of a culture can be just as serious, or even more serious, than the disappearance of a species of plant or animal. The imposition of a dominant lifestyle . . . can be just as harmful as the altering of ecosystems" (145). Even more striking, in this regard, is Fancis' steadfast defense of "indigenous communities and their cultural traditions. They are not merely one minority among others, but should be the principal dialogue partners, especially when large projects affecting their land are proposed," because for them land "is a sacred space with which they need to interact if they are to maintain their identity and values" (146). Compare that attitude with, say, the oil companies now destroying aboriginal land to mine Canada's tarsands.

But the pope is just as radical, given current reality, when he insists on beauty over ugliness. When he demands the protection from development of "those common areas, visual landmarks and urban landscapes which increase our sense of belonging, or footedness, of 'feeling at home' within a city that includes us and brings us together" (151), he is not just celebrating Olmstead—he's wading into, for instance, the still-simmering Turkish revolt that began with plans to tear down Istanbul's Gezi Park and replace it with a mall and luxury apartments.

Or when he insists on giving "priority to public transportation" over private cars (153). This was the precise phrase used by Jaime Lerner, the visionary mayor of Curitiba, Brazil when a generation ago he launched the world's best transit system. His vision of Bus Rapid Transit is now spreading around the world, and it works best precisely where it most inconveniences autos, by insisting on dedicated bus lanes and the like. It makes getting around as easy for the poor as for the rich; every BRT lane is a concrete demonstration of what the Latin American liberation theologians, scorned and hounded by previous popes, once called "the preferential option for the poor."

The pope is at his most rigorous when he insists we must prefer the common good to individual advancement, for of course the world we currently inhabit really began with Ronald Reagan's and Margaret Thatcher's insistence on the opposite. (It was Thatcher who said, memorably, "there's no such thing as society. There are individual men and women and there are families" and that's that). In particular, the pope insists that "intergenerational solidarity is not optional, but rather a basic question of justice, since the world we have received also belongs to those who will follow us" (159). Think of the limitations that really believing that would place on our current activities. And think too what it would mean if we kept not only "the poor of the future in mind but also today's poor, whose life on this earth is brief and who cannot keep on waiting" (162). We literally would have to stop doing much of what we're currently doing—with poor people living on the margins in mind, and weighing the interests of dozens of future generations, would someone like to write a brief favoring, say, this summer's expansion by Shell (with permission from President Obama) of oil drilling into the newly melted waters of the Arctic? Again the only applicable word is radical.

But as I say, we've seen this kind of neither-liberal-nor-conservative radicalism before—from critics like Schumacher or Berry or, in the formulation of New York Times columnist David Brooks, other "purveyors of 1970s-style doom-mongering about technological civilization."[2] Indeed any serious effort to alter or even critique the largest trends in our civilization is now scorned, often by the theoretical left as well as the right. Brooks is united with, for instance, N+1 editor Mark Greif, who in his recent *The Age of the Crisis of Man,* heaps contempt on those who would do precisely what the pope undertakes: "Anytime your inquiries lead you to say, 'At this moment we must ask and decide *who we fundamentally are . . .*' just stop. You have begun asking the wrong analytic questions for your moment. . . . Answer, rather, the practical matters . . . and find the immediate actions necessary to achieve an aim." In other words, don't talk about individualism versus the common good; talk about some new scheme for carbon credits.

This is the "real world" talking. At least since the Buddha, a line of spiritual leaders has offered a reasonably coherent and remarkably similar critique of who we are and how we live. The greatest of those critics was perhaps Jesus, but the line continues through Francis's great namesake, and through Thoreau, and Gandhi, and a million others. Mostly, of course, we've paid them devoted lip service and gone on living largely as before. We've come close to change—opinion surveys at the end of the epochal 1970s, for instance, showed 30 percent of Americans were 'pro-growth,' 31 percent 'anti-growth,' and 39 percent 'highly uncertain,' and President Carter held a White House reception for Schumacher. But Reagan's election resolved that tension in the usual way, and the progress we've made, before and since, has been technological, not moral; people have been pulled from poverty by expansion, not by solidarity. The question is whether the present moment is actually any different, or whether the pope's words will fall as seeds on rocky ground.

If there's a difference this time, it's that we seem to have actually reached the edge of the precipice. Schumacher and the visionaries of the 70s imagined that the limits to growth were a little further off, and offered us strong warning, which we didn't heed. So now we've begun to plunge.

Take water, which the pope addresses at length. We probably should not need his words to know that "access to safe drinkable water is a basic and universal human right, since it is essential to human survival" (30). We all know it should not be wasted, and yet waste it we continue to do because doing so is beneficial to the rich and powerful: for instance, the insurance companies that have planted enormous almond groves across California in recent years even as water supplies have started to shrink, or the agribusiness planters who continue to draw down the aquifers of the Midwest. In the same week that the pope's encyclical emerged, a huge new study showed that those aquifers were now overdrawn in regions that provide food for 2 billion people—the data comes from satellites measuring the earth's gravitational field, which means that the water losses are so large they're affecting the planet on that scale.[3] In the American West alone, the drought has become so deep that last year those satellites show the evaporation of 63 trillion gallons of groundwater, weighing 250 billion tons, enough weight that the Sierra Nevada mountains jumped measurably skywards.[4]

Or take biodiversity, where the pope rightly notes that "caring for ecosystems demands far-sightedness, since no one looking for quick and easy profit is truly interested in their preservation." But that alarm sounds somewhat louder when, in the same week as the encyclical, a new study in a prestigious journal found that extinctions were now happening at 114 times the normal background rate, and that the planet's "sixth mass extinction is already underway."[5] Given that empirical data, the pope's rare flicker of real anger—"who turned the wonderworld of the seas into underwater cemeteries bereft of color and life" (41) reads like more than boilerplate.

Francis' profound sadness about the inequality among people, and the toll it exacts on the poor, is also undergirded by remarkable new data that separates it from earlier critiques. The data shows right now that inequality is reaching almost absurd heights: for instance, the six heirs to the Walmart fortune have more assets than the bottom 42% of all Americans combined, or the two Koch brothers (together the richest man on the planet) have plans to spend more than the Republicans or the Democrats on the next federal election. If you want to understand why, say, the Occupy movement, or the early surge towards Bernie Sanders caught the usual political analysts by surprise, consider those facts. (And if you want to understand the surprise, the pope suggests that "many professionals, opinion makers, communications media and centers and power, being located in affluent urban areas, are far removed from the poor with little direct contact with their problems" [49].)

Above all, the empirical data about climate change make it clear that the moment is ripe for this encyclical. The long line of brown-robed gurus, of whom Francis is the latest, now marches next to a line of scientists in lab coats; instead of scriptures, the physicists and chemists clutch the latest printouts from their computer models, but the two ways of knowing seem to be converging on the same point. So far we've melted most of the sea ice in the summer Arctic, made the oceans 30% more acidic, and started the apparently irreversible slide of the west Antarctic ice sheet into the surrounding ocean. We are, to put it another way, systematically breaking the largest physical features on the planet, and we are doing it with rapid speed.

Given that, who's the realist? The pope, with his insistence that we need a rapid cultural transformation, or Brooks, speaking for the complacent, with his insistence that "over the long haul both people and nature are better off with technological progress." The point is, *there no longer is any long haul.* Those who speak, in the pope's words, the language of "nonchalant resignation or blind confidence in technical solutions" no longer have a leg to stand on. The "magical conception of the market" (190) has not, ultimately, done what Reagan promised; instead it's raised, for the first time, the very real specter of wholesale planetary destruction, of change that will be measured in geological time.

In that crisis, we can't afford any more years of false solutions that comfort the status quo. Brooks, for instance, makes the centerpiece of his attack on the encyclical the notion that the existing technocratic paradigm is, happily, expanding fracking, because burning the natural gas it brings up produces less carbon than burning coal. This is scientifically obtuse (an emerging body of evidence shows that fracking instead liberates vast quantities of methane, an even more potent greenhouse gas) and in any event the extent of the damage we've already done to the climate means we no longer have room for slightly less damaging fossil fuels; we simply have to make the leap to renewable power. And the good news is, that's entirely possible. Thanks to the engineers whose creativity the pope celebrates, we've watched the price of solar panels fall 75 percent in the last six years alone. They're now cheap enough that a vast effort, rooted both in pragmatic physics and social solidarity, could ensure before the decade was out that not a hut or hovel on the planet's surface lacked access to energy, something that the fossil fuel status quo has failed to achieve in 200 years. It would utilize small-scale entrepreneurs of just the sort the pope has in mind when he describes the dignity of work, but it would mean a very different world. Instead of centralized power in a few hands, the earth would draw its energy from a widely diffused and much more democratic grid. And building it in time would require aid to the poorest nations to jumpstart the transition. It would require, for instance, a world much like the one the pope envisions, where concern for the poor counts as much as, in Brooks' sad words, the "low motivations of people as they actually are."

Brooks, Reagan, Thatcher, summon the worst in us and assume that will eventually solve our problems. Pope Francis, in a moment of great crisis, speaks instead to who we could be. As the data suggest, this may be the only option we have left.

References

1. <http://www.politico.com/story/2015/06/jeb-bush-knocks-pope-on-climate-change-push-119084.html>.

2. <http://www.nytimes.com/2015/06/23/opinion/fracking-and-the-franciscans.html?_r=0>.

3. <http://www.nytimes.com/2015/06/26/science/worlds-aquifers-losing-replenishment-race-researchers-say.html>.

4. <http://www.washingtonpost.com/news/morning-mix/wp/2014/08/28/californias-drought-what-losing-63-million-gallons-of-water-looks-like/>.

5. <http://www.salon.com/2015/06/22/the_sixth_extinction_is_here_earths_species_are_disappearing_at_114_times_the_normal_rate/>.

[Editor's note: A shorter version of this article appeared in the New York Review of Books as "Pope Francis: The Cry of the Earth," June 18, 2015.]

PART
ONE

Commentaries

A 21ˢᵗ Century Manifesto
for Earth Democracy

Vandana Shiva

Most of the press reports of Pope Francis' encyclical that appeared before its formal launch reduced this path-breaking document with 246 paragraphs on the contemporary ecological and human crises to the four paragraphs on climate change (23-26). But *Laudato si'* is much wider and much deeper.

It is first of all a call for a change in consciousness and a worldview that differs from the entrenched paradigm of domination over nature and its destruction, to one where we see the Earth as our Mother, as our common home.

Laudato opens with St. Francis' prayer—"Praise be to you my Lord, through our sister, Mother Earth, who sustains and governs us, and who produces various fruits with colored flowers and herbs."

This resonates so deeply with the Indian philosophy of Vasudhaiv Kutumkan, the Earth Family. It resonates with the contemporary movement for the Rights of Mother Earth. It resonates with cultures and faiths across the world.

The encyclical is an invitation to "a new dialogue about how we are shaping the future of the planet" (14) and this includes biodiversity, air, water, oceans. It is clear that "to protect our common home we need to bring the whole family together" (13).

The encyclical goes on to say: "This sister now cries out to us because of the harm we have inflicted on her by our irresponsible use and abuse of the goods with which God has endowed her. We have come to see ourselves as her lords and masters, entitled to plunder her at will. The violence present in our hearts, wounded by sin, is also reflected in the soil, in the water, in the air, and in all forms of life" (2).

Soil is referred to frequently, including the contributions of soil and land degradation and of deforestation to climate change. And the pope reminds us that "we have forgotten that we ourselves are dust of the earth" (Gen 2:7). Navdanya's manifesto Terra Viva, released at the Expo in the Year of Soil is a celebration of Soil as the basis of our lives, of "humus" as the root of "human." We are the soil.

The encyclical is also very critical of the privatization of water and of the idea that lifeforms are just mines of genes useful to business. "It is not enough . . . to think of different species merely as potential 'resources' to be exploited, while overlooking the fact that they have value in themselves" (33). The intrinsic worth of all beings and all biodiversity is the ethics on which Navdanya is founded. That is why we say there should be "No patents on Seed " and "No patents on Life."

Laudato si' is cautious on the question of GMOs, but does point to the GMO threats to small farmers. And it indicates that through biotechnology and knowledge related to DNA, a handful of interests are controlling the fate of the Earth and humanity. "It is extremely risky for a small part of humanity to have control" (104).

Everything that will shape our freedom and survival is addressed in the encyclical. "Our freedom fades when it is handed over to the blind forces of the unconscious, of immediate needs, of self-interest, and of violence" (105).

Among the blind forces of the unconscious are the ideas of infinite, unlimited growth, of technological fundamentalism without precaution, assessment and responsibility, and of anthropocentrism.

"The technological mind sees nature as an insensate order, as a cold body of facts, as a mere 'given,' an object of utility, as raw material to be hammered out into useful shape. The intrinsic dignity of the world is thus compromised" (115)

Nature is not dead matter; she is alive. And when we destroy nature, she can destroy us. Our greed, our arrogance, blind us to this basic reality that women, small farmers, and indigenous cultures have understood. Diverse movements will be empowered by the encyclical. The only ones who are threatened are those who would like to continue their effort to establish their empire over the entire planet and the earth's resources, privatizing the commons, pushing free trade agreements like TPP (Trans Pacific Partnership) and TTIP (Transatlantic Trade and Investment Partnership), destroying democracy and people's rights, and destroying the earth that sustains us. And stupidly and recklessly, they call this destruction "economy." But economy is derived from "Oikos," our home, and refers to management of our common home, the theme of the encyclical. The selfish and narrow-minded who have commented that the pope should not interfere in the economy have deliberately forgotten, or distorted, what the economy is. The encyclical helps us remember that it is about love and care, not exploitation, greed, and destruction.

The encyclical observes that "the degree of human intervention, often in the service of business interests and consumerism, is actually making our earth less rich and beautiful, ever more limited and grey" (34).

It is by bringing beauty, true well-being, and the joy of living in harmony with nature to the center of human concern that the encyclical awakens our deeper humanity and consciousness. Being human is not worshipping the "god of money," or tools of technology, or the myth of progress defined as the conquest of nature and people.

Being human is to be deeply aware of all beings who share this beautiful and precious home with us. *Laudato si'* is based on integral ecology—the interconnectedness of ecology, society, and economy. This is the interconnectedness we tried to explore in Terra Viva.

In integral ecology, sustainability and social justice are inseparable. As the encyclical states, "a truly ecological approach becomes a social approach: it must integrate questions of justice in debates on the environment, so as to heal both the cry of the earth and the cry of the poor" (49).

This for me is Earth Democracy.

Pope Francis' Encyclical on
Care for Creation

Rosemary Radford Ruether

Pope Francis' encyclical on *Care for Our Common Home,* issued June 18, 2015, explores the radical edges of the issue of responsibility for creation in the light of current damage to nature by modern culture and technology. Francis cites important precedents of encyclicals on creation by his papal predecessors, Paul VI (1963-78), John Paul II (1978-2000) and Benedict XVI (2005-2013), all of whom spoke strongly on ecological concerns. Francis also lifts up the statements of his colleague in the leadership of the Greek Orthodox Church, Ecumenical Patriarch Bartholomew, who has spoken often and passionately of his concern for creation. For Patriarch Bartholomew, "to commit a crime against the natural world is a sin against ourselves and a sin against God" (8).

Francis particularly lifts up his namesake, Francis of Assisi, as the patron of ecological theology. Francis speaks of the saint as "a mystic and a pilgrim who lived in simplicity and wonderful harmony with God, with others, with nature and with himself. He shows just how inseparable the bond is between concern for nature, justice for the poor, commitment to society and interior peace" (10). Citing the 1960 encyclical of Pope John XXIII, *Pacem in Terris,* which was addressed not just to the Catholic Church, but to "all men and women of good will,"

16

Francis addresses his encyclical on creation to "every person living on this planet" (3). All human beings are called to be concerned for the well-being of creation. As Francis puts it, "I would like to enter into dialogue with all people about our common home" (3). He cites the bishops of South Africa as saying, "Everyone's talents and involvement are needed to redress the damage caused by human abuse of God's creation" (14).

Pope Francis then turns to what is happening to the earth, how the land and oceans are being polluted, and how the devastation to the planet particularly affects the poorest humans. Listing key themes of his encyclical, Francis says, "I will point to the intimate relationship between the poor and the fragility of the planet, the conviction that everything in the world is connected, the critique of new paradigms and forms of power derived from technology, the call to seek other ways of understanding economy and progress, the value proper to each creature, the human meaning of ecology, the need for forthright and honest debate, the serious responsibility of international and local policy, the throwaway culture and the proposal of a new lifestyle" (16).

Francis points particularly to the warming of the climate system as the global effect of human activity on the planet. Although he acknowledges that there may be other factors that are causing this warming, such as volcanic activity, yet he insists that human activity is its primary cause. "Scientific studies indicate that most global warming in recent decades is due to the great concentration of greenhouse gases (carbon dioxide, methane, nitrogen oxides and others) released mainly as a result of human activity. Concentrated in the atmosphere, these gases do not allow the warmth of the sun's rays reflected by the earth to be dispersed in space. The problem is aggravated by a model of development based on the intensive use of fossil fuels, which is the heart of the worldwide energy system" (23). For those conservatives in the United States and elsewhere who have objected to the pope pronouncing on technological and scientific subjects, where they presume him to be incompetent since he is a pastor, it is useful to realize that Francis in fact was trained in science and is quite knowledgeable in this field.

Francis analyses climate change in detail as a global problem with "grave implications, environmental, social, economic, political and for the distribution of goods" (25). He discusses the depletion of natural resources, particularly that of water. He points to the fact that water poverty particularly affects Africa where there is widespread lack of access to safe drinking water. This is worsened by the growing pattern of privatizing water, turning it into a commodity subject to the laws of the market. There is a general loss of biodiversity, the loss of woodlands and forests with the accompanying loss of many species needed for food and medicine. Not only the disappearance of larger mammals and birds, but many microorganisms necessary for the good functioning of ecosystems. This includes those "richly biodiverse lungs of our planet" (38), the Amazon and the Congo basins, and the great aquifers and glaciers, the ecosystems of tropical forests, the oceans, and tropical seas. These include the coral reefs which shelter millions of species. Finally, there is the decline of human life and the breakdown of society. Here Francis returns to his key theme that the deterioration of the environment particularly affects the poor. He shows in detail how poor communities are impoverished by the destruction of the environment, such as communities that depend on fishing when the waters on which they depend are polluted. This affects entire communities and even entire countries.

With poetic eloquence, Francis responds: "These situations have caused sister earth, along with the abandoned of our world, to cry out, pleading that we take another course. Never have we so hurt and mistreated our common home as we have in the last two hundred years. Yet we are called to be instruments of God, of Father, so that our planet might be what he desired when he created it and correspond to his plan for peace, beauty and fullness" (53). For Francis the issue is that "we still lack the culture needed to confront this crisis" (53). This lack of culture is reflected in the remarkably weak responses to this crisis in international meetings. This shows how international responses have been subject to agents of political and technological interests who refuse to face up to the radical issues involved. As Francis put it, "The most one can expect is superficial rhetoric, sporadic acts of philanthropy, and perfunctory expressions of concern for the environment, whereas any genuine attempts by groups within society to introduce change is viewed as a nuisance based on romantic illusion or an obstacle to be circumvented" (32). The pope also acknowledges that there are vehement differences of opinion of these issues, and it is difficult to have a unified conversation about what to do.

Having analyzed the damage to the earth and the lack of adequate response locally and internationally, Francis seeks to create a new culture for dealing with these issues by appealing to a "gospel of Creation." All human beings are created in the image of God. All creation was created "very good." Human dominion over creation is given for the purpose of caring for creation and bringing it to its fulfillment as "very good." This is not intended to be a domination that allows human to exploit creation, much less to degrade it. Not just humans, but all creatures in nature have value in their selves.

Human life is grounded in three fundamental and closely interrelated relationships, with God, with our neighbor, and with the earth itself. These three vital relationships have been broken, outwardly and within us. This rupture is sin. The harmony between the Creator, humanity, and creation as a whole has been disrupted by our presumption to take the place of God and refusing to accept our creaturely limitations. This is expressed in the distortion of dominion as a mandate to "till the earth and keep it" into domination. The original harmonious relationship between humanity with its neighbors and with nature was distorted into conflict. This is expressed in wars, violence and abuse, the abandonment of the most vulnerable and attacks on nature.

The earth is God's, not ours. We are called to repentance and conversion from our exploitation of one another and of the earth, into a restored attitude of care for one another and a process of bringing our relationships into that love and fulfillment in goodness which is our true mandate. Humans must respect the particular goodness of every creature and avoid distorted abuse in our relations with fellow humans and with the earth. We are called to facilitate the fulfillment of creation in that goodness which is our and creation's calling, culminating in that glorification of all things in the resurrection.

The ultimate destiny of the universe is in the fullness of God which has already been attained in the risen Christ. The ultimate purpose of all creatures, human and nonhuman, is not found in us humans. Rather, as Francis puts it, "all creatures are moving forward with us and through us toward a common point of arrival, which is God, in that transcendent fullness where the risen Christ embraces and illumines all things. Human beings, endowed with intelligence and love, and drawn by the fullness of Christ, are called to lead all creatures back to their Creator" (53).

Here Francis makes a notable development of the Christian hope for final resurrection. Traditionally the resurrection from the dead was seen as limited to humans; for many, to just their religious community of humans. Francis' theology of creation culminates in a resurrected glory that includes all of creation.

To sum up Francs' perspective in this remarkable encyclical: the ecological crisis is not "natural," or the result of some flaws in nature, but reflects human sin; the exploitation of nature by humans, and the misuse of human power, especially by the richest and most powerful sector of humans. Technology needs to be guided by ethics. Local cultures should be respected, especially indigenous cultures that have values of harmony with and care for creation. Religions need to dialogue with each other, as well as with sciences about the care for creation and the common good.

Francis concludes by calling for an ecological conversion of humanity. This conversion needs to happen on the level of individuals and local communities, but also globally. Not just humans, but all creation is incarnational. All created things manifest the divine. God is present in the whole universe. Humans need to convert their consciousness and way of life to the care for the creation, leading it and themselves to that fulfillment in resurrected glory in union with God

Thoughts on Pope Francis' *Laudato Si'*

Herman Daly

As a Protestant Christian my devotion to the Catholic Church has been rather minimal, based largely on respect for early church history and for love of an aunt who was a nun. In recent times the Catholic Church's opposition to birth control, plus the pedophile and cover-up scandals, further alienated me. Like many others I first viewed Pope Francis as perhaps a breath of fresh air, but little more. After reading his encyclical on environment and justice, dare I hope that what I considered merely "fresh air" could actually be the wind of Pentecost filling the Church anew with the Spirit? Maybe. At a minimum he has given us a more truthful, informed, and courageous analysis of the environmental and moral crisis than have our secular political leaders.

True, the important question of population was conspicuous by its near absence. In an earlier offhand remark, however, Francis said that Catholics "don't need to breed like rabbits," and pointed to the Church's doctrine of responsible parenthood. Perhaps he will follow up on that in a future encyclical. In any case, most lay Catholics have for some time stopped listening to popes on contraception. The popular attitude is expressed in a cartoon showing an Italian mamma wagging her finger at the pontiff and saying, *"You no playa da game; you no maka da rules."* Discussing population would not have changed realities, and would have aroused official opposition and distracted attention from the major

21

points of the encyclical. So I will follow Francis' politic example and put the population question aside, but with a reference to historian John T. Noonan, Jr.'s classic book, *Contraception*,[1] which sorts out the history of doctrine on this issue.

The big ideas of the encyclical are Creation care and justice, and the failure of our technocratic growth economy to provide either justice or care for Creation. Also discussed is the integration of science and religion as necessary, though different, avenues to truth. And yes, the pope supports the scientific consensus on the reality of climate change, but, media monomania to the contrary, the encyclical is about far more than that.[2]

Francis' voice is, of course, not the first to come from Christians in defense of Creation. In addition to his ancient namesake from Assisi, Francis also recognized Ecumenical Patriarch Bartholomew of the Eastern Orthodox Church who has, for two decades now, been organizing conferences and speaking out in defense of rivers and oceans, including the Black Sea. The Orthodox Church lost a generation of believers to Communistic atheism but is gaining back many young people attracted to the theology of Creation and the actions it inspires. Liberal mainline Protestant Christians and, more recently, conservative Evangelicals have also found their ecological conscience. So Francis' encyclical would seem to be a capstone that unifies the main divisions of Christianity on at least the fundamental recognition that we have a shamefully neglected duty to care for the Earth out of which we evolved and to share the Earth's life support more equitably with each other, with the future, and with other creatures. Many atheists also agree, while claiming that their agreement owes nothing to Judeo-Christian tradition. That is historically questionable, but their support is welcome nonetheless.

This theology of Creation should not be confused with the evolution-denying, anti-science views of some Christian biblical literalists (confusingly called "Creationists" rather than "literalists"). Mankind's duty to care for Creation, through which humans have evolved to reflect at least the faint image of their Creator, conflicts headlong with the current dominant idolatry of growthism and technological Gnosticism. The idea of duty to care for Creation also conflicts with the materialist determinism of neo-Darwinist fundamentalists who see "Creation" as the random result of multiplying infinitesimal probabilities by an infinite number of trials. The policy implication of determinism (even if stochastic) is that purposeful policy is illusory, both practically and morally. Creation care is also incompatible with the big lie that sharing the Earth's limited resources is unnecessary because economic growth will make us all rich. Francis calls this magical thinking. He skates fairly close to the idea of steady-state economics, of qualitative development without quantitative growth in scale, although this concept is not specifically considered. Consider his paragraph 193:

> In any event, if in some cases sustainable development were to involve new forms of growth, then in other cases, given the insatiable and irresponsible growth produced over many decades, we need also to think of containing growth by setting some reasonable limits and even retracing our steps before it is too late. We know how unsustainable is the behaviour of those who constantly consume and destroy, while others are not yet able to live in a way worthy of their human dignity. That is why the time has come to accept decreased growth in some parts of the world, in order to provide resources for other places to experience healthy growth.

In the last sentence "decreased growth" seems an inexact English translation from the Spanish version "decrecimiento," or the Italian version "decrescita" (likely the original languages of the document), which should be translated as "degrowth" or negative growth, which is of course stronger than "decreased growth."[3]

Laudato si' is already receiving both strong support and resistance. The resistance testifies to the radical nature of Francis' renewal of the basic doctrine of the Earth and cosmos as God's Creation. Pope Francis will be known by the enemies this encyclical makes for him, and these enemies may well be his strength. So far in the U.S. they are not an impressive lot: the Heartland Institute, Jeb Bush, Senator James Inhofe, Rush Limbaugh, Rick Santorum, and others. Unfortunately they represent billions in special-interest money and have a big corporate media megaphone. The encyclical calls out the opponents and forces them to defend themselves. To give them the benefit of the doubt, they may really think that Francis is rendering to God what actually belongs to Caesar's oligarchy. But neither Caesar, nor the market, nor technology created us, nor the Earth that sustains us. Thanks to Francis for making that very clear when so many are denying it, either explicitly or implicitly.

Endnotes

1. John T. Noonan, Jr., *Contraception: A History of its Treatment by the Catholic Theologians and Canonists,* Belknap Press, 1986. Noonan demonstrates the lack of a biblical basis for opposition to contraception, as well as the origins of church doctrine in secular Roman law, which was absorbed into canon law. The ancient Roman meaning of "proletariat" was "the lowest class, poor and exempt from taxes, and useful to the republic mainly for the procreation of children." Clearly contraception was not indicated for them, although tolerated for patricians. This literal meaning of proletariat as the prolific class was lost when Marx redefined the word to mean "non owners of the means of production." But the Malthusian connection with overpopulation and cheap labor has remained real, even if downplayed by Marxists as well as Catholics.

2. The pope's condemnation of carbon trading reflects a common mis-understanding of the cap-auction-trade policy, unfortunately shared by some leading climate scientists. See Joseph Heath, "Pope Francis' Climate Error," *New York Times,* 19 June 2015.

3. Thanks to Joan Martinez-Alier for pointing this out.

The Postmodern Pope

David Ray Griffin

Although Pope Francis is beloved around the world, his encyclical has been denounced in many circles. Critics have said that he should leave climate change to scientists; that his fears of destruction from global warming are exaggerated; and that he is anti-technological, even anti-modern.[1]

However, climate scientists say that the encyclical's science is sound; that its warnings are, if anything, understated; and that "science and technology are wonderful products of a God-given human creativity."[2]

The reason for attacks on the encyclical

The real reason for antagonism to the pope's encyclical is that it challenges the real religion of our age, which is what Francis calls "market fundamentalism," based on a "deified market." As one insightful commentator put it, the encyclical is "a radical . . . attack on the logic of the market and consumerism."[3]

The antagonism to the pope's critique of the market primarily involves the most profitable product in the market, fossil fuels. The pope says that the continued use of these fuels will result in "extraordinary climate change and an unprecedented destruction of ecosystems" (24). Accordingly, the use of fossil fuels "needs to be progressively replaced without delay" (165).

25

The attempt to discredit the pope's message has been led by individuals and organizations who rely on funding from fossil fuel corporations: Republican politicians, fossil-fuel lobbyists, and think tanks devoted to climate denial.[4]

The charge that Pope Francis is anti-modern was leveled by R. R. Reno, the editor of *First Things*. But the pope is more accurately called *postmodern*. Confusingly, Reno added this term to his list of charges against the pope, although Francis himself had used this term negatively, describing the postmodern world as one of "rampant individualism" (162).

However, the label "postmodernism" is used positively by some thinkers, especially Whiteheadians. Far from being anti-modern or restricting themselves to deconstruction, constructive postmodernists seek to retain the best elements of modernity while overcoming its destructive elements.[5]

Pope Francis as constructive postmodernist

In the remainder of this essay, I lift up elements in the pope's encyclical that parallel themes in constructive postmodernism.

- Climate change is most fundamentally a matter not of economics but of morality.

- Fundamental to climate morality is protecting human rights. For example, "access to safe drinkable water is a basic and universal human right" (30). This right should not be trumped by those who claim that they have the right to sell water for profit.

- Even more inclusively, climate morality is a commitment to the common good. "Society as a whole, and the state in particular, are obliged to defend and promote the common good" (157), and "[t[he climate is a common good, belonging to all and meant for all" (23).

- The common good is most fundamentally, as the title of the encyclical indicates, "Our Common Home." As George Lakoff has observed, "This simple phrase establishes the most important frame right from the start. Using the metaphor of the *'Earth as*

Home,' [Pope Francis] triggers a frame in which all the people of the *world are a family*, living in a common home."[6]

- Moreover, "The notion of the common good also extends to future generations." Indeed, "Intergenerational solidarity is not optional, but rather a basic question of justice, since the world we have received also belongs to those who will follow us" (159).

- Morality, furthermore, is not limited to our respect for human beings, present and future. Rather, all other species "have value in themselves," and "[e]ach organism, as a creature of God, is good and admirable in itself" (140).

- "It cannot be emphasized enough how everything is interconnected"—that "everything in the world is connected" (16), that "all creatures are connected" (42).

- Because of this interconnectedness, ecology must be an "integral ecology," which would combine respect for the intrinsic value of all species with protecting nature for future generations and overcoming poverty. The economy would not accept "every advance in technology with a view to profit, without concern for its potentially negative impact on human beings" (109) and politics would not allow special economic interests to trump the common good. An integral ecology would also include "reflecting on our lifestyle and our ideals, and contemplating the Creator who lives among us and surrounds us" (225).

- With regard to technological and economic development in particular, it cannot be considered progress if it "does not leave in its wake a better world and an integrally higher quality of life" (194).

- With regard to the Creator: Although Francis uses the traditional language of the "all-powerful God," he says: "The universe did not emerge as the result of arbitrary omnipotence" (77). Rather, "God's love is the fundamental moving force in all created things." Moreover, sounding even more like a process theist, the pope says: "The *Spirit of God has filled the universe with possibilities* and therefore, from the very heart of things, something new can always emerge" (80).

- The pope also does not portray Christianity as the only authentic and worthwhile religion. Rather, he speaks of religions in the plural, encouraging "religions to dialogue among themselves for the sake of protecting nature, defending the poor, and building networks of respect and fraternity" (201).

- Finally, not counting on divine omnipotence to save the planet from ecological disaster, Pope Francis says: "Global regulatory norms are needed to impose obligations and prevent unacceptable actions" (173). What is needed, he adds, is "an agreement on systems of governance for the whole range of so-called 'global commons'" (174). In fact, like his predecessor Pope John XXIII, Pope Francis says that "there is urgent need of a true world political authority" (175).

Conclusion

Although there are respects in which Pope Francis' encyclical cannot be affirmed by process thinkers, its central message can be supported with enthusiasm.

Endnotes

1. Matt Taibbi, "Why Are So Many Pundits Trashing the Pope? *Rolling Stone,* 27 June 2015; Lindsay Abrams, "David Brooks' Baffling Assessment of the Pope's Encyclical: Too Much Christian Love," *Salon,* 23 June 2015; R. R. Reno, "The Return of Catholic Anti-Modernism," *Frst Things,* 18 June 2015.

2. Emily Atkin, "What Did Actual Scientists Think of the Pope's Climate Encyclical?" *Climate Progress,* 18 June 2015; "Encyclical Letter Laudato si' of the Holy Father Francis on Care for Our Common Home."

3. Steffen Böhm "Pope's Climate Letter is a Radical Attack on the Logic of the Market," *The Conversation,* 18 June 2015.

4. On the efforts by the fossil fuel corporations to undermine climate science, see Chapter 11, "Climate Change Denial," in David Ray Griffin, *Unprecedented: Can Civilization Survive the CO2 Crisis?* (Clarity Press, 2015).

5. See David Ray Griffin, ed., *Spirituality and Society: Postmodern Visions* (SUNY Series in Constructive Postmodern Thought), SUNY Press, 1988.

6. George Lakoff, "Pope Francis Gets the Moral Framing Right," *Reader Supported News,* 27 June 2015.

A Liberal, Catholic Response

Daniel A. Dombrowski

The purpose of the following remarks is both to indicate the tremendous debt that is owed to the current pope for his thoughtful encyclical *Laudato si'* and to indicate the important work that still needs to occur in response to the environmental problems discussed by Pope Francis.

The greatest strength of the document, as I see things, is the close connection he draws between the current environmental crisis and unjust institutions, both political and economic. That is, there is a tendency for the natural environment and the human environment to deteriorate together. By unreflectively accepting current economic institutions we have paved the way for exploitation of the natural world. This one-dimensional mindset erodes a sense of the common good, such that even so fundamental a reality as water has been privatized and commodified along with almost everything else.

Francis' label for his own view is "integral ecology." The integration he has in mind, however, involves not only that careful attention be paid to the link between environmental problems and political/economic problems that militate against the Catholic Church's preferential option for the poor, but also the link between both of these and the need for an integral humanism or a renewed commitment to human fulfillment. What he has in mind is a thoroughgoing critique of the internal emptiness in the lives of postmodern people that drives them toward a mindless consumerism. Francis instead encourages pursuit of a simple life based on a contemporary, reflective *askesis* that is not so much body-hating as nature-loving.

From the above it should be clear that our way out of the contemporary environmental crises is not to be found in a blind confidence in technological solutions, in that the underlying problems are philosophical or spiritual. Francis is to be commended for admitting that in the past Christianity itself played into the hands of this spiritual crisis by leaning in the direction of anthropocentrism. But the *imago Dei* hypothesis does not necessarily lead to an anthropocentric dominion over nature. To be made in the image of God is actually a burden in that we are called to develop ecological virtues in addition to the normal moral virtues like moderation and courage.

Several traditional views are given new life by Francis in the context of this encyclical. One of these is the idea that a defensible right to property is not absolute, such that ownership rights to land are always subservient to the common good, especially to the needs of the poorest. Another is the Aristotelian/Thomistic idea of hylomorphism, which counteracts the disparaging of the body and nature that is encouraged by dualistic versions of religious belief. On the hylomorphist view, human beings are mindbodies or soulbodies, to coin some words that indicate the close connection between spirituality and embodiment in an incarnational religion like Christianity. Yet another idea is the emphasis on diachronic justice across generations, such that present consumption patterns can be seen as unjust treatments of human beings yet to be born. Finally, Francis is adamant that political corruption, which is odious under normal circumstances, is especially bothersome when it exacerbates environmental degradation and grinding poverty.

All of the above is meant to highlight the commendable features of Francis' view. Given the persuasive power of his office, environmentalists, whatever their religious or nonreligious beliefs may be, should be grateful for such a nuanced yet forceful statement in favor of immediate environmental action. Despite all of the positive features of his view, however, there are at least two areas that are problematic and that are in need of the sort of dialectical engagement encouraged by Francis himself.

First, there is an unresolved tension regarding nonhuman animals (hereafter: animals) in the encyclical. On the one hand, Francis is clear that *all* creatures should be loved and respected (42), hence we ought not to mistreat animals, in particular (92). This leads to an apparent condemnation by Francis of the practice of taking the lives of certain animals for their fur (123). That is, we should not cause animals to suffer or die "needlessly" (130). On the other hand, Francis permits us to use animals in order to provide for our "necessities" (130). Unfortunately, these necessities are not specified by Francis, nor does he tell us when the suffering and death we inflict on animals is needless. Hence, it seems that Francis is opposed to taking the lives of animals only if they are members of endangered species (123). It is thus not surprising that at no point does he extol the virtues of a vegetarian or vegan diet, despite the fact that switching to such a diet has a more beneficial environmental effect than switching from driving an SUV to riding a bicycle (e.g., it takes between fifteen to twenty pounds of grain fed to a cow to get one pound of beef). In fact, at one point (22) he indicates that herbivores are for the sake of carnivores (like us?). Species have value in themselves (Francis thinks that the extinction of an animal species is analogous to the extinction of a culture—145), but it is by no means clear in Francis if individual members of animal species have enough intrinsic value in order to be morally considerable (33).

Although animals are not *completely* subordinated to us (69), they are in fact in a condition of subordination. Quite frankly, I do not know what to make of Francis' criticism of anthropocentrism. It is clear that he is a theocentrist in that his critique of anthropocentrism is meant to have us consider the perfect being who is superior to us. But it is not clear if his critique of anthropocentrism has any notable implications for those "beneath" us (68, 115-16). That is, I think that Francis is more of an anthropocentrist than he is willing to admit.

If Francis is correct, as I think he is, that anthropocentrism involves both selfishness and moral arbitrariness, then getting clear about the implications of anthropocentrism for those sentient beings closest to us in the natural world is no trivial matter. In Francis' defense it can be said that he exhibits obvious care for other living beings (211), and he even accentuates Luke 12:6, where not even a single bird is forgotten (221), unless, of course, the bird is raised for the table. Human beings *do* need to eat, but it is by no means clear that they need to do so at the expense of sentient animals.

Second, Francis sidesteps the problem of overpopulation of human beings. Although he is to be commended for pointing out that one-third of all the food produced worldwide is eventually discarded (50), he is a bit glib in assuming that if we lived more simply and did not waste food (including meat), that a population of six billion people (soon to be twelve billion, then fifteen billion, etc.) is not in itself a problem. Once again, I think that Francis is more of an anthropocentrist than he is willing to admit. By contrast, on my view, which is consonant with the views of most environmental scientists, it is possible to have too much of a good (human) thing.

The issue of human population is obviously connected to Francis' attitude toward women, in general, and toward reproductive health issues, in particular. As is well known, the Catholic Church is one of the major impediments in large parts of the world to easy access not only to abortion but even to contraception. It is unfortunate that Francis does not engage these issues in light of his own ultimate social concern: the lives of the poor. That is, once women are granted political autonomy and are given meaningful control over their own bodies, population increase tends to slow, the children who are born tend to be healthier, and poverty levels decrease. In fact, the claims made in the previous sentence are nothing short of axiomatic among those demographers who have studied carefully the relationship between women's rights and poverty.

Although Francis cites different international earth summits convened to deal with environmental issues (e.g., the Rio conferences in 1992 and 2012), he does not cite equally important international summits convened to deal with the status of women worldwide, specifically with reproductive health issues (e.g., the famous Cairo conference in 1994, at which the Catholic Church played an obstructionist role). One gets the impression that on Francis's view we can ignore (or even impede) women's rights in the area of reproductive health and still make meaningful strides in ameliorating environmental degradation and extreme poverty. I am not convinced that he is correct about this.

In many ways Francis' way of thinking is a breath of fresh air. But regarding reproductive health issues the air is rather stale. He, not surprisingly, opposes abortion (117, 120, 131), but one nonetheless wishes that he would have made distinctions among fetuses at various stages of gestational development. He certainly could have done so even on traditional Catholic grounds. Saints Augustine and Thomas Aquinas, for example, defended versions of delayed hominization in which fetuses early in pregnancy were not viewed as human persons. The air is also stale regarding Francis' patriarchal tendency to refer to God as omnipotent Father (e.g., 73-77). To switch metaphors, the pope is certainly at the cutting edge regarding certain aspects of environmental and economic justice, but his analytic precision is unfortunately somewhat dull when the issues in question concern the relationship between justice (whether environmental or economic) and sex/gender.

In conclusion, it is heartening to see Pope Francis cite favorably the work of his fellow Jesuit, the great process thinker and scientist Pierre Teilhard de Chardin (81-83). Although with less than optimal enthusiasm, Francis introduces some degree of dynamism both into the concept of God and into the effort to understand our place in the overall scheme of things. Both religion and natural beauty have a rich past; because of Francis it is reasonable to hope that they will have a rich future as well.

The Pope's Encyclical from a Quaker Perspective

Anthony Manousos

The pope's encyclical *Laudato si'* is an historic and prophetic document that is already having a significant influence on the conversation about the global climate crisis. The leader of the Catholic Church, with a worldwide membership of over a billion people, cannot easily be dismissed, even by hard-core climate change deniers in our Congress. A chemist by training, the pope has taken pains to bring together some of the best minds in the Church to make this encyclical both powerful and well-grounded in science, scripture, and theology. In this encyclical Francis provides a theological framework for what he calls "integral ecology." He calls for a change of heart, an "ecological conversion," and proposes concrete actions, a change of lifestyle on both a personal and societal level. He addresses his encyclical not only to Catholics, but to all people of faith and conscience. Reading this encyclical, my "heart leapt for joy" (to use a phrase of Quaker founder George Fox). For years, I have held views similar to those expressed by the pope, but with the power and authority of his office he has articulated them in a way that is profound, comprehensive, and impossible to ignore.

Quakers are not much given to theologizing. Ours is an experiential and practical religion. Because of our peace testimony, we also tend to

35

look at the world through the lens of social justice and nonviolence. So I would like to examine the pope's encyclical from this perspective.

Letting our lives speak

The Quaker phrase, "Let your life speak," implies that what we do is often more important that what we say. What impresses me about Pope Francis (as well as Pope Benedict) is a practical commitment to living the church's social teachings. Following the example of his namesake, Pope Francis has chosen to live as simply as possible. During his papacy Benedict XVI undertook green initiatives that made Vatican City the "greenest state in the world" and earned Benedict the title "the green pope."[1] The Vatican's solar panels provide enough energy to sustain all 40,000 of its households. Pope Francis is simply preaching what Benedict practiced.

This reminds me of our Quaker lobby, Friends Committee on National Legislation (FCNL). In 2003, FCNL (the oldest religious lobby in Washington, DC) began renovating its Civil War era office and became the first LEED certified Green Building on Capitol Hill, with a vegetative roof, geothermal heating and cooling, light scoops, and other energy-saving measures. By modeling the change it would like to see in the world, FCNL has more credibility when it lobbies for environmental legislation. Inspired by this example, my wife and I made our home in Pasadena a model of sustainability. We installed solar panels and purchased a plug-in Chevy Volt, which reduced our electrical consumption by over 90% and our gasoline consumption by over 50%. We replaced our sprinklers with a highly efficient drip watering system. We replaced our water-guzzling grass with decomposed granite and mulch. And we installed a gray water system that recycles thousands of gallons of water from our washing machine and bathtub to water our 19 fruit trees. During a time when California is experiencing a drought of biblical proportions—the worst in 1200 years—we cut our water consumption by over 50% and still have a highly productive organic garden. An environmental journalist in local newspaper wrote about us, and now groups and individuals come to our home on a regular basis to see what we have done and are inspired to take similar steps.

I am pleased that Vatican City and the pope are taking practical steps on a much grander scale to demonstrate their commitment to what theologian John Cobb calls "an ecological civilization." When the pope preaches what the Vatican practices, his message is extremely compelling.

Social justice and sustainable cities

Francis' main concern is with the poor and marginalized—those who are suffering most from climate change and the pollution caused by industrial society. The pope's ecological vision includes not only wilderness areas, but also rural areas and cities—what he calls "human ecology." According to Francis, there is no separation between the human and the natural world. Cities affect the natural world, and vice versa. Francis' vision of a sustainable city is one in which all people—rich and poor—feel interconnected. Francis makes it clear that the word "ecology" comes from the Greek word meaning "home," and an ecological civilization is one in which every person is decently housed:

> Lack of housing is a grave problem in many parts of the world, both in rural areas and in large cities, since state budgets usually cover only a small portion of the demand. Not only the poor, but many other members of society as well, find it difficult to own a home. Having a home has much to do with a sense of personal dignity and the growth of families. This is a major issue for human ecology. In some places, where makeshift shanty towns have sprung up, this will mean developing those neighborhoods rather than razing or displacing them. When the poor live in unsanitary slums or in dangerous tenements, "in cases where it is necessary to relocate them, in order not to heap suffering upon suffering, adequate information needs to be given beforehand, with choices of decent housing offered, and the people directly involved must be part of the process." At the same time, creativity should be shown in integrating rundown neighborhoods into a welcoming city: "How beautiful those cities which overcome paralyzing mistrust, integrate those who are different and make this very integration a new factor of development! How attractive are those cities which, even in their architectural design, are full of spaces which connect, relate and favor the recognition of others! (152)

My wife Jill Shook, an Evangelical Christian who has written a book about faith-based affordable housing models, was thrilled to read this insightful passage. It reminded her of what T. J. Gorridge calls the "theology of the built environment": the values implicit in the ways our cities are planned and built. As people of faith, we need to make sure that not only our homes, but also our cities, reflect our theological and moral values. This is the core teaching of the pope's ecological vision.

War and the environment

Francis is following in the footsteps of Pope John XXIII. In 1963, just before his death, Pope John issued an Encyclical called *Pacem in Terris*, calling on all men and women (not just Catholics) to work for human rights, social justice, and nuclear nonproliferation. In his 21st century encyclical, Pope Francis calls on all people to care for God's creation and recognizes that one of the greatest threats to the environment, and to human betterment, is war:

> It is foreseeable that, once certain resources have been depleted, the scene will be set for new wars, albeit under the guise of noble claims. War always does grave harm to the environment and to the cultural riches of peoples, risks which are magnified when one considers nuclear arms and biological weapons. (57)

The pope is clearly aware that conflicts over resources, caused by climate change and political systems dependent on war, will escalate unless steps are taken to live sustainably. The military is one of the greatest polluters in the world, driving people from their homes and making their lands uninhabitable with land mines, cluster bombs, and a host of toxic chemicals. As a Quaker peace activist and environmentalist, I would argue that we cannot solve our ecological crisis if we don't dismantle the war system that pollutes and dominates the world.

Ending the war system may seem an even more daunting task than solving the environmental crisis, but we should not forget that religious activists (including Quakers and Evangelical Christians) played a major role in ending (or at least illegalizing) slavery, an institution as old and entrenched as war. A Quaker-inspired group called "War Beyond War," founded by David Hartsough, one of the leading Quaker peace activists of our time, has brought together scholars, activists, and experts in peace studies to explore practical steps to helping humanity transition from a war system to a peace system, from a culture of war to a culture of peace. As the pope makes clear, we need drastic, fundamental changes if human beings are going to survive beyond the 21st century.

This inward and social transformation will not be easy. As the pope wisely notes, we need to cultivate our inward life through prayer, meditation, and communion. Silent, unprogrammed worship is the heart of our Quaker faith, and the basis for our activism. We believe that through worship, we can more deeply connect with "that of God" in ourselves and in others, including those in the natural world. This leads us to compassionate action. I found especially moving Francis' prayer at the end of his encyclical:

> All-powerful God, you are present in the whole universe
> and in the smallest of your creatures.
> You embrace with your tenderness all that exists.
> Pour out upon us the power of your love,
> that we may protect life and beauty.
> Fill us with peace, that we may live
> as brothers and sisters, harming no one.
> O God of the poor,
> help us to rescue the abandoned and forgotten of this
>   earth,
> so precious in your eyes.
> Bring healing to our lives,
> that we may protect the world and not prey on it,
> that we may sow beauty, not pollution and destruction.
> Touch the hearts
> of those who look only for gain
> at the expense of the poor and the earth.
> Teach us to discover the worth of each thing,
> to be filled with awe and contemplation,
> to recognize that we are profoundly united
> with every creature

as we journey towards your infinite light.
We thank you for being with us each day.
Encourage us, we pray, in our struggle
for justice, love and peace.

Pope Francis has inspired and challenged us with a powerful and far-reaching vision, and his down-to-earth practicality. In September 2015, he plans to speak to the U.S. Congress, and in December 2015 he will address the United Nations. Drawing together faith leaders of diverse traditions, as well as reaching out to political leaders, the pope has proven himself to be a lobbyist *par excellence.* He has shown his political effectiveness by persuading President Obama to recognize Cuba. I hope he will prove even more effective in mobilizing the world to take action on climate change, the gravest crisis of our era.

References

1. <http://inhabitat.com/the-vatican-city-is-the-greenest-state-in-the-world/>.

Stewardship and the Roots of the Ecological Crisis

Brian Henning

In 1967 the historian Lynn White, Jr. published in the journal *Science* a controversial essay exploring "The Historical Roots of Our Ecologic Crisis." His contention is that the roots of the crisis, a crisis that was even then apparent, run deeper than the rise of modern science and technology. The Baconian quest to master and violently subdue nature was, he argues, only possible because of an underlying anthropocentric worldview which made such possibilities live. That worldview, White argues, can be traced to a particular dominant form of Western Christianity that "not only established a dualism of man and nature but also insisted that it is God's will that man exploit nature for his proper ends."[1] Western Christianity bifurcated nature, setting humans above the rest of creation. The world is merely a stage on which to play out humanity's quest for salvation. The play of life is for and about humans. "Despite Copernicus, all the cosmos rotates around our little globe. Despite Darwin, we are not, in our hearts, part of the natural process. We are superior to nature, contemptuous of it, willing to use it for our slightest whim."[2] "Especially in its Western form, Christianity is the most anthropocentric religion the world has ever seen."[3]

White's contention is that this underlying worldview created the conditions necessary for the possibility of the violent misuse of nature.

Note that his thesis is not dependent on showing the callousness of Christians. Rather, his claim is that the basic Christian worldview is now inseparable from the Western mindset and is appropriated independently of any religious belief. "Both our present science and our present technology are so tinctured with orthodox Christian arrogance toward nature that no solution for our ecologic crisis can be expected from them alone. Since the roots of our trouble are so largely religious, the remedy must also be essentially religious, whether we call it that or not."[4] Given this diagnosis, White's point is to demonstrate that without a more adequate worldview, the ecological crisis will have no solution. "What we do about ecology depends on our ideas of the man-nature relationship. More science and more technology are not going to get us out of the present ecologic crisis until we find a new religion, or rethink our old one."[5]

Importantly, White's goal is not to contend that Christianity is an *inherently* flawed worldview that must be abandoned. Rather, he suggests that within its own tradition there are resources for "rethinking." Specifically, White suggests that Western Christianity might overcome its dualistic narrative if it gave greater status to the views of St. Francis.

> Possibly we should ponder the greatest radical in Christian history since Christ: Saint Francis of Assisi. The prime miracle of Saint Francis is the fact that he did not end at the stake, as many of his left-wing followers did. . . . The key to an understanding of Francis is his belief in the virtue of humility—not merely for the individual but for man as a species. Francis tried to depose man from his monarchy over creation and set up a democracy of all God's creatures. With him the ant is no longer simply a homily for the lazy, flames a sign of the thrust of the soul toward union with God; now they are Brother Ant and Sister Fire, praising the Creator in their own ways as Brother Man does in his.[6]

> We must rethink and refeel our nature and destiny. The profoundly religious, but heretical, sense of the primitive Franciscans for the spiritual autonomy of all parts of nature may point a direct. I propose Francis as a patron saint for ecologists.[7]

My goal in this brief essay is not so much to defend White's controversial thesis,[8] but to use it as a context for appreciating the significance of Pope Francis' new encyclical *Laudato si'*. Considering it in the context of White's thesis will bring certain salient features into relief.

First, it is interesting to note that much of what White suggested by way of rethinking Chritianity has come to pass in the last half century. For instance, though due in no part to White, in 1979 Pope John Paul II did in fact make St. Francis the patron saint of ecology. Beyond this symbolic act, the Catholic Church's explicit discussion of the ecological crisis as a moral issue demanding serious consideration by all people of good faith begins with Pope John Paul II's 1990 world peace day speech, "The Ecological Crisis: A Common Responsibility."

> In our day, there is a growing awareness that world peace is threatened not only by the arms race, regional conflicts and continued injustices among peoples and nations, but also by a lack of *due respect for nature*, by the plundering of natural resources and by a progressive decline in the quality of life. The sense of precariousness and insecurity that such a situation engenders is a seedbed for collective selfishness, disregard for others and dishonesty.[9]

In this moving account, John Paul II begins to lay the foundation for connecting social and environmental justice, recognizing not only that harm to the environment disproportionately affects the poor, and that justice entails right relation not only between humans and their creator, but also necessarily between humans and creation. Furthermore, he recognizes that a consistent "ethic of life" must respect not only human life, but also nonhuman life. Finally, like White, John Paul argues that the ecological crisis is not a problem to be "managed" by the application of more science and technology. John Paul contends that the ecological crisis is ultimately "a moral problem." In this way he seems to agree that the ecological crisis is a manifestation of an inadequate worldview and that unless and until a more adequate conception of ourselves and our relationship to the natural world is conceived, the crisis will only worsen. This reaction went a great distance in affecting the "rethinking" called for by White. It reinterpreted human dominion of the Earth from despotic tyranny to benign stewardship. Humans being uniquely made in God's image now entails responsibilities more than privileges.

Though a dramatic and welcome shift in teaching, these statements often stopped short of recognizing that the nonhuman world has intrinsic value and is deserving of respect for its own sake. Some within the Catholic Church were concerned that recognizing the intrinsic value of nature would encourage misguided pantheistic worship of nature. The obligation to be good stewards of creation was ultimately owed to the creator and to present and future humans, but never to plants, animals, or ecosystems for their own sakes. Duties to nonhumans were left merely indirect. In this way, one might say that the Catholic Church shifted from the self-destructive anthropocentrism White discusses, to a more enlightened anthropocentrism. Whatever the reason, the Church's views had changed dramatically but had not yet abandoned the dualism which, according to White, is at the root of the ecological crisis. Though Francis had been named the patron saint of ecology, his democracy of fellow creatures was still excluded in favor of St. Thomas' Aristotelian-inspired *scala natura*. Despite now recognizing our dependence on the natural world and the need to respect its "integrity," humans are still set off from and above the natural world.

This hesitation to recognize the intrinsic value of all beings, human and nonhuman, has with Pope Francis finally been resolved. In his new encyclical, *Laudato si'*, he consistently and even emphatically recognizes that nonhuman organisms must be taken into account "not only to determine how best to use them, but also because they have an intrinsic value independent of their usefulness. Each organism, as a creature of God, is good and admirable in itself; the same is true of the harmonious ensemble of organisms existing in a defined space and functioning as a system" (140). Indeed, not only does he recognize that individual organisms have intrinsic value, but also the systems of which they are a part have value. In this encyclical Francis has for the first time unequivocally repudiated anthropocentrism and recognized that the natural world has value independent of its usefulness to human beings and deserves to be respected and protected not only for the sake of present and future humans, but also for its own sake. Nonhumans are owed both direct and indirect duties. Yet Francis is also quick to note that this should not be taken to imply a leveling "biocentrism."

> A misguided anthropocentrism need not necessarily yield to "biocentrism," for that would entail adding yet another imbalance, failing to solve present problems and adding new ones. Human beings cannot be expected to feel responsibility for the world unless, at the same time, their unique capacities of knowledge, will, freedom and responsibility are recognized and valued. (118)

Here we see Francis trying to be clear that in rejecting anthropocentrism he is not "yielding" to a biocentrism—or, he might have added, an ecocentrism. However, this position incorrectly assumes that "biocentrism" necessarily entails a flat or egalitarian axiology in which all beings are of equal value. Environmental ethicists are careful to maintain the distinction between moral considerability and moral status. Biocentrism is simply the view that if a being is living, then it is intrinsically valuable and deserves moral consideration for its own sake. Whether all living beings are *equal* in intrinsic value—have the same moral status—is a related, but distinct question, answered differently by different thinkers. In other words, Francis' target seems to be egalitarian forms of biocentrism that claim all living beings have value *and have it equally.* However, there are many non-egalitarian forms of biocentrism which claim that *all living beings are equal in having value, but not all have value equally.*

For instance, Nobel Laureate Albert Schweitzer's "reverence for life" ethic is perhaps among the most eloquent, though also the least systematically developed, versions of biocentrism. "Ethics thus consists in this, that I experience the necessity of practising the same reverence for life toward all will-to-live, as toward my own. Therein I have already the needed fundamental principle of morality. It is good to maintain and cherish life; it is evil to destroy and to check life."[10] At times, Schweitzer seems committed to an egalitarian form of biocentrism, arguing that "life as such is sacred. He [the ethical person] shatters no ice crystal that sparkles in the sun, tears no leaf from its tree, breaks off no flower, and is careful not to crush any insect as he walks." However, even this view need not imply a leveling axiological egalitarianism. Schweitzer recognizes that the "will-to-live" is in some ways "at variance with itself. One existence survives at the expense of another of which it yet knows nothing." Our moral obligation, Schweitzer contends, is to avoid injuring life "without being forced to do so by necessity."What is perhaps left ambiguous in Schweitzer is clarified in prominent proponents of biocentrism, such as the environmental ethicist Gary Varner, who explicitly defend a form of "biocentric individualism" grounded in an axiological hierarchy. [11] Biocentrism is fully compatible with a hierarchical conception of value.

Though the term is not mentioned by Francis, a similar analysis could be produced for "ecocentrism," which goes beyond biocentrism and also recognizes the intrinsic value of not only individual living beings, but also the systems of which they are a part. Indeed, though Francis does not use the term, he does seem to embrace a form of ecocentrism: "Each organism, as a creature of God, is good and admirable in itself; the same is true of the harmonious ensemble of organisms existing in a defined space and functioning as a system" (140). There are indeed some ecocentrists, such as the Sessions and Devall, who defend an "ecological egalitarianism" in which all beings are "in principle" equal in value. [12] However, there are others, such as Holmes Rolston, who defend a hierarchical form of ecocentrism that readily acknolwedges differences in degrees of value. [13] Perhaps the most expansive form of non-egalitarian ecocentrism is that grounded in the work of Alfred North Whitehead, who recognizes that everything in the universe has value for itself, for others, and for the whole. [14] The scope of our direct moral consideration excludes nothing. Everything has intrinsic value, but there are many degrees and grades of value achieved by different beings and the systems of which they are a part. Much of my own professional work has been dedicated to exploring the development of an ethic grounded in such a worldview. [15]

I belabor this discussion of biocentrism and ecocentrism in order to demonstrate that, contrary to Pope Francis' impression, there is no incompatibility between a thoroughgoing biocentrism or even an ecocentrism and a recognition of humans' "unique capacities of knowledge, will, freedom and responsibility" (118). The repudiation of anthropocentrism need not entail a great leveling that fails to recognize the real differences between different beings. A genuine biocentrism or ecocentrism is not only compatible with Pope Francis' call to shed an arrogant, unjustified anthropocentrism, but a resource.

In explicitly repudiating anthropocentrism and recognizing the intrinsic value of a world that deserves respect and protection for its own sake, Francis has in fact addressed White's most basic concern that "we shall continue to have a worsening ecologic crisis until we reject the Christian axiom that nature has no reason for existence save to serve man."[16] Francis is unequivocal in rejecting the insidious dualism which grounded our unjustified anthropocentrism. "Nature cannot be regarded as something separate from ourselves or as a mere setting in which we live. We are part of nature, included in it and thus in constant interaction with it" (139). Indeed, Francis explicitly recognizes that, as White contended, too often Christians have misunderstood the nature of their "dominion."

> Although it is true that we Christians have at times incorrectly interpreted the Scriptures, nowadays we must forcefully reject the notion that our being created in God's image and given dominion over the Earth justifies absolute domination over other creatures. (67)

> An inadequate presentation of Christian anthropology gave rise to a wrong understanding of the relationship between human beings and the world. Often, what was handed on was a Promethean vision of mastery over the world, which gave the impression that the protection of nature was something that only the faint-hearted cared about. Instead, our "dominion" over the universe should be understood more properly in the sense of responsible stewardship. (116)

Pope Francis's explicit embrace of a stewardship ethic is a welcome development. However, I fear that stewardship, taken out of the context of the encyclical as a whole, is likely to be misunderstood. The metaphor of stewardship rightly challenges the notion that the Earth is "ours," to be disposed at our lordly whim. Stewardship is always on behalf of another.[17] As stewards we are entrusted with responsibility for, not possession of, the Earth. We are stewards on behalf of the creator, and on behalf of future generations.

So far as this goes, it is a dramatic improvement. However, there is a danger latent within this metaphor. Too often it simply packages in a new form an unjustified anthropocentrism. A benign anthropocentrism, perhaps, but unjustified all the same. The evolutionary biologist Stephen J. Gould notes well the potentially problematic nature of the metaphor of stewardship

> Such views [of stewardship], however well intentioned, are rooted in the old sin of pride and exaggerated self-importance. We are one among millions of species, stewards of nothing. By what argument could we, arising just a geological microsecond ago, become responsible for the affairs of a world 4.5 billion years old, teeming with life that has been evolving and diversifying for at least three-quarters of that immense span?[18]

If one is not careful, stewardship simply becomes an extension of the "Promethean vision of mastery over the world" (116). This is to commit the sins of hubris and conceit. Nature does not need a benevolent caretaker to ensure its proper functioning; it does not need fixing. It has its own integral unity which, if allowed to flourish, functions quite well.

Fortunately, if taken in the context of the encyclical as a whole, it becomes clear that Pope Francis' conception of stewardship is more expansive than this. Stewardship is not akin to the sustainability movement, which too often is solely aimed at making sustainable a consumer lifestyle that robs from the poor even while it fails to satisfy those who are fortunate enough to have the resources to pursue it. Though less polluting forms of technology are needed, the ecological crisis is not a technical problem to be managed through the development of new technologies. The ecological crisis is, at root, an ethical and spiritual problem "which require[s] that we look for solutions not only in technology but in a change of humanity; otherwise we would be dealing merely with symptoms" (9).

The shift to an ethic of stewardship properly understood entails more that human beings reenvision themselves and their place in the natural world. Put differently, we are called to be stewards of ourselves, not of nature. We are not in charge of nature and our attempts to do so usually create more harm than good. Pope Francis' conception of stewardship is far more radical than it might first appear. "It is not enough to balance, in the medium term, the protection of nature with financial gain, or the preservation of the environment with progress. Halfway measures simply delay the inevitable disaster. Put simply, it is a matter of redefining our notion of progress" (194). To become good stewards is to become good stewards of ourselves, to devise ways of living that are in harmony with and respectful of the other beautiful forms of life on the planet. The great Catholic priest and cultural historian Thomas Berry described this task as the "Great Work" of this generation.

> The Great Work now, as we move into a new millennium, is to carry out the transition from a period of human devastation of the Earth to a period when humans would be present to the planet in a mutually beneficial manner.[19]

Whether the roots of the ecological crisis can be traced to Western Christianity (as Lynn White claims) or to modernity (as Pope Francis contends), both seem to be in agreement that the ecological crisis is ultimately a moral and spiritual problem that can only be addressed by embracing a worldview that repudiates an unjustified and arrogant anthropocentrism that separates us from and makes us contemptuous of nature. We must recognize that, although humans are truly amazing in their capabilities, we are fundamentally a part and product of the natural world and that, as intrinsically beautiful and valuable, every being deserves moral respect and appreciation. Pope Francis' encyclical is a clarion call to take up the Great Work before us.

> If we approach nature and the environment without this openness to awe and wonder, if we no longer speak the language of fraternity and beauty in our relationship with the world, our attitude will be that of masters, consumers, ruthless exploiters, unable to set limits on their immediate needs. By contrast, if we feel intimately united with all that exists, then sobriety and care will well up spontaneously. The poverty and austerity of Saint Francis were no mere veneer of asceticism, but something much more radical: a refusal to turn reality into an object simply to be used and controlled. (11)

Endnotes

1. Lynn White, Jr. "The Historical Roots of our Ecologic Crisis." *Science* 155, (1967): 1205.

2. Ibid., 1206.

3. Ibid., 1205.

4. Ibid., 1207.

5. Ibid., 1206.

6. Ibid.

7. Ibid., 1207.

8. For critical analyses of White's thesis, consult Robin Attfield, "Social History, Religion, and Technology: An Interdisciplinary Investigation into Lynn White's 'Roots'," E*nvironmental Ethics* 31, (2009) and Elspeth Whitney, "Lynn White, Ecotheology, and History," *Environmental Ethics* 15, no. 2 (1993): 151-69.

9. John Paul, II, "The Ecological Crisis: A Common Responsibility," 1 January 1990 <http://w2.vatican.va/content/john-paul-ii/en/messages/ peace/documents/hf_jp-ii_mes_19891208_xxiii-world-day-for-peace. html>.

10. Albert Schweitzer, "The Ethic of Reverence for Life," trans. John Naish <http://www.animal-rights-library.com/texts-c/schweitzer01.htm>.

11. See Gary Varner, *In Nature's Interests? Interests, Animal Rights, and Environmental Ethics* (Oxford: Oxford University Press, 1998).

12. Bill Devall and George Sessions, *Deep Ecology: Living as if Nature Mattered* (Salt Lake City: Gibbs Smith, 1985).

13. Holmes Rolston III, *Environmental Ethics: Duties to and Values in the Natural World* (Philadelphia: Temple, 1988).

14. Alfred North Whitehead, *Modes of Thought* (New York: Free Press, 1938), 111.

15. My most systematic attempt to develop a Whiteheadian inspired moral philosophy is in Brian G. Henning, *The Ethics of Creativity: Beauty, Morality, and Nature in a Processive Cosmos* (Pittsburgh: University of Pittsburgh Press, 2005). Other relevant work on this can be found in Brian G. Henning, *Riders in the Storm: Ethics in an Age of Climate Change* (Winona, MN: Anselm Academic, 2015); Brian G. Henning, *Beyond*

Mechanism: Putting Life Back into Biology, eds. Brian G. Henning and Adam C. Scarfe (Lanham, MD: Lexington Books, 2013); Brian G. Henning, "From Despot to Steward: The Greening of Catholic Social Teaching," in the *Heart of Catholic Social Teaching: Its Origins and Contemporary Significance,* ed. David Matzko McCarthy (Grand Rapids, MI: Brazos Press, 2009), 183-94; and Brian G. Henning, "Trusting in the 'Efficacy of Beauty': A Kalocentric Approach to Moral Philosophy," *Ethics & the Environment* 14.1 (2009): 101-28.

16. White, 1207.

17. For a more developed discussion of this point, see chapter 5 of Brian G. Henning, *Riders in the Storm: Ethics in an Age of Climate Change* (Winona, MN: Anselm Academic, 2015). See also, Robin Attfield, ""Trustees of the Planet," in the *Ethics of the Global Environment* (West Lafayette, Indiana: Purdue University Press, 1999), 44-61.

18. Stephen Jay, Gould, "The Golden Rule: A Proper Scale for our Environmental Crisis," *Natural History* 99.9 (1990): 24.

19. Thomas Berry, *The Great Work: Our Way into the Future* (New York: Broadway Books, 2000), 3.

An Ecological Pope Challenges the Anthropocene Epoch

Holmes Rolston III

I greatly welcome the recent encyclical: *Laudato si', On Care for Our Common Home*. One of the world's great leaders, and a popular one, insists that the human relationship to nature can and ought to involve love and appreciation, gratitude and care. The pope is, in words he almost himself uses, a biocentric holist.

Here is the way he puts it, recalling St. Francis:

> Francis helps us to see that an integral ecology calls for openness to categories which transcend the language of mathematics and biology, and take us to the heart of what it is to be human. Just as happens when we fall in love with someone, whenever he would gaze at the sun, the moon or the smallest of animals, he burst into song, drawing all other creatures into his praise. He communed with all creation, even preaching to the flowers, inviting them "to praise the Lord, just as if they were endowed with reason. (11)

> It is not enough, however, to think of different species merely as potential "resources" to be exploited, while overlooking the fact that they have value in themselves. Each year sees the disappearance of thousands of plant and animal species which we

will never know, which our children will never see, because they have been lost for ever. The great majority becomes extinct for reasons related to human activity. Because of us, thousands of species will no longer give glory to God by their very existence, nor convey their message to us. We have no such right. (33)

These convictions are set in a monotheist perspective, appropriately for the pope, but he does appeal to an "integral ecology" and to species biodiversity as having a worth of their own, under God, which we have no right to destroy.

We take these systems into account not only to determine how best to use them, but also because they have an intrinsic value independent of their usefulness. Each organism, as a creature of God, is good and admirable in itself; the same is true of the harmonious ensemble of organisms existing in a defined space and functioning as a system. (140)

The pope amply recognizes that humans need natural resources, but he is crystal clear that there are limits to exploiting natural resources, limits set by the intrinsic values of plants and animals. He continues:

If we approach nature and the environment without this openness to awe and wonder, if we no longer speak the language of fraternity and beauty in our relationship with the world, our attitude will be that of masters, consumers, ruthless exploiters, unable to set limits on their immediate needs. By contrast, if we feel intimately united with all that exists, then sobriety and care will well up spontaneously. The poverty and austerity of Saint Francis were no mere veneer of asceticism, but something much more radical: a refusal to turn reality into an object simply to be used and controlled. (11)

We are urged to keep "an openness to awe" and this checks an escalating techno-managerial approach. Such an approach by itself is "unable to set limits" to humanity's demands on nature. He links an underdeveloped environmental ethics with an overdeveloped economy. We don't just need better interventions in wild nature, we also need fewer interventions, and more respect for the complex, beautiful world that God has created and nature has evolved over the eons. We need more protected areas where the primary focus is on biodiversity preservation rather than economic exploitation (37).

The pope is careful to link human losses to biodiversity losses. In the long view biodiversity, when celebrated in awe and with a good of its own, proves also to bring benefits to us. Here is the way he puts it:

> The earth's resources are also being plundered because of shortsighted approaches to the economy, commerce and production. The loss of forests and woodlands entails the loss of species which may constitute extremely important resources in the future, not only for food but also for curing disease and other uses. Different species contain genes which could be key resources in years ahead for meeting human needs and regulating environmental problems. (32)

> Ongoing research should also give us a better understanding of how different creatures relate to one another in making up the larger units which today we term "ecosystems". . . . Although we are often not aware of it, we depend on these larger systems for our own existence. We need only recall how ecosystems interact in dispersing carbon dioxide, purifying water, controlling illnesses and epidemics, forming soil, breaking down waste, and in many other ways which we overlook or simply do not know about. Once they become conscious of this, many people realize that we live and act on the basis of a reality which has previously been given to us, which precedes our existence and our abilities. So, when we speak of "sustainable use", consideration must always be given to each ecosystem's regenerative ability in its different areas and aspects. (140)

The pope's "integral ecology" returns with his discussion of the importance of all things great and small. As ecologists often put it, little things run the world as much as big things. The natural world is a complex webwork:

> It may well disturb us to learn of the extinction of mammals or birds, since they are more visible. But the good functioning of ecosystems also requires fungi, algae, worms, insects, reptiles and an innumerable variety of microorganisms. Some less numerous species, although generally unseen, nonetheless play a critical

role in maintaining the equilibrium of a particular place. . . .
Nowadays, intervention in nature has become more and more
frequent. As a consequence, serious problems arise, leading to
further interventions; human activity becomes ubiquitous, with
all the risks which this entails. Often a vicious circle results, as
human intervention to resolve a problem further aggravates the
situation. For example, many birds and insects which disappear
due to synthetic agrotoxins are helpful for agriculture: their
disappearance will have to be compensated for by yet other
techniques which may well prove harmful.

We must be grateful for the praiseworthy efforts being made by
scientists and engineers dedicated to finding solutions to man-
made problems. But a sober look at our world shows that the
degree of human intervention, often in the service of business
interests and consumerism, is actually making our earth less rich
and beautiful, ever more limited and grey, even as technological
advances and consumer goods continue to abound limitlessly.
We seem to think that we can substitute an irreplaceable and
irretrievable beauty with something which we have created ourselves. (34)

We can put this pope as one with great doubts about any celebration
of our having entered a new geological epoch: the Anthropocene—when
global ecosystems are significantly impacted by human acitivities.

The pope has done his homework in ecology. For instance, he also
urges that we set aside conservation corridors linking protected areas
(35) and that we recognize the difference between tree plantations and
primary forests (39).

The pope is asking for a new worldview, not just improvements in
the prevailing systems. The driving cause of our environmental crisis is
an economic system out of control, not focused on providing sufficient
goods for people to live good lives, but devoted ever more intensive
commodifying of nature, in service to ever more consumption. Here
is his warning:

Environmental protection cannot be assured solely on the basis
of financial calculations of costs and benefits. The environment
is one of those goods that cannot be adequately safeguarded or

promoted by market forces. Once more, we need to reject a magical conception of the market, which would suggest that problems can be solved simply by an increase in the profits of companies or individuals. Is it realistic to hope that those who are obsessed with maximizing profits will stop to reflect on the environmental damage which they will leave behind for future generations? Where profits alone count, there can be no thinking about the rhythms of nature, its phases of decay and regeneration, or the complexity of ecosystems which may be gravely upset by human intervention. Moreover, biodiversity is considered at most a deposit of economic resources available for exploitation, with no serious thought for the real value of things, their significance for persons and cultures, or the concerns and needs of the poor. (191)

The pope insists that we must tame modern industrial capitalism; harness the economy in service to higher goals. Otherwise the logic of capitalism, endless development, even sustainable development, will degrade both wild nature and human life alike. Some critics have wondered whether the pope should have more directly addressed population growth, but that was something he could not effectively do in this encyclical. In the future the path is figuring out how less is more: "We need to take up an ancient lesson, found in different religious traditions and also in the Bible. It is the conviction that "less is more" (222).

In any event, if in some cases sustainable development were to involve new forms of growth, in other cases, given the insatiable and irresponsible growth produced over many decades, we need also to think of containing growth by setting some reasonable limits and even retracing our steps before it is too late. We know how unsustainable is the behaviour of those who constantly consume and destroy, while others are not yet able to live in a way worthy of their human dignity. That is why the time has come to accept decreased growth in some parts of the world, in order to provide resources for other places to experience healthy growth. (193)

A path of productive development, which is more creative and better directed, could correct the present disparity between excessive technological investment in consumption and insufficient investment in resolving urgent problems facing the human family. It could generate sensible and profitable ways of reusing, revamping and recycling, and it could also improve the energy efficiency of cities. Productive diversification offers the fullest possibilities to human ingenuity to create and innovate, while at the same time protecting the environment and creating more sources of employment. Such creativity would be a worthy expression of our most noble human qualities, for we would be striving intelligently, boldly and responsibly to promote a sustainable and equitable development within the context of a broader concept of quality of life. On the other hand, to find ever new ways of despoiling nature, purely for the sake of new consumer items and quick profit, would be, in human terms, less worthy and creative, and more superficial. (192)

For new models of progress to arise, there is a need to change "models of global development." This will entail a responsible reflection on "the meaning of the economy and its goals with an eye to correcting its malfunctions and misapplications." It is not enough to balance, in the medium term, the protection of nature with financial gain, or the preservation of the environment with progress. Halfway measures simply delay the inevitable disaster. Put simply, it is a matter of redefining our notion of progress. A technological and economic development which does not leave in its wake a better world and an integrally higher quality of life cannot be considered progress. (194)

This is an encyclical about environment and, equally, a fundamental socio-economic critique. There is remarkable wisdom here, ancient and contemporary, and many of us who have been saying these things for decades can rejoice in a new and powerful voice for saving the Earth.

Pope Francis' Ecological Conversion

Herman F. Greene

It is important when the Bishop of Rome addresses a letter, an encyclical, to all the bishops in communion with the Roman Catholic Church to guide them in relation to those in their care. It was *extraordinarily* important when Pope Francis published the encyclical *Laudato si' On Care for Our Common Home.*[1] Here are three things that make this encyclical exceptionally important:

- Joining social justice and environment.
- Offering an integral ecology.
- Calling for ecological conversion.

Joining social justice and environment

There has been a tension between activists who focus on environmental concerns and those who focus on social justice. Environmental activists are passionate that the most fundamental issue is the health of the planet, without which there can be no social justice. Social activists recognize the importance of a healthy planet but feel that social issues, such as poverty, inequality, working conditions, war, political participation, and gender and racial discrimination are more pressing. With respect to environmental concerns, they prioritize situations that cause immediate harm to humans, such as air and water pollution and toxins in the workplace. Environmental activism has suffered because of this tension. From the perspective of the encyclical, so has social activism.

People generally make a distinction between social and environmental concerns, with the social taking priority, except when a natural or environmental disaster gives urgency to environmental concerns. This inattention to the environment is almost taken for granted, so much so that many who are concerned, not giving due regard for the planetary scale of disaster that is possible, say, "People will not change until some disaster makes them change."

Only a little thought is needed to realize it can't be one or the other—healthy planet or social justice. Yet, how to effectively express the connection is difficult. This encyclical does this better than any writing I have seen. It does so by taking away the dualism between humans and nature.

Francis writes,

> When we speak of the "environment", what we really mean is a relationship existing between nature and the society which lives in it. Nature cannot be regarded as something separate from ourselves or as a mere setting in which we live. We are part of nature, included in it and thus in constant interaction with it. Recognizing the reasons why a given area is polluted requires a study of the workings of society, its economy, its behaviour patterns, and the ways it grasps reality. Given the scale of change, it is no longer possible to find a specific, discrete answer for each part of the problem. It is essential to seek comprehensive solutions which consider the interactions within natural systems themselves and with social systems. We are faced not with two separate crises, one environmental and the other social, but rather with one complex crisis which is both social and environmental. Strategies for a solution demand an integrated approach to combating poverty, restoring dignity to the excluded, and at the same time protecting nature. (139)

Then he proceeds to illustrate how we are not to deal with nature in one way and humans in another, but we are to relate to all in the same way. Francis calls for us to regard every being as having its own inherent value, and to relate to every being as a subject not an object. He notes,

"The biblical accounts of creation invite us to see each human being as a subject who can never be reduced to the status of an object" (81). And he follows this with "It would also be mistaken to view other living beings as mere objects subjected to arbitrary human domination" (140). "When we can see God reflected in all that exists, our hearts are moved to praise the Lord for all his creatures and to worship him in union with them" (87). He notes with approval that his namesake, St. Francis, called the Sun his brother and the Moon his sister.

Francis calls us into universal communion: "As part of the universe, called into being by one Father, all of us are linked by unseen bonds and together form a kind of universal family, a sublime communion which fills us with a sacred, affectionate and humble respect" (89). The same attention is to be given to all. For example, we should not be concerned with the trafficking of endangered species without also being concerned about human trafficking (91).

Because we humans are so integrated into the natural community, care for Earth and care for the poor go hand in hand. In explaining the major themes of the encyclical, Francis states, "I will point to the intimate relationship between the poor and the fragility of the planet, the conviction that everything in the world is connected" (16). He notes the disproportionate impact of pollution (20), environmental degradation (14), and climate change on the poor. With respect to the last, he writes:

> [Climate change] represents one of the principal challenges facing humanity in our day. Its worst impact will probably be felt by developing countries in coming decades. Many of the poor live in areas particularly affected by phenomena related to warming, and their means of subsistence are largely dependent on natural reserves and ecosystemic services such as agriculture, fishing and forestry. They have no other financial activities or resources which can enable them to adapt to climate change or to face natural disasters, and their access to social services and protection is very limited. (25)

He makes clear that the roots of environmental degradation and social injustice are the same: "The human environment and the natural environment deteriorate together; we cannot adequately combat environmental degradation unless we attend to causes related to human and social degradation" (48). "The same mindset which stands in the way of making radical decisions to reverse the trend of global warming also stands in the way of achieving the goal of eliminating poverty" (175), "'The mindset which leaves no room for sincere concern for the environment is the same mindset which lacks concern for the inclusion of the most vulnerable members of society. For the current model, with its emphasis on success and self-reliance, does not appear to favour an investment in efforts to help the slow, the weak or the less talented to find opportunities in life'" (196, quoting from his Apostolic Exhortation, *Evangelii gaudium* 24 November 2013). "A world of exacerbated consumption is at the same time a world which mistreats life in all its forms" (230).

Offering an integral ecology

At the outset, Francis makes clear that the reason for *Laudato si'* is to provide guidance in relation to environmental deterioration. He compares this encyclical to the encyclical *Pacem in Terris*, written by Pope John XXIII in 1963 when the world teetered on the brink of nuclear disaster. Like Pope John, Francis addressed a global problem, so he wrote "to address every person living on this planet" and "to enter into dialogue with all people about our common home" (3).

When Francis outlined the structure of the encyclical, he said he would begin by begin by reviewing various aspects of the environmental crisis drawing on scientific research. Next he would consider guidance from the Judeo-Christian tradition. Then he would "attempt to get to the roots of the present situation, so as to consider not only its symptoms but also its deepest causes. This will help to provide an approach to ecology which respects our unique place as human beings in this world and our relationship to our surroundings" (14).

He calls this approach to ecology, "integral ecology." He uses the ideas involved in this term "to advance some broader proposals for dialogue and action which would involve each of us as individuals, and also affect international policy," and to "offer some inspired guidelines for human development to be found in the treasure of Christian spiritual experience" (14).

Pope Francis is not the first person to have used the term "integral ecology," but he likely is the one who has made the term part of the global lexicon. Let's first look at the history of the term as presented by Sam Mickey and then at how Francis uses it. Here is what Mickey wrote:

> The phrase *integral ecology* emerged four times independently throughout the twentieth century. It was first used by Hilary Moore in a 1958 marine ecology textbook, in which Moore proposes that ecologies that focus on (synecology) and on their component organisms (autecology) should be supplemented by an "integral ecology" that would reconnect the ecosystem and its components into a whole. . . . In 1995, three different theorists used the word *integral* to call for such boundary-crossing approaches to ecology: the cultural historian . . . Thomas Berry, the liberation theologian Leonardo Boff, and the Integral theorist Ken Wilber. . . .
>
> For Berry, the historical mission of [our times, our Great Work] is "to reinvent the human," creating new modes of consciousness and conscience that participate in an integral Earth community. Such a community can only be built with the support of renewed engagements in many sources of wisdom, including those of contemporary sciences, the world's religious traditions, indigenous communities, and women. . . .
>
> Deriving from the Latin word for a "whole" or "complete entity" *(integer),* the word *integral* bears connotations of unity or wholeness. Based on that definition, becoming integral with the Earth community suggests that humans would understand themselves as members of one single *yet* multiform community that includes all of the planers habitats and inhabitants, ideas and societies, humans and nonhuman.[2]

Francis is keenly aware of "relationality" and the meaning of "integral." We find terms such as these throughout the encyclical: relate, relationships, web of relationships, everything is interrelated, integrity of the earth, integral ecology, sustainable and integral development, bonds of integration and social cohesion, integrated into a broader vision of reality, in the service of a more integral and integrating vision, integral improvement in the quality of human life, find ourselves integrated and happy, potential for integration, integral and interdisciplinary approach, integral education.

In accord with Berry's advice, Francis draws on the wisdom of "contemporary sciences, the world's religious traditions, indigenous communities, and women." In speaking about the effective action local communities could take, he writes: "[Individuals and groups] are able to instil[*sic*] a greater sense of responsibility, a strong sense of community, a readiness to protect others, a spirit of creativity and a deep love for the land. They are also concerned about what they will eventually leave to their children and grandchildren. These values are deeply rooted in indigenous peoples" (179).

Also:

> It is essential to show special care for indigenous communities and their cultural traditions. They are not merely one minority among others, but should be the principal dialogue partners, especially when large projects affecting their land are proposed. For them, land is not a commodity but rather a gift from God and from their ancestors who rest there, a sacred space with which they need to interact if they are to maintain their identity and values. When they remain on their land, they themselves care for it best. (146)

It is noteworthy that in his visit to Ecuador following publication of the encyclical, Francis "called for increased protection of the Amazon rain forest and the indigenous people who live there, declaring that Ecuador must resist exploiting natural riches for 'short-term benefits,' an implicit rebuke of the policies of President Rafael Correa."[3] Pope Francis walks his talk.

While apparently indebted to and influenced by people like Leonardo Boff, who is well known to Latin American Catholics, and by Berry (perhaps through Boff's writing),[4] Francis gives a distinct meaning to integral ecology. Its focus, as stated above, is "an approach to ecology which respects our unique place as human beings in this world and our relationship to our surroundings" (15). In this sense, it could be called human ecology, but that is not the term he chose or the full meaning he gives to integral ecology. It is an ecology of the full dynamics of Earth, universe, cosmos, and the divine.

Concerning earthly affairs, Francis is clear on the meaning of the Anthropocene, though he does not use that term. Human activity now affects all of life and is a prime force in nature—in the larger sense this activity is nature acting through humans. He begins the section of the encyclical on integral ecology by stating:

> Ecology studies the relationship between living organisms and the environment in which they develop. This necessarily entails reflection and debate about the conditions required for the life and survival of society, and the honesty needed to question certain models of development, production and consumption. It cannot be emphasized enough how everything is interconnected. (138)

It may come as a surprise to some that he "jumps" from "ecology" to "models of development, production and consumption." His explanation is "it cannot be emphasized enough how everything is interconnected" (138). This *is* integral ecology, everything is interconnected. There is no more human, on the one hand, and nature, on the other. Further it is human models of development, production and consumption that are giving rise to the environmental deterioration which is the subject of the encyclical.

The section of the encyclical titled "Integral Ecology" comes after a lengthy examination of the ecology in the more commonly understood sense of the study of other-than-human life and life systems and, pointedly, of the human causes of environmental deterioration. Francis begins the section by stating: "Since everything is closely interrelated, and today's problems call for a vision capable of taking into account every aspect of the global crisis, I suggest that we now consider some elements of an *integral ecology*, one which clearly respects its human and social dimensions" (137). He then discusses integral ecology under the headings of

- environmental, economic and social ecology
- cultural ecology
- ecology of daily life
- the principle of the common good

Pope Francis has offered to all humans an integral ecology. As previously noted, he is not the first to use the term, but he likely is the one who has put the term into the global lexicon. This is one of the most important contributions of this encyclical.

Calling for ecological conversion

A critic of the encyclical derisively noted that the pope Francis was the first to call for ecological conversion rather than conversion to the Christian faith and doctrine. One might respond that this was because this encyclical was not an evangelical document issued for the purpose of Christian conversion but rather involved Catholic social teaching, how Catholics should respond to issues in the world. Yet to give this interpretation would be to miss the import of Francis' very intentional choice of the term "ecological conversion."

Francis cites Pope John Paul II's *Catechesis* (January 17, 2001) as the originator of the term.[5] Then he writes of ecological conversion of Christians:

> The ecological crisis is also a summons to profound interior conversion. It must be said that some committed and prayerful Christians, with the excuse of realism and pragmatism, tend to ridicule expressions of concern for the environment. Others are passive; they choose not to change their habits and thus become inconsistent. So what they all need is an "ecological conversion," whereby the effects of their encounter with Jesus Christ become evident in their relationship with the world around them. Living our vocation to be protectors of God's handiwork is essential to a life of virtue; it is not an optional or a secondary aspect of our Christian experience. (217)

Next he expands the meaning of ecological conversion to extend to communities including nonChristians:

> Social problems must be addressed by community networks and not simply by the sum of individual good deeds. This task "will make such tremendous demands of man that he could never achieve it by individual initiative or even by the united effort of men bred in an individualistic way. The work of dominating the world calls for a union of skills and a unity of achievement that can only grow from quite a different attitude." The ecological conversion needed to bring about lasting change is also a

community conversion. (219, quoting Romano Guardini, *The End of the Modern World*, 65-66)

Even broader meanings of ecological conversion come from reading the encyclical as a whole. Francis writes of universality in a new way. As previously mentioned, he writes of universal communion with all humans and all creatures. He also states, "We require a new and universal solidarity" (14), water is a universal human right, people should not live in ways in which their lifestyles cannot be universalized, and there needs to be a universal destination (distribution) of goods. At the political level, there is a need "to devise stronger and more efficiently organized international institutions, with functionaries who are appointed fairly by agreement among national governments, and empowered to impose sanctions" (175). All of this is needed because of the "radical change which present circumstances require" (171). "A strategy for real change calls for rethinking processes in their entirety, for it is not enough to include a few superficial ecological considerations while failing to question the logic which underlies present-day culture" (197).

For all people ecological conversion means seeing Earth community as a living whole. Old ways of thinking that rely on technological fixes and repetitive intervention in nature are still based on understandings of the world as a collection of objects to be manipulated. They fail to see that humans and other living beings are subjects, and that Earth is a living organic system. Civilizational change is needed, from industrial civilization to a civilization of love and life.

For Christians, ecological conversion involves greater emphasis on creation. In the Christian Trinity, God the Father is the Creator. Thus, all things in the universe have a divine origin, and God called the created order good. Francis reminds Christians of the creative activity of Christ understood as Logos in John 1, where it is written, "Through him all things were made and without him nothing that was made has been made"; and further, this Logos became flesh and the mystery of Christ is at work in the natural world as a whole (99).

For Christians an ecological conversion is needed to be present to God's activity in creation, and the need for this is urgent: "The work of the Church seeks not only to remind everyone of the duty to care for nature, but at the same time 'she must above all protect mankind from self-destruction'" (79, quoting from Pope Benedict XVI's Encyclical Letter, *Caritas in Veritate* [June 29, 2009]).

Conclusion

Addressing the deterioration of the environment is not simple. I have a friend who jokes that the good thing about the environment is one can never get off the subject. It is this exactly that makes addressing environmental deterioration, and explaining what is needed to address the deterioration, so difficult. If it were only a matter of technical fixes and interventions, then Francis would have been able to chide people on weak responses and then call for these fixes and interventions. Instead he needed to present an integral ecology in its biological, geological, theological, philosophical, social, political, economic, cultural and personal dimensions. In my opinion he did this better than it has ever been done.

Pope Francis has helped us all (1) by joining social justice and environment; (2) by offering an integral ecology; and (3) by calling for ecological conversion.

Endnotes

1. The encyclical is dated May 24, 2015. It was published on June 18, 2015.

2. Sam Mickey, *On the Verge of a Planetary Civilization: A Philosophy of Integral Ecology* (New York: Rowman & Littlefield International, 2014), 16-17 (footnotes omitted).

3. Jim Yardley, "Pope Francis, in Ecuador, Calls for More Protection of Rain Forest and Its People," *New York Times,* 7 July 2015.

4. Sam Mickey, "Pope Francis and Integral Ecology," *Becoming Integral Blog,* 18 June 2015 <http://becomingintegral.com/2015/06/18/pope-francis-and-integral-ecology/> (accessed July 8, 2015).

5. In that document Pope John Paul II wrote:

> If we scan the regions of our planet, we immediately see that humanity has disappointed God's expectations. Man, especially in our time, has without hesitation devastated wooded plains

and valleys, polluted waters, disfigured the earth's habitat, made the air unbreathable, disturbed the hydrogeological and atmospheric systems, turned luxuriant areas into deserts and undertaken forms of unrestrained industrialization, degrading that "flowerbed"—to use an image from Dante Alighieri (*Paradiso*, XXII, 151)—which is the earth, our dwelling-place.

We must therefore encourage and support the "ecological conversion" which in recent decades has made humanity more sensitive to the catastrophe to which it has been heading. . . . At stake, then, is not only a "physical" ecology that is concerned to safeguard the habitat of the various living beings, but also a "human" ecology which makes the existence of creatures more dignified, by protecting the fundamental good of life in all its manifestations and by preparing for future generations an environment more in conformity with the Creator's plan.

A Bright Hope for the Depressed Globe

Andrew Sung Park

The encyclical letter of Pope Francis *On Care for Our Common Home* is a comprehensive and amazing document for the wellness of the human family and the whole globe. It contains six chapters: pollution and climate change, the gospel of creation, the human roots of the ecological crisis, integral ecology, lines of approach and action, and ecological education and spirituality.

Following his role model, Saint Francis of Assisi, Pope Francis cares for the nature of God's creation and for the poor and downtrodden, living "in simplicity and in wonderful harmony with God, with others, with nature and with himself" (10). This encyclical was issued to point out "how inseparable the bond is between concern for nature, justice for the poor, commitment to society, and interior peace" (10).

In this reflection on his encyclical, I will rather zero in on Francis' ecological thought. His warning against unlimited economic growth is a greatly needed message for our time: "In any event, if in some cases sustainable development were to involve new forms of growth, then in other cases, given the insatiable and irresponsible growth produced over many decades, we need also to think of containing growth by setting some reasonable limits and even retracing our steps before it is too late" (5). Such a reckless economic growth has misled the human family to this state of the world of ecological disruptions.

Pope Francis' aspiration for new models of global development converges with Lester Brown's ecological model. According to Brown there are two contrasting views of the state of the world: an economic view and an ecological view.[1]

Economists analyze and interpret trends with reference to development, investment, and savings. From such viewpoints, they have little reason to be concerned about limits of nature on human economic activities. They ignore the carrying capacity principle that is so fundamental to ecology. In this economist view, technological advancement will push back any limits of nature on economic developments.[2]

Contrary to this economic view, ecologists look into the organic relationship of living beings and things with each other and their environment. In ecology, all growth processes are confined with the limits of the natural boundaries of an ecosystem. Ecologists clearly notice the damage to natural systems and assets from irresponsibly expanding economic activities. They hold that the obsessive pursuit of economic growth will eventually bring forth economic collapse.[3]

This encyclical recommends new ways of green growth:

> We know how unsustainable is the behaviour of those who constantly consume and destroy, while others are not yet able to live in a way worthy of their human dignity. That is why the time has come to accept decreased growth in some parts of the world, in order to provide resources for other places to experience healthy growth. (193)

It is worthy to note that this encyclical inspires the decrease of unhealthy growth in certain areas of the globe. This growth is unsustainable, irresponsible, and insatiable. Furthermore, Pope Francis recommends new ways of measuring the progress of human civilization:

> For new models of progress to arise, there is a need to change "models of global development". . . It is not enough to balance, in the medium term, the protection of nature with financial gain, or the preservation of the environment with progress. Halfway measures simply delay the inevitable disaster. Put simply, it is a matter of redefining our notion of progress. A technological and economic development which does not leave in its wake a better world and an integrally higher quality of

life cannot be considered progress. Frequently, in fact, people's quality of life actually diminishes—by the deterioration of the environment, the low quality of food or the depletion of resources—in the midst of economic growth. In this context, talk of sustainable growth usually becomes a way of distracting attention and offering excuses. It absorbs the language and values of ecology into the categories of finance and technocracy, and the social and environmental responsibility of businesses often gets reduced to a series of marketing and image-enhancing measures. (194)

I really like Pope Francis' "new models of progress" and his rejection of "halfway measures" (194). I almost hear him saying, "Do away with the rhetoric of halfway measures," He urgently asks the world to change its doomed course before it is too late. He denounces the world of wanton economic growth, strongly advocating true and actual sustainable growths. His vision for a new measuring standard of global development affirms the ecological view and the foresight of John Cobb and Herman Daly.

In *The State of the World 2001,* Lester Brown of the Worldwatch Institute lauds a new index of global progress developed by Herman Daly and John Cobb. It is called "the Index of Sustainable Economic Welfare (ISEW)."[4] This index goes far beyond the deficient norms of GNP and even the Human Development Index (HDI) devised by the United Nations. Based on a scale of 0 to 1, the three indicators of HDI gauge longevity, knowledge, and the command over resources needed for a decent life. Longevity denotes life expectancy at birth, knowledge means literacy rates, and the command over resources is measured by gross domestic product (GDP). Since these indicators show national averages, they do not directly involve distribution inequality, but they indirectly reflect the distribution of resources by including longevity and literacy. For example, a high average longevity indicates general access to health care and to suitable supplies of food.[5]

In contrast, ISEW is "the most comprehensive indicator of well-being available, taking into account not only average consumption but also distribution and environmental degradation."[6] After fine-tuning the consumption component of the index for distributional inequality,

ISEW counts several environmental expenses associated with economic mismanagement, such as depletion of nonrenewable resources, loss of farmland from soil erosion and urbanization, damage of wetland, cumulative damage from ozone production, cost of commuting, and cost of air and water pollution. This index also calculates "long-term environmental damage."[7] Brown acclaims its thoroughness: "ISEW is the most sophisticated indicator of progress now available, although its use is constrained by lack of data."[8] It is necessary for the UN to study ISEW carefully and to utilize it partially or wholly by obtaining indispensable ecological data so that we may measure true global progress and may move toward a hopeful direction. This encyclical and ISEW confront and rectify the misleading indicator of the global development of economic views.

Its limitations:

• Despite its comprehensive and caring spirit, this encyclical is silent on the issue of sexism when it treats the dualisms of nature/human, matter/spirit, and mind/body (98). Such dualisms have led us to exploit nature and women in the church and in society.

• Concerning cultural ecology, Pope Francis stresses the importance of the preservation of local cultures: "Ecology, then, also involves protecting the cultural treasures of humanity in the broadest sense. More specifically, it calls for greater attention to local cultures when studying environmental problems, favouring a dialogue between scientific-technical language and the language of the people" (143).

• I appreciate the pope's call for greater attention to local cultures. I wish, however, along with the importance of local cultures he could emphasize the significance of local economy that boosts local business, undermines transnational business, and debunks the economic view.[9] Strengthening each other, local economy, local culture, and local ecology are inseparably interwoven in the health of a community.

• It is admirable that Pope Francis includes the voice of Ecumenical Patriarch Bartholomew of the Orthodox Church in his encyclical. He embraces the creation theology of the Orthodox Church that demands the repentance of our sin of climate change (8). Even though Pope Francis is impressively inclusive and ecumenical, he left out the voice of Protestant leaders. In fighting for the restoration of the health of our deeply wounded earth, at least all Christians must work together.

In spite of these shortcomings, Pope Francis' encyclical addresses not only the holistic global progress for the human family, but also the humane treatment of animals and care for nature. His encyclical for ecological care does not derive from the fear of the destruction of creation, but from his genuine concern and love for God's creation. Instilling a fresh hope in the gloomy world, his climate encyclical opens a new chapter of the involvement of the ecumenical church in the actual environmental changes of our home earth.

Endnotes

1. Lester Brown, "The New Order," *State of the World 1991,* edited by Lester Brown, et al. (New York: W.W. Norton & Co., 1991), 5.

2. Brown, 5.

3. Brown, 5-6.

4. Most of the detailed work and writing of the ISEW was carried out by Cliff Cobb and is included in *For the Common Good: Redirecting the Economy Toward Community, the Environment, and a Sustainable Future,* Herman E. Daly and John B. Cobb, Jr. 2nd ed. (Boston: Beacon Press, 1994), vii.

5. Brown, 9.

6. Brown, 10.

7. Brown, 10.

8. Brown, 11.

9. Herman Daly and John Cobb have potently articulated the issue of local economy in their book, *For the Common Good.*

The Jesuit Pope

Ignacio Castuera

Pope Francis' encyclical exhibits the powerful combination of profound piety and scrupulous study. Much is made of the adoption by Cardinal Bergoglio of the name of the Saint of Assisi for his papal appellation but it must never be forgotten that Francis, the author of *Laudato si'*, is a Jesuit, a Latin American Jesuit.

The head of all Jesuits is often referred to as the "black pope" because of the great influence this person has had in history and because of a tension with the Vatican in spite of the vows of obedience that all Jesuits take. The mere idea of a Jesuit pope had been almost anathema until Jorge Bergoglio became, bishop, cardinal, and finally Pope Francis.

The Jesuits, founded by Ignatius of Loyola soon after the Protestant Reformation, have had a history of dedication to action and contemplation. This powerful combination brought them into conflict with secular forces from their inception. Many a Jesuit ended up persecuted, jailed, executed (or murdered) by the powerful and wealthy wherever the Jesuits went. The order was suspended, then reinstated by the Vatican, expelled from Latin America, and, through a strange twist of fate, admired and feared by the Portuguese.

Voltaire was an enemy of religion and of some philosophy. Most people are aware that in *Candide* neither the church nor Leibniz (Dr. Pangloss in the novel) fare well. For Voltaire this was not the best of all possible worlds and he constantly tried to show that belief in God was a sign of faulty logic and science. When the great Lisbon earthquake took place Voltaire quipped (misrepresenting the truth) that it was strange that all the churches were destroyed in the earthquake, but God spared all the brothels. In fact the Jesuit church in Lisbon, St. Roque, was not destroyed, and that gave the Jesuits great power since popular religiosity led many to believe that God favored the Jesuits. The civil powers in Portugal were jealous of the influence of the Jesuits, and several of the Ignatian leaders ended up jailed and executed or murdered.

In Latin America, Pope Francis' brothers have suffered through the centuries. Most recently, in 1989, six Jesuits were assassinated (along with their housekeeper, Elba Ramos and her 16-year-old daughter Celina) by government forces in El Salvador for the role the Jesuits were playing in supporting and educating the poor. This concern for the marginalized is reflected in *Laudato si'* in the interconnection between the damage to the earth and the cheapening of human life. The Jesuit martyrs of El Salvador shine through passages of this courageous encyclical. Ignacio Martín-Baró, Ignacio Ellacuría, Segundo Montes, Juan Ramón Moreno, Joaquin López y López, Amando López, PRESENTES!

There is another Jesuit whose influence must not be forgotten, Pierre Teilhard de Chardin. In fact, his presence is implicit in the scientific rigor reflected in the statement by Pope Francis. Pundits who thunder against the pope for lack of scientific soundness are simply wrong. The pontiff availed himself of the best of scientific knowledge at hand because that is part and parcel of the Jesuit training. Jesuits are *"Men Astutely Trained"* as the title of the book on the education of American Jesuits by Peter McDonough so cleverly states and so thoroughly demonstrates in the pages of his tome. Jesuit education is lifelong, it does not end with ordination and many Jesuits have several graduate degrees.

Teilhard de Chardin was priest, paleontologist, and philosopher. He is an intellectual first cousin of Alfred North Whitehead, and with another French thinker, Henri Bergson, forms the triumvirate of the philosophy of organism. *Laudato si'* is filled with "organistic" references that can easily be connected to Teilhard de Chardin's *Hymn of the Universe, The Divine Milieu,* and his beautiful *Mass on the World.*

Written on the Feast of the Transfiguration in 1923 the Mass clearly conveys that all the earth, and not just Christ, must be seen as permeated with the divine. The paragraph I will quote also mentions the labors and the sufferings of the world that are being offered as the sacramental oblation, echoing *Laudato si'*, the poem, and prefiguring *Laudato si'*, the encyclical.

> *Since once again, Lord—though this time not in the forests of the Aisne but in the steppes of Asia—I have neither bread, nor wine, nor altar, I will raise myself beyond these symbols, up to the pure majesty of the real itself; I, your priest, will make the whole earth my altar and on it will offer you all the labors and sufferings of the world.*

The concept of the divinization of the universe permeates *Laudato si'* because its author, though named Francis, is thoroughly Ignatian.

The Game-Changer in the Vatican

Joseph Prabhu

When Cardinal Jorge Bergoglio of Argentina was elected pope by the College of Cardinals in March 2013 and chose a name in honor of St. Francis of Assisi, the choice was significant. It was the first time in the history of the papacy that the name was chosen, and it signaled both a message and a personal style to go along with it. In choosing the same name as the 13th-century Umbrian saint, Pope Francis was pointing to an engagement with the world rooted in love for both the created world and those whom the human world marginalizes, those whom Franz Fanon once called the "wretched of the earth." Francis has said he wants the Church to be like a field-hospital, tending to society's outcasts and also to the wounds inflicted by humanity on the earth; a church of and for the poor. The manner matching the message is one of simplicity, candor, straightforwardness, and humility. By invoking his Umbrian predecessor, Francis was indicating that the Church exists to serve the world and its needs, and not to succumb to the all-too-common temptations of worldly power and materialism cloaked in "spiritual" guise. And while he did not don the rags of the *poverello*, Francis eschewed the grandeur of the papal palace and chose instead a modest suite of rooms in a Vatican guesthouse, the Casa Santa Marta. He dresses in a simple white cassock adorned by a pectoral cross.

The first full-fledged text in which Pope Francis articulated his vision for the Church came in his November 2013 Apostolic Exhortation, *Evangelii Gaudium*, (The Joy of the Gospel), in which he clarified the mission of evangelization in the contemporary context. While that text was written in the form of a pastoral letter addressed primarily to the 1.2 billion members of the Roman Catholic church, it nonetheless touched on many themes that are spelled out more fully in the recent encyclical—concern for the poor, the obligation to establish just and sustainable social and political orders, the priority of the common good over individual self-interest, and the imperative to see societal wealth more in terms of rich and relational human lives, rather than in monetary terms. With his penchant for straight talk, Francis questioned the priorities of a world where it is not considered newsworthy that an elderly homeless person dies on the streets, but it is a prominent news item when the Dow Jones average loses two points. *Evangelii Gaudium* primarily addressed the need for ecclesial reform and renewal that would better equip the Church to fulfill a radical change of priorities and the tasks associated with them—in words often ascribed to St. Francis, to "preach the Gospel, and if necessary, use words."

Laudato si', dated May 24, 2015 (the Feast of Pentecost in most Christian churches), and officially published June 18, 2015,has been much anticipated for more than a year. It was well known that Pope Francis consulted widely with an array of thinkers and activists, spanning environmental scientists, economists, theologians, philosophers, policymakers, and advocates for change. The document reflects that broad scope and multidisciplinary, multi-level focus. Nonetheless, it is not an academic treatise but a pastoral appeal addressed not just to Christians but to all people, reflecting both the universal nature of the ecological crisis in which we find ourselves, and the need for a universal response at different levels—political, social, and personal. This is manifested in the subtitle of the encyclical *On Care for our Common Home*. It is an urgent call addressed to humanity at large for changes in outlook, consciousness, practices, and lifestyle. Needless to say, a document as ambitious and as deliberately pondered as this one merits careful study and thoughtful response. Francis clearly feels that this is a watershed moment in human evolution. He has issued a summons to pay heed and to change our ways.

This brief essay represents just a few preliminary reflections evoked by a first reading of the text. There are several noteworthy features of the encyclical on which I shall comment, before engaging with a few issues at somewhat greater length.

First, an encyclical, in contrast to, say, an exhortation or a pastoral letter, signifies the highest level of teaching in the Catholic Church and becomes part of the official social teaching of the Church. The rigorous preparation and the wide consultation point to the fact that these are not just the personal views of the pope but represent a broad spectrum of opinion, much of which is cited in the endnotes. A whole team of experts was brought together under the able leadership of Cardinal Peter Turkson of Ghana, the President of the Pontifical Council for Justice and Peace. This team produced a first draft, which then went through many revisions. Nevertheless, it is the pope's vision and spirit that permeate the text. He goes to great lengths to acknowledge candidly that it is neither possible nor desirable to get a complete consensus on these matters, and indeed invites further reflection, dialogue, and discussion. The encyclical is now an official statement of the Church.

Second, this is the first encyclical in the history of the Church that addresses the environment, and to my mind it ranks up there with *Rerum novarum* of Pope Leo XIII in 1891, which dealt with the rights of labor and capital in the modern economic system, and *Pacem in Terris* of Pope John XXIII in 1963, which concerned itself with the arms race and nuclear nonproliferation in particular. Mention should also be made of the powerful encyclical, *Evangelium vitae* (The Gospel of Life) issued by Pope John Paul II in 1995, which in many ways is a precursor to *Laudato si'*. When historians write the history of Catholic social teaching, I wager that *Laudato si'* will be seen as one of the most significant encyclicals of modern times, a profound statement dealing with fundamental questions of the purpose and destiny of creation and of humans within it. Leonardo Boff, one of the grandfathers of Latin American liberation theology, has dubbed it "The Magna Carta of Integral Ecology."

Third, for all its profundity, it is written in a simple, direct, and warmly appealing style, reflecting the desire of Francis for it to be widely

read, studied, and discussed. While the personal popularity of this pope
might initially draw people, perhaps out of curiosity, to the text, its
literary craft and sincerity, not to mention the importance of its subject
matter, might well induce a wide readership to go further and read it
through. In the short period of time since its publication, it has already
evoked much discussion. Indeed this very volume, edited by one of the
most renowned and prominent eco-theologians of our time, Prof. John
B. Cobb Jr., is further testimony to its importance.

Fourth, while it engages with many pressing scientific, political,
ethical, and economic issues, *Laudato si'* is primarily a spiritual and
devotional text. It begins with the famous *Canticle of the Creatures* of St
Francis, *Laudato si', mi' Signore,* ("Praise be to you, my Lord) and ends
with a long prayer, which concludes with the lines:

> O Lord, seize us with your power and light
> help us to protect all life,
> to prepare for a better future
> for the coming of your Kingdom
> of justice, peace, love and beauty.
> Praise be to you!
> Amen

Indeed, part of its literary skill is that it is able to enfold scientific,
moral, and political arguments within a theological and devotional context, signaling that for Francis, theological talk about God is inextricably
and necessarily linked with reflection on human destiny and the fate of
the earth. I see it as a text within the Franciscan devotional tradition,
translating St. Francis' robust and challenging spirituality for our times.
All too often, St. Francis is presented in art and popular representa-
tions as a sentimental, innocuous figure who preached to the birds and
swooned over the sun and the moon. What is overlooked, and what
Pope Francis picks up, is how counter-cultural his espousal of poverty
was, and how in our own day the "poor in spirit" might be better able to
hear the cries of the earth than those intoxicated by the "technological
paradigm" and dreams of material progress.

Fifth, it is a significantly ecumenical document, drawing on a wide range of wisdom— Christian, Jewish, and Muslim—and also on deliberations in conferences in many parts of the world. The pope makes special mention of the Ecumenical Patriarch Bartholomew of the Orthodox Church, one of the most respected religious voices on the environment (see paragraph 7). It is also noteworthy that the three people invited to officially launch the encyclical on June 18, 2015, were the above-mentioned Cardinal Peter Turkson, President of the Pontifical Council for Justice and Peace; the Orthodox Metropolitan John Zizioulas of Pergamon, one of the outstanding environmental theologians of our day; and Professor John Schellnhuber, Director of the Potsdam Institute for Climate Change. Already in Buenos Aires, Francis was well-known for his close ecumenical ties with Rabbi Abraham Skorka and Imam Omar Abboud. Recognizing the global nature of the eco-crisis, the pope here reaches out to all people, religious and secular.

Sixth, in spite of the ecumenical and multicultural references in the encyclical it is important to remember that Francis, as an Argentinian, is the first pope from the Americas. And indeed this is a very Latin American document marked by the style and temper of Latin American liberation theology. Not only are there ample references to at least three important conferences of Latin American bishops in Medellín (1968), Puebla (1979) and Aparecida (2007), there is a characteristic liberationist methodology adopted in the encyclical which I might summarize as: observe, analyze, listen deeply to the cries both of the earth and the poor, and then act for freedom and dignity. This is reflected in the composition of the text. Chapters one and three are respectively entitled, "What is Happening to our Common Home" and "The Human Roots of the Ecological Crisis"; chapters two and four address "The Gospel of Creation," and "Integral Ecology"; and, finally, chapters five and six speak to "Lines of Approach and Action" and "Ecological Education and Spirituality."

Having commented on some broad features of the encyclical I want to make two slightly more extended remarks, the first theological and the second political-economic.

In an influential article in 1967 entitled "The Historical Roots of Our Ecologic Crisis," the historian Lynn White Jr. laid the blame for

our environmental crisis largely on Christianity, with its account of
creation and its anthropocentric worldview. Both of these legitimize
human insensitivity and indifference to the natural world and our consequent exploitation of nature. But precisely because the roots of the crisis
are religious in nature, the solution must also be "essentially religious,
whether we call it that or not." He concludes his essay thus: "We must
rethink and re-feel our nature and destiny. The profoundly religious, but
heretical, sense of the primitive Franciscans for the spiritual autonomy
of all parts of nature may point a direction. I propose (St.) Francis as a
patron saint for ecologists."

Some 50 years later, Pope Francis has heeded Lynn White's call for
an "alternative Christian view" along Franciscan lines that might ground
and empower a healthy natural and social ecology. He writes early in the
encyclical: "I do not want to write this encyclical without turning to that
attractive and compelling figure, whose name I took as my guide and
inspiration when I was elected Bishop of Rome. I believe Saint Francis
is the example par excellence of care for the vulnerable and of an integral
ecology lived out joyfully and authentically. He is the patron saint of all
who study and work in the area of ecology . . . He shows us just how
inseparable the bond is between concern for nature, justice for the poor,
commitment to society and interior peace" (10).

In his exegesis of the two creation accounts, Francis is at pains to
show they have been incorrectly interpreted to imply dominion over the
earth and nature. He emphasizes the injunction in Genesis 2:15, where
we are enjoined to "Till and keep the earth," where "tilling" refers to
cultivating and ploughing, and "keeping" implies caring, preserving, and
sustaining. And he then concludes this biblical reflection with the words:
"peace, justice and the preservation of creation are three absolutely interconnected themes, which cannot be separated and treated individually
without once again falling into reductionism. Everything is related" (92).

Francis then buttresses this integral ecology with what I might call
an integral theology. What we call the Divine cannot be separated from
the human and the cosmic, or else we fall into the dualisms of the divine
and the human, and of the human and the natural which, theologically
speaking, are precisely what have enabled the ecological crisis. But while

the Divine, the Human and the Cosmic should not be separated, it is not entirely clear how they should be related. Traditional Christian theology has usually seen the Divine as ontologically preeminent and to the extent that humans are created in his or her image, some of that ontological preeminence rubs off on us, which in turn leads to the human domination of nature. Metaphors of "care" and "stewardship" still carry an anthropocentric charge, and however much such anthropocentrism might be tamed in asking us to care to "till and keep the earth," we have not yet moved to a truly "integral theology."

A more promising candidate for such an "integral theology" is the cosmotheandric vision of Raimon Panikkar where the Divine, the Human, and the Cosmic exist in co-constitutive relationality and have no individual and independent ontological status. As Panikkar puts it: "There is no matter without spirit and no spirit without matter, no World without Man, no God without the universe, etc. God, Man, and World are three artificially substantivized forms of the three primordial adjectives which describe Reality."[1]

Allied with this theological weakness in *Laudato si'* is a related cosmological inadequacy. The modern form of *Homo sapiens* emerged in the last 200,000 years. Human history has to be placed within the 14 billion years of the universe's existence and the 4.5 billion years of the earth's existence. Modern industrial civilization is a mere two hundred or so years old, and yet has managed to destroy in that short interval many of the life forms and much of the bio-diversity built up over the life span of the universe. Metaphors of "care" and "stewardship" acquire context and depth, and are themselves questioned, when placed within the histories of the earth and the universe. The account of the interplay between human and evolutionary history provided by Thomas Berry and Brian Swimme in *The Universe Story*, and the "deep history" of *Homo sapiens* given by Yuval Harari in *Sapiens*—to provide just two examples of what is becoming a fast-growing field—allow us to see and to understand more vividly our human place in nature and our belonging to it. This body of important research is relatively neglected in *Laudato si'*, an understandable omission given its already sizable length. Nevertheless, this research might call into question both our anthropocentric tendencies and our hyper-present imaginations, fueled by technologies that speed up time and constrict space.

While I am not an unqualified admirer of the pope's theology, I am, however, a strong supporter of his notion of integral ecology. "We urgently need a humanism capable of bringing together the different fields of knowledge, including economics, in the service of a more integral and integrating vision. Today, the analysis of environmental problems cannot be separated from the analysis of human, family, work-related and urban contexts, nor from how individuals relate to themselves, which leads in turn to how they relate to others and to the environment" (141). There is a tendency at times to see the environmental crisis as a largely scientific-technological one having to do with reliance on different forms of energy. Questions of poverty and inequalities of power and wealth, by contrast, are seen as a largely socio-political crisis. The pope shows clearly the error of this way of thinking and demonstrates how both the social and environmental crises are inextricably linked and are part of one complex problem. This perception is clearer to a person from the Southern hemisphere, because much of the extraction of oil, gas, and coal, and much of the deforestation required to feed modern industries have come either from the South or from other areas previously under colonial control. In particular it is important to see how a rapacious capitalist economic system, which relies on the accentuation of desire and on consumerist lifestyles for its profits, drives the relentless extraction of resources and the exploitation of the earth, which most severely affects the poor.

Reading Francis' critique of the modern industrial system brought back memories of a remarkably similar critique assayed more than a hundred years ago by Mahatma Gandhi, who in his 1909 tract, *Hind Swaraj*, comes up with a similar set of criticisms of the modern techno-economic system. Gandhi likewise saw it as materialistic, soulless, and fundamentally violent toward both nature and human life. It mistakes material comfort for progress, constant motion for purposeful movement, restlessness and distraction for vitality and dynamism, speed for efficiency, and consumerism for an improved quality of life. In Gandhi's analysis as well, the ones who pay the highest price for these mistakes are the earth and the poor. In a similar vein, Pope Francis writes:

Once more we need to reject a magical conception of the market, which would suggest that problems could be solved simply by an increase in the profits of companies or individuals. Is it realistic to hope that those who are obsessed with maximizing profits will stop to reflect on the environmental damage which they will leave behind for future generations? Where profits alone count, there can be no thinking about the rhythms of nature, its phases of decay and regeneration, or the complexity of ecosystems which may be gravely upset by human intervention. (190)

Much has been said about the need for cooperation between science and ethics as part of an integral ecology, but it seems to me that what the analyses of both Gandhi and Francis reveal is the co-responsibility of modern economists, who increasingly see their discipline as part of the mathematical and natural sciences instead of the social and moral sciences where it truly belongs. The very word "economics" comes from the Greek words *oikos* (household) and *nomos* (law or rule), and from Aristotle to as recently as Keynes, economics was seen as a moral science. The father of modern economics, Adam Smith, was a professor of moral philosophy at the University of Edinburgh, and his famous book, *The Wealth of Nations*, which describes some of the workings of the market as an institution, depends heavily on a prior book *The Theory of Moral Sentiments*, which emphasizes the importance of trust in society and of cooperation. Both economics as an academic discipline and economists who advise governments, corporations, banks, and other policy-shaping institutions, have had, I would argue, a largely baleful effect on modern society for which they have not been held accountable. It is not that there have not been critiques of modern economics and economists, as for example in the work of Amartya Sen, Jeffrey Sachs, Joseph Stiglitz, Herman Daly, Tim Jackson, and many others. It is rather that these critiques have had relatively little impact on the nature of the discipline and on mainstream economic thinking. It is to be hoped that *Laudato si'* will add fresh impetus to a long overdue reevaluation of the discipline and its sadly distorted and misplaced priorities.

Any thoughtful person looking at our world today cannot be filled with much optimism. Violence, poverty, and instability of many different kinds mark our situation, and it is easy to succumb to despair. It is, therefore, especially valuable and refreshing to encounter a text which is both clear-eyed and sober in its analysis and yet manages to be hopeful. This is, of course, a quite different thing from optimism. Within a brief compass, I have tried to provide some preliminary reflections which I shall in time, together with many others, deepen. There are strong signs that *Laudato si'* is serving as a rallying cry and a summons to contemplation and action, of which this book itself is a reflection. It seems best to let Pope Francis have the last word:

> Many things have to change course, but it is we human beings above all who need to change. We lack an awareness of our common origin, of our mutual belonging, and of a future to be shared with everyone. This basic awareness would enable the development of new convictions, attitudes and forms of life. A great cultural, spiritual and educational challenge stands before us, and it will demand that we set out on the long path of renewal. (202)

Endnotes

1. "Philosophy as Lifestyle," *Philosophers on Their Work* (Bern: Peter Lange, 1978), 206.

Falling in Love with the Earth:
Francis' Faithful Ecology

Jacob J. Erickson

In an unassuming 1967 edition of *Science*, a medieval historian from the University of California argued a now infamous thesis in my own field of religion and ecology. "Christianity," Lynn White, Jr., wrote, "is the most anthropocentric religion the world has seen." The notion of "dominion," he argued, allowed human beings to exploit the ecological world in unprecedented ways.[1]

White's argument set off a decades-long firestorm, engaging activists, environmental ethicists, and Christian theologians alike.

But what most people generally forget about that now-canonical article is in the final eight paragraphs. After charging the cultural influence of Western Christian thought, White then argues for an equally *religious* response. "Possibly," he offers, "we should ponder the greatest radical in Christian history since Christ: Saint Francis of Assisi." The 13th century saint, who preached to birds and wolves, who referred to cosmic and elemental entities like fire as "Sister," might serve as a model, White argued, for a different kind of Christianity, a kind that can care for the earth seriously, in humility.

Like many scholars in my own field of religion and ecology, I woke up yesterday morning with another Francis—this one a pope—on my mind.

The Vatican had just officially released *Laudato si', Praise Be to You*—the first official papal encyclical to address the reality of climate change.

Pope Francis' letter, of course, appears in the midst of a great cloud of witnesses on religiously motivated ecological justice. The Patriarch of Constantinople, spiritual head of the Orthodox Church, known by many as the "Green Patriarch," appears several times in the encyclical. Catholic liberation theologians like Ivone Gebara and Leonardo Boff's work is unparalleled. Many leaders from other Christian denominations and world religions are discussing global warming and now the encyclical in earnest. Lutheran theologians like myself are using this letter in acts of ecclesial and planetary solidarity to prepare for the 500th Anniversary of the Reformation in 2017.

Scholars and environmental activists speculated for months (and not wildly) about the contents of the letter: its portrayal of climate change, its reflection on the human causes of climate change, its reflection on planetary science, its depiction of human life and sexuality, its understanding of everything from fossil fuels to water to biodiversity.

As I read through *Laudato si'* I saw much of the speculation confirmed. Pope Francis reflects on our various ecological ills. He reflects on anthropogenic/human-caused global warming, water scarcity, biodiversity loss, the dangers of unlimited consumerism, the dangers of unlimited and overused technology, "a misguided anthropocentrism," economic growth, and the list goes on.

We hear those litanies of devastation often these days and simple reflection on global warming can send anyone into a spiral of ethical helplessness and moral ambiguity. But there's something in the rhetorical feel, the affective language of this letter that might help pull a reader through.

The letter's laments are couched in the language of praise. Francis the pope lures the reader in with the poetry of Francis the saint. The encyclical reads,

> Saint Francis of Assisi reminds us that our common home is like a sister with whom we share our life and a beautiful mother who opens her arms to embrace us . . . This sister now cries out to us because of the harm we have inflicted on her by our irresponsible use and abuse of the goods with which God has endowed her. (1)

The gendering of language in this letter deserves its own extended reflection. But as I woke yesterday and read these opening words, Lynn White's article came tumbling back into my imaginative world. And White's argument for Saint Francis appears oddly, historically prescient (or at least influential) when a pope takes the name of that ecological saint and creates one of the most influential texts on religious environmentalism to date. Even if, we might say, the encyclical isn't perhaps as environmentally radical as White (or even I) might have wanted.

Still, what I'm haunted by most in reading this letter is its poetic genius in connecting seemingly disparate realms of life. Not a few have remarked to me about the encyclical's balance of tragedy and human sin alongside love, hopefulness, joy, and possibility. It seems that the letter is nothing less than a love letter, an invitation to love God and the creation in which human beings live out their lives in ecological interaction. The rhetoric and prose itself lends Pope Francis' vision to that very human context of learning appropriate loving communion, joy, and beauty.

Beauty carries a lot of ethical weight in this encyclical. Despite the vast ecological devastations, the letter evokes the beauty of our ecological contexts in its descriptions and its logic argues that seeing that beauty urges respect of other creatures. Learning to see beauty in the everyday is an intrinsic part of an ecological conversion to the earth. (Think of it this way: By my count the word "ecology" occurs thirty-three times in the encyclical. The word "beauty" occurs twenty-seven times.)

Another point of connection is the theme of integral ecology. In a nod to liberation theology and Leonardo Boff in particular it seems, *Laudato si'* refuses to make the choice between human and ecological life a zero sum game. Pope Francis writes,

> Today, however, we have to realize that a true ecological approach *always* becomes a social approach; it must integrate questions of justice in debates on the environment, so as to hear *both the cry of the earth and the cry of the poor*. (49)

The letter is concerned throughout with poverty. The pope goes so far as to say that the earth *is* one of those marginalized and demanding moral attention: "the earth herself, burdened and laid waste, is among the most abandoned and maltreated of our poor" (2).

Many popular dialogues about social justice and ecological justice pit these concerns against each other; this letter argues them to be of mutual, related concern.

Finally, as a constructive practice of hope, the encyclical argues time and time again for earth as a kind of "commons"—the encyclical itself is subtitled *On Care for Our Common Home*. The letter urges disparate communities—geographical, intellectual, and religious—to dialogue together for the sake of planetary action. The common home theme incorporates all of creaturely life—animal, plant, human, elemental. And such a perspective urges intergenerational ethical reflection on all who will compose the planet before and after us—how do we work together, planetarily, for the sake of our commons?

I'm bringing out these themes quickly as a kind of moral and because of the desire these connections tease out. When folks in the United States aren't mired in distracting debates on climate change denial and politically motivated refusals of science, we tend to talk about ecological crisis in terms that are hard to assimilate. We talk about the vast structural powers of atmosphere and anthropogenic change. We talk about the complicated ocean acidification that dissolves away at livable ecologies. We talk about the swirls of energy from fossilized fuels and various structural oppressions that energize climatological change.

The problems overwhelm our imaginative creativity to respond. Nothing can be done; the earth is doomed. Or, even, "the earth will go on without us, so what?"

I think what a message like Pope Francis' does is remind us of the deeply *ordinary* human and moral dimensions of ecology and climate change.

The words remind us of our *responsibility*. By connecting the affective themes of love or beauty, the integrally human and ecological, and passion for our common home, powerful ecological treatises like this one remind us that global warming is just as much about the *abstract* oppressive and climatological power as it is about the *intimate* oppressive and climatological powers that shape our everyday lives. And that working within everyday structures can help in creating justice and navigating the future.

I've come to believe that our climate crises are crises of planetary intimacy. I don't mean that we've lost a romantic relationship with nature that we need to recover. (That kind of imagination is just another anthropocentric misconstrual of creaturely life.) What I do mean is that everything of our contemporary crises also occurs in the intimate and risky relations of everyday life. Learning to address that intimate enfolding of life and creatureliness is one of our best hopes. Learning how to love the earth, how to build homes together in precarious climates, how to reconsider daily lives, how to daily protest structural economic systems, how to consider our animal interactions—all that is what creating a planetary resilience is about. This encyclical, as I read it, is simultaneously an act of love, an act of protest, and a hope for resilience.

Perhaps in bringing our crises of climate down to earth, to the very intimacies, desires, and relations of our bodies, Pope Francis' encyclical offers a way forward. Perhaps when we feel earth, affectively, lovingly in the everyday—in all of its vibrancy and tragic beauty—we'll be better able to do the work we so desperately need to do.

Endnotes

1. Lynn White, Jr. "The Historical Roots of Our Ecologic Crisis" Science, New Series, Vol. 155, No. 3767 (10 March 1967), 1203-07

[Editor's note: This article was first published in Religion Dispatches, *June 19, 2015.]*

That We May Sow Beauty

Sandra Lubarsky

From start to finish, *Laudato si'* brims with references to beauty. Emphasizing the relationship between "the infinite beauty of God" and the "beauty of the universe," Pope Francis declares the natural world to be a place of beauty. *Our common home* is ablaze with beauty, lit up by God's beauty and radiant with the beauty of each created being. In speaking so clearly about beauty in his encyclical, the pope lifts up the importance of beauty both to his theology and to the goal of an "integral ecology."

To introduce beauty into the ecological discussion, indeed to make it a central ingredient, is to develop a truly radical response to the dominant "techno-economic paradigm" (53). In fact, the pope's aesthetic turn is so radical as to go largely unappreciated, in itself a demonstration of the power of the techno-economic paradigm to delegitimize non-monetary value. In the dominant paradigm as it is now, beauty is a merely subjective valuation, a private judgment of little account in the broader system of calculation. But Pope Francis recognizes that a "different cultural paradigm" (108), one that challenges the reduction of value to utilitarian use, calls for the reintegration of aesthetics into our way of thinking and a reconnection of aesthetics with ethics.

In emphasizing the aesthetic dimension of life, Pope Francis assumes a more comprehensive—and more traditional—understanding of beauty and aesthetics than is currently assumed by either the general public or the professional art world. Though he mentions poetry, architecture, music, and landscape, Francis does not limit aesthetics to these arts or to art *per se*. In "A Prayer for Our Earth," he appeals to God for "the power of your love, that we may protect life *and* beauty" (246, my emphasis). It is this association between life and beauty that is at the heart of his logic. Beauty is important to integral ecology and to spirituality because it is an aspect of vitality—of God's life force and of the vivacity permeating the natural world. And beauty is a marker of quality of life, as well. "It is not enough to seek the beauty of design," writes Pope Francis. "More precious still is the service we offer to another kind of beauty: people's quality of life" (150). Both pollution and poverty diminish beauty and both deplete life. Pope Francis is acutely aware that they often appear together so that the poor suffer a twofold privation.

Pope Francis turns to St. Francis as a model for developing his aesthetic-ethical frame for integral ecology. He begins by noting that St. Francis' response to the world "was so much more than intellectual appreciation or economic calculus" (11). Guided instead by a vibrant sense of kinship with all living creatures, St. Francis participated in the world as a subject engaged with other subjects. He met the wondrous range of these unique lives with affection and care, experiencing the world as a community of subjects in relationships of mutuality. In contrast, our modern worldview maintains that our primary human relationship with other forms of life is between human subjects and nonhuman objects. Encouraged by both Cartesian metaphysics and an economics based on rational choice theory, we reduce nonhuman life to a resource for human appropriation. Rather than affection and concern, we aim for possession, control, profit, and utility. We reduce the richness of life to calculable riches that can be measured and tallied. We rely on reason and economics at the expense of affection. The consequence is as Pope Francis describes: no longer speaking "the language of fraternity and beauty in our relationship with the world, our attitude [is] that of masters, consumers, ruthless exploiters, unable to set limits on their immediate needs" (11).

Convinced by the beauty of each member of the created order— and thus the intrinsic value the natural world—St. Francis refused to reduce nature to an object for human manipulation. He interpreted the beauty of the world as a manifestation of God's presence, a "glimpse" of God's "infinite beauty and goodness" (12). Pope Francis affirms this view, acknowledging nature's beauty as both a teaching about God and a path to God, and beauty as the value intrinsic to the created world and each created being.

The techno-economic paradigm presupposes an absence of intrinsic value in the natural world. This assumption is bolstered by the modern conceit that all value is nothing more than an individually and socially constructed judgment imposed on our experience of the objective world, not derived from it. To renew the sensibilities of St. Francis with his perception of nature as a place of living beauty and to affirm with the Eastern church that beauty names "the divine harmony" as it appears in the world—"as in the shape of a church, in the sounds, in the colours, in the lights, in the scents" (235)—is to strike at the heart of the techno-economic paradigm. The pope's emphasis on beauty is no mere gesture toward the service beauty has given the church and no dutiful bow to the tradition of the sacred arts. It is a theological and philosophical challenge to the techno-economic image of the natural world as devoid of intrinsic value. In affirming the world's beauty, Pope Francis discredits the modern reduction of the natural world to an object for human control and use.

Pope Francis rightly maintains that an affirmation of the entwined values of "fraternity and beauty" so remarkably expressed in the life of St. Francis is essential to overcoming the misconceptions and limitations of the current dominant paradigm, to realigning ourselves with the natural world, to developing an integral ecology, and to sustaining the created order. In acknowledging the beauty of the natural world, life-sustaining value is anchored *in* the world and the absolute power of economism is broken. It becomes possible to restructure our relationship with nature and with one another in ways that promote rather than disable life, that "sow beauty, not pollution and destruction" (246).

PART
TWO

Reception

A Song-Inspired Narrative of Resistance

David Carlson

Pope Francis' encyclical letter to "the whole human family" (13) is permeated with *song*. *Laudato* opens with a brief couplet from St. Francis' *Canticle to the Sun* and closes with an exhortation to Christians: "Let us sing as we go. May our struggles and our concern for this planet never take away the joy of our hope" (244). A third of the way through, most of the entire *Canticle* is included verbatim (88). Its sheer exuberance resonates throughout the pope's message. *Laudato* is song-inspired.

Here, I would like to suggest, first, that the pope's message can be read as a *song-inspired narrative of resistance*. And second, that *song*—broadly speaking—is necessary for the new thinking and the many configurations of dialogue that *Laudato* calls for in order for them to come forth and be manifest. Briefly stated, song—in both musical and nonmusical form—is essential for integral ecology.

A song-inspired narrative of resistance

Laudato is clearly a narrative that has much in common with other clear-eyed, yet hopeful, critiques of the purely instrumental use of nature's resources and the reduction of the value of human life to the cycles of production and consumption across the earth. I have in mind, for example,

Rebecca Todd Peters' critiques of four theories, or narratives, of globalization: the resistance narratives of earthism and of postcolonialism opposing
the dominant narratives of neoliberalism and of social equity liberalism.[1]

Pope Francis does not reject markets per se (see, for example, 94,
129, and 180), but rather rejects "the interests of a *deified* market" (56,
italics added) and opposes "a magical conception of the market, which
suggest that problems can be solved simply by an increase in the profits
of companies or individuals" (190). Similarly, *Laudato* does not stand
against technology as such (see, for example, 102 and 103), but instead
calls for "resistance to the assault of the technocratic paradigm" (101).
Pope Francis sees a resistance generated by "a distinctive new way of
looking at things, a way of thinking, policies, an educational programme,
a lifestyle and a spirituality" acting together (111). But he is no Luddite.

Indeed, *Laudato* could be called *a spirituality of resistance*. Philosopher Roger Gottlieb has developed this fruitful concept over several
years of teaching and writing.[2] In his view, resistance entails, in the first
instance, opposing "superior and threatening powers, in a context of
injustice, oppression, or violence." To resist is to take a stand, to act. To
do so from a "spiritual point of view," Gottlieb cites several expressions
from the wisdom literature of centuries, such as "Open your heart to the
pain of the world, without fear or judgment," and "Give love in a dark
time, when everything seems hopeless." However, he points out that
the equanimity which spiritual wisdom and practices may engender risk
becoming mere nostrums unless compassionate and resolute resistance
to injustice and violence result.

Laudato, however, does not center its message in terms of what
it opposes in human affairs but rather in its idealized vision for life
on earth: namely, *a civilization of love*—grounded in *integral ecology*.
Laudato calls for an ecology of the environment, economics, society,
culture, daily life, and spirituality. All elements are interconnected. In
particular, the well-being of nature and humankind are inseparable.
Pope Francis approvingly quotes the Earth Charter's vision: "Let ours
be a time remembered for the awakening of a new reverence for life, the
firm resolve to achieve sustainability, the quickening of the struggle for
justice and peace, and the joyful celebration of life" (207).

Song—in both musical and nonmusical form—is essential for integral ecology.

The power of music to effect personal and social transformation is widely recognized. One outstanding example is the impact of the poem "Amazing Grace," later set to a hymn tune, upon William Wilberforce and the eventual abolishing of the slave trade in Britain. Another is the undeniable contribution that the song, "We Shall Overcome," has made in sustaining the civil rights movement in the United States during the 1960s and to this day.

I wonder: Are there comparable tunes that might help unify a worldwide movement toward a "civilization of love"? Is there a tune of caring for our common home—a melody so simple and meaning-filled that 7-year-olds in Colorado, the Congo, and China could sing the same melody with the same words in their native tongues? If not a single tune, perhaps a family of melodies with words from different cultures will emerge that say/sing the same message differently—a pluralism of unity without uniformity.

But does music exhaust the core meaning of "song"? Apparently not. St. Francis' *Canticle of the Sun* is variously described online as a religious song, a hymn, a prayer, and a poem. Although several composers have set this praise-filled canticle ("little song") to music hundreds of years after its composition, this canticle clearly stands on its own in *Laudato* (and elsewhere) without musical accompaniment. I think the same can be said for this "canticle" composed in our time:

> i thank You God for most this amazing
> day: for the leaping greenly spirits of trees
> and a blue true dream of sky; and for everything
> which is natural which is infinite which is yes
> (i who have died am alive again today,
> and this is the sun's birthday; this is the birth
> day of life and of love and wings: and of the gay
> great happening illimitably earth)

how should tasting touching hearing seeing
breathing any—lifted from the no
of all nothing—human merely being
doubt unimaginable You?
(now the ears of my ears awake and
now the eyes of my eyes are opened)[3]

Thus, the lines between song and poetry are blurred. Some say more and regard poetry *as* song.[4]

On this view, poetry can legitimately join song in musical mode in expanding the space for new thinking and multiple forms of dialogue to care for our common home. Moreover, poetry in everyday language, grounded in this place, this planet, is called for. And finally, poetry and song that articulate commitment, steadfastness, and lament (in addition to praise) are sorely needed for the long journey ahead. Here is one example; let us recognize others and share them.

My heart is moved by all I cannot save:
so much has been destroyed
I have to cast my lot with those
who age after age, perversely,
with no extraordinary power,
reconstitute the world.[5]

[Note: These reflections owe much to my colleagues in the track Organizing for Change and Sustaining Involvement at the international conference, "Seizing An Alternative: Toward An Ecological Civilization," held in Claremont, CA on June 4-7, 2015. Professor Roger Gottlieb, Worcester Polytechnic Institute, served as chair. Rev. Thandeka led a session that emphasized the central importance of song. Ms. Carol Blaney provided the excerpt of Adrienne Rich's poem displayed above.

Endnotes

1. Rebecca Todd Peters, *In Search of the Good Life: The Ethics of Globalization* (New York: Continuum, 2004).

2. See, for example, Roger Gottlieb, *A Spirituality of Resistance: Finding a Peaceful Heart and Protecting the Earth* (Lanham, MA: Rowman & Littlefield, 2003) and *Political and Spiritual: Essays on Religion, Environment, Disability, and Justice* (Lanham, MA: Rowman & Littlefield, 2015).

3. e.e. cummings, "i thank You God for most this amazing," in *100 Selected Poems* (New York: Grove, 1959).

4. The philosopher Martin Heidegger, for one. In his 1946 lecture, "Why Poets?" in *Off the Beaten Track,* trans. and ed. by Julian Young and Kenneth Haynes (Cambridge: Cambridge University Press, 2002), Heidegger asserts that the vocation of the poet is to reach into the abyss of the "world's dark night." He writes: "To be a poet in a desolate time means: singing, to attend to the track of the fugitive gods. This is why the poet, at the time of the world's night, utters the sacred" (202).

5. Adrienne Rich, an excerpt from "Natural Resources," in *The Dream of a Common Language: Poems, 1974-1977* (New York: Norton, 1978), 67.

A Change in the Climate of Climate Change?

Jim Conn

More Americans believe in angels than in climate change. Still, a poll released earlier this year indicated that more Americans than ever now think that climate change is happening, that it is caused by human activity, and that world leaders have a moral obligation to do something about it.

So why are we getting so little action? If a large majority of people actually thinks our only home, the Earth, suffers from human behavior, then shouldn't our personal and public actions reflect that reality? Oh, sure, lots of people drive electric cars, but lots more drive SUVs. I know that California has implemented a "cap-and-trade" program that will limit the future growth of carbon in the air, but the state has not banned fracking, which wastes water and hurts our air quality. And I know that the federal government has been setting higher goals for vehicle mileage—although it also leases the Artic seas to Shell for further oil exploration. We can't have it both ways.

Changing our personal behavior doesn't seem like an imperative either, or it feels useless. Driving a low-emission, high mileage small car while dodging the SUVs on Ventura Boulevard doesn't make my efforts feel very important.

Many religious people think that it is all in God's hands anyway. God created it; God can take it away. It's all in the Big Plan. If you're not religious, there's another attitude that also keeps many people from focusing on the health of the planet. These people believe that science will provide a solution to this problem. In an age of science, they are certain that there must be a technological fix and that some researcher somewhere will stumble across it in the nick of time. Maybe we will colonize another planet or even another solar system.

As activists—people who believe in justice and who think we are responsible to make it happen—so many urgent and immediate issues demand our attention that ensuring the survival of the Earth becomes only one among many. Immigration rights, low-wage working families, blue-on-black violence, incarceration, sexual diversity, women's control over their health, the list goes on. These issues feel important, and they are. Involvement with them also makes us feel as if our individual actions make a difference, and they do.

But behind these important matters, human-caused climate change looms as a threat that jeopardizes everything. If the only home of human life in the cosmos is our mother the Earth, then all our efforts for justice live or die with her fate. How she fares will measure the ultimate success of our work. Her survival is the frame—the big picture—that we must consider in all our individual and collective actions. Every issue must reference and complement the effort to save Earth.

In the meantime, the corporations with the largest financial stake in the status quo and its current direction raise doubts about the very premise of climate change. Through corporate-funded think tanks and research institutes, they challenge the "human-caused" part of the climate change formula. They encourage people to distrust environmental researchers, causing just enough hesitation to shift the argument from the realm of science to the arena of politics and the economy.

For the huge stakeholders like Exxon or Shell, the strategy is to befuddle and block. Curtail the extraction of fossil fuels, they challenge, and the economy will shrink—and our quality of life with it. They argue that it is the responsibility of elected officials to ensure that does not happen. By challenging science, they shift the action from moral obligation in the face of certain calamity, to a political process bogged down by endless debate in legislative bodies they can control.

Perhaps the encyclical by Pope Francis will give us the moral shove we need to make this matter urgent. The piece declares that climate change is caused by human activity and that we have a moral obligation—as governments, as corporations, as individuals—to secure a safe future for life on planet Earth. This upsets the powers of energy extraction, just as it encourages the earth's advocates. If we are lucky, and the angels are on our side, the pope's words will push us to do nothing less than save the earth. Our lives and the lives of our children and their children depend on it.

[Editor's Note: A version of this first ran in Capital & Main. *It is reprinted here by permission.]*

Encountering Francis: Barriers to Action

Carolyn T. Brown

In the encyclical *Laudato si'*, Pope Francis has recast the environmental crisis in spiritual terms, calling us to deep care for the earth and all its creatures as our thankful response for the holy gift of life. He has bypassed the world's powerful institutions, some of which are dysfunctional or morally corrupt, and invited us as individuals into deep dialogue to address the destruction we have wrecked on the earth and on each other. We have worshipped false gods—technology, the financial system, material goods, and others, and without much thought have desecrated the earth. Wisely, Pope Francis offers no simple solutions to the complex, interconnected issues but rather calls each of us to use our human creativity to head off the catastrophe looming ahead.

How will we summon the creativity, the willingness to change our ways? What impediments and resistance will we create to undermine compassionate action even while we strive to implement it?

I was not totally surprised that a pope who had taken up the mantle of St. Francis would evoke the holy man's canticle to brother sun and sister moon, brother wind and sister water, in speaking to the environmental crisis. The popular garden figure of gentle St. Francis feeding little animals belies the ferocity of his biography. In fact, Francis abandoned family riches, lived a life of extreme poverty, and without compromise set out to reform a morally corrupt church. Therefore, when Pope Francis took on his name, he caught the interest of this lapsed Presbyterian. Then when he refused the red shoes and the lavish papal apartments, I thought, surely something is up. And it was.

From my church-going days I remember Christ's admonition: "let he who is without sin cast the first stone." So rather than begin by accusing those most responsible for the problems, I feel called to consider my own culpabilities and ask why I have been slow to perceive the divinity of the natural world, and even slower to show full compassion to the poor and meek, who may inherit the kingdom of heaven but suffer disproportionately in this fallen world of earth.

I grew up in a modest house in New York City where, as a child, I delighted in hunting for four-leaf clovers, studying the ants, and watching the clouds from a comfortable perch on my father's lawn. I attended a university set in one of the most beautiful natural landscapes in the United States, and one spring experienced the death-rattling tumult of gigantic chunks of ice hurtling through the gorge on the day the frozen ice broke free from the lake upstream. I have been no stranger to nature. Yet not until I moved to a house with windows on all sides overlooking a tree-filled natural park did I begin to experience each day the wonder of the natural world. The tulip poplar tree over my outdoor deck amazes me with its demands. In the fall it drops leaves, of course, but also all winter it showers branches. In the spring it dusts me with green pollen, then births new leaves, drops green flowers, and its crowning glory—hurls sweet sap on everything, rendering the furniture and the deck floor a filthy looking black. It also blesses me with its very greenness and cool shade. Until I experienced a tree at this visceral level, through sight, sound, and yes touching the unending debris, I never really sensed how much nature, how very much the earth herself is alive. That required unrelenting experience. It is odd in the saying, but my tree taught me to bless the earth and praise God.

So with the poor. As an upper middle class American, I rarely encounter an obviously poor person, and when I do the context is usually a request for funds. I am sure that there are working poor who staff some offices in my government agency, but workplace protocols disguise that. When confronted by a beggar on the street, I may try to imagine how a beautiful little infant came to live in such a state, but I have no intuitive understanding of that person's likely story. How much harder it is to connect with the humanity of those I have never seen. The refugees fleeing war or hunger are pictures in the newspaper, not people directly experienced. Of course I give to worthy causes, I vote for politicians who seem more compassionate than their rivals, and every usable item that I discard goes to a charitable outlet. I mocked, with a touch of self-righteousness, the political candidate for U.S. president who did not know how many multi-million dollar houses he owned—was it seven or eight? And as the descendent of American black slaves, I do claim some insight into historical suffering. Yes, I can imagine poverty, I can imagine hunger, I can imagine living in fear and aching despair. Nevertheless, even though my own life has not been free of difficulty, I have never suffered extremes of poverty or miseries of horrendous scarcity with my own body, in my own experience.

So when I hear Pope Francis' call to respect the divinity of the earth and that of each human being, I know something of the impediments and resistances that people of goodwill but little experience of either will bring to the response. Of course we can behave better, and many are doing just that, at least with respect to the environment, but it is a great challenge to offer our hearts as well as our heads to the business of loving "mother sister earth" and loving our unseen brothers (and sisters) as ourselves.

The imperative of preventing ecological catastrophe demands that we respond fully with every force we can muster. If necessary, hands must do the work now, and we can hope that hearts, our own as well as others', will follow later. Time may be short. Yet I think that elusive thing known as "political will" depends in part on seeing with our own eyes and hearing with our own ears. What plans will those of us who live in privilege lay to ensure that we experience the livingness of the earth and the suffering—as well as the resilience and dignity—of those who have scarcely enough to survive?

In 2011, I spent a week in Assisi, Italy, as part of the Fetzer Institute's "Global Gathering" that convened several hundreds of people in that place to reflect on the multiple ways that love and forgiveness manifest in professional work. The gathering was amazing; it informed and inspired. But what also seized my soul was walking the hilly cobblestoned streets, the site of St. Francis' work, seeing the stone bed where he slept, and contemplating the Giotto paintings in the Basilica that document his life. I experienced a holy presence in the monastery that he built for his spiritual companion St. Clare in the very room where others have seen "appearances." I felt a holy presence of energy as I slowly circum-navigated his tomb. During that week, for me, St. Francis moved from being an historical figure to becoming an emblem for living knowledge of spiritual force.

In my career as a federal government bureaucrat I was trained to anticipate problems and remove obstacles, and so I bring that habit of mind to the ecological crisis. Most of the world's leadership at the regional and national levels and below lives in cities, as do the elites in the arenas of government, finance, commerce, and so forth. Their wealth, just as my more modest means, insulates them from the exquisite beauty and ferocious terror of the natural world, and it protects, as in fact it was designed to do, from the physical vulnerabilities and psychological burdens of poverty. At a spiritual level, great privilege also impoverishes; to a certain extent they/we really have little idea what we have done and continue to do.

So perhaps the greatest challenge in allowing the encyclical to trans-form us, even in small ways, is that the direct knowledge that would energize us lies beyond easy reach. Climate change is too incremental to be seen on a daily basis, and the poor, well, they live "someplace else." Even as we bring our particular talents and engage the issues with our rational minds—and we do need to do this—perhaps we can also enlarge our imaginations and extrapolate from the small sufferings in our immediate experience to the large sufferings of and across the earth. Perhaps we can allow the force of the two Francises to enter our lives and act on our consciousness and our souls.

A Letter to His Holiness Pope Francis

Thandeka

Your Holiness:

At first glance, your claim in *Laudato si'* that "Once we start to think about the kind of world we are leaving to future generations, we look at things differently"(159)—seems overly optimistic.

Social context is not given adequate account. A case in point.

Recall the story about the 10 billion tons of toxic garbage illegally buried by the Camorra mafia in their own region near Naples for billions of dollars in profits (January 29, 2014, *New York Times*).

When one of the mobsters involved in the dumping operation thought about the carcinogenic effects of the toxic garbage on himself, his family, his community, and their future, he complained to his Camorra boss, saying "We're polluting our own house and our own land. What are we going to drink?"

"You idiot," the boss replied. "We'll drink mineral water."

The dumping continued and the complaining mobster, most likely, became the compliant thug. Refusal was not an option here. His life and the well-being of his wife and family would have been at risk *now* rather than in the future.

Similarly, our social context does the same thing to us. If we refuse to comply with the demands of our jobs that make us active agents in despoiling the earth, we risk losing our jobs, our income, our homes, our families, and even our lives. Just saying "no" is not an option for many of us when the socio-economic fabric of our culture requires us to acquiesce.

On second glance, however, we find the actual context for your claim, which is not secular, but mystical. Your entire letter is written as an invitation to and thus a mental exercise in Christian spirituality.

In your words: When we experience an "interior impulse" (216) which brings about a "change of heart" (218) accompanied by "an alternative understanding of the quality of life [that] encourages a prophetic and contemplative lifestyle" (222) we feel an "intimate connection between God and all beings, and thus [feel] that 'all things are God'" (234). And this feeling stops the toxic show, because not even a mobster dares to dump on God. No Catholic wants to make God angry.

Thus your main point. The kind of spiritual thinking you are calling for requires community. This way of thinking, as you put it, is greater than the insight of one individual or the sum of individual good deeds. Networks of these communities, you tell us, together foster a spirit of generous care.

Placed in this vast spiritual context, you are clearly the shepherd tending to his flock.

But something still seems amiss.

You have not given Catholics and other religious persons a game plan that simply galvanizes these communities to spark spiritual experiences anew in their members, but one that also lays out the concrete steps that must be taken to link these religious communities together so that, billions of persons strong, they take to the streets to demand new work and life protocols as part of their spiritual practice.

Take Cuba, for example. Or more precisely, please take Cuba as a test case for such an action plan.

The floodgates of hell—American dollars for industrial farming and so much more—will pollute Cuba's pristine rivers, damage its protected coral reefs, destroy forests, decimate the network of organic farms, create vast beach resorts and a consumerism culture, and wreck other forms of environmental havoc as closer ties with the U.S. imperil Cuba's habitats (*New York Times*, July 3, 2015).

You can stop this future from happening now.

Gather together the region's cardinals and bishops.

Organize their congregations to ensure new spiritual depth.

Link these churches with other congregations and community groups to care for their earthly home.

Your unswerving voice for the poor of heart and spirit, and for sustainable economic and social wellbeing for us all has turned you into a global rock star.

Rock us into action.

The Purposive Orientation

Cliff Cobb

Like all papal encyclicals related to Catholic social teaching, *Praise be* is both continuous with and different from previous encyclicals. It is continuous in its concerns about poverty, international debt, and global inequity, as well as the insistence that financial speculation and injustice, not overpopulation, are the major causes of human misery. *Praise be* also incorporates a *telos* for human society in the form of "human dignity" that has a long history. Since classical liberalism and neoclassical economic theory deny the possibility of any social purposes that can transcend the sum of individual desires or preferences, the teleological element in Catholic social teaching is one of its great strengths. One might wish that Catholic teleology would derive more from Teilhard de Chardin and less from Aquinas, but as an antidote to excessive individualism of liberal thought, *Praise Be* is a good start.

The major difference between *Praise be* and previous encyclicals is the inclusion of the nonhuman world, including the earth's climate. This is not a perfunctory statement that humans should care for the earth by acting as good stewards. That would not represent much of a departure from the past. What is new is the urgency with which this encyclical calls for us "to recognize the need for changes of lifestyle, production and consumption" (23). After listing the multiplicity of environmental and social crises that are looming before us, Part I concludes with: "we can see signs that things are now reaching a breaking point, due to the rapid pace of change and degradation" (61). This encyclical is a call to take action, not merely to adopt resolutions full of "green" rhetoric (49). It harshly condemns diplomats and their national governments for failing to take decisive action: "It is remarkable how weak international political responses have been" (54).

The central theological precept of this encyclical is humility. We need to face our limitations as humans and "leave behind the modern myth of unlimited material progress" (78). That myth has gained power as human technology has developed greater capacity and as the subjugation of other forms of life has become more complete. Having eaten from the tree of knowledge of good and evil, we have fashioned ourselves as the lords of creation, assuming at all times that what we create is good. At this stage, the recognition that the humanly created order imposes tremendous costs on both humans and nature appears to be the one piece of knowledge that is still lacking.

Integrating humility into modern culture is probably not possible. That is to say, modern thought, which presupposes the capacity of the human mind to solve any problem through the analysis of smaller elements, is inherently arrogant. The technological imperative (or what the encyclical calls "the technocratic paradigm") also proposes that any technical change that solves a military or commercial problem will be a benefit and should be pursued. Indeed, a large portion of commercial inventions are spin-offs from military applications.

One of the most important ideas in the encyclical is synergy—the interactive effect of one or more elements, for good or for ill. Thus, *Praise be* states: "The human environment and the natural environment deteriorate together; we cannot adequately combat environmental degradation unless we attend to causes related to human and social degradation" (48). Later, it expands on that idea: "Ecological culture cannot be reduced to a series of urgent and partial responses to the immediate problems of pollution, environmental decay and the depletion of natural resources. There needs to be a distinctive way of looking at things, a way of thinking, policies, an educational program, a lifestyle and a spirituality which together generate resistance to the assault of the technocratic paradigm" (111).

The synergistic approach to problem solving is entirely different from the compartmentalized approach of modern mechanistic thought, which breaks problems into pieces in order to solve them separately. Thus, some social scientists focus on poverty, others on environmental policy, but few, if any, look for ways to solve both problems together. The possibility of integrated solutions is repudiated as a matter of principle, even by some of the most ardent foes of limitless growth. Since Catholic social teaching has not developed the principle of synergy, *Praise be* merely alludes to it without developing it further. Nevertheless, the use of the term "integral ecology" suggests that this could be one of the most important principles to evolve from this document.

What is most needed at this stage of history is a philosophy that offers a collective purpose, one that could guide the work of both social theorists and activists. Classical liberal political theory recognizes purposes only at the level of individuals pursuing privately defined aims. That is the basis on which economic growth is ultimately defended— the increased ability of individuals to achieve their purposes. Public purposes, such as the survival of the nation, are considered only insofar as they are represented in individual preferences. (An example might be: How much would you be willing to give up in research on heart transplants or personal computing power to increase the probability of the survival of the nation by 0.1%?) Catholic theology has long offered an alternative way of formulating the purpose of social policy: human dignity. This provides a standard by which to judge laws and institutions that is independent of changing individual preferences.

The Catholic understanding of a *telos* or purpose is valuable as a model, but it is unduly restrictive. In fact, its focus solely on human well-being or dignity is one source of the current ecological crisis. This encyclical makes a valiant effort to go beyond the bounds of the inherited *telos* of Catholic theology, but the following statement reveals the difficulty: "Every act of cruelty towards any creature is 'contrary to human dignity'" (92). The necessity of expressing the suffering of nonhuman animals in terms of human dignity is rather awkward. It would be much better to affirm a purpose that encompasses the dignity of nature rather than trying to subsume the value of nature under human dignity.

Ultimately, *Praise be* fails to be sufficiently radical. By that, I do not have in mind the common use of "radical" to mean "critical of capitalism." *Praise be* is, indeed, sharply worded in its denunciations of the excesses of capitalism. Nevertheless, I would argue that capitalism is a symptom of the problem we face, not the deeper cause. To be radical means going to the root, which is precisely what *Praise be* seeks to do. It makes an important start by emphasizing the human relationship to nature, but the need for action goes much further.

A fundamental cause of the many crises that afflict humanity at the moment is the physical separation of most people from the cycles of nature. More than half of the people of the world now live in cities. In the most technologically advanced nations, as much as 80 to 90 percent of the population is now urbanized. Such statistics are important in representing the scale of the problem, but to understand the nature of the problem, we need to look behind the statistics at the cultural and psychological effects of living in cities.

One important, and often overlooked, result of urbanization is that the average person no longer grows up with a diversity of plants and animals, including soil biota, as a normal part of the daily routine. Thus, human and animal waste are not seen as an important element in natural cycles but simply as pollution, something to be flushed away or gathered in plastic bags and put in the garbage. In short, our routine experience involves as much separation from natural processes as possible. With the exception of the large number of pets and houseplants in urban apartments, a city dweller now deals almost exclusively with humans. This lack of knowledge cannot be corrected by "education" in the usual sense of formal schooling. Indeed, the industrial model of schooling that currently prevails around the world is intimately tied to the dissociative nature of modern knowledge. Few students will ever learn to appreciate nature in a sterile building, using a curriculum that favors abstract knowledge. The means contradict the ends.

In the past twenty years, cultural practices have created a higher level of alienation that goes beyond treating nature as an abstraction. Now, even human contact has diminished. Humans increasingly interact with symbols on a screen rather than directly with other people. This is convenient, and it allows friends and family members to stay in touch with each other at long distance. But the dominant effect is to create a barrier to direct human interaction. We are all familiar with the absurd and humorous situation in which people sitting next to each other communicate through text messages. As a result of the electronic communication revolution, other humans, as well as all aspects of nature, are increasingly experienced as digital abstractions.

The phenomena associated with urbanization and digitization are widely regarded as psychological issues that do not rise to the same level of concern as such pressing problems as climate change, economic inequality, crime, or other issues that become headline news. Yet, if we project current trends forward, it should become clear that the transformation of human consciousness caused by urbanization and digitization is going to make solutions to the "big problems" impossible. Already, there are signs that people who have been raised with digital consciousness dismiss social and environmental problems as "coding errors." A whole generation has been raised to believe that reality begins and ends on the computer screen. Even before that, we are faced with two generations of young people who tacitly believed that food comes from grocery stores. The more enlightened and sophisticated members of the new generation recognize that food should be grown "organically," but that still remains an abstraction that has more do with labeling practices than with the survival of earthworms or bees. Being "organic" is seldom perceived to be a condition that involves the structure of the entire agricultural system, from production to marketing, much less a concern for the soil and its life forms.

At this stage in human history, these extreme, but normal, forms of alienation should have made clear that the experiment in liberal thought has been a failure. The celebration of the human spirit as a property of individuals has led to a set of consequences that now threaten to destroy the very thing we celebrate. Liberalism sought to free each of us as individuals from the constraints of nature and social convention in order to pursue our own ends, with the expectation that this would lead to character development. That was the hope of the Enlightenment: with the aid of liberal arts education, each individual would develop his or her full potential. It was, and still is, a noble ideal, and yet it was a house built on sand. The dissociative consequence of removing people from their natural setting was present from the beginning, but it was not immediately noticeable. Indeed, it remains a hidden problem today, even when the signs of it are so obvious.

The rise of fascism was another sign that something was wrong with the liberal ideal. Many people throughout Europe and the United States (not just Germany, Italy, and the other Axis powers) were attracted to a philosophy that offered a collective, national purpose. Many variants of socialism have offered the same hope—a purpose for which people could work together instead of merely pursuing their own private ends. Even if those options were flawed in many ways, and even though they offered only minor improvements in the human relationship to nature, they reveal a longing for connection that is not met by liberalism.

Catholic social teaching has also been offering an alternative to liberalism for over a century. Despite its flaws (primarily its unwavering affiliation with Aristotelian-Thomistic categories of thought, in contrast to a more biblical foundation), it may still offer the best starting point in Western thought with which to rethink the most basic principles of civilization. That is to say, it begins with purpose, and it now recognizes that nature must be part of that purpose in some way.

The purpose of ecological culture, as described in *Praise be*, might be thought of as maximizing wisdom within the context of preserving biological complexity. This challenges not only industrialism but also the individualistic principles of liberalism. It goes beyond the traditional Catholic emphasis on human dignity, but it does so by integrating the new elements in *Praise be*. Most importantly, it challenges all of us to imagine new institutions by which to strive for human wisdom in an ecological context.

In the case of education, for example, we might question whether industrial-style schooling can ever impart wisdom, particularly in an urban setting. Does that mean abandoning universities and all forms of schooling that presently exist? Perhaps so. They are oriented toward the production and dissemination of instrumental knowledge, but they are designed in such a way that wisdom, particularly ecological wisdom, can play no role. This does not mean that we should throw out the knowledge previously gained or cease to develop it. But if the purpose of educational institutions was deemed to be the "production" of wisdom, their internal structure would have to change dramatically.

In similar fashion, the goal of an economy would shift from efficiency (a means orientation that intentionally avoids common goals) to activities that were conducive to a specific purpose—the development of wisdom. Instead of supporting rules that make transportation faster, clothing more plentiful, and investment more profitable, the logic of a legal and regulatory framework would be oriented toward adequacy and diversity of regional (sub-national) output, equality in the distribution of economic surpluses, and conditions that make production itself a source of learning. Cost accounting would be supplemented in the decisions of production units by legally enforceable requirements that life-cycle and social accounting principles must be adhered to. Some type of reflective process, similar to ones used in Amish communities, could be used by public jurisdictions to determine which types of new technologies should be allowed. Even socialism has never truly clarified the purposes that an economy is supposed to serve. Most socialists have thought only in terms of worker management and more equal distribution of wealth, not the ultimate social aim of all production and consumption.

In keeping with the goal of re-connecting both life and education with ecological processes, it is almost certain that the current process of urbanization would be reversed. Unless people actually live in a context in which daily decisions are related to the natural environment, the latter will remain an abstraction. Ecological culture must necessarily be one in which human behavior adapts to local conditions rather than one in which natural differences are eliminated in order to adapt nature to human desires. That is a very difficult condition to create in cities, where people mostly interact with technology, not nature.

The process of de-urbanization, however, reveals why the process of changing course in a radical way is going to be like trying to unravel a string that is tangled up and knotted. The problem we face is actually worse because we cannot simply undo what we have done. The complexity and interconnectedness of the pathways of habit, knowledge, and energy will make efforts to untangle the knots difficult and perhaps self-contradictory. Thus, the reversal of urbanization cannot be simple and direct for several reasons. First, a "back to the land" movement would fail because the preconditions for its success are largely missing. For example, plow-animals do not exist in large numbers in many parts of the world, and even if they did, few people would know how to use them. In general, cultural knowledge in most societies has been focused on urban problems for more than a century. Most urbanites simply do not know how to live outside the city. Second, even if it were possible to peacefully and intelligently transfer one or two billion people from cities to the countryside, the result might be a rapid growth of human population. The single largest factor limiting population growth in recent decades has been rapid urbanization. For the entire history of civilization, rural areas have had higher fertility than cities. Thus, the process of de-urbanization could easily lead to a reversal of recent declines in fertility around the world.

All of these speculations are far too radical to even think of putting them into practice in the near term. Nevertheless, we must all begin thinking in categories with which we are now unfamiliar if we are ever to make a transition to a livable future. The fact that the problems facing humanity cannot be solved in a direct, linear fashion is precisely why modern culture needs to be displaced by a culture of wisdom. Our current intellectual tools may not be adequate, but we can hope that the tools developed in a world based on wisdom will be.

Listening to the Impoverished

David Ongombe

At the heart of the papal encyclical stands an amazing proposal for an "integral" ecology embracing the environment, the economy, and the whole of political and social reality. By that holistic vision, the pope counters a complex combination of realities that reinforce our current world civilization, with its unbelievable destruction of both human beings and the nonhuman world. The courageous writing of the pope condemns this civilization. He sees that its "ecological management" is based on superficial and fragmentary rationalism and a continuing dualism. It employs technology in the service of capitalism. Confronted by the concept of "integral ecology" many slogans, such as *"mondialisation"* (globalization) and *"communauté internationale"* (international community), as well as the actual international organizations for the protection of the environment, must be radically reconceived.

Current practice and theory pits one part of the world and its people against the whole of humanity and its environment (its home). This current dangerous and "un-integrative" management of ecology is encouraged by ignorance and indifference. It is in fact an unacceptable mismanagement, expressing ill will, and injustice. It expresses the control given to the most economically powerful to exploit the weakest. The most scandalous result of all of this is the massive destruction of the poorest and a rapid lessening of the possibility for the survival of humanity.

The pope sees that there is now a torture of nature and humanity on a planetary scale. Some of the responsibility for this unbelievable situation is individual and some is collective. The extent depends on the actors' capacities to influence events around the world. This torture has various components, such as invasion, colonization, wars, slavery, dictatorships, racism, and genocide. It results in the unilateral enrichment of superpower countries; the exponential growth of the richest exploiting powers. It often destroys the food systems of whole people in order to add to the wealth of those who are already rich.

Certainly such universal torture can be described as "unjust genocide." It involves a toxicity imposed on nature by a perversion of its own components. The human will, politics, economics, and technological projects are linked as a *system* manipulated by the strongest hand—often for ideological purposes. When such a system excludes the principles of social justice and equity, it certainly neglects what the pope sees: that the clamor of the earth is internally related to the clamor of the poor people. Those two clamors constitute an appeal for a holistic or integrative ecology.

Commitment to the ideal of integral ecology is vital for new, innovative, revolutionary, and genuinely ecological management. Such work requires an interdisciplinary dialogue. It must lead to revision of our basic concepts imposed by the dualistic rationalist civilization that has shaped our sense of reality and its human component.

Many scholars, working in different disciplines, have already shed light on what an integral ecology involves and requires. Alfred North Whitehead, Charles Hartshorne, John Cobb, David Griffin, Herman Greene, and many others have pushed ahead in research. They have created centers for interdisciplinary dialogue to promote the thinking needed to develop integral ecology. The intercontinental impact of their ideas is expressed in the creation of organizations providing various possibilities for dialogue among Chinese, Japanese, Korean, Indian, Latin American, European, and African peoples around ecological questions related to a holistic vision. From those intercontinental streams new ideas are being discussed in different formulations, assuming the intuition of a deep and integral ecology: green ecology, ecozoic vision, ecological economics, regenerative ecology, deep ecology, African integrative and differential ecology, and ecological civilization.

The pope's intuitions about ecology could be rapidly advanced if he engaged in dialogue with proponents of process thought and ecozoic civilization and the traditional philosophies of other continents. To talk about an integral ecology, one must recover and promote the sensibilities of peoples of different continents. In this way these peoples could be active contributors, not only the beneficiaries, to the development of a catholic idea of integral ecology. They would be true partners in the dialogue. Many indigenous cultures around the world can provide fundamental resources for this ecological revolution (integrative) for which the pope courageously spoke. I have found Whitehead's philosophy to be one of the best tools for facilitating dialogue.

We shall not know how to move forward in this integral ecology without a rigorous criticism of dualistic rationalism. Derrida can help us understand how an ethnocentric ideology has imposed planetary torture, using the justification that it has provided economic and technological progress and a kind of unilateral protection. Numerous rationalist dualistic thinkers have considered some of the world's people to be "deprived of rationality." This has been used to justify their absence from the decision-making that has managed the planet. Their silencing is one of springs of the integrative ecology crisis. The result is that laws favor the richest nations while the birth rate is highest among the poorest.

An Aesthetic Revolution of Love

Sheri D. Kling

Prejudice should not have us criticize those who seek ecstasy in music or poetry. There is a subtle mystery in each of the movements and sounds of this world.

The quote above from the 9th century Sufi poet and mystic Ali al-Khawas is not the only surprising treasure in Pope Francis' encyclical letter *Laudato si': On Care for Our Common Home.* Reading this document as a theologian, artist, and student of the work of Alfred North Whitehead, I was also surprised to find an abundance of themes that are common to Whitehead's thought. Pope Francis eloquently writes of the intrinsic value of creation and a natural world with its own purposes, that everything is interrelated and interdependent, and that the human and natural environments will deteriorate or flourish together. He decries the reductionistic, materialistic, and individualistic culture based on a modernist worldview that has contributed to the destruction of the environment and the loss of species. He bemoans the economic commodification and objectification that replaces aesthetic value and craftsmanship with disposable monocultures. Moreover, Pope Francis describes the earth and its inhabitants as an interweb of trinitarian relations and calls us to a spiritual conversion based on such values as love, harmony, and beauty.

There is much in this document on which I could comment, but having just finished organizing a section for the Seizing an Alternative conference on the transformative power of the arts, it is through the aesthetic lens that I wish to respond. I do so not only because there is, of course, an aesthetic quality to the natural world that we can appreciate, but also because I believe that it is only through the arts that a vision compelling enough to be a catalyst for conversion can be offered. We care for what we cherish, and we cherish what we love. In short, I believe that what we require now is an *aesthetic revolution of love* to spur us over the barricades of ecological inaction, apathy, and despair. Environmental activists have heaped up mountains of data about climate change, mass extinctions, and other environmental disasters with little effect on much of the general public. Maybe Whitehead was right when he said that "it is more important a proposition be interesting than that it be true"[1] because, as David Ray Griffin noted, "unless it is interesting, thereby becoming a 'lure for feeling,' no one will care whether it is true."[2]

Whitehead believed that God was concerned about the "zest for life" or the "intensity" that all beings experience, and that the world is aiming for enjoyment. For him, God was the "lure for feeling" or the "eternal urge of desire,"[3] operating as a "divine Eros urging the world to new heights of enjoyment."[4] For Whitehead, the highest value is Beauty (an idea much more nuanced than our typical understanding of that term), and it is this feeling-soaked aesthetic that lures us forward. Pope Francis recognizes that beauty provides a counterpoint to "self-interested pragmaticism" and writes that "If someone has not learned to stop and admire something beautiful, we should not be surprised if he or she treats everything as an object to be used and abused without scruple" (215). Whitehead also mentions peace and harmony as other aims of God, but, ultimately, "the teleology of the Universe is directed to the production of Beauty,"[5] which includes "the most material and the most sensuous enjoyments."[6]

Surprisingly, John Calvin also linked beauty with passion and desire. According to Beldon Lane, Calvin turned the idea of the *theatrum mundi* on its head by seeing God not as a Divine Playwright determining all of the action onstage, but as its principle actor, dressed in Nature's garments, seeking to move us to love and desire for God's self. For Calvin, it is God's alluring performance through Nature's wonders and the passionate response of all beings that actually create the world. Here we find the *eros* of relatedness as a fulcrum around which actualized existence turns. No wonder the pope insists that we are "made for love."

While Pope Francis most frequently describes God as Father, all-powerful, and the ultimate "owner" of creation, God is also experienced in a tender way, as a presence that cares for the world and its creatures. Pope Francis draws from Saint John of the Cross who thought that the goodness in creation also existed "eminently and infinitely" in God and that finite things, being intimately connected and enlivened *by* God, could be experienced *as* God. For Saint John, God is the Beloved who is encountered in mountains, valleys, trees and birds (234). I find this image of God as Beloved and as capable of being met in the natural world to be more compelling, more alluring, for the spiritual conversion that is called for.

In *Laudato si'*, God is described as able to be discovered in all things, and intimately present to each being. Nature is a "certain kind of art," a source of "wonder and awe," and God is an author who "has written a book whose letters are the multitude of created things, manifestations of God" (85, quoting John Paul II's *Catechesis*). "Nature," writes Pope Francis, "is filled with words of love, but how can we listen to them amid constant noise, interminable and nerve-wracking distractions, or the cult of appearances?"(225). Christian spirituality and community relatedness are presented as part of the solution, and humans are described as having an innate "openness to what is good, true and beautiful" (205). Even in the midst of some of the most destructive forces of poverty and overcrowding, love proves itself to be the more powerful force. Even in such conditions, an "experience of communitarian salvation" (149) can spark creative responses.

But creativity is not just available as a response to the world engendered by bonds of love; in fact, creativity is at the very heart of things, through the work of the Holy Spirit. Though art is mentioned only infrequently in the text, there are many instances when aesthetic values are lifted up. Jesus' nondualism and harmony with the world are connected to his willingness to work with his hands, "in daily contact with the matter created by God, to which he gave form by his craftsmanship" (98). Beautiful architecture is contrasted with "megastructures" and a culture focused on mass acquiring and disposing of cheaply made goods (113). We are drowning in plastic and megabytes but starved for meaning and joy; at risk is our very "historic, artistic and cultural patrimony" (143) as we wallpaper the globe with a consumerist monoculture.

This very topic was discussed in our conference track called "Imaginal Communities: The Power of Place in Art and Story," and it is this kind of collaborative spirit between communities, artists, and storytellers that I believe can provide the "aesthetic education" and motivation that will be necessary for us to take the leap toward integral ecology with strong commitment. As Pope Francis notes, "This patrimony [of nature as well as of history, art, and culture] is a part of the shared identity of each place and a foundation upon which to build a habitable city . . . there is a need to incorporate the history, culture and architecture of each place, thus preserving its original identity. Ecology, then, also involves protecting the cultural treasures of humanity in the broadest sense" (143).

Pope Francis calls for many different types of dialogue, including the realms of politics, economics, religion, science, and local and national policymaking, and I would argue that it is crucial for the artists and storytellers to be at the table for each and every one. When the pope asks for a "universal awareness" that can be translated into "new habits," an "awakening of a new reverence for life," and an "ecological conversion" (207), I honestly do not believe any of those will happen without the aesthetic lures for feeling that can draw us toward the "great motivations which make it possible for us to live in harmony, to make sacrifices and to treat others well" (200). I have heard of studies showing that people who read fiction develop more compassion, and I can think of no other means as effective in breaking open human hearts as art. If it is indeed true that "a sense of deep communion with the rest of nature cannot be real if our hearts lack tenderness, compassion and concern for our fellow human beings" (91), then it is time to enlist the artists in the "bold, cultural revolution" (114)—what I'm calling the *aesthetic revolution of love*—to which we are called. Surely the "ecstasy in music or poetry" can lead us to discover the "subtle mystery in each of the movements and sounds of this world" (233, quoting Ali al-Khawas).

Endnotes

1. Alfred North Whitehead, *Process and Reality,* 1929, corrected edition, ed. by D. R. Griffin and D. S. Sherburne (New York: The Free Press, 1978), 259.

2. David Ray Griffin, *Archetypal Psychology: Self and Divine in Whitehead, Jung, and Hillman* (Chicago: Northwestern University Press, 1990), 15.

3. Whitehead, *Process and Reality*, 344.

4. John B Cobb, Jr, and David Ray Griffin, *Process Theology: An Introductory Exposition* (Philadelphia: Westminster Press, 1976), 26.

5. Alfred North Whitehead, *Adventures of Ideas,* 1933 (New York: The Free Press, 1967), 265

6 .Whitehead, *Adventures of Ideas,* 257.

Appreciation and Questions

Roger S. Gottlieb

For the many of us—clergy and laypeople, academics and plain citizens, in the U.S. and throughout the world—who for decades have been saying that the environmental crisis calls for a religious perspective and an activist religious response, Pope Francis' bold words are a wonderfully welcome addition.

At least three things give those words special weight: first, as the years pass the reality of both global warming in particular and the other dimensions of the crisis (including the vast scale of pollution, species loss, and environmental illness) have become increasingly clear. Second, Pope Francis has established himself as a humble, intelligent, and authentic spiritual leader. If political conservatives resent his critique of capitalism, and cultural conservatives wish he would condemn homosexuals, an awful lot of other people (Catholic or not) see him as a man trying to live up to the traditional Christian virtues of love, forgiveness, and humility.

Third, and perhaps most important: Francis is clearly and unambiguously (for the most part, at least, while skirting population control) calling a spade a spade: he rejects consumerism and unfettered capitalism, anthropocentrism and turning the earth into "an immense pile of filth." He does not take refuge in vague generalities or idealistic appeals to unthreatening platitudes.

As an essentially secular person, I am delighted. Every (serious) environmentalist needs every other (serious) environmentalist. If there was ever an "issue" on which religious and secular, scientists and critical theorists, people of all races and nations and cultures might agree, it is this one.

We are left, however, with some serious questions. The first one is to what degree anything said by the pope, or any other religious leader from the head of the World Council of Churches to the Patriarch of Orthodox Christianity, will make a difference. Some years ago I read that American Catholics use birth control at the same rate as nonCatholics. As a predominantly Christian country the overwhelming consumerist and militarist U.S. is clearly paying scant heed to biblical admonitions against wealth, violence, revenge, or arrogance. As one woman from Italy interviewed on the radio said about the his environmental stand: "I like this pope—so I will do what he says." The implication being, of course, that if she didn't like him she might not.

In the end it may be that for the vast majority of people religious virtues are simply too demanding to live up to. Loving your enemy (even loving your neighbor), overcoming desire, truly seeing Allah as the *only* God (as opposed to wealth, power, or masculine privilege), and so forth are observed much more in the breach than in reality throughout the world's religious communities. Perhaps the values and virtues of religious environmentalism—care and respect for other creatures, concern for the future of the earth, carefully avoiding any industrial policy which harms the most vulnerable—are just too hard to follow as well.

The second question concerns the behavior of the Catholic Church itself: its vast wealth and property, the institutions it directs, the level of consumption of its leading figures (from bishops and cardinals to the presidents of Catholic universities and heads of Catholic hospitals). How much property could be sold, with proceeds going to green the ones that are left? How many cuts in salary or benefits would the top men be willing to accept in order to do their part? What kinds of sacrifices will the Church advocate for its better off members throughout the world: that they should eat more locally, stop consuming meat, drive less, fly less, challenge existing ecologically destructive policies and powers, and start being really careful with everything they throw "away"? Where is the church's wealth invested and when will that wealth be disinvested from the fossil fuel industry? When will powerful lay members of the church, what we Jews call the "big givers," hear that wealth derived from global warming or other forms of pollution is no more acceptable than wealth derived from prostitution rings or drug sales?

The sad truth is that the Catholic Church, like the university where I teach, like almost all the concentrations of wealth and power in the world, depend heavily on an economy and industrial system that are environmentally destructive. It is certainly fine and fitting for Francis to scold governments and corporations and greedy consumers. But the scolding must include his own huge community, and given his position a series of detailed environmental guidelines—perhaps not orders but definitely stronger than mere suggestions—need to follow.

Finally, there are the related questions of hope and despair. While the pope's declaration is one among many positive signs, the overall tendency in environmental matters has been continuing deterioration. The sheer quantity of refuse we've deposited in earth, air, and water; the crushing number of extinguished species; the rising costs to economies, cities, villages and islands. As well, and most significant, the way the majority of the most powerful commit themselves to only minor variations in business as usual. What is a realist to do but despair of our species?

Theists have one advantage over those of us whose sense of the sacred is limited to the natural universe. This advantage resides in the belief that there is, at the heart of existence, an Intelligence and Intention that is fundamentally on the side of goodness, love, and care. Like the cowboys who used to ride over the hill to come to the rescue at the end of the movies I saw as a child, belief in God serves as a beacon of trust that Someone, Somehow, is On Our Side.

Exactly how this will work out in practice is somewhat vague, and surely every believer is aware of all the times—the wars, plagues, famines, abused children, and genocides—when at least in the short run only evil triumphed. Yet we do not have to know *how* God is on our side to be comforted by the thought that She is. Indeed it is one of the characteristics of both institutional religions and non-denominational and eclectic spirituality to believe that whatever happens in the short run, by a mysterious cosmic calculus every good act matters—somehow. While some will talk of Heaven and others of Karma, and others not know what to say, there is a trust that it makes some kind of difference to live with love, even if we cannot see what kind of difference that is. Again: those of us who are, for want of a better term, "naturalists," can have no such faith or hope.

Yet perhaps, and here I speak simply for myself, the ultimate outcome is not what matters most. Ask yourself: if you possessed a completely accurate crystal ball that could foretell the future with unerring accuracy; and the ball showed you a future in which completely acidified oceans, near constant overwhelming droughts and floods, tens of millions of climate refugees, and decimated agriculture have all come true—well, what then?

Would it then make sense to give up our work, leave the fridge door open, buy a gas guzzler, stop teaching and writing and talking to people we know and demanding that governments and corporations and churches and universities change their ways? Even if we won't win, should we stop trying to live with love?

I don't think so and in whatever ways we disagree about God, Heaven, Scripture, or the role of gender in religious institutions, I am reasonably sure the pope doesn't think so either. Let our work continue. Let us live lives of love. Whatever the future holds, it's the best way to live today.

Dialogue between Paradigms (Anthropocentric/Biocentric, Technocratic/Ecospiritual)

John Quiring

Nobody is suggesting a return to the Stone Age, but we do need to slow down and look at reality in a different way. (114)

Culture war polarization makes it easy to miss third-way thinking in *On Care for Our Common Home.* If a lingering presumption that "radical environmentalism" is leftist divides reactions to the pope's letter, both sides will ignore its invitation to *everyone* to dialogue (201) about future scenarios (collapse or sustainability), components (resources, pollution, population), and factors of causation and remedy (worldview, agriculture, religion, technology, science, modernity, economics, politics, etc.). But if "[i]deological diversity remains a hallmark . . . of the whole spectrum of radical environmentalism,"[1] the left-wing and right-wing can explore coalition. And, if "[e]veryone's talents are needed to redress the . . . abuse of God's creation" (47), how might environmental critics be enlisted?

Multiple readings and assessments were bound to arise from the 246 paragraphs in *Our Common Home.* By responding to conservative dismissal of the letter, I seek to document a possible third-way reading.

Something of a dialogue is thereby rendered. *The Guardian* response was "most astonishing";[2] "stunning" said *The Nation* editor.[3] But many conservatives were dismissive. The very first words I heard about the letter were on a road trip in South Carolina—listening to radio talkers. Later—googling for a transcript of what I'd heard—I found more reactions. But how closely had the letter been read? How carefully can *anyone* read it in a culture of omnipresent media spin and counter-spin (47), drowning out voices of wisdom and reason?

Rush Limbaugh said: "Il Papa . . . is basically saying to . . . environmentalist wackos, . . . they're going to have to also . . . become anti-abortion, which they won't. . . . The consensus of scientists is bought and paid for. . . . The earth is not warming. We're in the midst of a 10-year cooling cycle."[4] Another way to look at it, I suggest, is: There's something for *everyone* in the letter. Indeed, it is pro-life!—though in more ways than one. Again, isn't all science funded—government *and* corporate?[5] NASA says "nine of the 10 warmest years since 1880 have been in the last decade."[6] "The first five months of 2015 topped the warmest such period on record for the globe."[7]

Again: "The Pope's . . . Marxist Climate Rant" will be 'Leaving **"Everybody . . . Living Equally In Misery"'** . . . **and he's** "directing mankind to worship the Antichrist" . . . "talking about some super government" . . . It's "blasphemous to call our ancestors . . . greedy thieves."[8] Is it Marxist to affirm "justice, peace, love and beauty" (47) or "credit, insurance, and markets" (94)? But is it capitalist to teach the "universal destination of goods" (93) and "a social mortgage on all private property" (93)?

Equal misery or climate justice? The letter says, the "time has come to accept decreased growth in some parts of the world, in order to provide resources for other places to experience healthy growth" (193). Is it ranting to say "Doomsday predictions can no longer be met with irony or disdain" (161)? Again, polarized focus on *climate* policy-particulars obscures the letter's call for attention to matters *beyond* politics and economics, technoscience and reproductive health—e.g., "liberation from fear, greed, and compulsion" (9).

World Government? Is super-government called for—or subsidiarity:[9] "global consensus . . . for . . . problems which cannot be resolved by . . . individual countries" (164). But did not the near-collapse of trans-national finance (175) in 2008 indicate the need of counter-vailing pow-er—a "true world political authority" (175)? And an "antichrist" (1 Jn 2:22) does not contemplate the "Trinitarian Lord . . . in the beauty of the universe" (246).

Again, was the letter ghostwritten by Al Gore, Karl Marx, and Teilhard de Chardin?[10] No—by the Pontifical Council for Justice and Peace.[11] Peggy Noonan's warning that the church has been known to side with the wrong science[12] allows the letter's refusal of climate skepticism to obscure its more fundamental employment of a family-values meta-phor—one common home for a universal family. *The Weekly Standard* warned against the encroachment of state-supported "Environmental Religions:" "The climate change crusade gains a prominent leader," it lamented.[13] But, libertarian economist Robert Nelson sees a larger chal-lenge to confront—the "holy war" between "economic religion" and "environmental religion."[14]

Alas, the pope's letter about "our common home" was bound to be trashed by *some* "conservatives" because—in the course of its politiciza-tion—the environmental challenge came to be seen as a single-interest, anti-conservative movement best handled by well-financed NGOs.[15] But a *five*-wave history of U.S. environmentalism, with global echoes, has yet to be widely internalized: (1) wilderness conservation, (2) activism and legislation, (3) greening of technology and business, (4) radicalization, (5) pragmatic pluralism.[16] The third wave includes green conservatives.[17]

What is pragmatic pluralism? "Given the complexity of the ecological crisis and its multiple causes, we need to realize that the solutions will not emerge from just one way of interpreting and transforming reality . . . no branch of the sciences and no form of wisdom can be left out" (63). By encouraging dialogue between sciences and religions (201), instead of polarizing debate and gridlock on "geosystem" (34) issues, the letter probes causal factors *beyond the usual suspects*, inviting readers to consider "the rich contribution which religions can make towards an integral ecology and the full development of humanity" (62).

Sheer overreach?[18] So you might still be thinking, "But, how much can a pope know about science, technology, ecology, economics, and politics? Shouldn't he stick to his business?" Arguably he does, but he gets there by first noting the limitations of specialization (201), and after climbing out of the wreckage, so to speak, of colliding secular proposals and counter-proposals. Necessarily touching on so many points—"[g]iven the complexity of . . . causes" (63)—exposes him to misunderstanding from more sides than one. Perhaps philosophy of religion's expertise in managing polarized perspectives (e.g., believer/unbeliever) provides a context for mediating the letter's contrasting of **mindsets**: egoist, objectivist, reductionist, instrumental vs. mystical, relational, trandisciplinary, "open systems" and "emergence" (81).

Dialogue? Because "there is not one . . . solution" (60), the encyclical calls for a new, open **dialogue** (201), including **everyone** (14), not just environmentalists (201) and scientists (143). Why *open* dialogue? Because otherwise we can remain isolated with partial perspectives that leave us with incomplete information (138), and temptation to absolutize our own specialization (201). "A fragmentation of knowledge and isolation of bits of information can . . . become a form of ignorance, unless . . . integrated into a **broader vision**"(138).

So what is the dialogue about? The nature of reality—to "look at reality in a different way" (114) than most of us do most of the time. *And how is that?* We "turn reality into an **object** simply to be used and controlled" (11). Again, that's "[a]n instrumental way of reasoning, a purely static analysis, in the service of present needs" (195). *And why is that a problem?* It implies that "we have stopped thinking about the **goals** of human activity" (61), beyond day-to-day existence.

And what more is there than what's in front of our face? A larger perspective reminds us that "everything is connected" (117), "interrelated" (120). Earth is "our common home" for millions of species—past, present, future. "Nature cannot be regarded as something separate . . . or . . . a mere setting in which we live. We are part of nature, included in it" (139). But "our common home" is being mistreated (53), "falling into disrepair" (61), and we can "discover what each of us can do about it" (19). Unquestionably, biologically "we are one single human family" (52). Notions of "common good" and "intergenerational **solidarity**" (158-9) represent human oneness at the moral level of analysis. To reinforce human oneness at the level of choice, we need to worry that ecology alone won't have significant results "unless we struggle with deeper issues" like "What kind of a world do we want to leave to those who come after us?" (160)—indeed "the world we have received also belongs to those who will follow us" (159).

Then what? Only after we have arrived at that level of awareness—discernable not only by popes and religions but by other perspectives—philosophical, psychological, artistic—are we in a position to appreciate that "[v]ariable **future scenarios** will have to be generated between . . . **extremes**—biocentric and anthropocentric (118). *To biocentrists* the encyclical warns that we probably can't sustain support for other vulnerable and defenseless species and individuals unless we "acknowledge the worth of a poor person, a human embryo, a person with disabilities" (117). *To anthropocentrists* the encyclical warns that "when human beings place themselves at the center," all else becomes relative" (122). Thus, for all their genuine truth, power, and productivity, "when well directed" (103), science, technology, and markets can become unbalanced and destructive in the context of the globalized, "omnipresent technocratic paradigm and the cult of unlimited human power" (122), blocking access to any "different cultural paradigm" (108).

What would be an alternative paradigm? As "the **external deserts** in the world are growing, because the **internal deserts** have become so vast" (217), we can learn or rediscover "**another form of progress and development**" (191): For the poor—"growth marked by moderation;" for the rich—"less is more" (222). That is, if the consumption of the rich has negative "repercussions" on the poor (51), the developed countries can assist underdeveloped countries toward sustainable development (52).

The pope's business, then, is evaporating "that unhealthy anxiety" that lays waste the world (241). *How so?* By demonstrating "a spirituality of that global solidarity" (240) that embeds individuals in humanity, humans in life, institutions in a culture of life. It teaches *the transcendent meaning of ecological ethics* (210), embodying the Franciscan vision of "the union of all creatures" (244), employing the metaphoric complex of one "universal family" (89)—one species, one life of mother Earth (92) and father God (96)—for "a future . . . shared with everyone" (202).

Endnotes

1. Franklin Rosemont, "Radical Environmentalism," in *Encyclopedia of the American Left*, ed., M. Buhle, P. Buhle, and D. Georgakas (New York: Garland, 1990), 629.

2. <http://www.theguardian.com/commentisfree/2015/jun/18/guardian-view-on-laudato-si-pope-francis-cultural-revolution>. Accessed 7/5/15.

3. <http://www.washingtonpost.com/opinions/pope-francis-takes-aim-at-the-worship-of-markets/2015/06/23/06f64588-18f9-11e5-ab92-c75ae6ab94b5_story.html>. Accessed 7/5/15.

4. <http://www.rushlimbaugh.com/daily/2015/06/18/the_pope_throws_the_left_a_curve>. Heard on South Carolina radio 6/18/15; accessed 7/1/15.

5. <https://en.wikipedia.org/wiki/Funding_of_science>. Accessed 7/3/15.

6. <http://climate.nasa.gov/climate_resources/10/>. Accessed 7/3/16.

7. <http://www.weather.com/news/climate/news/earth-warmest-january-may-2015>. Accessed 7/6/15.

8. <http://mediamatters.org/research/2015/06/18/conservative-media-vs-the-pope-the-worst-reacti/204037>. Accessed 6/26/15.

9. <http://americamagazine.org/issue/laudato-si-joins-tradition-catholic-social-teaching>. Accessed 7/3/15.

10. <http://remnantnewspaper.com/web/index.php/fetzen-fliegen/item/1819-why-i-m-disregarding-laudato-si-and-you-should-too>. Accessed 7/5/15.

11. <https://en.wikipedia.org/wiki/Laudato_si%27>. Accessed 7/5/15.

12. Peggy Noonan in *The Wall Street Journal*, 6/12/15. <http://mediamatters.org/research/2015/06/18/conservative-media-vs-the-pope-the-worst-reacti/204037>. Accessed 7/5/15.

13. <http://www.weeklystandard.com/keyword/Laudato-Si>. Accessed 7/5/15.

14. Robert H. Nelson, *The New Holy Wars: Economic Religion versus Environmental Religion in Contemporary America* (University Park: Penn State University Press, 2010).

15. <http://www.thebreakthrough.org/images/Death_of_Environmentalism.pdf>. Accessed, 7/3/15.

16. To the four-wave history in Mark Dowie, *Losing Ground* (Cambridge: MIT, 1995) can be added a fifth wave: "Pragmatism" and "Environmental Pluralism," J. B. Callicott and R. Frodeman, eds., *Encyclopedia of Environmental Ethics* (Detroit: Gale, 2009): I: 384-87 and II: 174-77.

17. Roger Scruton, Chet Bowers, John Bliese, Gordon Durnil, Rod Dreher, Wendell Berry, E. F. Schumacher.

18. <http://www.cruxnow.com/church/2015/06/25/pope-francis-has-spoken-on-the-environment-will-us-lawmakers-listen/>. Accessed 7/3/15.

Care for our Common Home and the Degrowth Movement: A Message of Radical Transformation

Barbara Muraca

Introduction: an encyclical for degrowth!

Last year I had the extraordinary good fortune of being part of an incredible event: the Fourth International Conference on Degrowth for Ecological Sustainability and Social Equity that took place in Leipzig, Germany. It was conceived, organized, and coordinated by a large group of very young activists and scholars and attended by over 3000 participants, while 7000 followed the conference via internet. According to what some scholars call prefigurative politics, the group tried to live up to the principles that they envisioned as core guidelines for a future society beyond the dictate of economic growth: gender equality, basic democracy and consensus-oriented decision-making, basic income, (re)distribution, self-management, reduced working hours, and care (shared child care during meetings, ongoing supervision to avoid one-sided overworking, convivial meals, care of emotions and the needs of the body, and so on).

A heterogeneous, vivid, and audacious social movement has originated from the conference in Leipzig and has joined the wider Degrowth movement that originated in Southern Europe almost 10 years ago.

Degrowth activists and scholars see in the current economic and ecological crisis a great chance to start changing things in a more radical
way: for them degrowth is not simply a way of coping with economic
shrinking and recession, but a radical transformation of the basic institutions of our societies, in order to render them independent from the
growth-addiction.

Reading the encyclical I was impressed by Pope Francis' radical
position in criticizing the Western model of development and explicitly
referring to the (moral and political) need to degrow for the countries of
the Global North. This is necessary in order to give space to the Global
South to grow enough to guarantee a minimal standard of living to
their populations (193). When I first heard about the encyclical and was
asked to write a comment about its relation to the degrowth movement,
I thought that it would not be a particularly interesting question, as the
movement is characterized by a strongly secular perspective. Although
the conference was *inter alia* supported by different noncommercial
foundations and social groups, including NGOs, inspired by Christian
values, the general background of many conference participants was
orbiting around a new, creative, and original form of leftist anarchism.
While this approach is not incompatible with the perspectives of the
encyclical, I had not expected the "people of Leipzig" to give to it much
consideration. Rather, I assumed that the encyclical would play a crucial
role only in the countries of the Global South, especially Latin America,
the Philippines, and Africa, which have a large Catholic presence. Moreover, Latin America especially hosts a long lasting historical tradition
of liberation theology, which seems to be the main inspiration of the
encyclical itself.

While I am still convinced that this is the case, I was wrong in
my quick judgment about the encyclical's influence on the European
Degrowth debate. While writing this comment, I ran into a contribution
by Oscar Krüger on the Blog of the degrowth conference; Krüger analyses
the encyclical in detail and connects it to the main ideals and principles
of the degrowth movement.[1] This was a comforting surprise. The
discussion of the need for a radical transformation of societies towards
degrowth, intended as a path of justice, solidarity, and conviviality, is

actively engaging with the proposals advanced in the encyclical, while at the same time also considering differences and disagreements.

Let me, in what follows, share a few thoughts about what the degrowth movement is all about and why I do think that the encyclical embodies an original, surprisingly radical, and promising perspective along this path.

From growth to degrowth

Economic growth has played for a long time a crucial role in stabilizing modern industrialized societies: it has secured prosperity for today and for future generations, guaranteed employment, social mobility, and tax revenue for the Welfare State. In other words, it has worked like a magic wand for social pacification and political stability.

However, such a form of dynamic stabilization by means of growth implies a steady process of expansion and acceleration. The growth machine is very much like a crazy bicycle that not only has to keep moving, but has to accelerate in order not to fall down.

Now we are faced with a crisis of this paradigm. It is not only due to ecological limits that growth is no longer a feasible path. Rather, the very logic of constant increasing, accelerating, and expanding undermines the basic conditions of reproduction of society. Moreover, holding onto growth at any cost reverses the promise originally attached to growth into a dramatic exacerbation of environmental and social conflicts all over the world.

While growth-based societies that stop growing fall from crisis to crisis into endless recession, increasing inequality, and destitution, degrowth represents for activists and scholars not simply a way of coping with a shrinking economy. Rather, degrowth calls for a radical transformation of society and its basic structures. The challenge is how to build a just and cohesive democratic society that is no longer dependent on economic growth for its stabilization and legitimation.

However, the societal transformation that degrowth envisions cannot be the mere implementation of a blueprint dictated by political leadership or technocratic governance, but has to emerge slowly from the different forces and voices in our societies. It should emanate from self-organized, small-scale, networked forms of resistance, subversion, and creative new visions and social experiments.

Social transformation encompasses at least three dimensions that are interdependent and interconnected. First, the structural and institutional dimension encompasses economic relations, relations of power and domination, and institutions. By drawing on Whitehead, I consider institutions and social structures in a wider sense as the *coagulation* and *sedimentation* of long-term, repeated patterns of belief, actions, and collective practices that over time became habitualized, established, and even sclerotized. They have grown into material structures that are strongly efficacious on present and future possibilities. This is why we tend to take institutions, material, and social structures for granted as something powerful and unchangeable. This is why TINA-narratives— the English term for There Is No Alternative—are successful in delegitimizing resistance and hope. Indeed this is true: There is no alternative *within the given framework*. Thus, real(istic) alternatives demand a different framework.

The second dimension encompasses both collective and individual practices and includes the agency of societal actors. Again with Whitehead, we can say that—all determining conditions notwithstanding— novelty and creativity are inscribed in the fabric of the actual world. On the one hand, practices are rendered possible, sometimes even generated and supported by institutions. On the other hand, in the long run, they create new institutions, by means of a process that I term coagulation, sedimentation, and repetition. Through practices, possible alternative modes of living, ideals and creative experiments gain materiality, as they are embodied into something that goes beyond the merely cognitive representation of envisioned alternatives.

The third and most important dimension of the cultural and value-related societal transformation is what some call the "Social Imaginary." This refers to a deep, collective self-understanding that confers sense to shared institutions and practices. It justifies what we do in the face of others, legitimates reciprocal expectations, keeps a society together. The Social Imaginary is the result of a long-term stratification of meanings, but also of the influence of elites and of social struggles.

Challenging the Social Imaginary is a necessary dimension for social transformation. In times of crisis like the one we are experiencing, established beliefs and commonly accepted justification of our actions start shivering. When, for example, the promise of prosperity attached to growth stops working, we are faced with a contradiction between the meaning we used to attach to our actions and their actual outcome (for example, working hard no longer leads to social improvement for oneself or one's children—we keep running in the treadmills no longer in order to move forward, but to stay in place and not to slip back). Institutions and their shared meanings lose their legitimation. This is both a time of danger and an opportunity for positive change.

The Social Imaginary changes when we start shifting the meaning of established values. It is not so much about reversing or rejecting them. It is about a slow and subversive move of reinterpretation and re-signification. Think of values in the Global North such as freedom: it is taken to mean individual freedom and arbitrariness in shaping one's personal life style. And yet it bears in itself the potential for the idea of collective autonomy, and it can be re-signified to mean reclaiming the capacity to decide not only about our life styles, but also about the conditions of our common living. Ivan Illich—surely one of the great inspirations of the encyclical—once wrote: "Prisoners in rich countries often have access to more things and services than members of their families, but they have no say in how things are to be made and cannot decide what to do with them. They are degraded to the status of mere consumers."[2]

Social struggles for emancipation and against discrimination also play a major role in shifting the shared Imaginary, and societal experiments can be the leverage for transforming it. As concrete utopias social experiments anticipate future possibilities and already contribute to creating the space in which these possibilities can be experienced, lived, and tested—they are prefigurative, prophetic, and performative. They are laboratories where social innovation is literally forged and where people participating in them can find there the power and the motivation for resisting, building alliances, and continue the transformation in other areas of life.

Societal experiments can become what Ernst Bloch called concrete utopias and thus perform the social transformation that they envision.

In contrast to an abstract utopia that is merely wishful thinking, a concrete utopia envisions the *real-possible*, what is already slumbering in the interstices of our actual world.

This is why concrete utopia needs what Bloch calls a militant optimism that is different from a naive hope for change. It means identifying the potentials and tendencies for transformation that are hidden in the present time and actively seizing them and rendering them visible; in other words, acting as a kind of catalyst enzyme that makes them stronger.

Concrete utopias have both a *prophetic* and a *performative* power: they envision alternative Imaginaries no matter how hidden behind TINA-narratives. The prophet is the one who seeks and sees the single righteous person to save the city. Alternative Imaginaries are embedded in the contradictions of the present following a sort of 'and-yet' logic: the real is open. Whatever *is* bears more in it than what is actually realized.

I mentioned before the example of the re-signification of freedom. We do not need new values and new meaning. We can look instead into the different layers and contradictions that existing, established values carry with them. In other words (and again with Whitehead), every pattern of the fabric that we call reality hosts several different threads. Less visible threads can be taken and woven into new patterns, and, in the long run, into a new, different fabric.

Concrete utopias do not only envision alternatives. They also *embody* them in the numerous laboratories in which new spaces are created and protected for actual experimentation and for new experiences. We need to know how it feels to live differently—otherwise we cannot figure it out.

This is why—finally—concrete utopias are spaces in which we can collectively learn about our desires; we can provisionally suspend, and thus start questioning, pseudo-desires and the satisfaction of needs imposed by the existing structures. But for starting a serious debate about needs and desires we need protected areas where we can experience and test alternatives.

The encyclical as vision for a radical transformation of society

The encyclical not only explicitly questions the Western model of development, based on and justified by economic growth. As the blog contribution on the degrowth page states, it also presents an incredibly well founded analytical reconstruction of the structural and systemic dynamics that have supported and kept in power the hegemonic paradigm of technocratic, growth-oriented, inhumane development that we have been witnessing all over the world in the last centuries. I am quoting here a larger passage from the blog on the degrowth page, because it shows a very deep insight into the encyclical and its relevance to the need for a transformation that is more radical than many of us might like to hear.

> The paradigm the cultural revolution needs to overthrow is clearly identified: "the deepest roots of our present failures [...] have to do with the direction, goals, meaning and social implications of technological and economic growth" (109). And although the encyclical proposes a variety of measures that individuals can practice in their daily lives, it is just as clear that a form of politics is required in order to truly unearth these roots (e.g. section IV). This saves the encyclical from falling into either of two common traps: First, it avoids making individual (consumer) behaviour either the primary culprit or the privileged site for intervention. Although greed and short-sightedness are condemned over and over again, such behaviour is nonetheless understood as systemically engendered by deeper structures, which would then reasonably be where an intervention needs to put its real focus (e.g. 203). Second, it likewise avoids making technology either culprit or hope in any simple way; science and technology are said to become problems only insofar as they are taken up [...] *according to an undifferentiated and one-dimensional paradigm*" (106). Thus avoiding two traps of depoliticizing productivism within a paradigm where "our politics are subject to technology and finance" (54), Francis calls the central task of the required revolution "a matter of redefining our notion of progress," since "[a] technological and economic development which does not leave in its wake a better world and an integrally higher quality of life cannot be considered progress" (194).

Such a structural analysis is of great importance: while going beyond the appeal to individuals to change their personal behaviors it clearly displays the dynamics that keep them chained to the pervasive logic of growth, acceleration, and competition. Moreover, the encyclical warns us against the naïve faith in technological fixes that relies on the illusion of global scale solutions. Rather, it stresses the fundamental role of bottom-up actions, small scale agriculture, peasants' movements, and the radically different understanding that indigenous people have of the relation between society and nature.

The encyclical is radical in sketching what in other contexts is called 'political or social ecology': the environmentalism the pope talks about is not the idealized wilderness conservation tradition of the Global North, in the name of which, more often than not, local and indigenous people in the South are evicted from their homes. He aligns himself with what activists and scholars in political ecology have been calling for years 'the environmentalism of the poor,' the struggles of the poor for their livelihoods, including their fundamental self-understanding of the relation to what *we* call nature and they call territory, home, or land. Ecology is not so much about nature, as Pope Francis writes, as something separated from society, but it is about society, its conditions of reproduction, its meaning, and its perspectives for the future. This is why, as the blog author further writes, "the environment that appears in Francis's encyclical is not detached from those working poor. Instead, it is an environment which can only be apprehended once we 'realize that a true ecological approach always becomes a social approach; it must integrate questions of justice in debates on the environment, so as to hear both the cry of the earth and the cry of the poor'" (49). The encyclical is an explicit call for politics of redistribution, both at a national, and at a global level.

Indeed, the encyclical cracks open the mantras of technocratic, economistic, and neoliberal TINA-narratives, and opens a dimension for imagining alternatives in the first place. It radically questions the most obvious assumptions that justify our way of living and the way our societies are supposed to function.

Relations of power are at the core of the text; for example, the problem with genetic modification of living beings is differentiated and accurate. The encyclical focuses on the real dimension of asymmetries of power and on the disempowerment of peasants all over the world. In so doing, it directly echoes the keynote speech that Vandana Shiva gave at our June 4-7 conference "Seizing an Alternative." Along this line, Pope Francis states that social and environmental issues are structurally not separable, not any more. He takes sides with the poor of the world: he gives voice to their cry for justice while at the same time emphasizing their creativity in the daily struggle for surviving and defending a different mode of relations among each other and to the world. By stressing the ecological debt of the North to the South, Francis indirectly points out the scandalous ignominy of financial debts that are devastating poor countries in all parts of the world. He claims the impending necessity of re-embedding markets into society, by subordinating the economy to politics, while at the same time stressing the importance of subsidiarity, local autonomy, and the important role of communities. The struggle of indigenous people for food sovereignty and self-management can be heard in the background of his message.

Technology is read along the line of great thinkers like Illich, according to whom the kind of tools a society chooses to employ and develop determines its political, institutional, and ethical fabric. This is why for Illich the decision about the role, limits, and meaning of technological development has to be embedded in participatory processes, to which all citizens have access and an active and substantial voice. In contemporary industrial societies, humans are driven into a drug-addiction-like state, in which they lose their autonomy (i.e. the capacity to creatively deal with problems and find solutions adequate to the context) and are delivered to the systemic and technical forces of the development machine. Instead, according to Illich, we need 'convivial tools' that serve politically interrelated individuals rather than managers, tools that enhance human creativity and enlarge the space of freedom, autonomy, and self-determination, instead of restricting it by imposing their own logic. Conviviality means for Illich 'individual freedom realized in personal interdependence' and relates to the quality of human relations, substantial freedom in terms of collective self-determination, and ongoing deliberation about the ends and forms of the commonwealth. Whether tools are convivial or oppressive does not depend much on their level of technology, but on how far they infringe the freedom and autonomy of the collective relating to them.

The encyclical also challenges our common understanding of work and enlarges it to include more than just traditionally paid work. However, what it fails to see and to address is the need for a radical rethinking of the distinction between so-called productive and (re)productive work. In fact, by implicitly reiterating the traditional role of families and the gender division of labor, it misses one of the most pressing steps for a successful societal transformation: reconsidering (re)productive activities as the essential basis for all societal processes, which instead have been exploited and denied valorization by the capitalistic mode of production. So-called reproductive activities include all forms of care, including the services delivered by ecosystems in regenerating water, soil, and air. Challenging the paradigm of modern capitalistic societies requires a radical redistribution of care beyond any traditional gender attribution and fixed social roles. As the German economist Adelheid Biesecker provokes her audience: "half of the care work belongs to you, men! Claim it back, now."[3] In our society, care activities are externalized to those who are weak or oppressed (women, mostly from the Global South along what feminists call global care chains, the poor, immigrants). The transformation we urgently need will have to lead to a radical redistribution of all socially meaningful and necessary activities among all the citizens. There is no radical shift in the collective Imaginary if we do not start challenging the traditional "contract" among the genders and the idea of a separation between care and production. The renegotiation of needs, desires, and social relations cannot neglect patriarchal forms of domination. The very paradigm of growth, ongoing marketization, and productivism that is questioned in the encyclical is rooted in the patriarchal oppression and the exploitation of bodies, vital energy, and desires of marginalized people.

Pope Francis is only one step away from this understanding when he claims the shift towards a relation of care for the environment and the Earth. Caring for our common home will never work if we do not re-conceive care and care relations beyond patriarchal domination.

Conclusion

To conclude, the encyclical is a masterpiece in developing a new Imaginary for envisioning a radical transformation of society. It does not invent new principles or values, but (re)calls deeply rooted ideals that are shared by many different traditions within and beyond Christianity. He challenges obvious assumptions and breaks open the possibility of thinking along different paths than the dominant TINA-narratives. However, thinking alternatives is not enough: we have to experience and live their very possibility in initiatives, projects, struggles, social projects. The encyclical is a strong empowering message for local groups, churches, and communities engaging in courageous forms or resistance. If different traditions and social groups across countries and spiritual traditions start building alliances for a new, promising future on our shared planet, there is hope.

Endnotes

1. <http://www.degrowth.de/de/2015/06/laudato-si-as-signalling-towards-degrowth/>.

2. Ivan Illich, *Tools for Conviviality* (London: Marion Boyers, 2001), 11.

3. Comment made at the Fourth International Conference on Degrowth for Ecological Sustainability and Social Equity, <http://www.degrowth.org/4-international-conference-on-degrowth-in-germany>.

References

Muraca, B. *Gut Leben: Eine Gesellschaft jenseits des Wachstums.* Berlin: Wagenbach, 2014.

Bloch, E. *Das Prinzip Hoffnung.* Frankfurt a. M, 1976.

Levitas, R. *The Concept of Utopia.* Bern: Peter Lang Verlag, 2010.

Biesecker, A. "(Re)productivity: Sustainable Relations both between Society and Nature and between the Genders."*Ecological Economics* 69, 1703–11.

Changing My Mind on Technological Education

Lília Dias Marianno

In this effort to join Pope Francis' team on care for our common home, I will focus on the last part of his encyclical: "educating for the covenant between humanity and the environment" and "ecological conversion" in Chapter VI. He introduces the chapter with the following words:

> Many things have to change course, but it is we, human beings, above all who need to change. We lack an awareness of our common origin, of our mutual belonging, and of a future to be shared with everyone. This basic awareness would enable the development of new convictions, attitudes and forms of life. A great cultural, spiritual and educational challenge stands before us, and it will demand that we set out on the long path of renewal. (202)

When I read these words I think about humanity in every sense and age, and most of all, about the world of work, where human beings spend the biggest part of their lives.

From an educator's experiences

Some weeks ago I finished, for the third time in the last eight months, a class entitled Psychology and Sociology of Work, with students in mechanical engineering graduating from the university where I teach. In the last meeting I do a collective evaluation, where each student gives oral responses to questions like: what was the most positive and the most negative aspect of this course? Which expectation did you have before the classes? Were your expectations met, frustrated, or overwhelmed? Which topic was more important for your professional education and for your personal life, as a human being?

Every time I apply this final evaluation, the students give the same type of answers about the learning they will bring to the rest of their professional and personal lives: 1) capability to understand another person as that person is, 2) the understanding to be less self-centered and more attentive to other people needs, 3) "get rich" is not the best solution for their lives; it is more meaningful to bring some purpose to the things they will do, 4) the possibility to use their talents as engineers to make the lives of poor people easier, 5) to use their creativity to build innovation, transforming reality around them, mainly in extremely poor communities.

A course with an emphasis on psychology and organizational behavior has a curriculum conducive to introducing several TED Talks about leadership, conflict management, ecology of relationships, vulnerability, shame, innovation, sustainability, identification, and so on.[1] But I need to remember that I am talking about students 20-24 years old. They are natives of the technological generation, born after the 90s and under the domain of computer screens and keyboards. They represent the "best" of the technological generation: individualistic, too quick, less attentive to peoples' needs, high self-esteem. They never will be the best example of austerity and solidarity.

So, why are they naming the humanitarian and moral sensibility topics as the best thing they learned in these classes? Their answers were not political, but deeply felt on an emotional level. How can we compare them with data from big corporations? Corporations are, at least in theory, focused on lucrative objectives instead humanitarian direction.

The business world is geared to efficiency and is bound to oppose two aspects of Pope Francis' encyclical where he comes across as very combative: 1) excessive consumerism as a lifestyle and 2) the waste of natural resources, enriching the rich and impoverishing the poor.

Moral sensibility in corporations: is it so impossible?

Five years ago I attended a forum for human resources managers, promoted by the Council of Professional Ethics for Administrators. The
forum had this title: "The People's Manager for the XXI century." At
that time I was facing a big change in my career. I had been a professor of theology for fifteen years and a big financial breakdown forced
the layoff of many of us. I had the option to turn back to my original
field of administrative education, and I did it, but I was very anxious
and nervous because I couldn't imagine how I could bring my fifteen
years' experience teaching people to serve the Lord Jesus to this "Judas'
road." I felt like I was being transformed into a disciple of Mammon
(the god identified by Jesus as the father of the "love of money, the root
of so many evils"). I had an inner feeling that I was betraying Jesus'
great commission. But in that forum the lecturer (the CEO of a big
corporation) talked about creating sensibility in organizations. It was a
paradox, and I was really curious to know how he could convert people
from the mindset of profitability to people concerned with the needs of
vulnerable human beings.

I had heard that workplace spirituality had gained importance in
the last decade in studies of organizational behavior. But in my mind,
I was thinking about the generational conflicts among Baby Boomers,
Generation X, Generation Y, and Generation Z. This last one was identified as more accelerated, technological, and selfish than Generation Y.
I was really curious. At the end of conference, I asked how he was able to
promote and develop sensibility in his companies, and, how could I do
it now, if my young Gen Z students are just concerned with their own
careers and suffer from too-high self-esteem? How could they be taught
to attend to other peoples' needs, if this is not on their list of priorities?

Without any theological intention, that experienced CEO answered
me using something I had learned in the theological field: "Take these
guys and turn them into contemplative people. Promote art on the
schedule of corporate activities. The companies where I was most successful were those where I was able to create opportunities to do art or
to contemplate art. Movies, dramas, chorales, everything that touches
sensibility you may introduce into the daily life of the company."

I could do it! I learned how to do it with Saint Francis, my favorite person in Christian history, after Jesus Christ. Because Francis learned contemplation with Jesus, who said: "Consider the sparrows and the lilies." The same Francis that inspired the pope's name. The CEO was telling me: sensibility is possible to teach in the heart of the big companies: they are people. "Corporations are people," as they like to say.

My personal conversion to a contemplative human being

In that same year, feeling myself as a betrayer of Christian commission, and obligated to make a radical change in my professional life, I turned my attention to spiritual disciplines, especially silence, pilgrimage, meditation, prayer, and contemplation. I spent several weekends in personal retreats, searching God's guidance for my next steps. My friends in these solitary walks were flowers, trees, their shapes, their grooves. I passed long hours imagining the centuries of history behind those trunks, listening to the several sounds of different birds singing in the sunset, trying to find peace and serenity to make the correct decision for my and my kids' lives. Unemployment converted me into a contemplative person. And during those walks I found many friends doing the same movement. Contemplative exercises are spreading in persistent and discrete ways but simultaneously at several points on the planet. Many friends, outsiders, were doing the same thing in their own countries, seizing upon a spiritual movement, lead by the wind of the Holy Spirit.

I benefited so much through these contemplative experiences that I decided to create a place in my congregation where people could come to learn about "contemplative spirituality for the active life."[2] We had some classes in Christian origins, culture, and posmodernism. We studied the common roots of several Christian movements, the poststructural and postmodern moments of history, the loss of references and values, and the atrocities of humanity against humanity in the two big World Wars, with the contemplative life as a guide to our essence. Contemplative disciplines lead us to reintegrate with nature, without mysticism, but with the comprehension that to be created beings was not to be the "lords of creation."

In our contemplative exercises, we used to pass 10-15 minutes in total silence, just watching birds building nests, insects with hundreds of colors, butterflies with thousands of different designs, flowers of different colors and sizes. All these exercises brought "hard people" to tears.

Contemplative life develops our sensibility as that CEO suggested to me, and as he had done inside corporations. And when he told me that, I felt hope. I could stay in corporations reaching people through their own essence and spirituality. I was not a Judas, a betrayer, anymore!

I began to use these resources in the business world, in the education of administrators, human resources managers and engineers, and I could see the "machines cry." My use of process thought and its organic way to treat relational topics was a marvelous consequence of my personal and profound conversion into an ecological human being.

Translating into educational opportunities

Pope Francis seriously affirms:

> Amid this confusion, postmodern humanity has not yet achieved a new self-awareness capable of offering guidance and direction, and this lack of identity is a source of anxiety. We have too many means and only a few insubstantial ends. . . . Many things have to change course, but it is we human beings above all who need to change. (203)

I am totally convinced that a strong investment of energy and resources in educational processes, transcending the technical limitations, will promote bigger integration between different generations and will be in dialogue with the ethical, moral, and existential values that we must teach, if we wish to see a change in humanity.

As educators we know that it is much easier to educate a child to new paradigms than to repair the old habits of adults addicted by them. There are many efforts to correct the problems generated by our environmental neglect and wrongful understanding of our place in this world. These efforts must intensify, stand, and prevail. But a parallel intensive investment in the new generations must be made in a persistent and insistent way. Our youth and children are more uncomfortable with the environmental and social demands made on them than were we, their predecessors. They were born at a time when environmental concerns were more widely discussed, that is, since the 90s.

For this reason, big corporations cannot focus on just absorbing them into the workplace. These new talents are people with big technological skills, but they also have a deeper sensibility to respond to environmental concerns. Big corporations must be concerned not just with the rules of ISO 9000 (production quality managing) family, but most of all with families of ISOs 14000 (environmental managing) and 26000 (social responsibility managing).

Arriving in our offices we have a whole generation of young professionals very demanding and more perspicacious than we ever could be. They are invading the job market. If the big corporations do not respond to the meaning of this "wave," they risk being considered irrelevant for decades. These young professionals don't look for a job just because they will receive a very good salary there. They want quality of life. Many of them prefer to have a low salary if this will bring them to a life where they will contribute to the common good. They are looking for purpose. Some tests I have done show they don't want to work in companies that pollute waters and land, or that don't promote racial and gender equality.

Partnering with corporations in the education of new generations

As an example of how it is possible for big corporations to invest in innovative education for the future generations, I want to mention a project where I am particularly involved. It is in the robotics field, promoted by FLL (FIRST Lego League), a nonprofit program for youngsters from 9-14 used in the USA, Canada, and many other countries, including Brazil. FIRST means *For Inspiration and Recognition of Science and Technology.*

The objective of this project is to celebrate science and technology among the young, using real social needs out of their contexts and backgrounds. A different theme, related to science and the international community, is proposed by FIRST, and an international competition is promoted under those themes. The themes of 2014 and 2015 were respectively Education and Trash Track (reverse logistic and residual recycling).[3]

In the competition, the children are stimulated to use the principles of engineering to create a robot of materials developed by Massachusetts Institute of Technology, in partnership with LEGO Mindstorms. Its function is to develop several tasks inside the chosen theme for that year. In their own local realities, young students are stimulated to innovate with ideas and solutions for the problems in their own contexts, using the ludic impulse as a resource for learning and innovation.

This project is called *Robotic on the Schools #inovareaprender* in public schools in Macaé County, in Rio de Janeiro State, in Brazil. The city has enormous environmental and social demands. It is an important site of global production of oil and gas and powerful corporations in subsea oil exploitation are based there. The city is seen as the Brazilian capital of oil and hosts one of the biggest exhibitions in the world (Brazil Offshore). Corporations have a huge power to transform reality when they take seriously their social responsibility.

In the 2014 FIRST Championship, ten of Macaé's public schools (public schools in Brazil means education for poorest children) sent teams and four of them received prizes. That year the theme was education, and the winning robotic project was created by a 9-year-old child dealing with the problem of two classmates of his with dyslexia.

As they are poor children, their families had no money to send these boys with major learning difficulties to a special school. Their classmates, concerned with their needs, developed a robotic project (the size of a glove) with special light sensors to help people with dyslexia read. Blind people also benefited from this project.

This integral creativity that benefits vulnerable people to those involved with these projects is possible but is really rarely used. I have taken part in several projects that changed lives and minds of people irrespective of their social and environmental relations. Conversion is indeed possible.

It was my honor to be invited to coordinate one of these teams involved with the project Robotic in a School promoted by FIRST, bringing together different generations of students: the poor children of public school in Macaé and young engineering graduate students. This project started in 2014 and involved 10 public schools and 150 children. The goal was to replicate the results. I can imagine the impact on environmental management in the next decades promoted by these children of today, who had the opportunity to be stimulated to create good solutions by big corporations.

Awakening children, loving our youth, making corporations sensible

Ken Robinson states that our children are living at a time of the greatest stimulation to creativity in human history, but we are doping and numbing their creativity, classifying them as hyperactive and troubled children. Ritalin is being administered in unprecedented amounts. We do all in our power to have our children sedated and sleeping. At this point I remember the old words of Whitehead in *The Aims of Education,* understanding the warning light of danger he recognized early in the last century. Whitehead declared that our educational curricula were quite inappropriate for the learning processes of children. Ken Robinson is doing a postmodern reading on what happens with those children whose rhythms of learning are not respected, as Whitehead suggested.[4]

Instead of putting our children to sleep, we should learn how to guide their energies and their innovative potential to build a new common house for the whole creation. They are paying attention to the demands around them, more than previous generations. "Hey, teacher, keep those kids awake!"[5]

And, what about the youth? They are passing over their best time of creativity. Research shows that the contemporary generation of youth is not reaching the full flourishing of its creative potential; in fact, they are experiencing a palpable reduction of creativity. What can we do for them?

Daniel Pink, in his book *Drive*, advises us to give a sense of purpose to the things we want them to do. Purpose, as motivation, works better than monetary rewards. Even if we are living in days of extreme consumerism and materialism, as Pope Francis states, this is still our big challenge with the youth: they are not moved only by money (one more paradox of a postmodern age). There is potential in the realization of purpose that is not well utilized in them. When the youth understand that they really can help to change life of people around them, some transformation will come.

If the children can learn, if the youth can learn, and if the corporations are able to learn sensibility, what are we waiting for? Is it necessary to have more faith than a mustard seed to do it? We really need faith to do it!

Investment in a humanizing education, focusing on the sensibility of university students, teaching them to attribute value to their professional careers—not by the amount of money they make but by the amount of transformation they can achieve in their jobs—and most of all by showing them the relevance of purpose in their lives, showing them the degree of transformation they can achieve with their actions, this is to use the best of their youthfulness. The young generation wants to change the world, but we have been spending too much time discussing their personalities and repressing their impulsive and impatient initiatives because they are not good for "the bottom line."

To invest more love in our educational processes for children and youth, to awaken the children, we need to stop numbing them with pills for hyperactivity and invest more energy on their innovative potential. To instill a greater sense of purpose in our youth for their professional performance is to design a more level and hopeful road toward the building of a new common house. Love is never too much and always brings positive results. Let us make contemplative, sensible corporations. Let us use the mystique of this zeitgeist.

As I started with some encyclical words. I want to finish with another quotation:

> Yet all is not lost. Human beings, while capable of the worst, are also capable of rising above themselves, choosing again what is good, and making a new start, despite their mental and social conditioning. . . . No system can completely suppress our openness to what is good, true and beautiful, or our God-given ability to respond to his grace at work deep in our hearts. . . . A change in lifestyle could bring healthy pressure to bear on those who wield political, economic and social power. . . . "As never before in history, common destiny beckons us to seek a new beginning . . . Let ours be a time remembered for the awakening of a new

reverence for life, the firm resolve to achieve sustainability, the quickening of the struggle for justice and peace, and the joyful celebration of life". . . . . We are always capable of going out of ourselves towards the other. . . . If we can overcome individualism, we will truly be able to develop a different lifestyle and bring about significant changes in society. . . . Environmental education should facilitate making the leap towards the transcendent which gives ecological ethics its deepest meaning. It needs educators capable of developing an ethics of ecology, and helping people, through effective pedagogy, to grow in solidarity, responsibility and compassionate care. . . . Only by cultivating sound virtues will people be able to make a selfless ecological commitment. . . . Education in environmental responsibility can encourage ways of acting which directly and significantly affect the world around us. . . . Ecological education can take place in a variety of settings: at school, in families, in the media, in catechesis and elsewhere. Good education plants seeds when we are young, and these continue to bear fruit throughout life. . . . I appeal to everyone throughout the world not to forget this dignity which is ours. No one has the right to take it from us. (205)

Endnotes

1. I am referring especially to lectures with insights for ethical positions, especially the following:

- Joseph Greeny—Changing Behavior <https://www.youtube.com/watch?v=6T9TYz5Uxl0>

- Erica Ariel Fox—Internal Negotiators <https://www.youtube.com/watch?v=C6dWnYoFDdo>

- Bunker Roy—Barefoot University <https://www.youtube.com/watch?v=oC5FMJlD_EQ>

- Brené Brown—Power of vulnerability <https://www.youtube.com/watch?v=iCvmsMzlF7o>

- Brené Brown—Listening the shame <https://www.youtube.com/watch?v=psN1DORYYV0>

- Daniel Pink—Motivation: Drive <https://www.youtube.com/watch?v=bIhHrL73d4s>.

2. I am borrowing the subtitle of Phileena Heuertz' book: *Pilgrimage of a Soul: Contemplative Spirituality for the Active Life* (Downers Grove, IL: Green Press/InterVarsity, 2010).

3. For further detailing about FIRST LEGO LEAGUE, see: <https://pt.wikipedia.org/wiki/First_Lego_League>.

4. Ken ROBINSON: "Changing Education Paradigms" <https://www.youtube.com/watch?v=zDZFcDGpL4U>.

5. From the Pink Floyd classic, "Another brick in the wall."

Climate Change: The Devil vs. the Pope for the Fate of the Planet

Andy Shrader

L et's talk about the devil and the pope, just for argument's sake.
If you are the devil and want to corrupt good people by the millions, you might create public relations campaigns funded by corporate entities driven by the sole mission of creating wealth for shareholders. (Keep in mind that greed is one of the seven deadly sins, defined well by Thomas Aquinas in the 11th century: "Greed is a sin against God, just as all mortal sins, in as much as man condemns things eternal for the sake of temporal things.") These greed-based PR campaigns lie to good people about cigarettes, gun control, plastic bags, education, food, GMOs, and climate change.

When something like the Emanuel AME Church shootings occur and innocents die, these types of PR campaigns result in people buying up guns like crazy because of widespread lies about new gun control efforts. It happened after Sandy Hook; it's happening now. Which seems to me to be a mystifying reaction to a tragedy.

When I was leading the campaign to ban plastic bags in Los Angeles, all these "reports" came out citing health issues with reusable bags. Those reports, it turns out, were mostly funded by the American Chemistry Council (which represents big oil, big plastics, and big chemistry), and,

161

when you poke around into these so-called studies, you find that they are not peer-reviewed, often not written by scientists, and often misquote actual scientists or misrepresent events that occurred. For instance, an Oregon girls' soccer team got sick, they said, by eating food out of a reusable bag which, in their biased estimation, meant that reusable bags are therefore dangerous. The scientist who wrote the study, Bill Keene, was misquoted in the corporately owned newspapers that ran the story under the headline, "Contaminated reusable grocery bag causes gastric illness outbreak" and emphasized the non sequitur that "Worldwide, the virus . . . caus[es] the deaths of 200,000 children annually." In his email response to me, Keene said: "This story has nothing to do with disposable bags, reusable bags, or anything similar. It is about how when norovirus-infected people vomit, they shower their surroundings with an invisible fog of viruses—viruses that can later infect people who have contact with those inanimate objects (fomites). In this case it was a reusable bag AND ITS CONTENTS—sealed packages of Oreos, Sun Chips, and grapes—but it could just have easily been a disposable plastic bag, a paper bag, a cardboard box, the flush handle on the toilet, the sink, the floor, or the nearby countertops." It was certainly not a coincidence that the story ran the same month the Los Angeles City Council was deliberating its eventually successful plastic bag ban.

Now the GOP, a party that purports to speak for conservative religious people of the United States, is going after Pope Francis, trying to discredit him and the reasoning behind his historic encyclical on climate change. On one side: people who are massively supported by the oil and gas industry, corporate entities driven solely by a greed-based focus to create wealth for shareholders. On the other side: the man who is supposed to be close to God, divinely chosen, who is quite possibly working to counteract the devil's machinations, and who is speaking up in order to protect the poor and underserved communities who will be the most adversely affected by an already changing global climate.

Who do you believe?

Integral Ecology and China

Ronald P. Phipps

No discussion of the development of integral ecology can fail to mention China. China 1) was a victim of protracted aggression during World War II; 2) suffered its protracted civil war; and 3) experienced the retrogressive impact of millennia of feudalism. As a result China was in a state of economic, social, and ecological disaster in the 1940s. There is no need to document the well-known heartbreaking poverty, discord, and inertia that gripped the Chinese people, when China was known as the "Sick Man of Asia." Professor Joseph Needham, in his monumental work *Science and Civilization in China*, documented the creative genius of the Chinese people, which had put ancient China at the forefront of discovery and innovation. That genius was stifled and thwarted for centuries.

As chairman of the U.S.-China Peoples Friendship Association of Seattle, I and other scholars worked to overcome the estrangement of China and the U.S. and to establish peaceful relations that would allow mutual learning between these two important countries. In the course of these efforts I led one of the first delegations of Americans to visit China, after the establishment of the Peoples Republic of China (PRC). We witnessed the reconstruction of China and the values and aspirations initially guiding that reconstruction.

During the first visit, our delegation went to a chemical factory in Shanghai. The factory leaders told us how that factory had been polluting the land, the nearby river, and the atmosphere. They showed how, through diligent efforts, they had transformed those pollutants into 99 useful products. Their justification for their efforts was, "We must serve the people and that includes protecting the environment. Our main interest is not to make a profit but to promote the strategic well-being of the Chinese people." During the 1960s to the mid-1970s, some factories were implementing policies of "Capturing Carbon" and transforming pollutants into useful products.

We also saw many projects of reforestation in China. Following the establishment of the PRC, there was a widely known slogan from Mao Tze Tung: "Make China Green." Many foreign visitors to China were deeply impressed at the farm systems, which appeared to us as meticulously tended, exquisite gardens. I planted pine trees in China. Since the devastation of wars, feudalism, and natural disasters had left China backward and weak, such efforts were incomplete, and results were mixed.

By the dawn of the 21st century, China's President Hu Jintao called for the establishment of an ecological civilization. In the preceding two decades, China became known as "the Factory of the World." The ethos of these decades has been described by Chinese scholars as "GDP worship." As China became known as the Factory of the World, it also became known that the toxicity of China's agricultural land and water systems and the pollution of its atmosphere were severe. These facts have aroused deepening concern among the Chinese people, within whom a demand for an ecological civilization is most deeply and intimately felt. Pollution, even in economically highly polarized societies, is a very democratic phenomenon. All strata of Chinese society are feeling the imminent threat of pollution that has pervaded, like a flood, a large number of regions, both urban and rural, reaching to all nooks and crannies within those regions.

Despite the growing awareness of the threat to the environment, human health, and agricultural production, China continues to open coal mines and build massive numbers of coal factories. China has created the 2nd largest economy in the world, which is now the largest contributor to greenhouse gases. The link between climate change, global warming, and pollution has not been adequately articulated within China.

In talks at ecological conferences, Chinese scholars have expressed their deepening interest in understanding systemic causes. Such understanding is the necessary foundation to crafting systemic changes that will restore a healthy and sustainable environment, maintain biological diversity, and rebuild endangered ecological systems in China and the world.

During the 10th International Whitehead Conference, an eminent Chinese scholar discussed China's effort to better integrate ancient Chinese traditions, Western traditions, and Marxism, which remains ostensibly the reigning political-economic ideology in China. During this discussion, I proposed that China needs, as a guiding principle to such integration, "6 plus 1." By "6 plus 1" I meant that each of these traditions has negative and positive features. For example:

1) Chinese traditional culture gave birth to very profound poetry, engineering, architecture, science, wisdom, and a culture of respect, humility and graciousness. At the same time, it presided over a feudal system which brought deep suffering to China's peasants and workers. There were periods of massive starvation and intellectual stagnation during which adventures of discovery, innovation, and creativity largely disappeared. China's ancient culture and ideology were steeped in rigid hierarchical relations, stern subordination, and authoritarianism.

2) The Renaissance of the West brought a burst of intellectual inquiry, scientific discoveries, innovation, and liberation of the productive capacities inherent in the world. It also led to economic polarization, social conflict, and the environmental degradation facing our planet.

3) Marxism, for its part, brought to the world a sense of the urgency to achieve social and economic justice. But it also engaged in erecting walls against religion and other moral traditions rather than building bridges to them, even when they shared Marxism's concern with justice and equality.

For each of the three systems there are positive features to embrace and develop. But each has its negative features to repudiate and avoid. Hence, 3 times 2 equals 6. However, in addition to a synthesis, an integration of these 6 factors, China needs another factor, which is to bring a fresh and independent analysis of the positive and negative realities and trends within China and the world. Without objectivity, positive transformation is impossible.

During recent decades China blindly imitated the car culture of the U.S. and the infrastructure of dispersion that separated home, work, shopping, and recreation, weakening local and rural communities. The move to urbanize China has threatened family traditions so cherished by Chinese cultural tradition and is creating the economic and cultural degradation of the countryside as well as many forms of disharmony within China's urban centers.

Mindless materialism, rapacious consumerism, and the obsession with social and economic status have played a huge role in China's attaining its status as the number one global contributor to greenhouse gases. If, and when, there is emulation and blind imitation of the vices, rather than the virtues, of external models, social disharmony, instabilities, and degradations inevitably follow.

We live in a global era of: 1) economic polarization; political plutocracy; and monopoly; and, 2) "the illusion of no ceilings." That is, some have led the world to believe that there are no ceilings to real estate values, to stock market valuations, to consumption levels, to economic polarization, and no limits to the degradation of the air, land, and water systems of our planet. These are global problems, but they are also China's problems.

In the realm of physics there is the phenomenon of dense hyperentanglement of photons. In the realm of social reality we are in an era of the dense hyperentanglement of 1) mindless materialism, 2) obsessive consumption, and 3) the idolatry of money, things, and status. Such entanglement holds the globe in its tight grips. We must unravel this hyperentanglement to prevent a deep catastrophe. Such creative transformations are vital to both China's future and that of the human family. We may bear in mind an ancient Chinese saying as we seek to achieve an integral ecology: "In the Heavens above are many stars. On the Earth below, one People."

Within our profoundly integrated world community, it has become essential for both China and the U.S., major sources of the global environmental crisis, to become the epicenters of solutions of these global problems.

The "Great Connectors"—modern modes of communication and transportation—have facilitated an inexorable global movement towards greater integration and interdependence. The great advances in pure science, engineering, and design have led to discoveries and innovations that have created tremendous productive capacity. While the international community must embrace these potentialities, it must learn to balance, integrate, and restrain the use of those technological potentialities. Just as modern military potentialities for destructiveness must be restrained in order to preserve global peace, the preservation of the health of the global environment demands discipline, balance, and restraint of economic activities. Achieving that balance and restraint rests upon the foundation of a transformed vision of human nature. This requires overcoming the estrangement of humanity and nature, which underlies the abuse of nature. This abuse has set in motion processes that imperil the survival of all highly developed species of life.

The stress placed upon our Earth ultimately threatens both the global economy and the survival of the complex forms of life that have emerged through evolutionary processes. Those processes have led to increasing biological complexity and the evolution of an unparalleled breadth of teleological activity on the basis of which the sense of beauty, truth, adventure, wonder, and creativity reside. That value and beauty of life has arisen in a context of bio-chemical and geophysical complexity and fragility.

We must work to mobilize and unite everyone who will join the movement for integral ecology. To do so, we must mobilize the youth of the world. This is an intergenerational and urgent struggle. But it will be successful to the extent that the idealism, the energy, the knowledge of the ecological crisis, and the commitment of youth participate in the creative, transformative, and systemic changes.

To rescue the planet from the spiral of abusive degradation we will need alternative forms of energy as well as alternative social and economic systems based upon alternative values. A movement for integral ecology must weave together need and hope. No creative transformation can be either achieved or sustained without hope.

The movement to restore ecological balance, health, and sustainability has been going on for the past half century. There are thousands
of scholars, hundreds of universities, numerous governmental agencies,
tens of environmental organizations, religious leaders, poets, scientists,
and even businesses developing clean energy sources who have spoken in
Europe, the U.S., China, South America, and elsewhere about this accelerating crisis. There have been great pioneers in numerous countries who,
during past decades, have raised these issues with powerful documenta-
tion, compelling evidence, and carefully reasoned appeals for constructive
change. The movement for what the pope aptly calls "integral ecology" is
like a mighty river with thousands of tributaries, some large and others
small, some powerful and others weak, all from various places, that are
flowing into this mighty river. Neither arrogance nor egoism are called
for given the severity and intractability of these problems.

The tremendous appeal and hopefulness of Pope Francis' encyclical
on the environment is intertwined with his personal humility. Pope
Francis integrates what he preaches and practices in the most compelling,
moving, and inspiring manner. There are numerous charming stories
that can be told of this harmony. Let me tell one I heard in September
2014, after a private tour in Buenos Aires that focused on the pope's
life. Our friend is a member of the Argentine church formerly led by
Cardinal Jorge Bergoglio. Before his installation as pope, he emailed his
shoemaker in Buenos Aires and said, "They want me to wear the red
silk slippers, but I refused. However, my old black slippers have holes
in their soles, can you please make me a new pair for the ceremony?"

We humans also have many holes in our souls. We, too, must be
made new and whole. The pope's encyclical takes its name from a poem
by St. Francis and I conclude with a poem as well.

> The Poet
> (i)
> I stroll in silence
> Through a Japanese garden
> Countless curves, contrasting curves, opening to
> Exquisite forms of water, greens, rocks

(ii)
Upon the steepest paths
To the Apex
The poet chooses to journey

(iii)
Only from the pinnacle
Can the poet discern
The Communal and Integral Beauty
Of the Earth
Or perceive
The fragility and fleetingness
Of all Beings, in Flux

Every Creature Is Sister and Brother

Inspired by Pope Francis' encyclical,
On Care for Our Common Home, *Laudato Si'*

Bob Hurd
Melody inspired by
O'Carolan's *Sí Bheag, Sí Mhór*

1, 7. Ev' - ry crea - ture is sis - ter and broth - er to us, ____
2. Ev' - ry crea - ture is sing - ing the good - ness of God, the
4. Ho - ly Spir - it come kin - dle a fire in our hearts, ____
5. From the grain of the har - vest, the grapes of the press, ____

made through the Word of God, spo - ken in love.
Love ____ that moves ____ the sun and the stars,
wis - dom and cour - age to take na - ture's part.
we bring to Christ ____ these gifts now to bless.

made a - new when the Word a crea - ture be -
giv - ing us eyes to see, be - yond ____ our -
Come a - wa - ken your peo - ple from ____ their
Let them be gifts that show our care for the

came bear - ing cre - a - tion's tra - vail ____ and pain.
selves, this great com - mun - ion in which we dwell *(To 3.)*
sleep this re - deemed world ____ to guard and keep.
earth, la - bor that serves ____ the com - mon good. *(To 6.)*

BRIDGE

3. When we fill up the heav-ens with heat that des-
6. When the hun - ger-ing child___ cries out to be

troys,   and plun - der earth's boun - ty and   sick - en the soil,
fed,   what par - ent would give her a   stone___ for bread?

those who suf - fer the most are the poor and the least,
How can   we, then, de - prive___ our child - ren to come

ev - er first to be harmed__ by short-sight - ed   greed.___ *(To 4.)*
of the   fruits of the earth, ___ our com - mon home?___ *(To 7.)*

PART

THREE

What Now?

Encycling: One Feminist Theological Response

Catherine Keller

Usually a catastrophe has at least the capacity to shake folk into fast action and cooperation. This climate crisis approaches with a more treacherous temporality: it is too fast and too slow. Too fast to prevent irreversible destruction; too slow to make it a top priority even of those who do not deny it.

Just a few days after the release of the encyclical I happened to be wandering in Glacier National Park. I was delighted finally to see these glaciers and enjoy perfect weather for the hike. The ancient icefields were nestled glistening in the Rockies, emanating a gorgeous foreverness. They sit there in their icy stillness, melting at rates that keep shocking the USGS team—scientists tuned to geological time—who measure them.[1] Only by reading just afterward did I realize that they are simply doomed: the remaining 25 of the original 160 glaciers will be gone in two decades. Forever. The Himalayas, upon which depend not only tourist joy but the water and therefore food supply of much of India and China, has a bit more time, and so a bit more opportunity to be rescued.

The weird slowfast time of the planetary catastrophe—of fire and ice, of water and soil, of atmosphere and all who breathe—is not readable as "global warming" except by way of mind-melting abstractions like the annual global average temperature shift of less than a degree. And this subtle catastrophic pace only shows itself as "climate change" in and as the space of an entire planet. Nor does the space read as "ours" except when "we" are the species. But to be a species demands a sense of collectivity, even of universality, that cuts against the more vivid sense of human difference and disparity—for much of the right or of the left. So to parlay this crisis into the needed mass response seems much harder than other more than national crises, like, say, a World War. This maddeningly abstract slowfast planetarity demands of us a new sense of global public.

And this is why we need theology. There is perhaps no more comparably vivid, global vocabulary for thinking about—all times and places, all at once. For thinking, first of all, about us as creatures of an integral earth, for thinking about obligations that no national or local or group ethos can trump, for facing oncoming planetary catastrophe—apocalypse—and for proclaiming the chance, in the face of it, of a new earth.[2] At least, there is outside of theology no more planetarily extended vocabulary that retains at the same time ancient currency, profound ancestral resonances, and ongoing symbolic force. That has a globally audible moral voice. That therefore might just have the capacity, mainly through various still living and often traditional Christian communities, institutions and cultures, to change enough minds and to impact enough choices.

For the most part, however, the conservative majority of churches remains untouched by or actively reactionary toward the emergent networks of ecologically-minded Christians. Ecotheological traditions have their own deep ancestry and planetary networks, but they remain fragile minorities, affiliated with feminist, liberation, proces, and other dissident traditions, and are prone to drift discouraged or disenchanted from the exhausted oldline institutions that support or tolerate them. The asymmetrical schism runs right through some old denominations, most manifestly through Roman Catholicism. Theology in its various ecological and interreligious registers keeps trying but has not been equal to the challenge.

This is why we need the pope.

The genius of *Laudato si'* will be studied—recycled, encycled—for generations (if we have them). More importantly, it will, it must, exceed the first news cycle to make its impact felt *now*, and the intensive interest of nonCatholics and lapsed Catholics in it, or I should say, the *affirmative* interest, displays its nonparochial reach. If I had to summarize its strength, I would say something like this: Pope Francis enfolds social justice and ecological viability into a document, simultaneously persuasive in its climate science and its socio-economic analysis, with biblical and creedal theology; therefore, his "integral ecology" can reach at once a global public, of any religion or lack thereof, while most specifically targeting the Christian, and particularly Catholic, constituency that is answerable to him. But what makes all this matter, now, is that *Laudato si'* answers to the slowfast time of climate catastrophe.

The Roman Catholic tradition changes through time at, well, glacial speed. And now its icy stability has been brought to bear—with the cadenced processional of statements from papal precedent never distracting from the ecosocial momentum of the argument—upon the immediacy of the crisis. Often it plays upon the dual temporality: in one paragraph. For instance, it "shows the urgent need for us to move forward in a bold cultural revolution." And yet: "Nobody is suggesting a return to the Stone Age, but we do need to slow down and look at reality in a different way, to appropriate the positive and sustainable progress which has been made, but also to recover the values and the great goals swept away by our unrestrained delusions of grandeur" (114). And so there is the need at once for a contemplative slow-down and an urgent acceleration.

Otherwise our actions will be dispersed in fragmented, virtuous efforts that do not collect the momentum, that do not produce the collective movement, "the bold cultural revolution," which alone can make the difference. And without that revolutionary collectivity, the urgency is dissipated through the smooth functioning of "the alliance between the economy and technology," which "ends up sidelining anything unrelated to its immediate interests. Consequently, the most one can expect is superficial rhetoric, sporadic acts of philanthropy, and perfunctory expressions of concern for the environment, whereas any genuine attempt by groups within society to introduce change is viewed as a nuisance based on romantic illusions or an obstacle to be circumvented" (54).

This is relentlessly nuanced rhetoric, exposing the ruses, the green-washing, the dismissive realisms that slow climate awareness down to its current international failure. And so we must "slow down and look at reality in a different way" (114) if we are to see it, and to see through the high-speed distractions that are slowing down the needed change.

The pope is calling for a new sense of planetary consciousness, dependent upon his radical ecumenism—that is, his call to all human beings, in their endless diversities. It is not a matter of reducing the difference, which means ultimately indifference. It is about gathering differences into alliance. He puts it precisely: "We need to strengthen the conviction that we are one single human family. There are no frontiers or barriers, political or social, behind which we can hide, still less is there room for the globalization of indifference" (52).

Of course when a pope calls down the metaphor of the family, we feminists run for the exits. Not without reason, as I will consider later. But in this millennium I have found that I must keep my own feminism—with its fast reactions—from sidelining the other major issues, particularly of global economics and its ethnic implications, that can now only be addressed in the context of climate change. Yes, then, to think ourselves as a species within the evolutionary tree of life means something very like recognizing our family resemblances. This is not a declaration that we are all "one," nor that we might now embrace each other in a great family reunification. The family of our species remains not only endlessly variegated in its differences but fundamentally dysfunctional in its legacy of collective abuse, exploitation, *patriarchy*, racism, classism, etc. And no less, therefore, a family: but all the more disturbingly so. Yes, sinfully. There is no exit from our "common home."

El Papa Francisco is calling for an immense reflective process in which we may think together in new ways and with multiple metaphors about this very togetherness. "Just as the different aspects of the planet—physical, chemical, and biological—are interrelated, so too living species are part of a network, which we will never fully explore and understand. A good part of our genetic code is shared by many living beings. It follows that the fragmentation of knowledge and the isolation of bits of information can actually become a form of ignorance, unless they are integrated into a broader vision of reality" (138).

Francis has with brilliant precision implicated the method of a fragmentation of knowledge in the breaking apart of planetary life. The newness of the answer requires a slowfast thinking—not new at all for process thinkers, Whiteheadian or Teilhardian, for ecofeminists, or for followers of Saint Francis—of radical material interdependence, gathered into the "integral ecology." Attention to the "cry of the poor and the cry of the earth" (49) will prevent the vaporization of the vision into a merely abstract connectivity. And attention to its edges of unknowability—"which we will never fully explore and understand"(138)—is not only a matter of rigorous scientific openness but of a mystical nonknowing. "We believe in the dimension of 'not-knowing,'" wrote Ivone Gebara years ago, "that makes us humble and at the same time more combative in order to gain respect for differences and the possibility of building an interdependent society."[3] Ecofeminism would be a pale thing without this Roman Catholic sister.

Speaking of sisters, I am struck by the parallelism of the pope's call to slow down and think the connectivity of the common home with another voice of ecological prophecy. In her crucial new text *This Changes Everything: Capitalism vs. the Climate*, Naomi Klein writes that "any attempt to rise to the climate challenge will be fruitless unless it is understood as part of a much larger . . . process of rebuilding and reinventing the very idea of the collective, the communal, the commons, the civil, and the civic after so many decades of attack and neglect."[4] She is an activist tuned to the "bad timing" of the slow surface and the alarming speed of climate change. And in her sense of urgency she remains clear that activism will fail without a shift of "worldview." For capitalism in its global development has depended upon the defeat of the idea of the common. And the academic left, sadly, has colluded whenever it pits the notion of "difference" against the collective or "particularity" against the communal. What is needed is the recuperation of the collective as the dwelling place of difference. Interdependence means neither dependence nor independence but a complex family of divergent particulars.

Klein places her hope neither in a sovereign state nor in greener techno-economies, but in the new movement she calls Blockadia—unprecedented alliances forming recently of indigenous groups, local farmers, eco-activists, citizen groups. (It has been especially active in the Pacific Northwest and Australia in blocking the shipment of coal.) And she makes no references to religious movements against capitalism, like liberation theology, or to eco-theological alliances. Her voice is purely secular.[5] So I find extraordinary the fact that her sense of hope in the face of inevitable climate disaster and mounting capitalist depredation antic-ipates the key papal move precisely. This can be briefly demonstrated: "The double jeopardy of social injustice and global warming should not discourage us. Climate change, with its rising flood waters—"could become a galvanizing force for humanity, leaving us all not just safer from extreme weather, but with societies that are safer and fairer in all kinds of other ways as well. . . . It is a matter of collectively using "the crisis to leap somewhere that seems, frankly, better than where we are right now."[6] In other words—in the face of the one-two punch of capi-talism and climate, the catastrophe itself can be the catalyst.

And hear the parallel answer of the pope: "The same mindset which stands in the way of making radical decisions to reverse the trend of global warming also stands in the way of achieving the goal of elimi-nating poverty" (175). The economic enemy of the common home is unambiguous. It was interesting to watch powerful Catholic Republi-cans reacting to the encyclical, like Rick Santorum and Jeb Bush, who normally love church hierarchy, scramble to restrict papal authority to private faith, stripped of political and of scientific meaning. Just like secular humanism does.

Indeed I would consider the encyclical a rare reason for real hope: not just the hope that it proclaims for a cultural revolution, but the hope generated by the fact that this voice—with more moral authority than any other single voice on the planet—is channeling the double cry of the double jeopardy of the poor and of the earth. And so it amplifies the double possibility of a systemic alternative. This hope is not the same as *optimism*. The pope's own hope is not optimistic: "Doomsday predictions can no longer be met with irony or disdain. We may well be leaving to coming generations debris, desolation and filth" (161). As Bruno Latour, facing global warming, paraphrases Dante at the gates of hell: "Abandon hype all ye who enter here."[7]

Does hope itself then double or does it divide when one considers the radical difference of its sources? A set of movements is forging new alliances for the sake of climate justice, from the bottom up. And on the other, simultaneously, there resounds the voice from the very top, from the top of the top—with angelic fanfare—right down to the misery and filth of the planet. But certainly top-down. And to most ears, theist or atheist, the gesture of a power from above that may descend, or condescend, to help us is just what one would expect from theology, Catholic or otherwise. In this context I can only whisper in such ears that process and feminist theologies have for half a century worked, often in tandem with biblical exegesis, to deconstruct from the deep within of faith itself the divinization of top-down power, its hierarchy, its patriarchy . . .

Oh dear. There is no way around a certain papal patriarchalism, is there. And it does run all the way up to its paternalist Heaven. At a certain point well into the encyclical, one encounters paragraph 75: "A spirituality which forgets God as all-powerful and Creator is not acceptable. That is how we end up worshipping earthly powers, or ourselves usurping the place of God, even to the point of claiming an unlimited right to trample his creation underfoot. The best way to restore men and women to their rightful place, putting an end to their claim to absolute dominion over the earth, is to speak once more of the figure of a Father who creates and who alone owns the world. Otherwise, human beings will always try to impose their own laws and interests on reality."

This is that omnipotent Creator whom process theology has from His [sic] origins recognized as incoherent in the face of creaturely suffering. Why not the call, the lure of God, that sin ignores and betrays—rather than a coercive force that will surely step in and save the planet for us if it is in His Plan? This incoherence may only get compounded by the idealization of the patriarchy of ownership: God the Father as proprietor of the world. Of course, these properties are being lifted up, as they not infrequently are by well-meaning theologians, to take down the human delusions of grandeur, the arrogance and greed that funds every oppression and also drives climate change. Paragraph 75 reads to me as something added not just to reassure but to mobilize a constituency, perhaps the crucial constituency of this document, that is not yet on board with the earth and the poor—but might yet swing. It does make me wince, though, having read 74 paragraphs in almost uninterrupted companionability with el papa.

This must be noted, then, before our feminism turns us icy: that paragraph is the worst of the theo-patriarchalism of the document, and it is itself embedded in a capacious eco-theological reflection that is astute in its biblical interpretation. It has taken on the problem of the Gen. 1 "dominion" passage, beloved of every anti-environmentalist and climate denialist organization. He locates it within his larger theological analysis of the triune sin against our "three fundamental and closely intertwined relationships: with God, with our neighbour and with the earth itself."

> The harmony between the Creator, humanity and creation as a whole was disrupted by our presuming to take the place of God and refusing to acknowledge our creaturely limitations. This in turn distorted our mandate to "have dominion" over the earth (cf. Gen 1:28), to "till it and keep it" (Gen 2:15). (66)

Here is an invaluable move, one that I missed despite having written a book focused mainly on Genesis 1! I always argue that in this text touting the divine delight in every creature ("God saw that it was good," over and over) there is no way that you can read the "have dominion" as "have your way with it—use, use up, demean, ignore, destroy, and exterminate the species." Dominion does not mean domination but responsibility. Not to mention that the culminating reward of the dominion is Gen. 1:29f: you get to be vegans, like all the others who breathe! But Francis splendidly couples and several times repeats the linkage of "have dominion" with "till it and keep it" from Gen. 2, and clarifies that "keeping" "means caring, protecting, overseeing and preserving" (62). He persists (at much greater length than the patriarchal paragraph is afforded) to lay out numerous ecological mandates of the biblical text.

Therefore, I certainly intend to teach this text to the very students to whom I am—at the same time—introducing the alternative metaphors of a God whose power is not classically omnipotent but lovingly omnipotential, requiring us to actualize it responsibly and creatively. A God Jesus addressed—a novelty then—as "Father," a radicalization of intimate relation, whom we now for the same reason refer to as Love, Mother, Father-Mother, Poet of the Universe, Friend, the Enfolding, or just—mysterious Infinity beyond names and beyond knowing. The endless nameability and unnameability of the divine is as sister Elizabeth Johnson made dauntlessly clear key to the work of feminist theology.[8] And it allows me to include citations of many ancient texts and some recent ones that use paternal language.

Contradiction?

No, complicity. Indeed, a very protest/anti feminist complicity with this pope whose mission has defined itself as one great protest on behalf of the poor and the earth. Great, and not infallible. And in this case I admit to recognizing that even the bit of the encyclical I disagree with is needed: if he omitted it, or indeed if he spoke (in the tongues of angels) the language I long to hear, beyond paternity, possession, omnipotence, beyond the constrictions of women's choices and callings, his encyclical would not have a chance of making the difference it might just make, not just preaching to the eco-choir, but to traditionally Roman Catholic populations.

We must not wait to agree on all our namings, not even on all our burning issues. There isn't *time*. At stake is the future of livable life for us all. The whole dysfunctional family. And in the meantime the most vulnerable among us, often women, will be thrown by droughts and meltings and fires, collapsing coastlines and islands, agricultures and cultures, into rapidly intensifying jeopardy. Might we then all consider joining—in our acute differences—this com-plicity: folding-together in collective mindfulness of the complications of our wondrously fragile and complex earth system? It isn't a matter of putting off our issues of gender and sex and race and ability, let alone class, but of colluding in the spirit of the grassroots movements and their dynamic entanglements. Then we can keep talking, arguing, contesting particular priorities— amidst difference there are always shifting deferrals—without delaying commitment to earth-keeping. As Klein puts it, "the environmental crisis—if conceived sufficiently broadly—neither trumps nor distracts from our pressing political and economic causes: it supercharges each one of them with existential urgency."[9]

Under planetary pressure, and with a little help from the pope, we just may form an alliance in the name of the universe and its source. In *their* complication they extend endlessly beyond our comprehension—but they give us timely clues. And in the fastslow temporalities of this encyclical, appealing to old texts and to possible futures, the movement down from above forms a vortex with the movements interlinking us and all our social contexts from below. Catastrophe, etymologically, comes from *kata-strophe*, a "turning down." Might we let the catastrophe we face turn us down, not in a great terminal meltdown, but in a *turning down to earth*? Where we already are, earthlings dwelling in the context of all our contexts. Then catastrophe becomes catalyst for the cultural revolution we need.

Early in the encyclical, after just two paragraphs, the human gets a magisterial clue as to our widest context. It comes with a single italicized sentence: *"Nothing in this world is indifferent to us"* (2). This is neither traditional Catholic teaching nor natural science. It sounds more like process thought or the new materialism, with a vibrant materiality composed of responsive interdependencies that entangle any observer and anything observed. But not indifferent?

Really, what do the glaciers as they melt care for us, or indeed the ancient strata of the stony earth upon which they reside? Right, they don't care, they don't have conscious concern. And neither do most of us, for almost all the rest of us, most of the time. We are too vastly limited to care for the rest, except—on principle. And in faith. But this need not render us indifferent to any.

In particular moments the vibrant interplay of our differences shines through—a stranger's grin, an owl's glare, a glacier's sparkle. And then we recognize difference as the precise opposite of indifference. Difference does not separate but relates. If indifference occludes difference itself—it is because the world is wrought of entangled differences. And these differences matter—in their interdependencies across every stratum of geology, chemistry, biology. Indifference is the opposite of difference. It conveys a world of separables and exploitables and expendables, blind and wasteful of the ways, willy nilly, we recycle each other endlessly. But there is no room for "the globalization of indifference" (52) in this house of many mansions, this complex homeostatic system, Gaia, sister-mother, our body of bodies, this momentously encycled earth-home.

Laudato si'.

Endnotes

1. Christopher White, *The Melting World: A Journey Across America's Vanishing Glaciers* (New York: St. Martin's Press, 2013).

2. Catherine Keller, *Apocalypse Now and Then: a Feminist Guide to the End of the World* (Boston: Beacon, 1996); cf. my update of apocalyptic theopolitics in *God and Power: Counter-Apocalyptic Journeys* (Minneapolis: Augsburg-Fortress, 2005).

3. Ivone Gebara, *Out of the Depths: Women's Experience of Evil and Salvation* (Minneapolis: Augsburg-Fortress, 2002), 132. For an exploration of the tradition of mystical unsaying (the apophatic or "negative theology") with reference to ecopolitics, see my *Cloud of the Impossible: Negative Theology and Planetary Entanglement* (NY: Columbia U. Press, 2015).

4. Naomi Klein, *This Changes Everything: Capitalism vs The Climate* (NY: Simon & Schuster, 2014), 460

5. See Naomi Klein's response to the encyclical, *New Yorker* 11 July 2015, which concludes: "The most powerful example of this capacity for change may well be Pope Francis's Vatican. And it is a model not for the Church alone. Because if one of the oldest and most tradition-bound institutions in the world can change its teachings and practices as radically, and as rapidly, as Francis is attempting, then surely all kinds of newer and more elastic institutions can change as well. And if that happens—if transformation is as contagious as it seems to be here—well, we might just stand a chance of tackling climate change."

6. Klein, *This Changes*, 7

7. Bruno Latour, *Facing Gaia: Six lectures on the political theology of nature. Being the Gifford Lectures on Natural Religion, Edinburgh, 18th-28th of February* 2013 <https://docs.google.com/file/d/0BxeTjgod3jSSSXZH-TU9Yb3FlYms/edit?pli=1>.

8. Elizabeth Johnson, *She Who Is: The Mystery of God in Feminist Discourse* (New York: Crossroads: 2002).

9. Klein, 153.

Climate Change Brings Moral Change

Mary Evelyn Tucker

Pope Francis is clearly one of the most popular people on the planet at present. With his love for the poor, his willingness to embrace the outcaste, and his genuine humility he has captured the hearts of millions—Christian and non-Christian alike. He has inspired minds as well by his willingness to take on difficult issues such as ecology, economy, and equity, which he sees as inextricably linked. Indeed, these three interwoven issues are at the heart of his papal encyclical released this week. An encyclical is a letter to the bishops and all church members. It is the highest level of teaching in the Catholic Church, and this is the first encyclical on the environment in the history of the Church.

First, he addresses ecology. Pope Francis, following in the tradition of Francis of Assisi, celebrates the natural world as a sacred gift. He does this with his reference to St. Francis' "Canticle of Brother Sun, Sister Moon" in the title of the encyclical *Praised Be.* The kinship with all creation that St. Francis intuited we now understand as complex ecological relationships that have evolved over billions of years. For Pope Francis these relationships have a natural order or "grammar" that needs to be understood, respected, and valued.

Second, he speaks about the economy. Within this valuing of nature, the pope encourages us to see the human economy as a subsystem of nature's economy, namely the dynamic interaction of life in ecosystems.

Without a healthy natural ecology there is not a sustainable economy and vice versa. They are inevitably interdependent. Moreover, we cannot ignore pollution or green house gases as externalities that are not factored into full cost accounting. This is because, for Pope Francis, profit over people or at the expense of the planet is not genuine profit. This is what has happened with fossil fuels causing climate disruption.

Third, he highlights equity. From this perspective, working within the limits of nature's economy can lead to thriving human societies. In contrast, exploiting the Earth and using oil and gas without limits has led to increased human inequities. Ecosystems are being undermined by climate change and the wealthy most often benefit. The pope recognizes that such an impoverished economic system results in impoverished and unjust social systems. Thus, for him, the poor must be cared for as they are the most adversely affected by climate change.

In all of this the encyclical is not anti-modernity, but hopes to reconfigure the idea of progress. "Not blind opposition to progress but opposition to blind progress" as John Muir said. The pope refers to this perspective when he speaks of a throwaway economy where humans are saturated in materialism. He sees the need for genuine progress where the health of both people and the planet can be fostered. Thus as the head of the Pontifical Academy of Justice and Peace, Cardinal Peter Turkson, has said, "We need to learn to work together in a framework that links economic prosperity with both social inclusion and protection of the natural world."[1] This linkage of ecology, economy, and equity is what is Francis calls an "integral ecology," and it is central to the encyclical.

Such an integral ecology clearly requires interdisciplinary cooperation as we find our path forward on a planet of more than 7 billion people. We need to understand more fully the challenges the world is facing in terms of economic development and environmental protection. These are not easy to reconcile. Indeed, the international community has been seeking answers since the Earth Summit in Rio in 1992 set forth a framework for sustainable development. The world is ever more in need of an integral ecology that brings together a fresh understanding that people and the planet are part of one interdependent life community. Such an integral ecology affirms the cooperation of science and ethics, knowing that our problems will not be solved without both. It is clear that climate change is requiring moral change.

The papal encyclical, then, represents a new period of potential cooperation. In the Yale Forum on Religion and Ecology we have been working for two decades with hundreds of scholars to identify the cultural and religious grounds in the world's religions for a more diverse environmental ethics to complement environmental sciences. Between 1995-2004 we organized ten conferences at Harvard and published ten volumes to examine how the world's religions can contribute their varied ethical perspectives for a sustainable future. At Yale School of Forestry and Environmental Studies we have been broadening this dialogue and building on the work of environmentalists, policy makers, and economists. The papal encyclical will be a fresh inspiration for these and numerous other efforts that are bringing together ecology and ethics for the flourishing of the Earth community. To this end we look forward to working together with the Center for Process Studies which, in addition to numerous publications, has convened conferences in both the U.S. and China to advance the goals of ecological civilization.

Endnotes

1. <http://en.radiovaticana.va/news/2015/04/28/cardinal_turkson_ together_for_stewardship_of_creation/114012>.

Achieving Pope Francis' Vision: Being a Part of the Transformation

Tina Clarke

When I read Pope Francis' encyclical on the environment, climate, and equity, I was filled with hope and happiness. His call to action is a game-changer for the most important survival issue ever to face human civilization. Transitioning the world from fossil fuel combustion to renewable energy and efficient use of energy—stopping runaway climate change—is the greatest challenge of our time, and it can be done, if we act quickly. Our success, over the next precious few years, will determine the well-being of human societies and the survival of earth's ecosystems, for the next one thousand years and beyond.

The pope's leadership is a great gift of support to people all over the world who are working to transition their communities and societies. Together we can take action at many levels to modernize energy technology, retrofit society for sustainability and resilience, save ecosystems (especially those that sequester large quantities of greenhouse gases), preserve biological diversity, restore soil fertility, and reduce consumption of energy-intensive food and products. It's time to redesign and remake our communities, change the rules of the economic game in our nation, and care The most important focus is to end the burning of coal, oil, tar sands, and other "dinosaur fuels" as quickly as possible.

The pope's call for transformation is based in modern science and engineering. Clearly the Vatican is getting excellent information from scientists and researchers in the fields of energy efficiency and renewable energy, because his encyclical reflects the conclusions of thousands of experts in wind and solar power, energy efficient technologies, food and hunger, and environmentally related sciences. Around the world engineers have shown that transitioning to safe, clean, reliable, renewable energy and energy efficient technologies is not only achievable, but also affordable and desirable for economic, health, and equity reasons. Economists have bolstered the case for renewable energy and efficiency investments.[1] As of 2014, the installed costs of many energy efficient technologies, wind turbines and solar panels are now lower than any non-renewable energy source—coal, oil, natural gas, tarsands, and nuclear power.

For example, Mark Jacobson of Stanford University and The Solutions Project[2] and Amory Lovins of The Rocky Mountain Institute,[3] have shown that affordable wind, solar, and water power can provide the world with many times more energy than it needs, affordably and reliably.

Regarding the role of efficient technologies, the Swiss Government and a leading technology university in Europe, ETH Zurich,[4] have shown that decarbonizing society (virtually eliminating fossil fuel use) can be readily achieved by implementing energy efficient technologies and modest amounts of wind and solar power. One area of research, the "2000 Watt Society," demonstrated that the world's poor could increase energy use to 2000 watts per person per day with renewable energy. Meanwhile people in wealthier countries could reduce their energy use down to 2000 watts per person per day by switching to energy-efficient technologies and manufacturing processes. (2000 Watts per person per day is one-third the level of energy currently used in Europe, and one-sixth the energy used in the U.S.) Thus the pope's vision of a more equitable sharing of energy and world resources has thus been proven as both possible and the best path into the future.[5]

The combination of safe, clean, renewable energy sources (wind, solar, and water power) and energy efficiency upgrades are solutions that need to be implemented in every community in every industrial society. The more quickly industrial societies transition to locally generated renewable wind and solar energy, and to high-efficiency heating, cooling, transportation, lighting, manufacturing, communications, and other technologies, the more likely the world will be able to avoid runaway climate change. Action by citizens in industrial societies is essential to enable the rise of ecological civilization.

If our action is essential to achieving global change and to sustaining our communities, how do we achieve it?

At least since the rise of hierarchical, agriculturally dependent societies 10,000 years ago, groups of people have achieved social change by connecting with each other: forming groups, organizations, and movements to achieve their goals. People have achieved change by rolling up their sleeves and doing it themselves. They've achieved change by informing others, by changing attitudes, and by calling for commitment to principles and values, as Pope Francis has now done.

In the modern era, groups of people have changed society by organizing politically (political parties, election education and get-out-the-vote, advocacy and lobbying of elected officials, media coverage, public movements) and organizing economically (guilds, cooperatives, trade unions, business associations, shareholder resolutions, land trusts, consumer campaigns, etc.). They have also put themselves on the line, risking injury or unpleasant or even risky forms of pressure against themselves. And, unfortunately, many have resorted to violence or damage when they see no other option, or not been willing to wait, or to cooperate, with the larger society to achieve change.

Martin Luther King, Jr. called violence, "the least redemptive" form of social change, championing all the other methods as essential alternatives. When change is not achieved peacefully, we can expect greater human suffering.

All of the peaceful methods of social change require vision and collaboration among significant numbers of people. Behind every major decision by a decision-maker is a movement or collaboration of people who have been working hard to make change happen. Social change is a game of numbers—getting "enough" people involved. Good information is important, but when people come together to act, with clear goals, from a foundation of principles, and with commitment to collaboration, larger, more visionary change is possible. This is another reason why the pope's encyclical is so important: he is bringing a much larger number of people together by calling upon over a billion Roman Catholics to study and act. By acting together we have a greater chance of achieving the big, important technology changes in time.

Not only are people more powerful and successful when we act together toward a common goal. Scientists at MIT and elsewhere call the wisdom that emerges from our focused collaboration the "collective genius." It turns out that we are smarter together.

Acting together is essential at every level of society. Whether national, state, local, business, or another level, social transformation is dynamic, interactive and unpredictable. Instead of choosing just one level of decision-making as "the" essential level, we are wise to identify what decisions need to be made at which level, who has the power to make those decisions, and what tools best fit the task.

The climate crisis needs our action at all levels. National policies set the rules of the economic game: who gets accolades, who gets funding and other economic benefits, who is monitored, who is fined, and who goes to jail. Right now governments around the world, including our own, are giving coal, oil, gas, nuclear, and other polluting sources of energy hundreds of billions of dollars in subsidies. Unless citizens act— insisting on free market discipline and fair competition, at least—the transformation to a stable climate will not be possible.

Until ten years ago, action at the community level had largely been overlooked or invisible. Many individuals, organizations and municipalities were working on climate issues, sustainability, food, renewable energy, and energy efficiency. But most of these efforts were seen as marginal, as "environmental." and not strongly related to the mainstream of daily life.

In 2004-2005 in the U.K., a permaculture teacher named Rob Hopkins, along with friends and students, began exploring the idea of "transitioning the from oil dependency to community resilience." They formed a "Transition Town" to work together to increase local food and local energy production, to reduce needs for products and resources imported from far away, and to increase mutual support, community caring and resilience. Transition Town Totnes began organizing events, gardening projects, community-owned renewable energy, use of the local currency from 917 A.D., resources for local entrepreneurs and businesses, and social events that brought people together to create whatever projects appealed to them. The group explored the social and inner, emotional challenges to changing our lives. They created a lot of fun, laughter, and friendship.

Dozens, then hundreds of people showed up. Hundreds, then thousands of people began participating in neighborhood, local economy, local food, home weatherization, and children's projects, and more. Public conversations and celebrations highlighted history, resilience, mutual support, positive vision, and local action to build a more vibrant, thriving future.

Soon neighboring towns were calling to learn what all the excitement was about in Totnes. The movement grew rapidly, virally, to upward of 1,000 Transition Initiatives in 2009 in the U.K. The idea of "transitioning" to "community resilience" and focusing on "positive action" in one's local place took off and blew around the world, changing the environmental movement.

How can a community transition from dependency to local strength and resilience? What enables "take-off" in a community?

To support communities in organizing projects and a community-wide initiative, many free resources are available at the global Transition Network.[6] Here are some fundamental components to get started.

First, find some people to form an "initiating" group to get things started.

Ask people who care deeply about the community and want to increase resilience and well-being to help bring people together to explore ways to lower our dependency on oil, natural gas, coal, tar sands, and other polluting energy sources. Ask at least 10-15 people to end up with a core group of 5-12. You may wish to officially register as a Transition Initiative to help the community understand what you're trying to do and to add credibility. Transition is an almost completely flexible structure for building your community's unique path into the future.

Second, discuss in the group the idea of changing how we think before asking others to change how they think and live.

A common mistake is to believe that we need to change others to "get them to do the right thing." Instead, community transformation is based on caring friendships and mutual support. Few people like to be told they should change! If all you do is make new friends and throw great parties to bring people together to share and support each other, that may be enough to get collaboration and projects going. In Transition we use Open Space Technology, in an adapted, shortened way, to support people to come together to create practical projects. Much good comes from simply building up our connections and ways of giving each other mutual support.

Third, identify some goals.

Make the focus of your group that you will get practical work done that improves everyone's quality of life, security, and well-being. Work for greater independence from imported energy and food. Host some fun and inclusive community events. Launch one or more new projects that deepen community connections.

Fourth, make a "Big List" of people and groups who care about community well-being.

Build a network of relationships that includes everyone—friends and neighbors, colleagues and critics—everyone who might care about the well-being of the people and place where you live. The "Big List" can also be where you collect information about who is already doing resilience work, who might be interested in particular projects and action (e.g. farmers market, bicycle coop, children's toy swap, etc.), what organizations are already building community resilience and reducing energy and food dependence, and what resources can help individuals and neighborhoods. Identify in the list: *People, Groups, Places, & Networks.*

Fifth, sort the Big List.

In a general, quick way, sort the people, places, groups, and networks into five very rough categories:

- *Aware & Active on the Climate Issue*
- *Aware of the Climate Issue, but not Active*
- *Neither Aware nor Active on the Climate Issue*
- *Not Interested*
- *Disagrees that the Climate Issue is Important to Address*

Do this quickly. Don't worry about accuracy. The goal is to increase efficiency in outreach, respect peoples' different perspectives, and thus better serve your community.

Sixth: Invite people on the list to connect, share ideas, and make practical work happen.

Invite people to connect—to share practical work ideas and to have parties! Your Initiating Group can create events, social gatherings, places in the community, and other social opportunities where people can meet, get to know each other, and discuss ideas for building resilience.

Each person in your community has different ways of thinking about the climate issue (or not thinking about it). In general, for the different categories, focus on the following.

- *Thank them. Ask them to give their gifts to build community resilience.*
- *Offer them easy projects they can do in short amounts of time.*
- *Design community events, projects and activities to help them with practical needs and to make life more fun.*
- *Invite to community events, but don't push. Don't exclude, but don't bother them.*
- *Learn what they think. Listen and Respect. If possible, dialogue, but don't get flustered, push or argue. Appreciate common values and build on areas of agreement.*

Seventh: Partner.

Reach out to local groups, places, and networks where local food, local energy, local economy, and other community resilience-building activities are happening. Meet with these groups and suggest that you promote their events and partner to create new projects. Build a network of collaboration in your community.

Eighth: Encourage everyone to give his or her gifts, have fun, and look for "common ground" with others in the community.

Community resilience is based on mutual support and relationships of trust with our neighbors. Rather than focusing primarily on the climate issue, the information, or whatever message we would personally like to give, we focus on relationship-building and collaboration around common goals or concerns. Listening, learning, respecting, and responding are more important to building a base of resilient relationships. Environmental information can come later.

Ninth: Organize events where people can talk to each other, create projects and build relationships.

Popular events include a fair, a series of panel discussions on different topics, or an Open Space Technology gathering to create practical projects. The key to a community-building, action-oriented event is a structure that supports small group conversations to form but allows people to move around. You want enough structure to help people with similar interests find each other, and have whatever conversations they want to have. Yet you don't want to impose content or topics on people beyond a general, big topic like "community resilience" or "reducing dependency on imported energy." Create the opportunity and structure so that people can identify the topics *they* want to discuss.

Tenth: Provide support, encouragement and appreciation.

The essence of the Transition model, and a key reason for its success, is the open-ended, participatory nature of local, community events, and activities. Rather than one organization telling people what they should do, we seek to support each unique person to give their gifts in community.

All levels of action are needed—personal, family, congregation, organization, local, state, and national—to help us transform our technology and resource use so that we do not destroy our planet home. Pope Francis has given us a vision of hope and a framework of values to guide our choices. Now, inspired by the love and leadership Pope Francis has shown, we can reach out to our neighbors and offer friendship. We can take initiative to start and grow practical projects, not wait for others to solve this greatest challenge from the top. We can invite conversation about how to reduce our dependency upon, and our use of, the world's resources.

Most beautiful of all, we can experience our own strength, our courage to give, and our abilities to forgive, to initiate, to collaborate, and to create a more wonderful home, as we do our part for the greater good.

Endnotes

1. <http://www.peri.umass.edu/energy/>.

2. <http://thesolutionsproject.org/>.

3. <http://www.rmi.org/>.

4. <https://www.ethz.ch/en/research/programmes-and-initiatives.html>.

5. See the 2000 Watt Society research, including <http://www.cer.ethz.ch/resec/news/Brochure_2kW.pdf>.

6. <www.TransitionNetwork.org> and Transition US, the U.S. affiliate <www.TransitionUS.org>.

Integral Ecology, Climate Justice, and the New United Nations Development Agenda

Rick Clugston & Karenna Gore

2015 is a promising year for mobilizing for transformative change. Governments will adopt a New (Post-2015) United Nations Development Agenda in September 2015 that will be guided by sustainable development goals (SDGs). Governments will meet in Paris (COP 21) in December 2015 to adopt a binding agreement on climate change. There is also a strong new energy in the dialogue within societies about culture, values, and lifestyle, harder to pin down but no less important to our capacity for change.

Pope Francis' encyclical (*Laudato si*) is a rallying point for ensuring that people understand the magnitude of the challenge facing us and for embracing the moral imperative to reorient our hearts and minds as well as our economic and social policies, to create a world that works for all. He terms this integral ecology, which "integrates questions of justice in debates on the environment, so as to hear both the cry of the earth and the cry of the poor" (49).

Following some background on the global processes, we highlight some key directions that Francis calls us to embrace to create a just sustainable and peaceful future. Then we explore mobilizing interreligious efforts to do deep justice based culture work including advocacy for critical policy changes.

Background: climate justice and the new United Nations Development Agenda

Climate change, the disruption and destabilization of ecological systems, is an assault on the well-being of life on Earth. COP 21 presents the most critical opportunity to avert the worst consequences of business as usual. It is our last chance for a meaningful binding treaty before it really is too late. It is critical for all of civil society to weigh in to secure a treaty that enables us to mitigate the worst consequences of unbridled fossil fuel-based development by immediately shifting to carbon neutral sources of energy. We also must assist in helping the most vulnerable communities adapt to the unavoidable consequences of our past and continued dependence on coal and oil for our energy needs. This is a matter of humanitarian urgency and also of national and global security. To quote the Secretary of the U.S. Navy, said, "We are beginning to move the Navy and the Marine Corps off of fossil fuels for strategic and tactical reasons, and because we ought to be a good steward of this planet and of its resources."[1]

Our difficulties in making a shift to sustainable energy for all can only be solved by adopting a new bottom line for economic development that incorporates planetary boundaries as it provides necessary goods and services for all. Anything less would overtly sacrifice future generations of humankind on Earth.

Climate change is an overarching symptom of an economic development model centered on short-term economic growth (i.e., increasing GDP). This model ignores the destruction done to natural resources and the well-being of the many people who are not in the circle of wealth distribution. This year is critical for action on curtailing the carbon emissions that cause climate change, but this must not cause that imperative to be seen in isolation from other related issues. The loss of biological and cultural diversity, the destruction of soil and water (oceans), and the status of women are some other symptoms, all interconnected, which must be addressed.

We must recognize that this crisis has already yielded a window of opportunity. As environmental and social deterioration has accompanied rapid economic growth, even the most established governments are recognizing the fact that "transformative change is needed," and "business as usual is not an option" (Secretary General's Interagency Task Force Report, 2012).[2]

In September 2015, world governments will adopt new, universal sustainable development goals that will incorporate the unfinished business of the Millennium Development Goals (MDGs) into a broader framework. SDGs are to be the guides (a sort of dashboard) for this transformative change. They are intended as a set of "action-oriented, concise and easy to communicate goals that could help drive the implementation of sustainable development." The 13 UN Intergovernmental Open Working Group (OWG) meetings led to the completion of the Zero Draft of the SDGs in July 2014. Then, various UN offices and civil society organizations analyzed these 17 goals and 169 targets and made recommendations for their improvement.

This extensive process (including the monthly intergovernmental negotiation sessions so far preparing for the Fall Post-15 Summit) has been remarkable in terms of the consensus for seeking transformative change. This will be guided by an integrated triple bottom line and determination to place the resultant new understanding of sustainable development at the center of national and international development, starting with United Nations' own agencies. In the monthly intergovernmental negotiations, governmental representatives have repeatedly affirmed the need for transformative change guided by a new framework for development that would eliminate poverty, promote the breadth of human rights, ensure equitable and inclusive economic growth—all within planetary boundaries.[3] (United Nations Sustainable Development Knowledge Platform, Sustainable Development Goals Report 2014, and other sources)

In shaping the Post-2015 sustainable development agenda, we must make sure that we are not just reinforcing the engine of unsustainable growth, under the guise of sustainable development. Providing more and more goods and services to an ever-increasing human population without crossing planetary boundaries is a fundamental challenge.

Pope Francis' challenge

Laudato si' challenges us to make three major shifts:

1. From narrow anthropocentrism to integral ecology, centered on the common good and the interconnectedness and dignity of all life.

2. Toward a just and equitable social order, emphasizing a new bottom line for development that replaces economic growth and short-term gain (GDP) with fuller measures of personal and planetary well being.

3. Toward a true global collaboration—a social movement, that is not about conversion but convergence grounded in shared global ethics.

Below are a few paragraphs from the encyclical, illustrating the pope's thinking on these matters:

> Authentic human development has a moral character. It presumes full respect for the human person, but it must also be concerned for the world around us and take into account the nature of each being and of its mutual connection in an ordered system. (5)

> It is not enough . . . to think of different species merely as potential "resources" to be exploited, while overlooking the fact that they have value in themselves . . . Because of us, thousands of species will no longer give glory to God by their very existence, nor convey their message to us. We have no such right. (33)

> Because all creatures are connected, each must be cherished with love and respect, for all of us as living creatures are dependent on one another. (42)

> The notion of the common good also extends to future generations. The global economic crises have made painfully obvious the detrimental effects of disregarding our common destiny, which cannot exclude those who come after us . . . We can no longer speak of sustainable development apart from intergenerational solidarity . . . Intergenerational solidarity is not optional, but rather a basic question of justice, since the world we have received also belongs to those who will follow us. (159)

The Earth Charter asked us to leave behind a period of self-destruction and make a new start, but we have not as yet developed a universal awareness needed to achieve this. Here, I would echo that courageous challenge: "As never before in history, common destiny beckons us to seek a new beginning . . . Let ours be a time remembered for the awakening of a new reverence for life, the firm resolve to achieve sustainability, the quickening of the struggle for justice and peace, and the joyful celebration of life." (207, quoting the Earth Charter, The Hague, 29 June 2000)

Together with the patrimony of nature, there is also an historic, artistic and cultural patrimony which is likewise under threat . . . Ecology, then, also involves protecting the cultural treasures of humanity in the broadest sense. More specifically, it calls for greater attention to local cultures.(143)

In this sense, it is essential to show special care for indigenous communities and their cultural traditions. They are not merely one minority among others, but should be the principal dialogue partners, especially when large projects affecting their land are proposed. (146)

Inequity affects not only individuals but entire countries; it compels us to consider an ethics of international relations. A true "ecological debt" exists, particularly between the global north and south, connected to commercial imbalances with effects on the environment, and the disproportionate use of natural resources by certain countries over long periods of time. (51)

Put simply, it is a matter of redefining our notion of progress. A technological and economic development which does not leave in its wake a better world and an integrally higher quality of life cannot be considered progress. (194)

A politics concerned with immediate results, supported by consumerist sectors of the population, is driven to produce short-term growth. In response to electoral interests, governments are reluctant to upset the public with measures which could affect the level of consumption or create risks for foreign investment. The myopia of power politics delays the inclusion of a far-sighted environmental agenda within the overall agenda of governments. (178)

Here I want to recognize, encourage and thank all those striving in countless ways to guarantee the protection of the home which we share. Particular appreciation is owed to those who tirelessly seek to resolve the tragic effects of environmental degradation on the lives of the world's poorest. Young people demand change. (13)

Society, through non-governmental organizations and intermediate groups, must put pressure on governments to develop more rigorous regulations, procedures and controls. Unless citizens control political power—national, regional and municipal—it will not be possible to control damage to the environment. (179)

What is development for?

Pope Francis would have us affirm that development—both economic and personal—is not primarily about short-term dominance and economic gain (thereby owning, consuming, and controlling ever more goods and services). Rather it is about building those conditions and capacities necessary for full human development for all in a flourishing Earth community.

The Earth Charter states: "We must realize that when basic needs have been met, human development is primarily about being more, not having more."[4]

Real transformative change will require the reorientation of development goals to support everyone's psychological and spiritual growth in the context of living in ways that all can live. Such growth is defined by Rami Shapiro as an "ever deepening capacity to embrace life with justice, compassion, curiosity, awe, wonder, serenity and humility."[5]

In the beginning of his encyclical, Pope Francis references the many statements of his predecessors on environment and development. In his *Encyclical on Social Concern* Pope John Paul II summed up well a spiritual perspective on development:

side-by-side with the miseries of underdevelopment, themselves unacceptable, we find ourselves up against a form of super-development, equally inadmissible, because like the former it is contrary to what is good and to true happiness. This superdevelopment, which consists in an excessive availability of every kind of material goods for the benefit of certain social groups, easily makes people slaves of 'possession' and of immediate gratification, with no other horizon than the multiplication or continual replacement of the things already owned with others still better.

This then is the picture: there are some people—the few who possess much—who do not really succeed in 'being' because . . . they are hindered by the cult of 'having'; and there are others— the many who have little or nothing—who do not succeed in realizing their basic human vocation because they are deprived of essential goods.[6]

True well-being for all can only be met if those with enough (perhaps with too much) decide to give what they really don't need to support sufficiency for the many who have too little. This is so that those impoverished can realize a good life and also to enable the regeneration of ecological systems that provide care for the whole community of life.

It is a recognition that we live within a mystery we cannot comprehend, and we will die; our only chance of awakening fully lies in creating a world that works for all, for we are interconnected, and the well-being of one depends on the well being of all. Many are experiencing a global commercial culture that is bankrupt of these values, even seemingly bent on destroying them. Yet, as Pope Francis memorably describes a "mist seeping gently beneath a closed door" (112), there is also a palpable, sentient humanity living within our global culture. *Laudato si'* is an inclusive, humble, and forgiving document. Let us encounter those who appear to resist its call in that spirit and continually open our conversation around the SDG's to new converts and also to all those who have not been included in the conversation thus far.

Not only the pope, but many Earth-systems scientists and cosmologists, nature poets and mystics, other religious leaders, and policy makers are converging on an understanding of Earth as a vulnerable, interconnected, and interdependent living system. We humans are a part of nature and dependent on the vitality of ecological systems for our well-being. Increasingly, scientists and practitioners of diverse spiritual traditions are awakening to Earth as a community of subjects that deserve our respect and care, especially in the Anthropocene. This is a convergence of new and old, scientific and spiritual, understandings, of who we are in the Earth community, and how we create mutually enhancing human Earth relationships.

What does this understanding of our interconnection with all life imply for how we live our lives, organize our communities and workplaces, revise our economic and social policies at all levels of government?

Transformative change

The encyclical's call for transformative change presents a fourfold challenge to religious and spiritual communities (actually to all communities) to reorient our perception and action focused on the following.

A. Make lifestyle choices to:

- Engage deeply and effectively in contemplative practices that awaken us to our great work, our vocations, where our deepest passions meet the real needs of the world.

- Experience our interconnectedness and interdependence with the whole living world, understanding diverse cultures and people, agriculture and wilderness, the cycles of life and the seasons, and the unfolding universe.

- Feel and act from compassionate concern for others, doing no harm and being conscious and responsive to the dignity and needs of all living beings.

- Live in ways that all can live, consuming no more than one's fair share of Earth's bounty—choosing products and services (e.g., food, energy, transportation, housing), in a way that strives to engage in systems that are ecologically sound, socially just, and economically viable (e.g., local, fair trade, organic, carbon and pollution neutral, humane).

B. Build communities and organizations centered on sustainable living and spiritual growth. Working together in our families, neighborhoods, congregations, and academic institutions, we can create resilient and anticipatory communities that give a taste of living in a way that all can live. Our work and home would emphasize the above four practices. Our processes of community and institutional decision making and conflict resolution would be open. They would enable all to participate and clarify their preferences and grievances and arrive at structures and solutions that further everyone's full human development in a flourishing Earth community. Our process capacities—to be humble, honest, and respectful; to not blame and to forgive; and to compromise for the good of all—are foundational.

C. Shift policy frameworks: Through voting, lobbying, and participating in political decision making at all levels, we can shift laws and policies to support future generations and the whole interconnected web of life. This means creating better measures of genuine progress than GDP, internalizing social and environmental costs in pricing goods and services, eliminating perverse subsidies, and creating ombudspersons and trusteeship structures at all governmental levels to effectively represent the interests of all members of the life community, current and future.

D. Participate in a truly collaborative, effective, social movement for ecojustice.

Not only does our materialist, ego-gratification-oriented consumer culture condition us to focus on owning and consuming more, it conditions us to operate as isolated, competitive egos focused on short-term personal and organizational profit and prestige. [We are at a social evolutionary moment analogous to when single-celled organisms in the primordial sea joined together in multi-cellular organisms with specialized functions in a new integrated whole. Then separate, individual cells developed fundamentally different modes of working together. Now we and our organizations must synergize our efforts to build the social movement to make those shifts in lifestyle, community, and professional practices, and also social policies, necessary to create a just and sustainable future.]

Working together on the Road Though Paris

Building on the constituency and the agenda from the Religions for the Earth Conference and the People's Climate March in September 2014, the Center for Earth Ethics (CEE) was created to advance the ethics, practices, and policies necessary to care for all members of our Earth community now, and for future generations. We, along with many other religious, spiritual, and secular organizations, are organizing for maximum impact for a climate justice treaty. Examples of active groups include the Forum on Religion and Ecology, Our Voices, Green Faith, the World Council of Churches, the Parliament of World's Religions, NAACP Environment and Climate Justice Initiative, and countless locally rooted community groups, visit our website <www.earthethics. org> for information on getting involved in the Road Through Paris.

Endnotes

1. Ray Mabus, Secretary of the Navy, Speech at Carnegie Council on Ethics in International Relations, 9 November 2010 <http://www.navy.mil/navydata/people/secnav/Mabus/Speech/Carnegie11910.pdf>.

2. <http://www.un.org/millenniumgoals/pdf/Post_2015_UNTTreport.pdf>.

3. <https://sustainabledevelopment.un.org/focussdgs.html>.

4. Preamble, Earth Charter <http://www.earthcharterinaction.org/content/pages/Read-the-Charter.html>.

5. Rami Shapiro, *Recovery—The Sacred Art: The Twelve Steps as Spiritual Practice* (Woodstock, VT: Skylight Paths Publishing, 2009), xiii.

6. John Paul II, *Encyclical on Social Concern* <http://w2.vatican.va/content/john-paul-ii/en/encyclicals/documents/hf_jp-ii_enc_30121987_sollicitudo-rei-socialis.html>.

Searching for a Second Enlightenment

Rick Smyre

An authentic humanity, calling for a new synthesis, seems to dwell in the midst of our technological culture, almost unnoticed, like a mist seeping gently beneath a closed door. (112)

The same mindset which stands in the way of making radical decisions to reverse the trend of global warming also stands in the way of achieving the goal of eliminating poverty. (194)

Put simply, it is a matter of redefining our notion of progress. A technological and economic development which does not leave in its wake a better world and an integrally higher quality of life cannot be considered progress. (175)

A strategy for real change calls for rethinking processes in their entirety, for it is not enough to include a few superficial ecological considerations while failing to question the logic which underlies present-day culture. A healthy politics needs to be able to take up this challenge. (197) –Laudato si'

From traditional to transformational

As I read *Laudato si'*, it was if I had returned to 1981 when I first read *The Turning Point* by Fritjof Capra, searching for a new and deeper way of thinking about reality and the future. I found the new language of biology and ecology, new concepts of complex adaptive systems, and many challenges to my system of traditional beliefs. My head hurt as my education in liberal arts at Davidson College and my study of science and technology at North Carolina State University conditioned my filter of how I saw the world.

Economics was market-oriented. Politics was focused on "sovereignty of the people" in a democracy. The study of psychology was centered on the evolution of individual self-sufficiency and self-actualization. Education emphasized content and more content, with evaluation based on "the right answer."

Fifteen years later, I read another book, *Dark Ages America,* by Morris Berman. I will never forget his warning that America needs to heed the fact that society is transforming, and unless we develop principles appropriate for a different kind of society and economy, ones that are globally interdependent and with the ability to adapt quickly to constant change, this society could enter a "dark age." At first I thought it totally out of sync with the times. America was at its peak after the fall of the Berlin Wall, the rise of new technologies that added growth and momentum to the economy, and for the first time in decades the national debt was reduced over a series of years.

Then came September 11, 2001, the Great Recession of 2007 and 2008, and the announcement of the sixth great extermination of species. In retrospect, Berman was prescient. As is true with all those ahead of their times, certain words have more meaning as the context of the times change. Not only that, I became a globalist.

As I read *Laudato si'* and thought of *The Turning Point* and *Dark Ages America,* it dawned on me that Pope Francis was looking through a historical filter similar to these visionaries. As I read his encyclical, four shifts of transformation from an Industrial Age to an Organic, Ecological Age came to mind:

- A shift from the norm of independence to interdependence.
- A shift from the norm of self-sufficiency to connected individuality.
- A shift from the norm of linear thinking to non-linear thinking.
- A shift from hyper-competition to deep collaboration.

Rethinking the future

My sense is that Pope Francis is creating a framework of principles and ideas that offer the opportunity for leaders and citizens at all levels to be able to align with the four fundamental principles listed above.

Consider the four quotes at the beginning of this paper. Consider them "dots of fundamental transformational ideas" that need to be connected to create a new framework to think about the future.

1. A new type of individual will emerge whose personal identity comes from connecting and co-creating with others to resolve issues, both current and emerging, that are complex and without a template or model by which to go. This will occur over several decades as a new type of "authentic humanity" shifts away from the need for power, great wealth, outcompeting and control.

2. A new way to think will begin to appear as people learn that there is not just one answer to a question or situation. Whereas love, integrity, deep caring, and intellectual honesty will maintain a value system steeped in tradition, other values (defined as that which is important) will transform how one sees the world to include interdependence, connective individuality, non-linear thinking, and deep collaboration). These values will gain momentum as more people and organizations begin to see a need to adapt to changing conditions. Thus the concept of "both/and" will become an important principle.

3. The concept of progress will slowly be redefined from a traditional focus on growth and increased material quality of life to one based on the biological principle of "dynamic balance" and sustainability using the principles and methods of "complex adaptive systems." This will include designing and framing parallel processes, seeding new ideas, watching what emerges and adapting to what works in a different type of society that will be constantly changing, interdependent, interconnected, and increasingly complex.

4. The concept of ecological systems that are able to adapt quickly will be at the core of organizing principles for the society and

economy. The concept of "innovation ecosystems" will become the basis for an economic culture open to everyone who is able to connect ideas, processes, and people. The concept of "a balance in ecological systems for nature and society (especially in the arena of politics and governance) will become key to insuring a vital and sustainable society.

5. As the focus on the importance of being interdependent increases, the ability to see emerging patterns before they become trends will be a key to the emphasis in the encyclical of the need to think holistically. We have been moving into an age of dynamic systems in which interlocking networks of people, processes and ideas will connect faster and faster, creating "ecosystems." Leaders will need to be able to identify "touch points" (where ideas and people initially can connect) and learn how to design systems of processes that allow new ideas to be seeded and grow in ways that cannot be predicted. This principle will become an important part of humanity's move to conserve nature's biodiversity, as more and more people understand that humanity is a part of the overall biosystem. In practical terms, the health of nature's ecology will define the health of humanity, and vice versa. Never before have we reached the tipping point of humanity's relationship to the natural world, whether manifested in climate change, loss of biodiversity, massive pollution, or increasing wealth gaps (indirect relationship). An overall reading of *Laudato si'* says "we are there."

Looking ahead

If I were asked to offer a subtitle for *Laudato si'*, I would introduce the phrase, "Searching for a Second Enlightenment." Throughout the encyclical new principles are introduced that are very different from the guiding principles that emerged during the one hundred years of the First Enlightenment (1725-1825). Although emphasizing the need to balance humanity's relationship to nature and the ecology for long-term survival, it is more than that. I interpret this encyclical as a call to arms for people of good will, especially faith-based people representing various religions to move beyond the narrowness of First Enlightenment ideas for the common good of the world.

In one part of the encyclical, there is an emphasis on the need to have global standards and connections and collaborations without regard to creed or nationality. In so doing, a new culture would emerge that would not focus on the differences of humanity, but give emphasis to the commonality of humanity, especially in relationship to God.

I concur that nations need to work in deeper collaboration to include dealing with challenges and problems at appropriate levels. This will help develop a culture open to new ideas and reflecting deeper collaboration in order to adapt quickly in consort with each other. However, based on my experience, I find a key element missing in Pope Francis' encyclical. It is the need to build "capacities for transformation" at the local level in parallel to building collaboration among nations for international cooperation. Without individuals at the local and regional levels learning how to introduce new concepts and methods that can be aligned with a constantly changing society and economy, there will be no understanding and support for large policy actions that are truly transformational.

My twenty-five years of experience learning how to seed new ways of thinking and action in local communities for comprehensive community transformation leads me to believe that there is a great opportunity for networks of people and organizations to collaborate, find "touch points," and build capacities for transformation. The kind of transformational change woven throughout Pope Francis' encyclical will need to emerge from individuals of good will of all ages who are concerned about our society and what we will leave to future generations.

With this in mind, I would like to offer a framework of key principles for a Second Enlightenment to be considered. The following has emerged from the dialogue of many people involved with our Communities of the Future work over twenty years. Consider it a starting point for dialogue that has many "touch points" with *Laudato si'*. Pope Francis is offering nothing less than a bridge for our transformation of history. May the stream of those who come to cross this bridge from all walks of life, diverse backgrounds and different life-filters represent a new DNA of historical transformation!

A Second Enlightenment

The following offers a new framework of key principles and ideas that we suggest can form a framework for a Second Enlightenment. Consider it a starting point and begin the dialogue.

Enlightenment	Second Enlightenment	Integral Society
independent (either/or)	interdependent (both/and)	systemic
self-interest	help each other succeed	concomitant good
linear thinking	connective thinking	synthesis & generation
static structures	modules, webs, & networks	dynamic adaptability
reductionism	holism	connective analysis
standard education & accountability	unlearning, uplearning, & nonlinear learning	transformative learning
meaning from materialism	meaning from creativity/spiritualism	balance of values
competititon	collaboration	generative development
prediction & certainty	anticipation & ambiguity	parallel, strategic, & adaptive planning
culture dumbed down	culture constantly upgraded	elegance in complexity
mix of goodness & skepticism	integration of reason & mystery	truth & discovery coexistent
debate	dialogue	future generative dialogue
one best answer	choices	concept of applied appropriateness
representative democracy	mobile collaborative governance	direct consensus democracy

Good News from the Global Footprint Network—and Bad News from the Fukushima Nuclear Disaster

Yoshihiko Wada

Ecological footprint indicator being promoted by civil society and scientists and being accepted by mainstream organizations

It is encouraging that pope's encyclical emphasizes the urgent need for transforming our civilization to "integral ecology." It is necessary to have a reliable and easy-to-use indicator to monitor the progress of our civilization toward the direction of integral ecology. The Ecological Footprint (EF) analysis is one of the most trusted and successful sustainability indicators available to assess this progress.

This indicator of the Ecological Footprint (EF) of a nation measures how many hectares of bio-productive land and water are necessary to support its economy or lifestyle and compares the results with the supply side: how many hectares of bio-productive land and water are available. The former represents the economy's demand for ecosystem services (such as production of renewable resources which we consume, and absorption of wastes which we generate). The latter represents the supply capacity of the ecosystems. The former is called Ecological Footprint (EF), and the latter is called Bio-capacity (BC). If EF, the demand side, is greater than the BC, the supply side, the economy is faced with

215

an "ecological deficit," and is not sustainable. This scientific tool, which assesses the balance between EF and BC, is called the Ecological Foot-print indicator. EF is a tool to analyze whether an economy is being managed within the means of nature.

Ecological Footprint calculations show that to sustain the human economy as a whole, 1.5 "Earths" are necessary. This indicates that the human economy as a whole has already exceeded the planet's Bio-ca-pacity and is running an "ecological deficit." Further growth generates more problems than benefits.

Another EF calculation shows that based on the Japanese average consumption rate, some 2.3 Earth-like planets are required. This was derived from comparing the Japanese per capita EF figure (4.2 global hectares) with the globally available BC per capita (1.8 global hect-ares). This means that Japanese citizens should cut their consumption by more than half. The EF results seem to have had some impact on overall Japanese awareness of the problem. World Wildlife Fund Japan (WWF Japan) and Ecological Footprint Japan (EFJ) have been active in promoting the EF concept and conveying the calculation results and its implications, using the phrase, "One Planet Living."

William Rees (Professor Emeritus of the University of British Colum-bia, Canada) and Mathis Wackernagel (President, Global Footprint Net-work, USA) are co-developers of the Ecological Footprint. They started developing this indicator in the early 1990s in Vancouver, Canada. In the ensuing 25 years, this sustainability indicator has gained recognition in many parts of the world. The Global Footprint Network (GFN) and other civil society organizations, such as WWF, have been working tire-lessly, pressuring mainstream organizations, such as the United Nations, and national and local governments, to adopt this indicator.

So far, eleven national governments have adopted the EF as one of their official sustainability indictors, namely, Switzerland, Japan, United Arab Emirates (UAE), Ecuador, Finland, Latvia, Luxembourg, Scotland, Wales, Indonesia, and the Philippines. Internationally, the European Union (EU) and the Association of Southeast Asian Nations (ASEAN) have been proactive in conducting studies on how the EF can benefit their member countries. The United Nations Environment Program's

Financial Initiative, in partnership with 14 leading financial institutions and the Global Footprint Network, has studied how to integrate environmental risks and resource constraints into country risk analysis. The Ecological Footprint plays a central role in this study.

In order to transform our current destructive civilization into Integral Ecology, it is necessary for us to make sure that our economy is being managed within the means of nature. The Ecological Footprint has been adopted in many of mainstream organizations and educational institutions throughout the world and has been instrumental in visualizing whether national economies are ecologically sustainable. This positive and hopeful trend can definitely facilitate the pope's admirable goal of achieving Integral Ecology.

Radioactive contamination of soil and ocean causing damage to human bodies of the most vulnerable in Fukushima and beyond

In Paragraph 160, the pope questioned what kind of world do we want to leave to those who come after us, to children who are now growing up? There is an extremely worrisome situation in Japan in this regard—the Fukushima Nuclear Disaster and its aftermath. The Tokyo Electric Power Company's Fukushima Dai-ichi nuclear reactors still continue to emit highly toxic radioactive water into the ocean. The soil in Fukushima and surrounding regions is being contaminated by highly radioactive fallout substances such as cesium and strontium.

Tree leaves and bark have been contaminated by those toxic radioactive substances. As time goes by, the contaminated leaves and bark have become the sources of contamination for forest streams, rivers and rice fields. Even the decontaminated land areas are being re-polluted again by the cyclical flow of contaminated falling leaves and bark. Even rain has been contaminated with radiation. The rainfall pollutes our homeland far away from Fukushima. The situation is hopeless and miserable.

During the 2020 Olympic and Paralympic site selection process, the Japanese Prime Minister Shinzo Abe, assured the world that "everything is under control." However, that was completely wrong. Abe is a deceiver. So far, unfortunately, the government has issue no official correction or apology.

The contaminated land and water have already damaged the health of children of age 18 or younger, the most vulnerable population, in Fukushima. For example, by May 2015, approximately 300,000 youths living in Fukushima have been examined. Among them, 127 youths have been diagnosed as having thyroid cancer or as having a high possibility of contracting this disease. This is somewhere between 60-75 times higher rate than the rate observed in 2010. The Japanese government and Fukushima Prefectural government have admitted the increased rate. They have never, however, admitted the causal relationship between the Fukushima nuclear disaster and the recently observed high rate of occurrence of the disease.

Both the violation of law and the infringement of human rights and dignity have been witnessed in Fukushima and beyond in terms of radiation exposure. For instance, the Japanese legal system clearly prohibits the general public from living in areas where radioactivity exposure is expected to be more than one milliSievert (milliSv) per annum. After the Fukushima nuclear accident took place in March 2011, however, the Japanese government has allowed the residents of Fukushima Prefecture and surrounding prefectures to live wherever radioactivity exposure is expected to be less than 20 milliSv per annum. Even infants and small children are put into this dangerous and unlawful situation. In fact, this 20 milliSv per annum standard is much higher than the 5.2 milliSvper annum which is applied to workers who are engaged in operating nuclear reactors and in medical radioactive facilities.

The Japanese government has decided that the evacuation zones should be lifted if these areas have been decontaminated and the annual radiation level is expected to be less than 20 milliSv per annum. Evacuees from these areas will no longer receive any compensation, because the government has determined that this contamination level is not hazardous to human health. Now that the government has declared their homes safe, evacuees will receive no compensation if they continue to live at what they consider a safe distance.

Why does the Japanese government have double standards for radiation exposure? The residents of Kyoto, for example, are not allowed to be exposed to radiation of more than one milliSv per annum, whereas the residents of Fukushima and neighboring areas are forced to expose themselves to radiation of up to 20 times that amount. Injustice prevails in Japan.

The current Japanese government has tried to re-start nuclear reactors in Japan, even though the causes of Fukushima nuclear incident have not been fully identified. They have installed new sets of nuclear regulations under a newly established governmental body, the Nuclear Regulatory Authority (NRA). The regulations are supposed to have incorporated the lessons derived from the Fukushima disaster. However, these regulations have been severely criticized for 1) failing to consider risks from eruptions of volcanoes and airplane crashes, 2) failing to consider simultaneous failures of devices, and 3) excluding appraisal procedure in terms of adequacy of evacuation planning, etc.

The existence of a powerful nuclear conglomerate in Japan and a global lobbying group to promote nuclear energy and nuclear weapons

Even if all of us, including our national governments, committed now to working toward Integral Ecology, we know that we face many disasters. How we face them will determine our chances of working through them to the world toward which the pope calls us. Japan has faced a disaster, but it has not dealt with it openly and honestly. Accordingly, the Japanese people are paying a high price. The reason for Japan's failure appears to be the power of those domestic and international forces that promote nuclear power and nuclear weapons. Perhaps the world can learn from Japan's failure and prepare to overcome, or at least counter, the opposition of those who profit from silence and misrepresentation.

The Japanese nuclear conglomerate consists of nine major electric companies, mega banks, heavy industries, major trading companies (for importing nuclear fuels and reactors), general contractors and subsidiaries, and the transportation industry, as well as commercial mass media. The Yomiuri News Paper, especially, has actively disseminated the myth of nuclear safety. The Japanese government, especially the Ministry of Economy, Trade and Industry (METI) sits in the center of this circle. Also, a number of conservative politicians are part of this group. Academic circles of the departments of nuclear engineering and nuclear physics in the universities also play significant roles of expanding knowledge base, advancing technologies, and educating students. Also, I would say that some yakuzas (the Japanese mafia), are part of this. They recruit workers in slum areas in large metropolises such as Osaka and Tokyo. The workers are dispatched to nuclear power plants and are engaged in high-risk repair and monitoring activities, being exposed to high level radiation. They are often fired just before they contract fatal diseases such as leukemia and cancer. They are often forced to write a letter saying they will not sue the company for health damages in exchange for small retirement allowances.

Nobody from this group, even TEPCO managers and METI officers, has been charged or punished for causing the Fukushima nuclear disaster. It seems to me that they committed a crime of "willful negligence."

The nuclear conglomerate openly and strongly urges the Japanese government to allow re-operation of many of the existing nuclear reactors. This obsession, stubbornness, and irrationality remind me of the Japanese imperial militarism and fascism which prevailed before the end of WWII.

The International Atomic Energy Agency (IAEA) and the International Commission on Radiological Protection (ICRP) work closely together to back up this Japanese conglomerate. They try to justify "peaceful" uses of nuclear technology in the world by inflating the benefits from the use of nuclear energy and by intentionally "under-estimating" the risks and damages associated with nuclear energy use, including uranium mining activities. They work to prohibit the "military" use of nuclear science and technology in the world, except for 5 nuclear weapons-possessing nations, namely, the USA, the UK, Russia, France, and China. This symbolizes the hypocritical character of these organizations.

Conclusions

In conclusion, I would like to thank the pope for highlighting the urgent need for us to transform our economy and civilization as a whole toward Ecological Civilization, i.e., Integral Ecology. The increasing recognition of the Ecological Footprint indicator in many parts of the world proves that we are moving in that direction. But, at the same time, we have to realize that we need to listen to the silenced voices of the victims of nuclear disasters not only in Fukushima, but also Chernobyl and Three Mile Island, as well as those contaminated places such as uranium mining sites in the Navajo Nation in the USA, rare earth refineries in China and Malaysia, and nuclear weapons experiment sites scattered around the world.

A Political and Spiritual Strategy to Save the Life Support System of Planet Earth

Rabbi Michael Lerner

Pope Francis' *Laudato si'* plea for environmental sanity and a serious recommitment to the Bible's call for humanity to be stewards of this planet earth just might make a huge difference by puncturing through the emotional depression that keeps most of the people of the earth paralyzed in face of the growing crisis.

It is not that people don't know about the environmental crisis that keeps us stuck in the societal paralysis that has prevented us from taking the dramatic and society-changing steps necessary to repair the destruction human beings have done to the life support system of the planet. It is rather that most people are unable to see any way out of the mess that global capitalism has created for us, and in which they participate through their consumption and through electing leaders whose environmental consciousness is limited by their unwillingness to challenge the fundamental economic and political system which has played a central part in creating the environmental crisis. So instead they sink into depression and denial.

Feeling hopeless about the possibility of the kinds of fundamental transformations needed to save the planet, much of humanity has chosen the ostrich strategy: deny the problem and focus instead on getting as much as one can for oneself in the decades ahead as the planet whimpers and falls into its own kind of deep emotional depression in response to the increasing destructiveness of the capitalist imperative to growth without limits and accumulation of money, power or things as the only meaning to life. Yet it is this very growth and accumulation of things, produced at the expense of the earth, that guarantees earth-destruction if not of the planet than at least of its life-support-system that makes human life on it possible.

The Democrats and most of the national environmental organizations have been a huge failure at developing a serious strategy to stop climate change and preserve the earth because they are not prepared to take on the capitalist system with its inherent dynamic that requires growth and requires endless conditioning of people to believe that they will achieve happiness and meaning in life through accumulation and growth.

Local environmental activists by-and-large (with important exceptions) have the same problem: they focus on narrow goals (getting more energy saving devices into middle income households or preventing fracking in their particular area) without trying to educate the people in their own organizations (much less those whom they reach out to in the course of their organizing) about the global system changes that are essential. And their reasoning is the same: raising those larger issues is seen as "unrealistic" and "likely to turn off potential allies," so instead they focus the issues so narrowly that their efforts do little to create the transformed consciousness that is the essential precondition for saving the planet.

When we at the Network of Spiritual Progressives have attempted to reach out to these organizations to discuss a more holistic and global strategy they have simply dismissed the idea as beyond their capacities.

Nor have they been willing to recognize that people impoverished by global capitalism around the world will not jump onto an environmental bandwagon proposed by the richest countries of the global North when the imperatives of feeding their families seem easier to meet by cutting down rain forests to grow cash-rich produce like cattle that will feed the global North's hunger for beef, pork, and other animal products. One reason we at the Network of Spiritual Progressives have advocated for a Global Marshall Plan whose contours we spell out at <tikkun.org/gmp>

is that we know that an essential part of any environmental strategy must be the elimination of global poverty, homelessness, hunger, inadequate education, and inadequate health care—all of which could be dealt with by the advanced industrial societies dedicating 1-2% of their Gross Domestic Product each year for the next twenty to the kind of plan we lay out (a plan which is based on the simple notion that "homeland security can better be achieved by a strategy of generosity than a strategy of domination"—an idea which must also be applied to how we respond to the earth itself).

The pope recognizes the centrality of eliminating poverty to an environmental program. So do many socialists, but socialist-style global redistribution of wealth is only a necessary, but not sufficient, condition for addressing the environmental crisis, because giving the poor more money to spend may only increase demand as long as we are operating within the materialist, looking out for number one, growth-as-necessary, more as better consciousness created by capitalist societies.

And that is why the pope is providing a unique kind of leadership. He is the first international spiritual progressive voice who can go beyond the "common sense" of global capitalism and articulate a different worldview.

The essence of the Spiritual Progressive world view, desperately needed by the environmental movement, is this: We need a New Bottom Line, so that all institutions, corporations, economic policy, governmental policies, our legal system, our education system, our media, and even our personal lives get to be assessed as productive, efficient, or rational not to the extent that they maximize money or power (the Old Bottom Line) but to the extent that they maximize our capacities to be loving and caring for each other and for the planet earth, generous and kind, promoting economic and social justice, treating everyone else on earth as equally valuable and equally entitled to share in the benefits of our planet and equally responsible to protect it, responding to others as embodiments of the sacred and not simply as means to our own ends, and responding to the planet earth and the entire universe with awe, wonder and radical amazement rather than simply treating it as a "resource" to satisfy human needs.

It is from this standpoint that spiritual progressives challenge the values that underlie global capitalism and materialist versions of socialism and instead chart a path to a fundamentally different global economic, political and social world. We at the Network of Spiritual Progressives have begun to do that with our proposed ESRA–Environmental and Social Responsibility Amendment to the U.S. Constitution (please read it at www.tikkun.org/esra).

The ESRA would ban all money from state and national elections except for public funding; would require public education about all aspects of the environmental crisis from k-graduate or professional schools; would require corporations operating or selling their goods and services in the U.S. with incomes above $50 million/yr to prove every five years a satisfactory history of environmental and social responsibility to a panel of ordinary citizens—or lose their corporate charter; would prohibit corporations moving out of the U.S. to avoid environmental or social responsibility; and invalidate any international treaties that might restrict environmental and social responsibility on the part of corporations operating in or selling goods and services in the U.S. Those corporations who fail this test would eventually be given to a new board of directors that could demonstrate how they would run the corporation with a satisfactory approach to environmental and social responsibility while still retaining their work force.

The ESRA offers a significant step toward creating a national movement with the vision necessary to change our direction in the U.S. and variants of it could be adopted to the political forms of other countries around the world. Of course it will be hard to pass this in the U.S. and other countries, but just as the struggle for the Equal Rights Amendment for women never passed but the struggle for it had a major transformative impact on how people viewed the issue of sexism, the struggle for the passage of the ESRA would lift the environmental movement from its narrow focus and open the question of the legitimacy of capitalist values and need for a fundamental challenge to the global capitalist system and its role in spreading and sustaining the materialism, selfishness, and "growth at all costs" values that underlie so much of what stands in the way of ending the global unconscious but nevertheless systematic assault on the life support system of the planet.

One reason why most Christian, Jewish, Muslim, Hindu, Buddhist, and most secular humanist organizations have not yet embraced this path is that, sadly, they are dependent for funding both from the capitalist class and from many in their membership who are attached to the materialist and looking-out-for-number-one worldview of global capitalist societies and hence dismiss any fundamental alternative as "unrealistic." All the more reason to rejoice that in the pope the world finally has a religious leader capable of developing a critique of capitalism without falling into the narrow economistic and materialist worldview that has characterized most Left movements. It is their economistic, materialist, and religio-phobic perspective that keeps most people on the Left from embracing the path of the spiritual progressive, even though in their hearts most people on the Left simultaneously embrace the values of the New Bottom Line (and were they to do so more explicitly, and get progressive organizations to publicly embrace and emphasize the New Bottom line the Left would be far more successful). It is tragic for the world and for the Left that it cannot seem to recognize that it would be so very much more successful if it would explicitly talk about building a world of love, caring, and generosity, and a world in which we responded to the universe with awe and wonder rather than looking at the earth and Nature as a bottomless cookie jar from which humans can take as much as we want without caring for the earth as a Subject and not an Object.

I only wish the pope would take the next step and call for a re-instituting of the Sabbatical Year (not every year one seventh of the people taking a year off, but once every seven years the entire people of a nation giving the earth a year of rest and giving all people in that nation a year to not have to work, forgiving all debts, and calling for reinstituting the Biblical call for a Jubilee every fiftieth in which the wealth of the world gets redistributed to eliminate whatever inequality has developed in the past 49 years. The Sabbatical Year would give humanity an opportunity to rest, slow down the frenetic pace of life driven by the internalization of the need to be more and more "productive" in terms of the Old Bottom Line and, instead, dedicate a year to intellectual, political, spiritual, and environmental renewal and reconnection to the magnificence of our awe-inspiring universe (no, not "conquering" outer and inner space but rejoicing in all that is). A weekly practice of Sabbath may give us a slight taste of what this might feel like, though done by the entire society for a whole year would dramatically multiply the psycho-spiritual and environmental benefits of a Sabbatical Year. Although this could be made to work in the U.S. even if no other country were to adopt it, eventually it would be easier if different countries had different years for doing this sabbatical year, so that one seventh of the planet was doing their sabbatical year each year, and the other countries helped supply the country that was having its sabbatical year whatever food, energy, and other items necessary for their sabbatical year to be successful. Even allowing ourselves to work out the details of this plan would be a contribution to developing in all of us a recognition that the earth has enough to sustain human and animal life if wisely cared for and deepen our commitment to overcoming the narrow worldview that societies based on the internalization of scarcity and "not enough" have to some extent succeeded in implanting in all of us.

Of course, the pope's stand is generating considerable opposition from conservative Catholics who have already found ways around the Bible's social justice teachings so that they could explain why they are champions of the rich and still call themselves Christians. All the more reason for the rest of us to embrace this Pope, even as we gently and lovingly chide him to consider applying his message of caring for everyone more fully by embracing full rights for women and homosexuals.

The best way to support the pope is to build an interfaith movement based on these values articulated in the New Bottom Line. It is only when people begin to see a spiritual progressive movement in the public sphere with a strategy for how to save the planet that is willing to challenge the fundamentals of global capitalism that they will be able to imagine overcoming their own passivity, emotional depression, and mistaken certainty that "nothing will ever make possible a new economic system." It is only when they see millions of us working together for a fundamentally different world that they will overcome this mistaken commitment to "being realistic" and instead recognize that "we never know what is possible until we join with others to struggle for what is desirable." So I invite you to become a member of the NSP[1]—Network of Spiritual Progressives—at <www.spiritualprogressives.org/join>.

You don't have to believe in God or be part of a religious or spiritual community to be a spiritual progressives—you only have to embrace the New Bottom Line articulated above—so the NSP is not only interfaith and welcoming people from every religious community in the world, but also welcoming to secular humanists and atheists who want the kind of world we are seeking.

But neither are we some flaky New Age-y kind of operation that believes everything will be fine if we just change our own hearts. We seek both an inner transformation and an economic, political, and societal transformation, and welcome those who will join with us in actually building a social change movement based on the principles of the New Bottom Line–a movement that is compassionate towards not only its own members but toward those who do not yet agree with us, a movement that is psychologically and intellectually sophisticated, and integrates humor, playfulness, joy, and love even as it seeks to challenge the institutions and economic arrangements that are destroying the planet. JOIN US, pretty please!

Endnotes

1. You can join the Network of Spiritual Progressives at www.spiritual-progressives.org, read about the Global Marshall Plan at www.tikkun.org/gmp, and read the full detailed version of the ESRA at www.tikkun.org/esra. For a fuller understanding of the spiritual progressive perspective, please read spiritualprogressives.org/covenant.

References

<www.tikkun.org>.
<www.tikkun.org/esra>.

Searching for Transcendence at the Hinge of History in the Context of *Laudato Si'*

Stuart Kauffman, Caryn Devins,
Roger Koppl & Teppo Felin

We are honored to present this essay in the context of the pope's recent encyclical, Laudato si'. This encyclical powerfully points to the very rapid deterioration of social, economic, and environmental systems. The recent, remarkable, Seizing an Alternative conference (June 4-7, 20145), dealt with many of the same issues, in particular, global warming and transformation to an eco-responsible civilization.

In the face of such looming calamity, our contribution, posted on the UN Academic Impact Site, and included in this book, is that the sustainable path forward will not be based on "designing" policy solutions but on changing our deepest held paradigms and beliefs. Climate change and other problems reflect our human values, and starkly and painfully reveal how far we have veered off course. It is hubris to believe that we can control the becoming of biosphere and Nature, even as we participate in them on a finite planet, or control the world population, with the same command-and-control, large-scale policies that have spawned such massive failure to begin with. The pope rightly calls for stewardship. Yet we must do so even while we face the truth that the world emerges in often unexpected ways. This is why we must persistently adapt and respond to the world we partially unleash, not fully *knowing what we unleash, with humility and wisdom, rather than petulantly demanding that the world adapt to us.*

Even if there are disagreements about the meaning and implications of climate change, what we do know in this moment is that we must adapt if we are to survive. And with seven billion of us, we can no longer survive by foraging. We need an economy, but one which creates and distributes wealth and human flourishing in Nature far more equitably. Our goal is to help and be part of a constructive conversation as to how we might do so, beginning with a fundamental shift in values and outlook. ~ Stuart Kauffman

The hinge of history

Perhaps we are too brave to begin boldly by saying that we are, to use historian Thomas Cahill's evocative phrase, at a "hinge of history."" Our thirty or more civilizations around the globe are weaving together in untold and untellable ways. We can, for the first time in history, truly afford sufficient wealth for all, even if opportunities and wealth are now grotesquely maldistributed. We can, for the first time in history, dare to consider what a global interwoven set of civilizations might become, whose highest values are our living experience. We must begin to think together, all of us, beyond our huge but more immediate issues.

The UN has articulated a set of Sustainable Development Goals, which include action on climate change and poverty eradication. These are urgent issues. Modern economic growth has lifted billions from grinding poverty and early death. And yet science has raised significant concerns over the environmental consequences of our current systems governing industrial production. It is possible that we are unleashing the largest extinction event since perhaps the Permian, thereby destroying the accumulated living wisdom of thousands of species with no thought that we almost surely cannot recreate what we are losing. How do we know that this vast, co-sustaining ecosystem that is all of the life on our planet may not partially, or completely, collapse? We have no idea.

Yet surely our hinge of history may be the most staggering opportunity the globe faces. If we do not talk about it, we cannot shape it. Yet we must do so through growth and transcendence rather than control and design, as we will explain further.

In this regard, one riveting period, the Axial Age, named by Karl Jaspers, from about 800 to 200 BCE demands renewed attention (see Bellah and Joas's *The Axial Age and Its Consequences*, 2012). In this period, 1000 years after writing was invented, the first enormous empires, Egypt, Mesopotamia, China, and the Indus Valley, exploded, with the capacity to accumulate wealth from the onset of agriculture. In this brief 600-year period across many cultures—Buddhism, Daoism, Confuscianism, the great Hebrew prophets, Jeremiah, Isaiah, Amos, Plato and Aristotle—all sought "transcendence" in different ways. For Confucius, ethical government; for the Buddha, enlightenment; for Plato, the good, the true, and the beautiful. All rose above early religions centered on the material welfare of the people—good hunting, good rains—to seek something higher, something transcendent. We are heritors to the Axial Age, which in the West gave rise to an arc of history beginning, perhaps, with Graeco-Hebraic civilization, then the dominance of the Christian Church, then the Renaissance with its soaring individuality, then Newton and the laws of physics, then the Enlightenment, then the Industrial Age, then modernity and post-modernity.

But are we satisfied with our era of modernity and postmodernity when it sometimes seems that our personal human dignity is threatened by global systems serving special interests more effectively than the commonweal? Have we become so many cogs in a great wheel that turns not for us?

Thus, the widest framing of our issues is what this hinge of history may afford us. But we cannot say what we will become, as we can at best unleash it and hope to wisely guide what we cannot predict. Though the pull of the present is powerful and entrenched, we must examine these issues together. We dare to hope this United Nations site may be a place for such broad discussions.

Against design

The UN Sustainable Development Goals seek nothing less than to resolve the most currently visible, intractable of human failures, from extreme poverty to climate change and political corruption. By the same token, these goals strive for certain pinnacles of human achievement, in the eyes of modernity. Such ambition may be dismissed as hopelessly idealistic, but it is laudable and necessary to aim high if we have any hope of solving the profound problems we face.

We believe, however, that goal-setting can either be enormously productive or a sure path to failure. We would like to share some lessons as to how these goals may be used most appropriately to effect true, lasting change in our beautiful, troubled world.

We argue that the UN goals are best viewed not as fixed objectives but powerful intentions to guide our actions in the present. To explain why requires a diversion into the abstract, from which we will return to offer some suggestions. In essence, we contend that it is impossible to design policies to implement fixed goals due to the inherent creativity of humanity and nature. Our evolving purposes will inevitably escape their moorings. Rather, we are more likely to reach success by seeking new opportunities in the existing evolving international and economic landscapes, and creatively wielding those opportunities to generate new possibilities not otherwise anticipated. In short, rather than creating a mold and seeking to fit the world within it, we argue that the mold should adapt to the unfixed world that we, often unknowingly, co-create. Instead of centralized, command-and-control policies, we advocate bottom up experimentation and evolutionary learning based on effective use of existing information, and our joint co-inventions, which are often not predictable in advance. In conflict situations, and in devastatingly poor regions, the envisioning of novel opportunities that may create unforeseen, "win-win" situations may lead to renewed hope and unexpected resolution. Witness Silicon Valley and the IT revolution—their becoming was unprestatable.

The notion that effective policies can be designed to achieve fixed goals—the reigning methodology of 20th century policy—is an illusion. The "design" mentality begins with identifying a perceived problem and choosing a fixed outcome that, properly implemented, the designer believes will solve the problem. The UN goals can potentially be seen in this light—a designer would say, for example, that world hunger is a problem and we therefore must ensure that every person in the world has a minimum quantity of food. Next, the designer would design and execute a particular policy to achieve that outcome, such as a particular food donation program as an example, expecting a stable relationship between the design and the outcome. The design would be seen as a sort of architectural blueprint, designed to alter social institutions in specific desired ways.

The problem with this approach, as we have seen with the large-scale failures of so many policies in the 20th century, is that society is not a machine that can be engineered in predictable or foreseeable ways. These "engineered" institutions do not sufficiently account for the evolutionary, creative nature of change. To see this, consider two cases: Alan Turing's mathematical idea of an algorithm enabled, but did not cause, the mainframe computer, which with the chip enabled, but did not cause, the personal computer, which enabled word processing, which enabled file sharing, which enabled the world wide web, which enabled online commerce, browsers, and Facebook. No one could have foreseen these latter opportunities when the Turing machine was invented.

As another example, unexpected loopholes can be found in any law, which open opportunities for new strategies with payoffs that were unforeseen to the law's designers. In turn, these new strategies require new laws, which again contain new loopholes. We cannot "design" this sprawling process of co-creation, but we must live it together wisely, accepting that we often do not know what we are creating.

Not only do we not know what will happen, we often do not even know what can happen. Rather, we are drawn, "sucked" into the very opportunities we create, even though we typically do not know what we unleash. Thus, we see that the faith in reason, the highest virtue of the Enlightenment, fails us in this instance, for reason cannot tell us what we enable.

Thus we question the idea that institutions operate in mechanical and predictable ways, like clocks we wind up and let go. In physical law-governed systems, all possible states of the system exist in a stable phase space, and all possible paths of the system are predetermined by entailing laws of physics. Much of modern economic theory builds on similar assumptions, where perfectly equilibrating markets and perfectly rational agents somehow exhaust all possibilities and sources of novelty.

But human and living, evolving natural systems are not governed by entailing laws. This is because the full range of relevant functional variables that may affect the system's evolution cannot be determined, let alone ascertained through any kind of logical reasoning. Without knowing all relevant variables, it is impossible to execute designs based on an accurate model of reality. This is known as the frame problem.

Because the space of possible outcomes of a given action is not fully known, it is impossible to predict with certainty what the reaction will be. Instead, actions enable adjacent possible niches, which become tools that politicians, regulators, business and others use in order to fulfill their own purposes. In the aggregate, this process creates new systemic behaviors that may ultimately subvert the action's initial purpose.

In other words, the fallacy of design is that the "frame" of the problem—the full set of relevant considerations (or uses and functions of existing assets and resources)—is assumed to already be known. For example, the United States Constitution was designed to balance competing factors. Federalism balanced the need for centralized decision-making with dispersal of power to safeguard liberty. Separation of powers was designed to divide power so that each branch would check the others. The Bill of Rights was intended to further protect unalienable individual rights. The constitutions of other nations have balanced these principles in distinctive ways, but all share a common faith, from Locke among others, in design. Yet in this era of deep governance crises, social unrest, and calls for new constitutional conventions, we should question the adequacy of any constitutional design.

We argue that all institutions, even the most fundamental, evolve so as to drift, even dislodge, from their original premises and purposes. Attempts to engineer these institutions will always fall apart in the long run. Rather, the concept of design itself is, like a desert mirage, a persuasive and comforting illusion. We can draw up blue prints to the smallest specification, but we cannot control the execution of our plans as they take on unanticipated new life within the adaptive networks that respond to them.

The futility of design implies a crisis of economic planning. How should governments design policies to achieve the UN Development Goals if design is an illusion? The stakes are too high for nihilistic or fatalistic responses. And the stakes are too high to blithely apply old-fashioned command and control models. At the same time, it is not satisfactory to abdicate collective action in the hope that "markets" can somehow achieve results that, while present in some cases, are not yet realized globally. In particular, we doubt that "privatization" should be viewed as our central tool in the pursuit of global development. We must somehow think and act beyond markets and states.

We must seek economic models that leverage the adaptive decision making of every actor in the system. We want each person's own inner force of will to be moved toward improvements and progress. Governments cannot hope to somehow direct the individual will of each individual citizen. But they can modify existing institutions to lean slowly in the direction of positive change.

But we have many overlapping institutions such that the institutional mix varies not only from nation to nation, but within nations as well. The precise institutional mix is always a local phenomenon. We should think of the UN development goals, then, as first and foremost guideposts for institutional adaptation at the local level. Improved health in one location may mean increasing caloric intake, while in another it means reduced caloric intake, and in a third it means indoor plumbing. It is important, therefore, to engage local knowledge and leverage local institutions to achieve our global ends.

Local governance of irrigation systems, for example, is essential to "ensure availability and sustainable management of water and sanitation for all." To cite a concrete and illustrative case, Lam (1998) found that Nepalese farmers were able to manage water resources effectively in part because of local governance mechanisms of their own making, which included annual meetings and frequent informal communications between farmers. Ostrom (2010) finds that in general, "farmer-managed systems are likely to grow more rice, distribute water more equitably, and keep their systems in better repair" that systems designed and imposed by a central government. And yet such systems are far from "privatized."

They are simultaneously voluntary, collective, and local. Similarly, women in urban markets in Ghana have formed small business collectives known as *susu*. "Trust and reputation are the essential elements in all of [these] informal arrangements, as this reinforces a system of reciprocal behavior" (Chamlee-Wright 1997, 140). Attempts to move these women to officially sanctioned markets and stalls backfired by rupturing the trust relations of the susu (150-51). Here again, voluntary, collective, and local seems to work best. Beware of formulas, however. The formula "voluntary, collective, local" admonishes us to start from where we are, to build on local institutions, to build on existing institutions. But it is of limited value in the design, for example, of spectrum auctions. Let us start from where we are, then, but avoid Procrustean solutions for human problems.

Ours, then, is a vision of global change through adaptive institutional change at all levels but first and foremost at the local level. It is not a vision of design, or command and control, or engineering and rational forecasts. It is a vision of enablement. We enable global change by enabling local governance.

So, given that conventional top-down, command-and-control policies are not the way to achieve the UN goals, how do we prevent these laudable ideas from languishing?" Perhaps we may gain insight from the eminent philosopher Alfred North Whitehead, particularly in his views of time, process, and the power of intention. In his book *Process and Reality*, Whitehead argued that the universe exists not as individuated substances, but rather entities existing as processes of becoming through time. However we may judge Whitehead's overall philosophy, we should take seriously his criticism of reductionism. The reductionist materialism that has dominated the philosophy of science since Newton, a paradigm that sees the universe in terms of cold, machine-like components existing in isolation, overlooks the layers of interconnected processes that drive the continuity of change.

In Whitehead's view, the influence of the past tends to be material and constitutes the framework from which the present and future evolve. Although Whitehead did not use this term, we argue, consistent with his theory, that the past provides "actual situations" that become "enabling constraints," which at once restrain and encourage the development of the future. In other words, the enabling constraints from the past ensure that we cannot mold the world from scratch but that we can build on what exists to create novel possibilities.

Whitehead argued optimistically that the future exerts its influence on the present, in the form of intention. Our intentions can act as basins of attraction that literally draw in the actions of the present, like balls rolling down the walls of a deep tub. We must recognize, however, that our intentions, and the realities they enable, can often create a widely divergent pattern of becoming, much like the evolving biosphere, political systems, and the economy. The balls may roll in differing directions and may clash and collide along the way. Diverse purposes and limited resources yield conflicts that always demand some form of fairness. Here we hope that finding new opportunities can be the source of hope and novel resolutions of these conflicts.

We cannot predict or prestate how our intentions may come to fruition, but through the strength of intention, invention, and compassion, we can bend the curve of the present.

What do intentions mean in the context of the UN goals for sustainability? We argue that rather than specific targets to be achieved through designed policies, these goals should be seen as values to guide human innovation. As individuals, institutions, and societies exploit opportunities in the adjacent possible, they can do so with an internal guiding purpose—the values embodied in the UN goals. Thus, rather than adopt rigid policies doomed to failure as realities shift, these entities may adapt their strategies according to new information. At the same time, we belong to diverse social groups with diverse goals that often come into conflict. We think there is no set moral answer to the resolution of these conflicts, even based on fairness, for we will always debate what is "fair" and our reflections on this are ever-evolving, from Hammurabi to now.

Putting this all together, we argue that we cannot design policies for specific goals. But we can exert our collective intention to influence the world. As in the Axial Age, we can transcend from our obsession with material well-being to human and spiritual values that may become the centerpiece of civilization. Such transcendence will require not logical reason and social engineering, but the embrace of spiritual values and the common conscience of humanity, which have been all but lost in modernity.

If individuals, institutions and societies are empowered to take action in their own sphere to effectuate these human values, despite inevitable conflicts of purposes, and with enduring hope to co-create solutions to bridge these conflicts, each action may accumulate with others in a forever evolving, unknowable becoming. At this global hinge of history, to do so requires enlightenment at a societal, even world, scale. The UN can serve as a crucial enabler of this process.

References:

Chamlee-Wright, Emily (1997). *The Cultural Foundations of Economic Development: Urban Female Entrepreneurship in Ghana.* London and New York: Routledge.

Lam, Wai Fung (1998). *Governing Irrigation Systems in Nepal: Institutions, Infrastructure, and Collective Action.* Oakland, CA: ICS Press.

Ostrom, Elinor (2010). "Beyond Markets and States: Polycentric Governance of Complex Economic Systems." *American Economic Review* 100(3): 641-72.

PART
FOUR

Elements of Integration

Pancho Populist's Encyclical

David Lewit

Pope Francis's resounding call to action on today's ecological and social ills, in language both plain and progressive, excites us—those of us adventurous enough or studious enough to have read critical science, ethics, or politics. And we are thrilled at his use of prescriptions such as "subsidiarity," "precautionary principle," "distributive justice," and "common good," as well as curses such as polluters' "pile of filth," slums' "hell on earth," "deified market," and "information overload." The former Argentine bishop Jorge Mario Bergoglio's tone is left-populist, winning for him in some circles in Mexico the affectionate nickname "Pancho" for his papal name, Francisco.

Forsaking the opulent quarters of former popes, this vicar of Jesus has come forth with the seeming innocence of the child who sees that the emperor has no clothes. That emperor is the corporate usurper of government, the overspecialized technologist, the insulated elitist, the addicted consumer. But Francis is no child. He learned well the lessons of the radical Msgr. Romano Guardini, and he appointed to his Pontifical Academy of the Sciences the esteemed theoretical physicist and complexity theorist Hans Joachim Schellnhuber—an atheist and birth control advocate who established the Potsdam Institute for Climate Impact Research. Schellnhuber probably drafted parts of this ecological/social encyclical and was one of three speakers at the document's presentation ceremony.

Despite a sprinkling of I's and we's in the encyclical letter, it tends to reflect the styles of the several distinct research groups contributing to its substance. The language at the beginning and in the last chapter is religious, as if drafted by theologians of the pontiff's council. But Francis' hand may be responsible for the lower case "him," referring to God, and the familiar "we," not the royal or editorial we. Early chapters might have been drafted by scientists of the Pontifical Academy of the Sciences, and much of the rest by sociologists of the Pontifical Academy of the Social Sciences and by philosophers in both Academies, with a sprinkling of poetry perhaps of the pope's favorites. Evidently bowing to Church tradition, virtually all of the 172 references are to churchmen's apt writings and speeches, belying the notion that radical hard science and social science are beyond the pale of Catholic clergy. Lacking in this document are stories and history; nevertheless it is forthright in scientific, holistic, and moral detail.

The encyclical's title, *Laudato si'*, are the opening words of the nature-bonding ode *Praise be to you, my Lord*, by Saint Francis of Assisi, which echoes the tone and ancient sentiments of the pharaoh Ikhnaton, the first monotheist and worshipper of Aton, the Sun. The two Francises honor all of nature as God's creation, calling the sun brother, the moon sister, wind and fire brother, and water sister—in the saint's poem quoted at Pancho's paragraph 87. If we add water's twin, sister forest, protection of the commons will be obvious. Public land defenders like Tim DeChristopher will be celebrated, not jailed; corporate land speculators will be chastened; and the angels will rejoice. So we can understand how Pope Francis chose to focus his strongest sentiments on the health of the ecosphere, including humans, and the responsibilities of people to promote it.

The encyclical ends with two prayers in poetic form by the pope himself, featuring these lines: *Enlighten those who possess power and money,/ that they may avoid the sin of indifference,/ that they may love the common good, advance the weak,/ and care for this world in which we live.* Here Francis is recognizing, but not tolerating, the existing power structure controlled by national or international elites, having characterized their behavior as "greedy" and "compulsive," recommending their transformation facilitated by "boycott" and promoted by ecological scrutiny of business ventures and projects with "the local population having a special place at the table"(183).

A new ecological Catholic order

So what are the principal thrusts of this encyclical, what can we add or prioritize, and how effective might it be in promoting health of the ecosystem and the common good of humanity? What can we do to ensure and speed action?

Focused on natural and human ecology, everything which Francis highlights is good but limited. Perhaps it is pushing, boldly, the envelope rigged by the powers that be but only to the limits of mass credibility. Still, that may be the optimum force which a pope may employ and still be useful. And it may be one or two steps advancing in the direction that ordinary people have already shown in opinion surveys to be preferred. Thus he condemns the leaders of industry who blast and pollute with impunity, demanding that they pay for restitution and prevention of further damage to the ecosystem and society.

The pope promotes the value of community and community differences and their value in urban planning, but praises "business [as] a noble vocation" without distinguishing or boosting local, independent or worker-owned, regulation-compliant businesses from free-wheeling transnational corporations. He demands corporate responsibility on the national level but also promotes international agreements without dealing with corporate manipulation of markets, media, regulation, or the agreements themselves.

Francis demonstrates a degree of magical thinking by quoting Matthew 20 to the effect that leaders should be servants of the people, while praising creative leaders (in technology) who are undeterred by regressive popular sentiment. He seems to take on faith that strengthening of community values will automatically reduce the "sins" of selfish business or financial elites. He elides the gross differences within localities among regressive and progressive factions—e.g., NIMBY, white supremacy, union exclusiveness, and religious fundamentalism—which may increase tensions, cause distractions, and blunt local reform.

To his credit the pope emphasizes that everything is connected, that human welfare depends on ecological integrity, which depends on mindful business and government, which depend on honest finance, which depend on individual watchfulness and virtue, which depend upon community, which depends upon technological adaptation, and so on. Where to intervene is a problem dealt with mainly by exhortation in favor of prevention. Still, with the pope on their side, strategy-minded progressive nongovernment organizations may be energized to overcome cultural lethargy and the selfish elites leading us to ecological doom.

Three imperatives

Overall, the pope highlights three imperatives in the service of the whole earth: human right to the means of subsistence, overcoming corporate selfishness and greed, and putting technology and "progress" in perspective. First, he affirms the psychological value of work and smallholdings which he considers a right. He implicitly condemns the large land holder for stealing God's earth. But not all people can be farmers, nor do urban dwellers necessarily have access to facilities and finance to engage in productive work. Unfortunately, he doesn't say anything about a guaranteed basic income for all—something fruitfully implemented locally in Canada, Namibia, and Brazil, and widely seen both as economical and as a fundamental solution to social and political ills.

Second, Francis would bridle giant corporations, especially their control of poor countries, through "financialization." "Saving [self-seeking] banks at any cost, making the public pay the price, foregoing a firm commitment to reviewing and reforming the entire system," he says, "only reaffirms the absolute power of a financial system, a power which has no future and will only give rise to new crises after a slow, costly and only apparent recovery" (189). In a related vein he continues, "The financial bubble also tends to be a produc[tion] bubble. The problem of the real economy is not confronted vigorously, yet it is the real economy which makes diversification and improvement in production possible, helps companies to function well, and enables small and medium businesses to develop and create employment" (189). Unfortunately, he says nothing about complementary currencies or public banking to assist the real economy.

The power of the pope's exhortation may be inferred from the knee-jerk silliness of criticism which immediately arose from "conservative" media pundits. Matt Taibbi in *Rolling Stone* cites one TV commentator who cries hypocrisy because the pope's Swiss Guard uses equipment supplied by arms corporations, while another jeers that the pope uses corporate-produced air conditioning to cool the Sistine Chapel. A featured columnist of the pretentious *New York Times* complains that the pope overlooks the benefits of gas fracking, for example, because its displacement of coal-burning emissions have somewhat reduced global warming. Never mind water consumption and pollution, sickness and displacement of rural families, and earthquakes.

Third, the "techno-economic paradigm" seems to worry Francis most:

> We are the beneficiaries of two centuries of enormous waves of change: steam engines, railways, the telegraph, electricity, automobiles, aeroplanes, chemical industries, modern medicine, information technology and, more recently, the digital revolution, robotics, biotechnologies and nanotechnologies. . . . It must . . . be recognized that nuclear energy, biotechnology, information technology, knowledge of our DNA . . . have given those with the knowledge, and especially the economic resources to use them, an impressive dominance over the whole of humanity and the entire world. Never has humanity had such power over itself, yet nothing ensures that it will be used wisely. . . Think of the nuclear bombs dropped in the middle of the twentieth century, or the array of technology which Nazism, Communism and other totalitarian regimes have employed to kill millions of people, to say nothing of the increasingly deadly arsenal of weapons available for modern warfare. In whose hands does all this power lie, or will it eventually end up? It is extremely risky for a small part of humanity to have it. . . .(102)

> The technocratic paradigm . . . tends to dominate economic and political life. The economy accepts every advance in technology with a view to profit, without concern for its potentially negative impact on human beings. Finance overwhelms the real economy. The lessons of the global financial crisis have not been assimilated, and we are learning all too slowly the lessons of environmental deterioration . . . (109)

The specialization which belongs to technology makes it difficult to see the larger picture . . . There needs to be a distinctive way of looking at things, a way of thinking, policies, an educational programme, a lifestyle and a spirituality which together generate resistance to the assault of the technocratic paradigm. (110)

Our symposium on "Economic System Transformation" at the "Seizing an Alternative" conference in Claremont also brought concern with technology's uses. Henry Lieberman and Christopher Fry, of MIT's Media Lab, promoted not only cooperation determined by the logic of variants of the "prisoners' dilemma" game but saw a happy and peaceful future 20 or 30 years out based on Makerism, wherein everybody (all can have equipment cheaply) can make with 3-dimensional printers whatever they want: communication devices, car parts, houses, food, other 3-D printers—creating plenitude and obviating social conflict. Little need for trade, police protection, government planning—nearing Utopia? How to reconcile this with the pope's view of the present as dystopia? Other discussants in the symposium accepted Making but not Makerism, so that technology would serve—not overwhelm—the needs of the poor, of the "lost generation" of youth, of neighborhood security, of democracy. Even corporations like Master-Card were said to be engaging such usage for common benefit, or risk corporate disappearance.

Another technologist, Lilly Irani from UC San Diego, who had to withdraw before the symposium, invented a digital system called Turkopticon whereby exploited contingent workers for Amazon (called Turks, after migrant workers in Germany) could organize to maximize bargaining power with this employer. Such conceptions create a sanguine outlook among technologists, contrary to the worries of sociologists such as Randall Collins who notes massive displacement of workers by automation, and unrest. Turkopticon and 3-D Making and thousands of other technological developments can contribute to the welfare of people and nature if the dystopian culture of the pope's "techno-economic paradigm" is addressed. The papal encyclical rightly aims to promote universal dialogue on technology and its changing relationships with economies and governance.

What might we add to the pope's concerns regarding the techno-economic paradigm or other ecologically and socially degrading concerns? Insights range from identifying systemic anomalies to broadly experiential and educational programs down to tactical innovations. We can think of events that might "unfreeze" dysfunctional institutions such as banks "too big to [let] fail," or military aircraft firms cozy with congress members, or crop seed monopolies dispossessing poor farmers, or military recruitment and training procedures, or profit-oriented charter schools. Or we can think of new or radically reformed institutions which might work in harmony with salutary institutions to promote humane objectives and values. Here are a few such ideas.

New institutions

First might be the revival and energizing of "Christian base communities," a key institution of liberation theology supported by Pope John XXIII in 1962 but quashed in the 1980s by Joseph Cardinal Ratzinger of the renamed office of the Holy Inquisition, later to become Pope Benedict XVI. Pope Francis, earlier critical of liberation theology, appears now to have lifted its suppression. Liberation theology emphasizes the "preferential option for the poor"—a value of Francis—while base communities implement a bottom-up revolution of political awareness and initiative among poor and oppressed villagers in Latin America through local in-home meetings reinterpreting the Bible for contemporary issues and responsibilities. As recently as 2007 there were 80,000 base communities in Brazil alone.

Although Pope Francis seems to prefer a nonpolitical approach to social change, the base community idea resonates with "participatory budgeting," a movement of popular municipal (and sometimes state) fiscal innovation and control started in Porto Alegre, Brazil, after the fall of the military dictatorship in 1989 and supported by local government in over 500 cities in South America, persisting despite setbacks due to corruption in the national political party of its origin. In that paradigm, already spreading to Chicago and New York City as well as parts of Europe and Africa, tens of thousands of citizens of a given city, especially the poor, participate in budget making and monitoring with tangible improvements in living standards. Judging from his encyclical, it is entirely possible that in time Francis will support such initiatives as base communities and participatory budgeting with greater rationale and enthusiasm.

These two new institutions have helped provide energy and organization for social change, which actually occurred as military institutions weakened. They are expanding as a new era blossoms in Latin America after centuries of conquest and entrenchment of military, church, and planter dominance. Bishop Bergoglio experienced that change in Argentina, as it was going on also in Chile, Brazil, Venezuela, and elsewhere. Yes, poverty and abuse of indigenous peoples are still rampant, but they are receding. With U.S. support, Iberian elites have been stubborn, but they cannot hang on forever in the face of change from below and also from East Asian corporate invasion. Movements can provide energy and primary organization for social change, but secondary organization—institutions—are necessary for stability. As long as old elitist institutions stand firm, only tension, and not flow, can occur.

Private property is at the center of the old system, and the right or claim to major property is assured by venerated laws and policies. The institution of patent and copyright as well as of deeds is at the heart of property "rights." If popular rights to the use and control of socially necessary lands, streets, transport, schools, books, science, medicines, forests, pastures, fisheries, airwaves, and so on are to be honored, "intellectual property" laws are to be abrogated. Lack of use of any of these determines austerity and poverty. Led by the governments of U.S., Europe, and Japan, national and international patent and copyright law has, in the last four decades, been co-opted and inflated by impersonal, opaque giant corporations in their compulsive quest for monopoly and cultural dominance.

Originally justified as the right of inventors to the fruits of their ingenuity, labor, and commercial development, patents are now bought up by giant corporations and their shareholders who exploit or sequester them for the sake of market share and profit rather than genius or common good. Today science-based patents and copyrights as in medicine and agriculture (e.g., genetic modification) are produced in universities, largely at public expense, and then become the property of corporations. Music and books created by individuals or bands are likewise monopolized for corporate gain. The culture they promote is standardized, mass culture lacking for the most part in disturbance of their owners or vision of alternatives. It is contrary to the values of Pope Francis, but his encyclical oddly says nothing about it. He will be challenged by China and other Asian countries which have flouted "intellectual property" laws for decades and whose policies may prove decisive in unfreezing those laws if not democratizing them. For humane alternatives to be established, the pope will be challenged to promote alternative property and use conventions. Otherwise corporate despoiling of the ecosphere and society will approach a catastrophic climax.

Changing the paradigm

What can lay individuals and associations do to turn this tide? Someone ought to compile the undoubtedly hundreds of ideas for system change, just as the sociologist Gene Sharp did with his 198 tactics for rebellion which were used in the color revolutions of Eastern Europe. Here I offer two: one technical and the other communitarian.

I am a social psychologist. Perhaps Pope Francis's call to action will inspire some psychologists to apply their technical expertise to systemic social change. Francis calls for new definitions of "progress" and condemns the ignoring both of "externalities" to conventional economic models and policies and of "monetization" of "costs and benefits." The salutary "triple bottom line" tries to account for social and environmental costs as well as economic, but fails to account for social benefits. Psychologists have long established criteria and constructed scales to measure emotions such as anger, pleasure, frustration, satisfaction, etc., in the brain, in isolation, and in social situations. These states can contribute to long-term emotional dispositions and behavior—some pro-social, some socially neutral, and some anti-social—having nothing to do with money or what money can buy.

Can psychologists devise measures for comparing such multi-faceted benefits and detriments of social, economic, and political policies? Will we change our notions of welfare and the common good? Of course the outcomes will differ for persons and groups of different kinds, but psychometrics—especially qualitative psychometrics —may humanize the otherwise narrowly materialistic perception of the effects of public and corporate policy. This could change our understanding of "winners and losers" in capitalist, state socialist, religious, indigenous, and other societies. In bureaucracies it may flip the roles of Minister of Finance and Minister of Culture. It may help in visualizing better systems.

Finally, can we improve—or revolutionize—human solidarity? With solidarity we can change political systems, as for example with Solidarnosc in Poland's transition from a form of communism to a form of democratic capitalism. In Boston in the 1990s and 2000s, church groups increased local political power by joining the Greater Boston Interfaith Organization (GBIO). This movement built solidarity by sending 30 or more members of any faith organization to formative local meetings where members systematically engaged, one-on-one, each visitor both at the meeting and in one member's home. Conversation was free, about the lives of the interlocutors themselves. Only after broad and deep personal solidarity was established did the members set neighborhood or city priorities and magnetize politicians to meet and listen and act on major issues such as health care, schooling, and housing.

More traditionally, the Islamic world community builds and ensures solidarity through the institution of the Hajj—the visit to Mecca required of every devout Muslim who can hitch-hike or scrape up airfare. The political outlook and determination of Malcolm X was changed toward universalist by his rubbing shoulders with every shade and nationality of pilgrim he was swirled with around the sacred Ka'aba. Despite major differences between denominations, the degree of cohesiveness and determination within militant Muslim groups continues to confound U.S./NATO military leaders.

Can the power of the Hajj be adapted to the building of solidarity among oppressed and other groups in U.S. cities? Black and white and brown kids meet in some schools and often become friends, but what about their parents whose groups are uni-racial or of uniform politics? Can churches and other social groups induce cross-town visitation among a critical mass of their members? No airfare is necessary to travel two miles to another section of town where folks are of different color, class, or religion. The Cross-town Hajj might be established as a seven-time interfaith religious obligation. "Religious" might morph into "civic" obligation, with intrinsic rewards as well as social and cultural engagement or even material rewards devised according to local ingenuity. With appropriate tools and programs, that solidarity may generate community and ecological change worthy of any pope's most persistent exhortations.

In conclusion, we must embrace Pope Francis for his emphasis, clarity, and pedagogy regarding systemic causation. Though his focal concern is the ecosphere—physical threat to all nature and humanity—he unhesitatingly speaks to powerful remote or masked causes of ecological destruction. These he shows to be an ownership and consumerist culture and its technophiles, allowing profit-oriented corporations and elites to manipulate governance, resources, production, and public acquiescence. His next letter can deal more pointedly with popular education and action to transform this culture for the common good.

Positive Solutions from a Plasma Physicist

Timothy E. Eastman

I am struck by the critique within *Laudato si'* of the common use (or abuse) of techno-science, accompanied by a call for fundamental rethinking.

In my experience as both scientist and science administrator, science and technology have had tremendous impact on our everyday world and continue to have profound possibilities for adding to our problems or for contributing to key solutions. Science alone is defined by methodology, not by content, although whole encyclopedias can be devoted to a wide range of results obtained by applying its methodology. Techno-science has led to new capabilities in transportation, communications, research, and education, etc. that have contributed greatly to the common good; however, the "dark side" of techno-science, emphasized in *Laudato si'*, has involved great dangers and abuse. Much of this dark side is not inevitable and, in my view, is not part of techno-science *per se*. Instead, various choices are made (political, economic, social) that amplify such negative impacts, which often seem to be the unintended consequences of market-based solutions or decisions out of context relative to any sense of an ecological vision or "integral ecology."

Such problems are all the more reinforced by prime beneficiaries of the status quo who claim that Adam Smith's "invisible hand" of capitalism can solve all problems while, at the same time, violating the spirit of their own rhetoric by encouraging major government subsidies for the status quo (e.g., globally \$5.3 trillion per year for petro-industry[1]), and actively discouraging investments in alternatives. Some alternative energy options have comparatively little means of support. For example, barely \$1M per year of solely private funding is currently invested in the promising alternative of Focus Fusion systems (see positive solution number 3 below). So far as techno-science is confused with this kind of manipulation, then it constitutes a false "god." Arguably, this arises at least in part from bad philosophy and bad economics. Certainly, such "bad faith" in a distorted application of techno-science is necessarily incomplete with respect to the full range of human experience and needs.

Context for techno-science

Even though science seeks invariant relationships that are context independent, their application is always in context of a particular application with attention to particular initial conditions and boundary conditions. Likewise, even though techno-science can be very useful for understanding how things work, such understanding rarely extends to basic "why" questions or the associated context of goals and purposes. Thus, it is a fundamental misconception to claim that science, technology, and their products should be treated as ends-in-themselves. Investments in techno-science, and its active pursuit, are always in context of some project, program, or end result. As a result, we need to analyze carefully associated goals and purposes. In many cases, such goals may actually be focused on optimizing profit margins for a few stakeholders with essentially no consideration of the common good. In contrast, *Laudato si'* calls for attention to the needs of the full range of stakeholders, including the "poor." Inevitably, ethical issues arise in multiple ways and the growing field of environmental ethics reflects this need. (See the "Environmental Ethics" entry at <iep.utm.edu>; also Brian Henning.)

Possibilities for positive solutions using science and technology

While *Laudato si'* provides a clear prophetic voice of the dangers of our present unsustainable trajectory, it balances this with a call for practical solutions and hopefulness. With this in mind, I list below some thoughts on how techno-science can be part of the solution instead of part of the problem:

Shift the present U.S. "defense" budget to focus on genuine defense needs instead of global projection of power; convert the 50% or more saved into research, solutions-oriented techno-science, and a wide array of projects to enable a dramatic shift towards a long-term sustainable economy. Total jobs gained would more than offset jobs lost in the arguably less-efficient military-industrial framework. Such conversion could be coordinated through a large-scale 21st century state-federal "WPA" program.[2] Feedback and decision-making could be structured as much more local in this framework (including effective feedback and open-access accountability) than that associated with the highly centralized military-industrial (and Wall Street) complex. Projects could be focused on quality of life, infrastructure, and needs for long-term sustainability. Many costs could be covered by the elimination of non-essential subsidies such as that for the petro-industry noted above. Concurrently, overall debt could still be reduced overall when combined with conversion of money supply and key banks from private control to direct accountability to the citizenry (Brown 2012). Invest in rapid conversion of agricultural systems, wherever possible, to perennial, polyculture crops from the current dependence on annual, monoculture crops. According to research carried out by the Land Institute (landinstitute.org), such conversion could reduce petroleum consumption nationwide by over 40% and enable drastic reductions in the use of problematic fertilizers and pesticides. The increased on-the-ground information requirements of perennial crops could potentially be met by adding many on-site jobs for information-skilled agricultural workers. The next agricultural revolution could then move away from the current agri-business, top-down model to a truly bottom-up, sustainable approach, effectively re-introducing the "family" farm.

Dramatically increase and "fast track" research and development (R&D) in humanistic studies that focuses on the underlying context of needs, goals, and purposes for the common good in addition to techno-science projects focused on the most promising alternative solutions for meeting our present global-change/sustainability challenge as articulated in *Laudato si'*. As one example, among many others, very modest investments in Focus Fusion experiments have recently led to break-through results, which indicate a possibility of clean, non-radioactive, widely available non-carbon fuels providing power supply at the equivalent of about 10 cents per gallon! If experiments this coming year prove successful, such systems could be practically in place by mid-century. Greater investment, of course, could greatly accelerate such development. Obviously, alternatives such as this could be a game-changer for energy supply worldwide and enable a rapid move away from petroleum-based fuel consumption. For details of this example, see focusfusion.org.[3] In conjunction with enabling new energy solutions, R&D in the generation of salt-free water (i.e., de-salinization) could be accelerated to identify improved (and locally practical) solutions to the worldwide need for clean drinking water. In parallel, new reduced-pollution industrial methods could be dramatically expanded (e.g., plasma-based surface cleaning and painting preparation versus current sand-blasting)[4]; plasma-enhanced melter systems for highly-efficient waste processing versus current "burning" (and pollution-prone) systems (Cohn 1997, 209-29); enhanced water and air-cleaning systems, the latter potentially up to city-wide scale (Prueitt 1997, 149-61). As well, enhanced efficiencies throughout our infrastructures (home, business, industry) could dramatically improve overall carbon footprint,[5] for example, by accelerating the deployment of fuel options (e.g., biofuels and liquid hydrogen) and electrical stations for hybrid, hydrogen-fueled, and electric-only vehicles.

Low-emissivity windows, which act like a mirror to heat waves but transmit visible light, have made impressive gains in reducing heating costs for many commercial buildings. In addition, new spectrally selective windows can now be made that pass visible light but reflect near-IR so as to "take the heat out of sunlight" and enable substantial reduction in summer air-conditioning bills—perhaps even to eliminate air-conditioning all together (Rosenfeld and Price 1997, 165-77). Special programs through utility companies could be established that accelerate the installation of such energy-saving options and spread costs and savings over time. Other examples of practical energy efficiency options for homes and businesses are discussed by Bill McKibben (*New Yorker,*

June 2015, 30-35). Even more advanced electrochromic (smart) glass windows or "super windows" are rapidly advancing in reliability (and reduced cost) that automatically (or by electronical control) change from clear to nearly opaque depending on lighting conditions (see Wikipedia "Smart Glass").

On feedback, assessment, and governance:

Many issues of global climate change, atmospheric chemistry, pollution, and related topics need to be understood inclusively because of how they affect systems at multiple scale, from the human level to the global Earth system. Although a few problems should be handled at global level, most practically viable approaches remain on regional or smaller scale. Such problems, as well, almost always impact everyone and the evaluation of solutions should attend to the needs and feedback of all stakeholders (and *Laudato si'* calls us to include the poor in this list!). As well, issues raised by environmental ethicists and other scholars should be included because techno-science solutions or business solutions, by themselves, are inevitably incomplete with respect to the common-good criteria.

As stated by Herman Greene,

> while acknowledging our dependence on it, we must, however, recognize that the industrial-economic system is fatally flawed. It does not offer a viable future for humans or nature, So, it must be re-built, but without a set of instructions. It must be re-designed, re-invented, re-constructed and re-newed. This involves every sector of society and every institution...Be sustained by the vision of ecological civilization. Act with the fierce urgency of now, yet be prepared for and committed to the long haul.

Global change effects are most clearly seen in long-time scales and are often difficult to recognize over short time scales; this aspect enables certain politicians to deny climate change effects even though the best peer-reviewed science (which attends to both short- and long-term time scales) is well established on many (not all) key aspects of these problems. Because primary accountability for political leaders is only short term, this difference of time-scale sets up a fundamental disconnect between the political sphere (short-term focus) and the needs for effective global change response (long term). The primary tool to offset this time-scale disconnect is that of providing effective feedback from relevant R&D to decision-makers. To better address the critical global-change problem, such feedback needs to be greatly enhanced (through both enhanced R&D and improved communication of such results to decision makers). As well, decision makers should be made more accountable for their response to such feedback (e.g., introducing new, independent evaluation and reporting systems, with results fully available to voters).

For decision-making from a regional to a global scale, some enhanced coordination methods are needed that go beyond the occasional meetings of international advisory bodies that generally have little or no authority. Although such efforts to provide persuasive influence to state actors should continue, perhaps an intermediate level of governance could be considered (recognizing the risks and problems of any global governance model). One example for this is the governance model for research in Antarctica, initiated with the highly successful Antarctic Treaty of 1959. Since that time, this Treaty system has expanded to a total of 50 countries (29 with a direct "Consultative" role) with new legal instruments developed including the Protocol on Environmental Protection (see *The Antarctic Treaty* site at <ats.aq/e/ats.htm>). Perhaps this successful Antarctic Treaty model could be applied in some way to the challenge of global climate change.

Conclusion

Responding to the prophetic voice of *Laudato si'*, we need a new sense of self-awareness that truly seeks the common good (see Daly and Cobb, 1994). *Laudato Si'* deals with the critical, global problems of climate change and sustainability in a unified manner, and in dialogue with multiple perspectives that comport with integral ecology for an ecological vision. This is the context within which science and technology issues should be addressed to enable its potential positive benefits, and to avoid the "dark-side" of techno-science engendered by a focus on growth versus sustainability, profits versus the common good.

Endnotes

1. Bill McKibben "Climate Warming as a Civilizational Crises," Keynote Address to Seizing an Alternative: Toward an Ecological Civilization, June 4-7, 2015, Claremont, California <pandopopulus.com>.

2. The U.S. Works Progress Administration (WPA) was a large and highly successful jobs program of the 1930's, which provided jobs for millions of otherwise unemployed workers.

3. My examples are primarily based on plasma physics, which has been my professional specialty. In addition, I am an investor with the Focus Fusion effort.

4. I am a shareholder with Atmospheric Plasma Solutions, which currently focuses on surface treatment and painting preparation applications (see aplasmasolution.com and plasmas.com).

5. Carbon footprint is historically defined as the total of greenhouse gas emissions caused by a person, product, event or organization (see Wikipedia entry).

References

Brown, Ellen H. *Web of Debt: The Shocking Truth about Our Money System and How We Can Break Free*. Third Millennium Press, 2012.

Cohn, Daniel R. "Hot and Cold Plasma Processing of Waste." *Plasma Science and the Environment*. Ed. W. Manheimer, L. Sugiyama, and T. Stix. Woodbury, NY: American Institute of Physics, 1997.

Daly, Herman E., and John B. Cobb, Jr. *For the Common Good: Energy, Environment, and Sustainability*. 1989. Boston: Beacon Press, 1994.

Greene, Herman F. *The Promise of Ecological Civilization*. Process Century Press. Forthcoming.

Henning, Brian. *The Ethics of Creativity: Beauty, Morality and Nature in a Processive Cosmos*. University of Pittsburgh Press, 2005.

McKibben, Bill. "Power to the People." *New Yorker* 29 June 2015.

Prueitt, Melvin L. "Convection Towers for Generating Electric Power and Reducing Air Polution." *Plasma Science and the Environment*. Eds. W. Manheimer, L. Sugiyama, and T. Stix. Woodbury, NY: American Institute of Physics, 1997.

Rosenfeld, Arthur H., and Lynn Price. "Recent Improvements in New Product Energy Efficiency." *Plasma Science and the Environment.* Ed. W. Manheimer, L. Sugiyama, and T. Stix. Woodbury, NY: American Institute of Physics, 1997.

Principles of Regenerative Agriculture for Ecological Civilizations

David Freudenberger and C. Dean Freudenberger

We gladly accepted the invitation extended to us by the Process Century Press to share this paper. Originally, we wrote it at the request of a professor teaching at China Agriculture University, Beijing. Then, following the 10th International Whitehead Conference, "Seizing an Alternative: Toward an Ecological Civilization" (June 4-7, 2015), we modified the paper in order to recognize the timely publication of Pope Francis' encyclical *Laudato si'*. This encyclical encouraged us greatly. The reader will notice several references to it. This paper reflects key issues that were discussed during the eight sessions of the Whiteheadian conference track: "Agroecology: Foundational for an Ecological Civilization.

The challenge

The 10,000-year history of agricultural civilizations is one of spectacular success and chronic failure. Agriculture is the foundation for the extraordinary rise of the human species, now seven billion in number. But this success has come at the cost of millions of hectares of biodiverse wetlands, grasslands, woodlands, and forests cleared for crops and pastures that led too often to soil loss and the collapse of societies (Montgomery 2012). Agriculture and humanity's command of fire (controlled combustion of bio- and fossil fuels) are the two great inventions and forces that have created the Anthropocene—an era where one species, humans, now affects all fundamental processes of the biosphere, including the air we breathe. These radical inventions have now enabled the majority of humanity to be freed from direct food acquisition or production. No other species has ever achieved such a liberation from the day to day grind and dangers food gathering. Industrial agriculture (the linkage between farming, industrial technology, and fossil fuels) now feeds half of humanity that live in extraordinarily vibrant and diverse cities.

Agriculture has from the dawn of recorded history fed the poet, philosopher, craftsmen, artists, and governing classes. But from the dawn of farming, the cultivation of grains (grasses and legumes) has been the most devastating hallmark of agriculture. Crop cultivation has required the plough to bare the soil that was once protected by forests, woodlands, or diverse grasslands. Fossil fuel farming developed over the past 100 years has simply accelerated the 10,000-year history of biosphere transformations (e.g., forest clearing). The industrial revolution, fed by coal and the manufacture of steel, has provided the tools for massive deforestation—chain saws, bulldozers, tractors, and global supply chains.

Industrial farming practices continue to erode soils far faster than they are naturally formed by geological, chemical, and biological processes (Montgomery 2012). Industrial agriculture is totally dependent on dwindling fossil fuels for soil cultivation, chemical fertilizers, pest control and transport. Vast monocultures of crops and confined livestock continue to drive millions of rural people into rapidly expanding cities that too often exhibit deep and unjust social divides.

There is an ever-growing urgency to evolve and nurture alternatives to such destructive practices and social inequities. To continue with contemporary systems of industrial food production will likely condemn millions of people to ecological and social collapse as has been repeatedly experienced throughout the history of agriculture (Montgomery 2012; Ponting 2007). As Pope Francis wrote in his recent encyclical "The exploitation of the planet's resources exceeds acceptable limits" (27).

This essay explores some of the emerging technological practices and required cultural norms of a radically new *regenerative* agriculture that must be the foundation of ecological and enduring civilizations.

Definitions

We use the term 'regenerative agri-culture' rather than 'ecological' agri-culture or 'sustainable' agriculture to emphasize that agri-culture must be a process of continuous renewal of soil fertility and adaptation to climatic variability and change. Agri-culture should not be seen as a steady state of optimized yields and profits, but rather a dynamic of life, death, and decay; learning, caring, and adaptation. We also chose to hyphenate agri-*culture* to emphasize that all nations are utterly dependent on the cultivation of foods. The harvest of wild foods was once important but likely supported only 5-10 million humans scattered across most all continents 10-13,000 years ago prior to the cultural development of farming and livestock domestication (Ponting 2007). Nearly all of contemporary humanity is a part of a underpinning *culture* of land clearing, farming, and food distribution. Agri-cultural practices, for better or for worse, are a profound reflection of what and who we are as a species. The culture of farming has radically transformed humanity from scattered groups of hunter-gathers to vast cities supporting a diverse array of occupations and amusements. But the culture of farming has also radically transformed the earth to deforested hills and muddy rivers.

Principles

We have found the metaphor of a three-legged chair (stool) to be a useful means of conceptualizing and communicating key elements of a regenerative agri-culture. We suggest that there are three fundamental legs or principles needed to support a truly regenerative agri-culture:

- Farming practices that continually protect biodiversity and renew soil.
- Political economies that continually renew rural communities.
- Cultures of gratitude, respect, and care.

For this essay, we can only briefly describe these supporting principles of a regenerative agri-culture and provide a few links to emerging examples.

Farming practices that continually protect and renew natural capital

The past 10,000 years of farming has been based on the plow that has ripped open soils once perennially covered by an incredible diversity of grasses, shrubs, and trees. Wherever the plow has been used, archaeological and historical evidence shows an immediate increase in erosions rates above natural (geological) soil renewal rates. The plow has simultaneously supported rapid rises in human populations but then, after a few centuries, frequent societal collapse and soil exhaustion (Montgomery 2012).

The plow must be abandoned. A regenerative agriculture will be based on soils that are always covered by living or dead vegetative cover (e.g. mulch). This is an awesome challenge to reverse farming practices that have been the foundation of all civilizations for so many millennia. Until recently it did not seem possible to abandon the plow. The majority of human food energy (starches and plant oils) comes from annual crops of grains and oil-seeds that require exposing the soil to extensive annual cultivation to prepare a seed bed and reduce competition from weeds. Over the past 50 years, with the advent of chemical herbicides, "no-till" or minimum-till cropping systems have been widely adopted where farmers have access to such agri-chemicals. However, such cropping systems may still not provide enough vegetative cover to reduce soil erosion to geologically natural rates (Montgomery 2012). Nor do we know what the long-term environmental and human health impact is of these evolutionary novel chemicals. "Caring for ecosystems requires far sightedness which are not immediately evident" (*Laudato si'* 36).

Until recently, it was not thought possible to develop (breed) perennial grains that only require cultivation for establishment and occasionally renewal. The prevailing scientific paradigm states that annual grasses (the majority of grain crops) invest in shallow roots, rapid growth, and many large seeds, but short life (months rather than years). In contrast, perennial grasses invest in large roots and an abundance of leaves to survive for many years, but the penalty is thought to be small and few seeds. Scientific theory held that there is a trade-off between lots of soil renewing roots versus few roots, but many seeds. It was thought that high seed-yielding perennial grains are biologically impossible (Glover 2010). However pioneering research over the past 40 years has shown that this theory is incorrect (DeHaan and Tassel 2014). High yielding perennial grain crops are possible to breed, but much more difficult and time consuming than breeding for large annual grains which the earliest farmers started about 10-13,000 years ago across multiple continents. Much progress is being made in developing a model perennial grain *Kernza*™ (a grass cultivar of *Thinopyrum intermedium*) and breeding a perennial sunflower is progressing (Tassel and DeHaan 2013).

A complementary approach is to simply incorporate large seeded but short-lived grasses (e.g., annual wheat, barley, or oats) into perennial grasslands. This approaches mimics how all-natural grasslands function—a scatter of annuals in amongst tussocks (clumps) of perennial grasses. In parts of Australia, this approach has been pioneered by farmers (not scientists) and called *pasture cropping* (White 2013). In autumn, annual grains are directly sown, with minimal soil disturbance (just a thin slot) into native pastures dominated by a locally evolved diversity of summer active perennial grasses. The traditional annual grains are grown over winter while the summer active grasses are dormant. The crops are harvested just as the native grasses become active with warming temperatures and longer day length.

For the first time in humanity's agri-cultural history, there appears to be viable alternatives to bare soil agriculture. At last there is hope that the plow can be abandoned and precious soil, the foundation of all civilizations, protected and renewed in perpetuity. Maximum yield per hectare, the "modern" measure of supposedly successful agriculture must also be abandoned in favor of maximum soil cover and root depth per ton of food produced.

Most humans are omnivores; we enjoy eating a wide range of animal meats, eggs, and dairy (adult humans are the only adult species than can digest milk; Lieberman 2013). Consumption of animal tissues high in protein is an important nutritional complement to grains, many of which are low in protein but high in starches and sugars. Animal-free diets (e.g., vegans) are possible, but rely on protein from annual pulses (crops like soybeans and chickpeas) that are high in plant proteins. Such crops, even if they can be bred to be perennial, must still be grown on land cleared of biodiverse native vegetation.

Humans are not herbivores. We cannot readily digest the most common carbohydrate, cellulose, that makes up all plant cell walls. But our ruminant livestock can. Sheep, cattle, and goats have evolved a remarkable symbiosis with a diversity of gut microbes that inhabit the large forestomach of these animals. These microbes are the only group of organisms that have evolved the capacity to break down the strong bound of the cellulose molecule. Our livestock species have a remarkable capacity to graze and browse upon a vast diversity of plants and then their gut microbes convert plant cell walls (cellulose) into energy for producing highly digestible meat, fat, and milk. Our livestock animals basically live off the energy rich metabolites of microbial digestion of cellulose. Our meat animals gain essential protein from digesting the microbes themselves. Ruminants, thanks to a symbiosis with a vast number and variety of gut microbes, can also detoxify a great diversity of plant toxins that make them inedible to humans.

Integration of grazing livestock with perennial crops must be an essential component of regenerative farming systems. Only our livestock, if well managed at the right densities, can consume a vast diversity of forages in perpetuity. Wetlands, grasslands, and woodlands do not have to be cleared and reduced to a monoculture of pastures. They can be sustainably grazed as biodiverse systems.

It is simply absurd that "modern" (industrial) agriculture has put our ruminant livestock into feed lots where humans spend an enormous amount of energy feeding them a monotonous ration of grains and forage crops (e.g., alfalfa/lucerne). Farmers and their machines now do the harvesting of forage monocultures rather than the cow or sheep with the evolutionary intelligence to select a balanced diet from a vast array of grasses, herbs and shrubs.

A regenerative supply of high quality animal protein is relatively straightforward. Simply let our beef and dairy cows out of the barn and back to the native pastures of woodlands, shrublands, and grasslands.

History has proven too many times that grazing animals can be enormously damaging to fragile plants and soils, so agricultural systems must evolve that allow livestock managers to have the flexibility to move livestock in and out of pastures in a manner responsive to seasonable conditions and the sensitivities of soils and its vegetative cover.

Protein from other animals groups (e.g., pigs, chickens, and fish) can be raised similarly—allow them to forage across naturally occurring foods. For example, chickens are being commercially raised on native perennial pastures where they consume a diversity of native insects and green shoots of grasses. But again, this requires a new agri-culture that fully understands and practices sustainable and flexible (seasonal) harvests and stocking rates.

Free range is considered to be lower yielding—so what? Most adults in affluent places consume far more protein then they metabolically require. We must relearn how to eat within the biosphere's limitations and gifts. Only rapidly growing children need diets high in animal and plant proteins (Lieberman 2013).

Political economies that continually renew rural communities.

Agriculture is a history of the subjugation of nature as well as the subjugation of people. There is little archaeological evidence of slavery amongst hunter-gatherer societies, but slavery appears time and again amongst agricultural societies. Industrial agriculture, thanks to the substitution slaves' sweat with fossil fuel, has greatly reduced the most brutal aspects of human subjugation, but most farmers remain poorly supported by modern societies and economies.

Even today, in highly educated societies, farmers are still not recognized as professionals with similar status and mandatory training and certification as medical doctors, lawyers, teachers, or tradespeople (e.g., mechanics, plumbers, and electricians). Farmers provide more health benefits (abundant food) than all the doctors and hospitals combined. Medicine utterly fails in the face of starvation. The vast majority of farmers in both rich and poor countries are lucky (exceptional) to have gone to school long enough to learn to read and write. We don't build statues of great farmers, only mere warmongers and other power aggrandizers (politicians). We adulate our great athletes and movie stars, but rarely thank a farmer for our next meal.

Truly regenerative farming practices are now, at last, possible but require uplifting of the farmer and renewal of the rural communities that support them. Farmers need the same access to education and professional development as we provide for the vast array of professions that support life in our cities. Access to electricity, public transport, telecommunication, and health services is just as important for farming communities as it is in cities. Rural-based universities and research institutions will continue to be essential for facilitating a transition to regenerative agricultural systems and landscapes. "Greater investment needs to be made at understanding more fully the functions of ecosystems. (*Laudato si'* 42). The full spectrum of arts and entertainment is needed to enrich and enliven rural life.

Regenerative agri-culture is not a rapacious factory of raw inputs, toiling workers, and food commodity outputs. Rather, regenerative agri-culture will evolve into diverse networks of people intimately involved in the food-nurturing process, distribution, and consumption. Farming needs to be a richly social process rather than just nameless business transactions on computer screens. Such culturally rich farming relationships are beginning to emerge in forms like local farmers' markets and community-supported agriculture where urban consumers co-invest with individuals or small groups of farmers in the risks and rewards of nurturing food from the good earth (Kumar *et al.* 2011). Regenerative agri-culture will reconnect informed consumers with the origins and lives of those people and communities tasked with the highly honored profession of farming.

Regenerative agri-culture will be nurtured and protected by laws and governing institutions that recognize farmland and its living soils must be held in trust for future generations, rather than a commodity that is speculatively traded for short-term gain. Farmers need the security of land-access rights, but in turn they must recognize that farming is a process of stewardship, rather than exclusionary ownership. Neither should farmland be seen as mere equity on which to become burdened with a lifetime of financial debt. Access to financial resources is essential to help our farmers invest in soil and landscape renewal and to buffer against climate variation from season to season. However, mechanisms need to evolve to ensure that debt does not lead to enslavement to financial institutions but, rather, to financial resources support creativity and security.

Institutions and consumers will recognize that agri-cultural landscapes are far more than a factory producing sugars, fats, and protein. Rather farmlands will be cherished, and land managers rewarded for providing a diverse range of ecosystem benefits including clean rivers and lakes, places for wildlife to flourish, and beautiful places to visit.

Laws and governing institutions will recognize the rights and welfare of all the animals that provide us with such tasty meals and fine fibers such as wool and cashmere. Life is dependent on death, but death of our food-producing animals must be swift following a life in which they live in productive comfort and without fear, stress, or abuse.

Agri-cultures of gratitude, dignity and care

The great philosophies and religions of both East and West have thought deeply about human relations with the cosmos but rarely dropped their gaze to the glorious life in the soil beneath their feet that provides them with their daily bread. The great philosophers of history have thought deeply and provided great guidance about human-to-human behavior, but seldom provided sufficient insights and guidance on human-to-nature relationships. Regenerative farming practices must be fully and strongly supported by cultural norms and practices that renew, rather than destroy.

Contemporary cultures based on individualism (me) and continuous growth in consumption (more) need to transform into cultures of "we" and "enough." The shallowness of individual gratification will be replaced by the rewards of supporting the collective good of both community and place (the environment). Ecological civilizations will be recognized by the dignity and care they bestow on their farmers and the land which sustains all people. Such civilizations will be founded on agri-cultures that sustain a deep sense of gratitude to the living soil and her plants and animals that provide human sustenance. History suggests there is unlikely to be an alternative. Our challenge is to broaden our ethical horizon for transgenerational welfare.

References

DeHaan, L. E., and D. Van Tassel. (2014). "Useful Insights from Evolutionary Biology for Developing Perennial Grain Crops." *American Journal of Botany* 101: 1801-19.

Francis. (2015). Encyclical letter. *Laudato si'*.

Glover, J. D., et al. (2010). "Increased food and ecosystem security via perennial grains." *Science* 328: 1638-39.

Kumar, S., J. Duell, A. Soergell, and R. Ali. (2011). "Towards Direct Marketing of Produce by Farmers in India: Lessons from the United States of America." *Journal of International Development*, 23(4), 539-47. <doi:10.1002/jid.1600>.

Lieberman, D. E. (2013). *The Story of the Human Body: Evolution, Health and Disease*. New York, Vintage Books.

Montgomery, D. R. (2012). *Dirt: The Erosion of Civilizations*. Oakland: University of California Press.

Ponting, C. (2007). *A New Green History of the World: The Environment and the Collapse of Great Civilizations*. Penguin Books, New York.

Van Tassel, D. and L. DeHaan. (2013). "Wild Plants to the Rescue." *American Scientist* 101 (3): 218.

White, C. (2013). "Pasture cropping: A Regenerative Solution from Down Under." *Solutions* 4 (1) <http://www.thesolutionsjournal.com/node/126>.

On Educational Reform

Marcus Ford

Pope Francis' encyclical on human-caused climate disruption, *Laudato si'*, is an extremely important and thoughtful document deserving of serious attention by all individuals who are committed to bringing about a more just and sustainable world. Its primary focus is on taking better care of our common home—the earth—and improving the lives of people everywhere, especially the poor. Its analysis is far ranging and many relevant topics are addressed, if only in passing. Among these topics is education. How we educate our youth and ourselves has profound implications for how we treat each other and the planet.

The central thesis of *Laudato si'* is that all things are related. Environmental issues are part of a larger picture, one that includes issues of social justice, healthy human communities, animal rights, economic development, education, moral values, and how we understand the world more generally—metaphysics. Human-caused global warming is not merely the result of how we currently produce energy; it is, more profoundly, symptomatic of a culture that has lost its way. The ecological crisis, Francis writes, " is one small sign of the ethical, cultural, and spiritual crisis of modernity" (119).

What we urgently need is a cultural revolution (114). We must replace our consumer culture with a culture that "encourages a prophetic and contemplative lifestyle, one capable of deep enjoyment free of the obsession with consumption" (222), and we must replace our culture of extreme individualism with a culture of care for one another and for the planet. We must reject the dogma that human happiness and well-being are closely associated with an increase in consumer spending, that endless economic growth is possible on a finite planet, that modern agriculture is sustainable and efficient, and that the natural world is devoid of intrinsic value. Humans are part of an ecosystem that has meaning and worth quite apart from the worth it has to the human economy. The human economy needs to be understood as a subset of something larger and more important, and it must operate in light of that wider context.

Transitioning from our current culture of economic progress and individualism to an ecological culture presents what Pope Francis terms an "educational challenge" (209). As the encyclical rightly notes, "The specialization which belongs to technology makes it difficult to see the larger picture. The fragmentation of knowledge proves helpful for concrete applications, and yet it often leads to a loss of appreciation for the whole, for the relationships between things, and for the broader horizon, which then become irrelevant" (110). Technical education is not sufficient; indeed, by itself it is destructive. "A science," Francis contends, "which would offer solutions to the great issues would necessarily have to take into account the data generated by other fields of knowledge, including philosophy and social ethics" (110).

Our public and private universities are not currently constructed to provide this kind of holistic, trans-technical, ethically infused education. In their current form they function to produce the "value-free" expert knowledge needed to perpetuate the technological culture that we currently have. Instead of helping us understand how our environmental and social problems are connected and how to transcend our desire for consumer goods, they reproduce and legitimate the un-ecological worldview that needs to be replaced. Instead of teaching that all things have intrinsic worth, they teach that reality is devoid of any intrinsic value and encourage us to find meaning in consumer goods and services. Universities, in other words, are a central part of the culture that is destroying our collective home. If they are to provide what is needed they will have to take a new form, embrace a new mission, and adopt a new worldview. As it currently exists, higher education is a major part of the problem that needs to be solved.

This view of higher education is extremely unflattering and likely to be rejected by most academics. It runs contrary to what we have been told and what we would like to believe. Higher education, we believe, is the key to a brighter personal and collective future. It is the means by which to get ahead. Higher education is not biased; it is objective. It does not promote a growing economy or the notion that consumerism is good. It does not promote a particular worldview. It simply tells the truth, without bias or prejudice. It provides information that people can use as they see fit. Higher education, we have come to believe, is making the world better.

And higher education could be a part of the solution—indeed it must be part of the solution—but it is simply not true that universities are culturally and metaphysically neutral. They are not neutral when it comes to the issue of technological progress and to the importance of growing our consumer economy. They are not neutral when it comes to the objective reality of ethical norms or the matter of intrinsic value (i.e., the value something has for itself). On all of these issues, universities—both public and private—take a strong stand. With only minor exceptions, they advocate for economic growth, personal wealth, personal autonomy, ethical relativism, and scientific materialism—a worldview that cannot explain a sense of meaning and purpose and is inconsistent with the entire project of higher education. This fact alone should make it clear that this worldview is inadequate.

In his encyclical Francis is critical of the media and the digital world. More often than not, he says, they [the media and the digital world] prevent individuals from "learning how to live wisely, to think deeply and to love generously" (47). He might well have said the same thing about our colleges and universities. "True wisdom," he says, "as the fruit of self-examination, dialogue and generous encounter between persons, is not acquired by mere accumulation of data which eventually leads to overload and confusion, a sort of mental pollution" (47).

We need colleges and universities that value and encourage wisdom as well as knowledge. If colleges and universities are to become a force for bringing about the kind of cultural change that is so urgently required, they will need to rethink their educational mission, their curriculum, and their worldview. They will need to see themselves not as economic engines and producers of value-free understanding but as institutions committed to wisdom and to passing along the values and skills of responsible citizenship and ecological stewardship.

Educating for wisdom, compassion, and ecological stewardship will require a different kind of curriculum than what now exists. We will have to recover old ways—and develop new ones—of teaching young people to think carefully about the world and their lives and about how to find happiness and meaning without destroying the planet and other cultures. We will have to move away from academic disciplines that were created to produce technical knowledge and away from programs of study that were designed to train workers for specific types of employment. We will have to move away from "value-free" information and place our knowledge within a moral framework.

This will not be easy. No human institution can easily and quickly redirect its focus and structure, and this is certainly true for universities steeped in a thousand years of tradition. Universities are very good at finding reasons for remaining essentially as they are while arguing that other cultural institutions—religious, political, and economic—must change. Perhaps now that the global situation is so dire, things will be different. Perhaps now it will become clear, even to academics, that our universities are very much a part of the culture that is destroying the planet. Perhaps now it will become evident that universities are uniquely positioned to bring about the kind of "cultural revolution" that is so clearly needed. Doing so will require that they themselves change radically. Were colleges and universities to redirect themselves, first and foremost, to "Care for Our Common Home" and all this entails, our collective future would be considerably brighter. Higher education *of a certain type* is absolutely critical in bringing about the kind of "cultural revolution" we so desperately need.

Management and the Care for Our Common Home

Mark Dibben

Politics and business have been slow to react in a way commensurate with the urgency of the challenges facing our world. Although the post-industrial period may well be remembered as one of the most irresponsible in history, nonetheless there is reason to hope that humanity at the dawn of the twenty-first century will be remembered for having generously shouldered its grave responsibilities.
Laudato si' (165)

Even setting aside its religious teaching correcting commonly held misconceptions of the place and role of human beings in the world, the papal encyclical is at the same time a formidable chastisement, a demonstration of systemic problems inherent to Modern Age political society and financial economy, and a powerful call for action. Much is made of the role of technology and business in causing the ecological crisis—and rightly so, there being inherent in the thinking an entirely erroneous belief that the Earth's resources are infinite and their exploitation is harmless. This thinking, which underpins technology-enabled globalization, consists of:

> [A]n undifferentiated and one-dimensional paradigm. This paradigm exalts the concept of a subject who, using logical

274

and rational procedures, progressively approaches and gains control over an external object. This subject makes every effort to establish the scientific and experimental method, which in itself is already a technique of possession, mastery and transformation. It is as if the subject were to find itself in the presence of something formless, completely open to manipulation. Men and women have constantly intervened in nature, but for a long time this meant being in tune with and respecting the possibilities offered by the things themselves. It was a matter of receiving what nature itself allowed, as if from its own hand. Now, by contrast, we are the ones to lay our hands on things, attempting to extract everything possible from them while frequently ignoring or forgetting the reality in front of us. Human beings and material objects no longer extend a friendly hand to one another; the relationship has become confrontational. This has made it easy to accept the idea of infinite or unlimited growth, which proves so attractive to economists, financiers and experts in technology. It is based on the lie that there is an infinite supply of the earth's goods, and this leads to the planet being squeezed dry beyond every limit. (106)

The pope is clear what the effects of this on the individual are: "Since the market tends to promote extreme consumerism in an effort to sell its products, people can easily get caught up in a whirlwind of needless buying and spending. Compulsive consumerism is one example of how the techno-economic paradigm affects individuals" (203). Even where challenges to the environment are understood, the pope notes, "the response to the crisis did not include rethinking the outdated criteria which continue to rule the world. Production is not always rational, and is usually tied to economic variables which assign to products a value that does not necessarily correspond to their real worth" (189) As a result of "the market tend[ing] to promote extreme consumerism in an effort to sell its products, people can easily get caught up in a whirlwind of needless buying and spending" (203). Up to a point, the pope is clear, too, as to the solution: "We need to reject a magical conception of the market, which would suggest that problems can be solved simply by an increase in the profits of companies or individuals" (190). There is the suggestion that to move beyond economism as the only alternative requires us to appreciate both the hidden costs of relying on non-renewable sources of energy and the impact on those who bear them, such that the moral side to consumption can be fully integrated into a changed lifestyle (195, 206).

The question is how? Despite frequent discussion of business and markets, the word 'management' is mentioned only once in the encyclical—in regards to "promoting a better management of marine and forest resources, and ensuring universal access to drinking water" (48:164). It would be tempting to suggest, therefore, that management has played no part in the crisis that we now face, much less in the way forwards. My contention, however is that management has been central to the problem, and, as we will see later, it is central to the solution also.

We are not the only species that engages in management. Most creatures engage in managing their environment, by making shelter—having special places where they rest and reproduce, finding and storing food, and even creating paths that run to and from the food and the shelter. Insects, spiders, birds, fish, reptiles, and mammals all practice management to some degree. Management is inherent in Nature. Indeed it seems to be almost naturally selected for. The Alpha pair of a Meerkat group, the dominant male and female in a chimpanzee community, the Silverback in a gorilla troop, to name just three community-dependent social animals, all have to be able to manage their respective entourages—boss them into line occasionally, yes, but also continually work to resolve disputes and thereby keep the group collective functioning effectively as a community, for the benefit of all within the community.

Yet of all the Earth's inhabitants it is *Homo sapiens* who is, perhaps unfortunately, the ultimate management practitioner. We seem to be capable of making the most decisions; we organize, manage, and use the technologies of tools and vocalizations to an extent unseen elsewhere in the natural world. The same is true of the way we also manage our personal behavior, others of our own kind, other species, and the environment so successfully (or not, as the case now seems to be). Managing, and thus management, is by the very force of Nature itself the only means we have for coping in and with our lives.

The difference between us and other animals is that, having invented currency to replace food and shelter and community as the primary value, we have ever-increasingly focused our management skills on making money, particularly since the Industrial Revolution. This most unnatural commodity has become our all-pervading focus, the measure of quality of life. More so even than the quality of life inherent in the Earth.

All species gather food; all species make shelters of some sort; all species make their own routes (some very short, others longer than our own) between food and shelter. Yet we have taken these natural acts of management to extremes, so that the making of shelters is about making money; the gathering of food is about making money; the travel is about making money. No other animal manages for the sake of consumption, that is, for the sake of obtaining more than it needs to live.

We have separated ourselves from the Earth, or so we have thought, in the search for growth as a proxy for quality of life. To the delight of the pharmaceutical corporations who manufacture antidepressant "happy pills"; happiness has declined while incomes have soared. As David Korten has explained (2015), corporations now rule the world and have done so, in fact, for some time. Management, as *Homo sapiens* has practiced it in recent times, in the Modern era, is about using people to improve the wealth of corporations, which offer goods (so positively called!) for human consumption as an end in itself. The implications of this purpose of management can be seen in many ways. Here are two: the drive for efficiency in organizations, and the use of knowledge and power by management.

To take the first of these, management in the Modern era would suggest that the best way, the most effective way, is the most efficient way. Certainly this is the driving premise behind much management thought as presented in academic management journals. If one looks to make every aspect of the organization as efficient as possible, then it will be as effective as possible. I, for one, am not sure this is correct. Whereas efficiency is straightforwardly rendered through balance sheets and other enumerable mechanisms of profit evaluation and quantifiable return on investment, effectiveness is rather more in the eye of the beholder. We can perhaps reduce it to effective use of someone or something to achieve an end goal, but then we are assuming agreement as to the end goal. We also have to clarify the question of "use." Even if we set this aside, certainly failure to meet the end goal implies a lack of effectiveness.

There is a tendency in many bureaucratic organizations for people to assume that the policies that govern the institution will prevent them from doing things, trying new ways of operating, or experimenting with ideas—and especially prevent genuinely putting new ideas into practice. This tendency arises from managers taking a traditional approach to their role as controllers whose main purpose is containment of expenses and maintenance of the status quo so as to deliver "core business." It creates the wrong atmosphere, an atmosphere of negativity, of avoidance of risk, of fear of failure. Very soon ideas are not even shared, let alone tried.

Things become even worse when managers really start to focus on deliverables, on things to be done above all else. That is, they focus on objectives—on objects. Very soon they see the people under them as objects to be used to deliver things. This is entirely in accordance with mainstream management thought. Yet when managers focus on the things, on deliverables, or when individuals are faced with a demand for results, very quickly their response is self-protection. A culture of "every man for himself" is all that can come from such an atmosphere. Very quickly, not just the effectiveness but also the efficiency of the organization unravels. At best, many of the people lose their jobs. At worst, the organization ceases to exist.

To turn now to the second, related, example, managers clearly have knowledge and power. The way in which managers traditionally use knowledge is as a means to control others. They gather as much knowledge about the organization and the people in it as possible, and retain as much of it as possible. The argument runs that managers engage in conversations with workers to discover what is happening and use that knowledge to control workers. They augment that power by withholding information from workers in order to expedite their wishes over and against those of workers. It is under these circumstances that the phrase "knowledge is power" arises as a lived reality. It is a troubling environment to find oneself in.

The response from people working under such circumstances is to withhold information, for fear that it will be used against them, and attempt to control their managers by being very careful about what information they do provide. And vice-versa. This turns the workplace into a playing field, and work into a game of charades, where no one tells the truth, where everyone tells stories. The reality is hidden beneath a cloak of what, to all intents and purposes, are lies. Trust is a very rare commodity, and people resort only to looking after themselves. Those who try to adopt a different stance, focused on the needs of others, are dismissed (metaphorically and occasionally also literally) as naïve. Anyone who has worked in an organization will doubtless recognize the picture just painted.

Where does this understanding of power and knowledge come from? As former Harvard Business School Professor David Korten argues (and as the papal encyclical also makes clear) the whole approach to business is based on a mix of two ideas. Korten terms one the "Distant Patriarch" belief—in which there is a view of God as the source of all agency and meaning. He calls the other the "Grand Machine" belief—in which there is a view that the universe is mechanistic, with no meaning, purpose or agency (60). As John Cobb has long argued (2014), and as the papal encyclical also makes clear, these ideas are unhelpful. Taken together, they encourage a managerial model built on the idea of managers invoking meaning, purpose, and agency where none existed beforehand, and being the architects of the organization. They think of themselves as gods of the universe they have created; a universe in which employees are creatures to be directed to a purpose they otherwise would not have. This brings about a real world ruled by corporations (profit-making organizations) managed by individuals with a dangerous sense of their own importance. All this results from a fundamental understanding of knowledge and power.

I would suggest all of the above is recognisable to anyone who has had the misfortune to work in an organization where Modern management is practiced. Unfortunately it is practiced in almost all business organisations! Clearly, then, Modern management is not leading toward an ecological civilization. We can no longer think about management in the way we did in the Modern age. That age, with its depletive relationship to Nature, as John Cobb has said (2014), is ending. Growth is now in sharp contradiction to sustainability, where sustainability means a genuine coexistence with the rest of Nature in a way that is regenerative of Nature. The current endpoint of human purpose, the wealth of corporations, and the false belief in consumption for happiness, will not matter as the Earth proceeds to recalibrate. What will matter is how we adjust our thinking and how we adjust our acting so that we can be in step with and supportive of that recalibration. We must think about management and the purpose of management in a new way.

To pause and recap, in the Anthropocene period of the Earth, humanity has developed the power to change the biosphere in ways only previously available to the geological aspect of Nature, its earthquakes and its volcanoes. The difference is that, whereas the chaos they cause, ultimately, has positive consequences for biodiversity, the sort of chaos *Homo sapiens* is presently causing does not. It's all negative. We need to change that. The question is how?

Alfred North Whitehead (1978, 5) was clear that his speculative philosophy ultimately requires us to complete the flight of the aeroplane; to land again "for renewed observation rendered acute by rational interpretation." I am here suggesting we in fact need to do more than just land the aeroplane. We need to let the passengers disembark. So that—after they have got their new formulations—they can do! We must ultimately focus on how to enable, enact; achieve change. So the question, again, is how?

It so happens that Management, and within this broad field, Leadership and Organization, is about Making Things Actually Happen. As Nigel Laurie, the founding editor of the journal I co-edit, tellingly entitled "Philosophy of Management," has said for many years, there is nothing that is going to replace management for understanding and crucially intervening in and changing the complex nature of our work and social lives. There is nothing called "Ungabunga" that is going to magically appear to replace Management. As any self-respecting Silverback Gorilla will tell you Management is natural; it is a Universal Feature of Purposeful Life.

As but one example close to the encyclical, consider an environmentalist who wants not just to understand the environment, global warming, the threat to the biosphere, but actually to change the way things are. She will necessarily and inevitably have to engage in environmental management. So it's time we did management properly, time we philosophers thought not just about what effect it is producing but actually thought also about how to change its focus. That would mean to change from its focus on growth, profit and GDP towards achieving the ends of another narrative. That narrative is what I term *humane becoming*, focused on the growth of people and their environment in a way that is not just sustainable but is truly regenerative—and thus beneficial to all of Nature. This requires us to appreciate the truly embedded reality of the manager and the managerial experience. That is, we must recognize that we as managers are embedded in communities of individuals. A Silverback is a Silverback precisely because of the community of individuals it is a part of, and because of the relations that exist not between them, but in the midst of them.

How might this refocus on the within-ness of a genuinely relational management play out in the way management understands people at work? It would genuinely invite and enable employees to become involved in the organization's approach to human resource management. It would develop and deliver not just policies, but also practices, that are regular, consistent, and fair. That is, management must provide a constructively positive stance in its dealings with its employees, and a genuinely inclusive ethics (as opposed to paying lip-service to the phrase). The result will be a culture soundly based on trust and selfless giving, precisely because it is properly underpinned by a thoroughly balanced (i.e. genuinely aware of the internal relations), relational understanding of people in terms of how they change and can adjust to changes in the workplace. In this way, and in contrast to the Modern organization, the constructive postmodern organization takes a process ethical approach as the appropriate way for the business to operate (see also Macklin et al, 2015).

A process perspective on managing people in the workplace is fundamentally to do with the virtues that will lead to and support desirable and constructive social interaction because it is focused on the employees, enabling people to approach their work experience aware that management qua the organization appreciate that quality of life transcends the organization itself. Management must move beyond the Modern either/or distinctions between life outside work and life inside work. This is about enabling people to "work towards a living whole in which each person plays a part" (Gare, 375). As Duston Moore notes, "value, experience, and subjectivity are always in the process of becoming, whereas intellectually complex events like human consciousness are particularly instances of the subjective experience of value" (274). In short, a constructive postmodern management practice rejects the undermining Modern fragmentation of life, work and culture. It moves beyond the economistic focus on profit and thereby takes a far more integrated view of corporate values being the sum of personal values.

For a manager to comprehend the real value of herself and others in such a living universe cosmology, requires her thoroughly to rethink her understanding of power and knowledge, away from what I call "the mini-omni god model" (2016) in which management is about the retention of knowledge to ensure power. Managers cannot continue to operate with—as the pope has indicated—a false worldview and a false premise that our exploitation of the world's resources is a function of the power God has given us. Instead it requires an approach to management as inherently "leaderful" (Wood and Dibben, 2015), in keeping with an understanding that the endpoint is not economic growth but is, rather, the *genuine* flourishing of human beings and indeed the biosphere more generally. This is important. If we are to discover, develop, or otherwise derive an ecological civilization, then that will be the result of managing towards it, and through it. There will be no route to it other than a managed one, and no way to preserve it other than through management. The management required is a philosophically informed process-relational management.

We need a self-less management deeply appreciative of the needs of others and intentionally looking to find and make the most of the good in others, for their benefit. Without this approach being more generally adopted it will not be possible to escape the enthralling nature of a 20th-century modern management as the means to acquire capital through economic growth. The challenge is significant. One manager in an organization adopting a selfless process management approach is not enough. She will be crushed, because what she says will be almost incomprehensible and cause tremendous problems. It would run entirely counter to the mainstream view. What is needed is a management practice that stems from deep consideration of the nature of management and its impact. This is philosophy as a very practical subject. The best managers, the best CEOs are philosophers. It is not possible for CEOs to operate successfully without a well-founded view of the world and their effect upon it, a view that they can convincingly communicate to others.

The problem lies partly in the orthodox ways of management thinking, founded in Cartesian ways of understanding nature and our place in it that the pope has so pointedly criticised. It lies also in traditional, secular, but biblically derived understandings of power and knowledge. These beliefs lead many managers to create an argument that is ultimately damaging to others and to the natural world. This can be felt in the difference between efficiency and effectiveness, in a time when mainstream management has come to see super-efficiency as the ultimate effectiveness. If, instead, we focus on effectiveness as something different from, and more important than, efficiency, then it is possible to think and act as a manager in a different way.

Process philosophy helps us in this endeavor. It argues not for fully determined happenings—efficient causation—but rather for an inherent freedom—effective causation. Management and many of its sub-topics must be thought of in a different way, a thoroughgoing (if inevitably incomplete) process relational way.

This way is more in keeping with, and regenerative of, Nature. It is a way that avoids the great clefts between Humanity and Nature, Mind and Body, and Subject and Object, in which we seem to exist. It looks to understand the manager in relation to herself, to other human beings, and the wider context. This can helpfully inform the ways we go about managing ourselves, others and the world we inhabit so that there is a genuine regenerative flourishing. Of course, this new understanding of management is ultimately focused on love, where love means (as Thomas Ord has defined it) "to act intentionally in sympathetic response to others (including God), to promote overall wellbeing" (29). That is to say, the act of management must involve a selfless focus on, yes, growth, but it is emphatically not economic growth. It is, instead, the intellectual and spiritual growth of the people in a manager's care, and the provision of the wherewithal to allow this to occur.

In order for humanity to "shoulder its vast responsibilities" (165), to hear and attend to "the cries of Mother Earth," Management for the New Age must concern itself with the selfless enablement of creative transformation, where selfless means not exploitative or extractive but contributive and integrative. We might thereby "include in our work a dimension of receptivity and gratuity, which is quite different from mere inactivity," find "another way of working, which forms part of our very essence," manage in a way that "protects human action from becoming empty activism," and avoid the "unfettered greed and sense of isolation which make us seek personal gain to the detriment of all else" (237).

Without comprehensively rethinking management in this way, Francis' call for action is likely to remain unanswered—and unanswerable.

References

Cobb, J. (2014). *Theological Reminiscences.* Claremont: Process Century Press

Dibben, M. (2016). *Recalibration: Towards a Process Philosophy of Management* Claremont: Process Century Press, forthcoming.

Francis (2015). *Encyclical Letter Laudato Si Of The Holy Father Francis On Care For Our Common Home.* Rome: Libreria Editrice Vaticana.

Korten, D. (2015). Korten, D. C. (2015) *Change the Story, Change the future: A Living Economy for a Living Earth—A Report to the Club of Rome.* Oakland, Ca: Berret-Koehler Publishers.

Gare, A. (2008). "Process Philosophy and Ecological Ethics." In M. Dibben and T. Kelly, eds. *Applied Process Thought Vol. I: Initial Explorations in Theory and Research.* Frankfurt: Ontos Verlag.

Macklin, R. et al (2015). "Process Ethics and Business: Applying Process Thought to Enact Critiques of Mind/Body Dualism in Organizations." *Process Studies* 43(2): 61-86.

Moore, D. (2009). "Propositions in Corporations: Unconscious and Non-Conscious Experience." In M. Dibben and R. Newton, eds. *Applied Process Thought Vol. 2: Initial Explorations in Theory and Research.* Frankfurt: Ontos Verlag, 2009.

Oord, T. (2010). *Defining Love: A Philosophical, Scientific, and Theological Engagement.* Ada, MI: Brazos Press.

Whitehead, A.N. (1978). *Process and Reality,* Corrected Edition. D. Sherburne and D. Griffin, eds. New York: The Free Press.

Wood, M. and Dibben, M. (2015). "Leadership as Relational Process." *Process Studies* 44(1): 24-47.

Management in the Context of
Integral Ecology

Vijay Sathe

John Cobb states: "The pope's encyclical points in the same direction as our conference. He speaks of integral ecology and we of ecological civilization. Both emphasize that to save the natural environment, and thereby the human species that depends on that environment, we must transform our society."

All of us who were lucky enough to attend the conference and listen to John and others would wholeheartedly agree. Among the most critical open questions is, *how*. How can we transform our society in the needed degree and direction quickly enough?

This is of course a massive undertaking to which many must contribute. My brief remarks are limited to what I have learned as a professor of management at the Drucker School over the last 30 years that may be relevant in effecting the required social transformation. My "headlines" are as follows:

"Sustainability" is now becoming incorporated into mainline management thinking. But, as the skeptics rightly assume, much of this is window dressing and greenwashing. However, there are a few serious attempts at real change. My colleagues and I have developed concepts to get companies to "tell the truth" about the real impacts of what they

286

are doing. We are engaging the management community to get them to talk truthfully about their small achievements and how far we collectively need to go to save the planet.

An increasing number of concerned top executives are telling us in private—though not as yet in public because of the fear of lawsuits from investors who do not see, or do not care—that they *support legislation and regulation* to promote measurable change to save the planet. After all, these top executives have grandchildren too, for whose future they are as deeply concerned as we are!

If one accepts the first two points, the critical question then becomes: How do we engage the increasing numbers of top executives who see the calamity that we see (but who have a legal responsibility to their stakeholders that we may or may not see) in a *fruitful dialogue* that moves us forward? I would respectfully submit that the well-intentioned rhetoric demonizing corporations that I witnessed on occasion at the conference is understandable but ineffective. It also diminishes us as human beings. Mahatma Gandhi was cited with admiration at the conference, and with good reasons that I wholeheartedly agree with. But the irony is that I doubt Gandhi would have endorsed demonizing the opposition. This is not the way he drove the British out of India. He did not demonize the British or wage war against them as others in India wanted, especially when the British were weakened and distracted during WW2. Instead he chose to support the British to rid the world of the evil that was Hitler, with the understanding that, to paraphrase: "The British are our friends. But they are like guests who have overstayed their welcome. After the war is over, we will ask them to leave." And leave they did, as friends.

I believe attempts to get corporations to change fundamentally by getting them to own up to the damage they are doing *and* by influencing public policy and regulation to level the playing field, so there is no competitive disadvantage in doing the right thing, are far more likely to succeed than casting corporations as demons to be fought. After all, the British East India Company is the model on which all modern corporations are built, so there is hope that they are more like the British than like the devil that Hitler was, and against whom Gandhi's methods, as he himself acknowledged, would not have worked.

In reading the pope's encyclical, I do not find anywhere in the 246 paragraphs even a hint of language that demonizes corporations, politicians, or anyone else. Everyone is addressed with respect and called forth to listen to their better selves for the common good. This, I hope, is the path we will choose as we move forward.

Missing at the conference almost entirely—and also almost completely in the management discussions on sustainability—is one of the root causes of what has placed our planet on a death march: CONSUMPTION. This is a biggie that no one wants to tackle, because it is just too hard to contemplate. I have been making a presentation on "The Elephant in the Room is Consumption" over the last three years and no one has challenged the premise that this is a root cause of the ills that we have wrought on the planet. But the two meta-challenges that must be tackled in order to address the root cause are just too hard to think about: (a) can the world's consumers be persuaded to consume less, especially of those things that damage the non-renewable resources of the planet, and (b) since jobs are tied to consumption, what happens to jobs and employment if we are able to get people to consume less? Recall that in the great recession of 2008-2009, consumers were implored to *buy more* to help the economy and job creation. My colleagues and I are engaging practitioners in various fields to find a way to address these seemingly insurmountable challenges.

The pope's encyclical does devote significant space (Chapter Six, I, Towards a New Lifestyle) to the dangers of excessive consumption and what must be done to address this fundamental challenge. It is to be hoped that this will provide the needed push to make progress on this front as well.

Laudato Si', the Idea of Property, and the Rule of Law

Howard J. Vogel

Pope Francis' letter to his church and to the world at large, *Laudato si',* calls us to embrace an "integral ecology" by recognizing the deep interconnectedness of ecology, economy, and equality. That is to say, we need to embrace the way in which our social life (equality) is deeply interconnected and dependent on the well-being of the Earth and all of its inhabitants and processes (ecology), so that we might rethink and reframe our relations with each other and the Earth (economy) in a way that participates in the renewing processes of the Earth as collaborative partners. Taking this call seriously will lead us to rethink every aspect of modern civilization, including its very foundations, the way we understand our experience of the land, and how we govern ourselves under the rule of law. In short, Francis has called us to understand and act on the knowledge that our interconnectedness runs all the way down to the subatomic level of the material world and includes the energy and spirit in which all are enveloped in what has been called our "planetary entanglement."[1] Out of that understanding Francis calls us to make peace with the land AND each other. To think and act in this way will lead us to a different understanding of the idea of property, as well the rule of law itself, from what has emerged in modern thought since the 17th century.

The rule of law is one of the distinctive features of our civilization. It recognizes the sanctity of each person by holding out the promise that all people are entitled to their "day in court" when they experience burdens or are denied benefits at the hands of the state or their neighbors. Thus, we say that the individual has "rights" which all others and the state are required to respect. The rights associated with the idea of property are among the most important individual rights. To be entitled to property is an important expression of an innate need and quest by humans for security that emerges in early childhood. It is not surprising that a central feature throughout the long history of property, law stretching back to the antiquity of Rome, is the *idea of possession*. Possession takes on meaning in property law because such law, rightly understood, involves *relations between individuals* rather than things—between those who possess property, often called owners, although they could be tenants, renters in our vocabulary, as well as non-possessors or non-owners. With possession comes the right to occupancy and the *right to exclude others* from the property

The idea of possession applies to both *personal* property, such as things we carry in our pockets, as well as *real* property, such as the land. The idea of possession as an important aspect of property law is part of common knowledge in the Anglo-American culture. Thus, for example, children at play can be heard to say "finders keepers, losers weepers" as they come upon something they value. Likewise, when they quarrel over whatever that something is that they found, they may be heard to say "I saw it first." And the precocious youngster in such a quarrel who has actually grabbed whatever it was that was found can be heard to say, "It's mine, because possession is nine points of the law." Perhaps you uttered these words in your own childhood play.

To be without a secure relationship to land where one can be at home is to be bereft of human agency, and human life in community with the land and each other. Hence the idea of property in law has grown to include a set of settled expectations for a person with a home on the land he or she is said to own, *to the exclusion of others*. But it has long been true in property law that there are certain *exceptions to the rights of owners*. Along with the settled expectations that come with land ownership, the idea of property is malleable and thus open to regulation by the state for the well-being of all.[2] For example, the law of "nuisance" requires that in certain limited situations, the impact of a possessor's use of the land on others in a neighborhood must be taken into consideration in conflicts between neighbors. Likewise, the idea that use of land must be considered in the larger context of the community gives the state power to regulate uses of land in a way that restricts private choices in order to serve the well-being of the entire community. Local zoning laws express this idea. But these well-known limits on land use have not been enough to protect the Earth from human actions that endanger the renewing processes of the Earth on which all depend.[3]

The costs to the Earth of the many extractive uses humans have engaged in are most often viewed as "externalities" to be excluded from the bottom line of the economic calculus that so often is the ultimate basis for making land use decisions. Thus, although the state has power to zone land use in a way that brings such uses into collaboration with the renewing processes of the Earth to the benefit of all, that power has often been used to merely "improve" the land, raising its tax value, through the action of some, to the detriment of the whole given the way the economic order has promoted an extractive rather than a collaborative relationship with nonhuman communities and the Earth on which all communities depend. Here we see how the *interconnection of ecology and economy* that Francis emphasizes has worked to deny *equality* in the destruction of the Earth and the ecosphere, with especially serious consequences for the poor. In short, the ecological crisis we face has been exacerbated by the conversion of the rule of law into an anthropocentric instrument that serves the unbounded human will of individuals in an extreme form of individualism that has undermined the larger community of life on which the individual depends. The dynamic intersection of property and industrial civilization, founded upon materialism and rampant consumption, has led to what Francis rightly calls a "throw away culture" to the detriment of the Earth and our life together.

The ecological crisis we face reveals the many ways the rule of law has become the handmaiden of the extreme individualism that now undermines the sanctity of the individual and the common good. This

is what Francis points to when he says that the result of human intervention is most harmful to the poor—but soon it will affect us all. The
participation of law in this harmful dynamic is expressed, if not entirely
caused, by the turn from classical natural law to modern legal positivism
as the frame of reference for understanding the phenomenon of law.

Natural Law theory reigned supreme from the time of the ancient
Greeks to the Enlightenment. This theory ultimately fell into serious
decline with the rise of utilitarianism which, in the 19th century, became
the basis of much modern legal positivist theory. Classical natural law
theory has as its distinctive characteristic the understanding that law
springs from and reflects enduring principles of universal application.
The source of these may be transcendent ideals, as in Plato, or the Divine
Law of God, as in the most systematic natural law thinker, St. Thomas
Aquinas. Positive law is understood by natural law theory as a human
endeavor that is law only insofar as it reflects the natural law. Classical
natural law theory takes the position that natural principles of justice can
be "discovered" and thus worked into positive law by the use of unaided
human reason. This theory ultimately places true law outside of human
limits but makes it accessible to human experience through the use of
reason. A significant feature of natural law is that it sets up the possibility
of determining whether human positive law is actually law by judging it
according to the criterion of the natural law. Thus the natural law lawyer
will declare, in the face or an apparently unjust positive law, that such a
"law" need not be obeyed since it is not law.

Legal Positivism was developed in the modern era by John Austin. It
is largely based on the utilitarian ideas of John Stuart Mill and Jeremy
Bentham. This theory of law embraces the idea that law is essentially a
general command of the highest political authority backed up by the
coercive sanctions of that authority. Further, it claims that law as a category of human behavior is distinct from morals. Thus law is understood
as imperative rather than indicative as in natural law. The conclusion of
the positivist is that law is morally neutral. Modern legal positivist theory
does not, however, deny that law has moral consequences but, rather,
rejects the idea that unjust laws are not law. The modern positivist view
of law has roots in ancient philosophy. The most immediate roots of

Austin's works are found in *The Leviathan* by Thomas Hobbes. Hobbes argued that law was the command of the absolute sovereign. For Hobbes this meant that the sovereign was superior not only to the subjects under the sovereign's law, but also that the sovereign was completely above law, unfettered in any manner by its constraints. The sovereign, for Hobbes an absolute monarch, was indistinguishable from a tyrant. Tyrannical though the power of the sovereign was to make and enforce law, Hobbes saw it as a necessity arising out of the state of nature. In the state of nature, the human was fraught by insecurity due to the threat to one's security posed by others in human society.

Modern legal positivism follows Hobbes by explicitly rejecting the notion that the members of a political society retain any rights not expressly recognized by the law of that community. Ultimately positivist theory stands opposed to the traditional concept of natural rights on the grounds that they are irrelevant and outside an empirical metaphysics. As Bentham put it, the notion of natural rights is "nonsense on stilts." In this light, individual rights, recognized under the Constitution of the United States, for example, are not natural rights, existing prior to the recognition given them by law. Prior to such recognition they are mere claims, which may be grounded in a variety of moral theories. That, however, does not raise them to legal status. Only the sovereign can do that.

Today a *deconstructive* postmodern critique of law expresses a deep skepticism about legal rules that also calls into question the idea of rights, natural or otherwise. This critique proclaims that "law is politics" and leaves us with no sense that law or politics might be animated by a purpose other than the will of those engaged in a struggle for dominance in the marketplace. The practicing lawyer is thus often left with a self-image of being no more than a hired gun, for sale to the highest bidder, in service of private will.

So what are we to do if we are to rescue the rule of law from its positivist captivity in service of extreme individualism separated from the reality of our planetary entanglement? *How might law be reformed to enable us to make peace with the land AND each other?* We must start with an acknowledgement that the critique of law is important for it shows us how law fails to live up to its possibilities for promoting justice and nurturing the life we share with the entire planet. From there we can begin to reimagine the possibilities of law in what has been called a *"reconstructive postmodernism."*[4] This can lead us to explore the possibility of thinking about the law in *neoclassical* metaphysical terms without going back to a pre-modern conception that would likely sacrifice the sanctity of the individual which modernity has brought forth. A neoclassical view of law would hold to the importance of the sanctity of the individual, but do so in recognition that t*he well-being of the individual occurs within community.* Thus, the rule of law protects the individual not as a person separated from the world, but rather as a "person-in-community."[5] Moreover, what has been called the "one commonwealth of life"[6] extending across the Earth is now a commonwealth made up of a "community of communities."[7] In this way we can fruitfully begin to rethink and reimagine the rule of law so that law can support us in collaborative partnership with the Earth and its renewing processes, rather than continue on the path that assumes we somehow own the Earth, and that we humans and our civilization can rise above and transcend the Earth itself. The transcendence that we can and do experience in our everyday life is experience we have in our relationship with and on the Earth that is our home, as well as with each other. If we are to get down to earth and come home before it is too late, our understanding of property and the rule of law needs to reflect this fact. To do this we could profitably learn from the wisdom of indigenous people for whom the land is of central importance as a relative to which they owe a duty of respect and care. Listen to the words of the Dakota poet and scholar Gwen Westerman, a direct descendant of several leading Dakota figures in 19th century Minnesota history, and imagine for a moment what the rule of law might become in the context of our planetary entanglement:

> Mni Sota Makoce. The land where the waters are so clear they reflect the clouds. This land is where our grandmothers' grandmothers' grandmothers played as children. Carried in our collective memories are stories of this place that reach beyond recorded history. Sixteen different words in the Dakota language describe returning home, coming home, or bringing something home. That is how important our homeland is in

Dakota regardless of where our history has taken us. No matter
how far we go, we journey back home through language and
songs and in stories our grandparents told us to share with
our children.

"Back home" implies a return, a cycle of returning, as if it is
expected, natural, a fact of life. Families gather around kitchen
tables and we remember the generations before us, or journeys
we make to or away from home. It is there, back home, where
we are trying to return, where we belong, where the landscape
is as familiar as our childhood beds and our mother's hands,
where our roots are the deepest. It is there, back home, where
we hear the repeated stories that make us who we are. So deep
is that connection to the land that the word for mother and for
the Earth are the same in the Dakota language: Ina.[8]

In these poetic words of communal dependency, Gwen Westerman
speaks of the deep reverence Dakota people have for their connection
with the land and each other. The wholeness of the people depends on
their relationship with each other and with the land. This recognition of
deep interconnectedness is expressed in the common phrase of greeting
offered by the people raised in the Dakota tradition to those they meet—
Mitakuyupi Owas'in (All My Relations).[9] This greeting expresses the deep
sense of interconnectedness of everything in the cosmos accompanied
by a deep respect (*Ohoda*) for it. Waziyatawin, a leading contemporary
scholar of indigenous history, herself a Wahpetunwan Dakota from Pezi-
hutazizi Otunwe in southwestern Minnesota, explains this phrase in the
following words:

> [W]hile [the phrase Mitakuyapi Owas'in] translates easily
> enough, the worldview associated with this phrase becomes
> apparent only when used in the context of the extensive network
> of other kinship terms. This is language that reflects the sacred-
> ness and interconnectedness of all creation and . . . [i]t is used in
> greetings, in prayers, in ceremonies, in speeches, and any other
> time one wants to call upon all or part of creation. Thus, uttering
> the phrase in English does not have the same depth of meaning,
> because in English, other spiritual beings are not referred to with
> a kinship term in everyday speech, even siblings.[10]

Dakota people, everywhere I have encountered them, explain this phrase as expressing the depth and quality of relationship that Dakota people have with each other in their extended kinship system and with the land, water, and skies in which the Dakota people encounter the Spirit. Out of this vast kinship, that includes the earth, the Dakota people understand they are called to a duty to act in a "good way" with a "good heart" for the well-being of all. In this way, *Ohoda* (respect) takes on an active meaning among Dakota people in the context of everything and everyone they encounter.

The challenge posed by the wisdom of the Dakota people has been embraced by Francis in *Laudato si'*. Can we embrace it so that the rule of law might be understood as a purposeful activity that enables us to reframe the idea of property and the rule of law so that we might creatively collaborate with the renewing processes of the Earth we encounter in our planetary entanglement in such a way that all might flourish together?

Endnotes

1. Catherine Keller, *The Cloud of the Impossible: Negative Theology and Planetary Entanglement* (New York, NY: Columbia University Press, 2015).

2. Laura S. Underkuffler, *The Idea of Property: Its Meaning and Power* (New York, NY: Oxford University Press, 2003),1-4.

3. Mary Christina Wood, "Part I Environmental Law: Hospice for a Dying Planet," in *Nature's Trust: Environmental Law for a New Ecological Age* (New York, NY: Cambridge University Press, 2014), 1-121.

4. David Ray Griffin, "Introduction to SUNY Series in Constructive Postmodern Thought," in John B. Cobb, Jr., *Postmodernism and Public Policy: Reframing Religion, Culture, Education, Sexuality, Class, Race, Politics, and the Economy* (Albany, NY: State University of New York Press, 2002) xiii.

5. Cobb, *Postmodernism and Public Policy,* n5,124-32.

6. Rex Ambler, a British Friend, wrote about this twenty-five years ago: "Befriending the Earth: A Theological Challenge" (*Friends Quarterly,* volume 26, 1990-1991), 17. Ambler's words are included in *Quaker*

Faith & Practice, Fifth Edition: The Book of Christian discipline of the Yearly Meeting of the Religious Society of Friends (Quakers) in Britain, 2013, in the section on the "Unity of Creation," para. 25.15.

7. Cobb, *Postmodernism and Public Policy*, n5, 137-42.

8 Gwen Westerman and Bruce White, *Mni Sota Makoce: The Land of the Dakota* (St. Paul, MN: Minnesota Historical Society Press, 2012), 13.

9. Waziyatawin Angela Wilson, *Remember This! Dakota Decolonization and the Eli Taylor Narratives* (Lincoln, NE: University of Nebraska Press, 2005), 62.

10. Wilson, *Remember This!* n10, 62.

A Revolutionary Pope Calls for
Rethinking the Outdated Criteria
that Rule the World

Ellen Brown

Pope Francis has been called "the revolutionary Pope."[1] Before he became Pope Francis, he was a Jesuit Cardinal in Argentina named Jorge Mario Bergoglio, the son of a rail worker. Moments after his election, he made history by taking on the name Francis, after Saint Francis of Assisi, the leader of a rival order known to have shunned wealth to live in poverty.

Pope Francis' June 2015 encyclical is called *Praise Be,* a title based on an ancient song attributed to St. Francis. Most papal encyclicals are addressed only to Roman Catholics, but this one is addressed to the world. And while its main focus is considered to be climate change, its 246 paragraphs cover much more than that. Among other sweeping reforms, it calls for a radical overhaul of the banking system. It states in Chapter V, Section IV:

> Today, in view of the common good, there is urgent need for politics and economics to enter into a frank dialogue in the service of life, especially human life. Saving banks at any cost, making the public pay the price, forgoing a firm commitment to reviewing and reforming the entire system, only reaffirms

the absolute power of a financial system, a power which has no future and will only give rise to new crises after a slow, costly and only apparent recovery. The financial crisis of 2007-08 provided an opportunity to develop a new economy, more attentive to ethical principles, and new ways of regulating speculative financial practices and virtual wealth. But the response to the crisis did not include rethinking the outdated criteria which continue to rule the world. (189)

A strategy for real change calls for rethinking processes in their entirety, for it is not enough to include a few superficial ecological considerations while failing to question the logic which underlies present-day culture. (197)

"Rethinking the outdated criteria which continue to rule the world" is a call to revolution, one that is necessary if the planet and its people are to survive and thrive. Beyond a change in our thinking, we need a strategy for eliminating the financial parasite that is keeping us trapped in a prison of scarcity and debt.

Interestingly, the model for that strategy may have been created by the Order of the Saint from whom the pope took his name. Medieval Franciscan monks, defying their conservative rival orders, evolved an alternative public banking model to serve the poor at a time when they were being exploited with exorbitant interest rates.

The Franciscan alternative: banking for the people

In the Middle Ages, the financial parasite draining the people of their assets and livelihoods was understood to be "usury"—charging rent for the use of money. Lending money at interest was forbidden to Christians, as a breach of the prohibition on usury proclaimed by Jesus in Luke 6:33. But there was a serious shortage of the precious metal coins that were the official medium of exchange, creating a need to expand the money supply with loans on credit.

An exception was therefore made to the proscription against usury for the Jews, whose Scriptures forbade usury only to "brothers" (meaning other Jews). This gave them a virtual monopoly on lending, however, allowing them to charge excessively high rates because there were no competitors. Interest sometimes went as high as 60 percent.

These rates were particularly devastating to the poor. To remedy the situation, Franciscan monks, defying the prohibitions of the Dominicans and Augustinians, formed charitable pawnshops called *montes pietatus*[2] (pious or non-speculative collections of funds). These shops lent at low or no interest on the security of valuables left with the institution.

The first true *mons pietatis* made loans that were interest-free. Unfortunately, it went broke in the process. Expenses were to come out of the original capital investment; but that left no money to run the bank, and it eventually had to close.

Franciscan monks then established *montes pietatis* in Italy that lent at low rates of interest. They did not seek to make a profit on their loans. But they faced bitter opposition, not only from their banking competitors but from other theologians. [3] It was not until 1515 that the *montes* were officially declared to be meritorious.

After that, they spread rapidly in Italy and other European countries. They soon evolved into banks, which were public in nature and served public and charitable purposes. This public bank tradition became the modern European tradition of public, cooperative, and savings banks. It is particularly strong today[4] in the municipal banks of Germany called Sparkassen.

The public banking concept at the heart of the Sparkassen was explored in the 18th century by the Irish philosopher Bishop George Berkeley in a treatise called *The Plan of a National Bank*. Berkeley visited America and his work was studied by Benjamin Franklin, who popularized the public banking model in colonial Pennsylvania. In the U.S. today, the model is exemplified in the state-owned Bank of North Dakota.

From "usury" to "financialization"

What was condemned as usury in the Middle Ages today goes by the more benign term "financialization"—turning public commodities and services into "asset classes" from which wealth can be siphoned by rich private investors. Far from being condemned, it is lauded as the way to fund development in an age in which money is scarce and governments and people everywhere are in debt.

Land and natural resources, once considered part of the commons, have long been privatized and financialized. More recently, this trend has been extended to pensions, health, education, and housing. Today financialization has entered a third stage, in which it is invading infrastructure, water, and nature herself. Capital is no longer content merely to own. The goal today is to extract private profit at every stage of production and from every necessity of life.

The dire effects can be seen particularly in the financialization of food.[5] The international food regime has developed over the centuries from colonial trading systems to state-directed development to transnational corporate control. Today the trading of food commodities by hedgers, arbitrageurs, and index speculators has disconnected markets from the real-world demand for food. The result has been sudden shortages, price spikes, and food riots. Financialization has turned farming from a small scale, autonomous, and ecologically sustainable craft to a corporate assembly process that relies on patented technologies and equipment increasingly financed through debt.

We have bought into this financialization scheme based on a faulty economic model, in which we have allowed money to be created privately by banks and lent to governments and people at interest. The vast majority of the circulating money supply is now created by private banks in this way, as the Bank of England recently acknowledged.[6]

Meanwhile, we live on a planet that holds the promise of abundance for all. Mechanization and computerization have streamlined production to the point that, if the work week and corporate profits were divided equitably, we could be living lives of ease, with our basic needs fulfilled and plenty of leisure to pursue the interests we find rewarding. We could, like St. Francis, be living like the lilies of the field. The workers and materials are available to build the infrastructure we need, provide the education our children need, provide the care the sick and elderly need. Inventions are waiting in the wings that could clean up our toxic environment, save the oceans, recycle waste, and convert sun, wind, and perhaps even zero-point energy into usable energy sources.

The holdup is in finding the funding for these inventions. Our politicians tell us "we don't have the money." Yet China and some other Asian countries are powering ahead with this sort of sustainable development. Where have they found the money?

The answer is that they simply issue it.[7] What private banks do in Western countries, publicly-owned and -controlled banks do in many Asian countries. Their governments have taken control of the engines of credit—the banks—and operated them for the benefit of the public and their own economies.

What blocks Western economies from pursuing that course is a dubious economic theory called "monetarism." It is based on the premise that "inflation is always and everywhere a monetary phenomenon," and that the chief cause of inflation is money "created out of thin air" *by governments*. In the 1970s, the Basel Committee discouraged governments from issuing money themselves or borrowing from their own central banks which issued it. Instead they were to borrow from "the market," which generally meant borrowing from private banks. Overlooked was the fact, recently acknowledged by the Bank of England, that the money borrowed from banks is also created out of thin air.[8] The difference is that bank-created money originates as a debt and comes with a hefty private interest charge attached.

We can break free from this exploitative system by returning the power to create money to governments and the people they represent. The strategy for real change called for by Pope Francis can be furthered with government-issued money of the sort originated by the American colonists, augmented by a network of publicly owned banks of the sort established by the Order of St. Francis in the Middle Ages.

Endnotes

1. Patricia Denise M. Chiu, "Francis, the Revolutionary Pope," *GMA News* 13 January 2015 <http://www.gmanetwork.com/news/popefrancis/story/402696/francis-the-revolutionary-pope>.

2. <https://www.jewishvirtuallibrary.org/jsource/judaicaejud_0002_0014_0_14150.html>.

3. <http://www.newadvent.org/cathen/14580a.htm>.

4. <http://ellenbrown.com/2015/02/10/why-public-banks-outperform-private-banks-unfair-competition-or-a-better-mousetrap/>.

5. <http://www.amazon.com/Hungry-Capital-The-Financialization-Food/dp/178099771X>.

6. http://www.bankofengland.co.uk/publications/Documents/quarterlybulletin/ 2014/qb14q1prereleasemoneycreation.pdf.

7. <http://www.amazon.com/Public-Bank-Solution-Austerity-Prosperity/dp/0983330867/ref=sr_1_1?s=books&ie=UTF8&qid=1371913558&sr=1-1&keywords=public+bank+solution>.

8. Richard A. Werner, "Can Banks Individually Create Money out of Nothing?—The Theories and the Empirical Evidence," *International Review of Financial Analysis* 36 (Dec 2014) <http://www.sciencedirect.com/science/article/pii/S1057521914001070>.

Building a Civilization of Love on the Foundations of an Ecological Civilization

Mark Anielski

Pope Francis' recent encyclical *Laudato si' mi' Signore* (Praise be to you, my Lord) is inspired by the invocation of St. Francis of Assisi. The new encyclical is an appeal from Pope Francis addressed to "every person living on this planet" (3) for an inclusive dialogue about how we are shaping the future of our planet. Pope Francis calls the world to acknowledge the urgency of our environmental challenges and to join him in embarking on a new path. This encyclical is written with both hope and resolve, looking to our common future with candor and humility.

The reference to St. Francis indicates the attitude upon which the entire encyclical is based, that of prayerful contemplation, which invites us to look towards the "poor one of Assisi" as a source of inspiration and as the example of "care for the vulnerable and of an integral ecology lived out joyfully and authentically" (10).

It is fitting that the pope took the name of Saint Francis of Assisi.

St. Francis is undoubtedly the patron saint of the environment and would be a champion for an ecological civilization and ecological justice. St. Francis was a model for how to love all of creation. He had a relationship with nature (birds, flowers, animals, and the land) having rejected the material and monetary wealth of his aristocratic father.

Francis espoused an ethic of right relationship with God and with nature. His Canticle to the Sun is a perfect reminder to us all that we are called to a harmonious and joyful relationship with nature; that a healthy environment is an extension of God's love.

Saint Francis reminds us that our common home is like a sister with whom we share our life and a beautiful mother who opens her arms to embrace us. The encyclical calls us to a collective cry to God for mercy as the earth cries for mercy. The path is one of humility and praise to the God who created all things and 'saw that if was all good.'

The pope uses the term "integral ecology" in Chapter 4 to explore a new paradigm of justice which means "the analysis of environmental problems cannot be separated from the analysis of human, family, work-related and urban contexts" (141), while solutions must be based on "a preferential option for the poorest of our brothers and sisters" (158).

The encyclical stresses the need for "honest and open debate, so that particular interests or ideologies will not prejudice the common good"(188). The Church does not presume to settle scientific questions or to replace politics, but it can promote dialogue on global and local governance, transparent decision-making, sustainable use of natural resources, as well as engaging in respectful dialogue with other people of faith and with the scientific world

In Chapter 6 the pope urges schools, families, the media, and the churches to help reshape habits and behavior. Overcoming individualism, while changing our lifestyles and consumer choices, can bring much "pressure to bear on those who wield political, economic and social power" (206) causing significant changes in society.

Environmental education has broadened its goals. Whereas in the beginning it was mainly centered on scientific information, consciousness-raising, and the prevention of environmental risks, it tends now to include a critique of the "myths" of a modernity grounded in a utilitarian mindset (individualism, unlimited progress, competition, consumerism, the unregulated market). It seeks also to restore the various levels of ecological equilibrium, establishing harmony within ourselves, with others, with nature and other living creatures, and with God. Environmental education should facilitate making the leap towards the transcendent which gives ecological ethics its deepest meaning. It needs educators capable of developing an ethics of ecology, and helping people, through effective pedagogy, to grow in solidarity, responsibility, and compassionate care.

This chapter calls for an "ecological conversion" highlighting St. Francis of Assisi as the model of "a more passionate concern for the protection of our world" (216), characterized by gratitude and generosity, creativity and enthusiasm.

Francis calls us to a new paradigm of ecological conversion! But how can we in the wealthier nations wean ourselves off our addition to materialism, our love of money, lives where wants exceed our needs for a good life, and where there is growing income and wealth inequality which threaten the social fabric of our communities? If we can overcome individualism, we will truly be able to develop a different lifestyle and bring about significant changes in society.

How can we move from a culture of greed (me, mine) to one of compassion, temperance (frugality) and shared responsibility? This will require a boldness to address the very spirit of modern capitalism: the nature of money itself.

If St. Francis were alive today he might be our leader to end the slavery of greed and the love of money by beginning with repudiating usury (charging interest on money creation) and introducing a money system that would be in harmony with maintaining healthy and flourishing natural ecosystems which will benefit humanity forever.

I believe St. Francis, like Pope Francis today, would agree with the proposition to create an ecological civilization. St. Francis understood that the right order of relationship in life was that all wealth and well-being come from God. That nature is an expression of God's love. His canticle to the Sun was a love song to nature. St. Francis taught us and those in power to remain humble and in thanksgiving to God who created all things, all creation with Love.

Francis' rejection of the worldly glamour of money and the material wealth of his father's textile trade in Assisi (Francis lived during the time of the crusades to Jerusalem) are role models for those of us today who want to return the world to a right relationship with the environment.

Francis would agree with us that the economy is a subsystem of a healthy natural world. Francis experienced the joy that in "giving it is that we receive." Francis had an acute and joyful relationship with the flowers of the field and the birds of the air. He understood the wisdom of the teachings of Jesus who reminded us that the lilies of the field and the birds have no concern or fear about the morrow as they live as if all will be well, and all is well.

St. Francis is the ideal patron saint of an ecological civilization and what I would propose as a civilization of love (something Pope John Paul II advocated). While some may view St. Francis' material frugality as extreme, he showed us that when we are in right relationship with the Creator and with nature (ecosystems) we experience a peace and joy that cannot be achieved in the accumulation of material things and money.

St. Francis would have been the ideal ecological economist understanding the right order of the well-being of the household (genuine economics) is closely aligned with the well-being of nature and ecosystems.

Indigenous cultures (First Nations in Canada) of North America share this same ethic; they remind us through their ceremonies of smudging (sweetgrass and sage), the peace pipe, the sun dance, and the sweat lodge that when we give thanks and tribute to the Creator for all that we have, then we have the chance to live a healthy economic life. I have had many experiences with First Nations elders who remind me that beginning with a thanks to the Creator for all that is gifted us results in meetings and relationships that seem to operate more smoothly.

Indigenous cultures teach us that our economic well-being cannot be separated from the well-being of the natural environment. To do so is a sign of insanity. In essence, our villages/cities and the environment are our common home. Indeed, the words economic and ecology share the same root word *oikos*, from the Greek meaning "home" or household.

We have created an economy based on the errant teachings of Ayn Rand (who inspired neoclassical economists such as Milton Friedman and Allan Greenspan), which is founded on a belief in individualism and greed rather than our natural human inclination of love, compassion, and altruism. We are hardwired to be in relationship with others and with nature.

Yet we are told that to survive in this harsh world, we must protect our own interests (hedonistic), hoard money, live a fragmented and contradictory life, and experience dis-ease. Each person tries to save himself or herself, in his or her own corner. Everyone follows his/her own interest. But there is a "community salvation" that starts from the inclusion of the weak, a valuable resource for an integral ecology.

The encyclical invites us to put into practice the common good: where the city and our environment are our common home.

Pope Francis' encyclical is a bold reminder to the world to heal our relationship with nature and Mother Earth and come back into "right relationship" (a Buddhist virtue). Moreover, we are to get the relationship with money and material wealth in the right order, as an integral part of a healthy ecosystem.

While I am encouraged by the pope's encyclical both as a professional ecological economist and a practicing Roman Catholic, I feel he has not gone as far in locating one of the key sources of our ecological crisis. I believe this source is our complex relationship with money and material things. In the wealthier countries (measured in terms of GDP per capita), we see a pandemic of fear about money; either not having enough or having too much. We seem addicted to feeding our wants even though most of our needs have been satisfied. We have, as Pope John Paul II said in 2003, come under a kind of spell of consumerism and materialism. He challenged the world to go beyond the current obsession (idolatry) with the market to building a civilization of love.

> Authentic development can never to attained solely through economic means. In fact, what has become know as the 'idolatry of the market'—a consequence of the so-called civilization of consumption—tends to reduce person to things and to subordinate being to having.

> This seriously detracts from the dignity of the human person and makes promotion of human solidarity difficult at best.

> Instead, recognition of the spiritual nature of the human person and a renewed appreciation of the moral character of social and economic development must be acknowledged as prerequisites for the transformation of society into a true civilization of love.

In this context we cannot fail to be concerned that an eclipse of the sense of God has resulted in an eclipse of the sense of man and of the sublime wonder of life to which he is called.

The tragic calamities of war and dictatorship continue to disfigure violently God's loving plan for humanity, so too the more subtle encroachments of increasing materialism, utlitarianism, and marginalization of faith gradually undermine the true nature of life as a gift from God.[1]

My other main concern with the teachings of Pope Francis is that he fails to address the fundamental driver of our economic systems and the basis of our ecological crisis, which is, in part, the very nature of our debt money system that currently consumes roughly 30-50% of global GDP in the form of hidden interest payments. The hidden cost of unnecessary interest costs in everything we buy and sell is the key reason that economies have to keep growing, measured in terms of GDP. Herman Daly taught me this in 1999 when I first met him while working on the update to the U.S. Genuine Progress Indicator (GPI). Herman compelled me to consider this issue the most important inquiry in my ecological economics career.

I have located the source of our economic growth addiction (more GDP) to the nature of money itself. The vast majority (98%) of modern money today is created in the form of private bank debts. When banks issue loans such as mortgages and when people carry a credit card debt balance, brand new money is created literally out of thin air. The problem with this system of money creation, which is called "fractional reserve banking," is that money creation is disconnected from real assets such as nature's capital. In a just, ecological civilization the creation of money would be tied to the goals of maintaining healthy and flourishing ecosystems. Ecological economists have contributed enormously to calculating the value of ecosystem services in the hopes of getting other economist to pay attention to the true value that nature's asset contribute to the economic well-being of society. Most of these ecosystem services, including the pollination services of bees, have no real replacement value in money terms. I can't imagine a day without bees when we would have to employ robots or paint brushes to pollinate plants! The idea that there would be sufficient money, human energy, and built capital to replace the services provided by bees (for free) is preposterous!

Most people have no idea that the total accumulated debt of nations and the world can never ever be repaid no matter how much the GDP grows. Through the power of compound interest the U.S. total outstanding debt (now $60 trillion) has been doubling every 7 years since 1981. In another 7 years, the U.S. will have reached $120 trillion. Even now the U.S. debt imposes on each U.S. citizen a burden of $0.35 in interest costs on every dollar spent in the economy for life's goods and services. This means the average American will work a third of their life just paying for the interest payments on the collective debt of the nation. What most don't realize is that this is completely unnecessary as money could be created without debt and without the interest burden if governments assumed this responsibility rather than private corporations (banks). The total amount of U.S. national federal debt of the government now costs the U.S. tax payer more in interest charges than what is spent on the annual military budget, the largest expenditure item in the budget.

What if 30-50 percent of our need to grow the economy because of unnecessary interest charges on un-repayable private bank debts were removed from the economic equation? We would quickly remove a significant amount of carbon imbedded in these interest costs, freeing up human energy and providing new and discretionary human energy and capacities to rapidly increase renewable energy capacity and retool our economy to achieve the goals of an ecological civilization.

Pope Francis has not yet entered into the thorny issue of monetary policy and the nature of money. Perhaps he is reluctant to provoke the "money power" (a term Thomas Jefferson, Andrew Jackson, and Abraham Lincoln used to refer to private banks) and challenge the world's bankers to a new moral and ethical standard of creating money without usury (charging interest) but for the good of the common wealth and humanity's well-being, rather than private gain.

I have proposed to Pope Francis in an open letter delivered to his office in the Vatican that he consider writing his next encyclical on money, usury (charging interest on debts), and fractional reserve banking. I quote Jesus himself in my letter who taught us that the Lord's Prayer should use the following words:

"Forgive us our debts, as we forgive our debtors."

At some point in history, the Church replaced the word "debt" with "trespasses." A trespass is certainly different from a debt; to trespass is to "enter the owner's land or property without permission."

I have proposed that the nature and power over money creation be fundamentally tied to the goals of healthy ecosystems; namely flourishing watersheds that yield good water supply. I have been working with a few First Nations in Canada including the Algonquin of the Ottawa (Adawe) watershed in Quebec to demonstrate how money creation could be linked directly to maintaining a flourishing watershed with vibrant ecosystem services. Instead of creating money in the form of debt (which effectively mimics the cancer cell consuming the energy of the host over time), money creation would be closely tied to maintaining clean water, clean air, habitat for birds and bees, and a steady state of natural resources for human needs (e.g. trees for building homes). I have demonstrated that when properly "valued" as a natural "asset" on the balance sheet of a Nation, healthy ecosystems can deliver a steady flow of economic benefits and ecosystem services in perpetuity.

St. Francis reminds us that he had to reject the money power of his father's merchant class in order to pay proper attention to the song of nature and to God. St. Francis understood that it is the love of money, not money itself, which was the source of his own dis-ease and distraction from being in right relationship with God and nature.

I look forward to a future encyclical when Pope Francis raises the issue of the nature and future of money. I have offered my services to help in authoring this next encyclical; one that will help to lead the world towards the vision for an ecological civilization.

Endnotes

1. John Paul II, "Address to the New Ambassador of the Czech Republic," 28 April 2003. <http://w2.vatican.va/content/john-paul-ii/en/speeches/2003/april/documents/hf_jp-ii_spe_20030428_ambassador-czech-rep.html>.

Foundations for an Eco-Ecclesiology

Rebecca Ann Parker

I am rejoicing! Pope Francis has clarified Christianity's love for this world. In the encyclical *Laudato si'*, "Praise Be," he soundly counters any notion that the core of Christianity is primarily "other worldly," unconcerned with the fate of the earth and its creatures. He grounds his encyclical calling for a global commitment to protect "our common home" in St. Francis' splendid canticle that lifts all creation in song. In doing so, Pope Francis brings forward an ancient, often-forgotten stream of Christian spirituality that can help us now as we face the devastating impact of humanity's ecological irresponsibility.

Well before the twelfth century when St. Francis called the sun brother, the moon sister and earth our mother, Christianity's earliest teachers reveled in a deep love for the sacred goodness of the earth. They taught that paradise—replete with refreshing waters and life-sustaining trees and plants—was not closed, not lost at the beginning of time, and not postponed to another world. Rather, its blessings and gifts permeated every region of the earth; Christ re-opened paradise, and humanity's spiritual responsibility was to receive the gifts of paradise with gratitude and use them wisely, so that just and abundant life would be available to all.

Hippolytus of Rome, writing in the second century, acknowledged that some thought paradise existed only in heaven, but he argued that the rivers and streams "which we can see today with our own eyes" flow from their source in paradise and demonstrate that paradise is not otherworldly but earthly. In the fourth century, Augustine, who called the world "a smiling place," taught that the seeds of God's first garden have now been scattered throughout the world, distributing the gifts of paradise to the whole of creation and enabling us to encounter paradise everywhere.

Paradise, in the understanding of ancient Christians, was not a place of innocence and purity—after all, the serpent dwelt in the garden and the earthly home for all life included the tree of the knowledge of good and evil. Paradise was a place that required struggling with evil and learning to know and choose the things that assure abundant life. As citizens of paradise, human beings needed to develop wisdom, maturity, and discernment to make life-sustaining choices, rather than choices that led to death. Bishop Ireneaus envisioned the Church, with its teachings, rituals, and ethical guidance to be a planting of "paradise in this world." Christian sanctuaries, as concentrations of paradise, were filled with vibrant images of life that evoked the Garden of Eden—blue rivers, green meadows, sparkling skies, spiraling vines laden with fruits, trees, flowers, fish, birds, animals, and beloved ancestors and saints gathered in the presence of the living Christ. No crucifixions were depicted during nearly the first thousand years of Christian history— blood sacrifice had no place in paradise. The purpose of the Church was to make paradise tangible and its blessings accessible. Through religious life together, communities of people were to learn and to practice how to live rightly in paradise. Rituals taught people to "taste and see that God is good," to know themselves as created in the image of God and to be anointed like Christ "to bring good news to the poor." Spiritual practices, such as distributing food to the poor and ministering to the sick, trained people in the virtues and ethics suitable to paradise. In our book *Saving Paradise*, Rita Nakashima Brock and I have called the cultivation of such spiritual maturity "ethical grace."

Ephrem of Syria, a fourth-century Eastern Christian who wrote thousands of lines of poetry on paradise while living in the war-torn borderlands between the Persian and Roman empires, spoke of paradise as "the life-breath of this diseased world." He celebrated the gifts of paradise—accessible in this present world—as a healing balm in the midst of wounding events and a source of sustenance for traumatized souls. "The soul pastures on God's beauties," he wrote and exulted:

> Paradise surrounds the limbs
> With its many delights:
> The eyes, with its handiwork,
> The hearing, with its sounds,
> The mouth and the nostrils,
> With its tastes and scents.[1]

These early Christian teachers lived with a sensibility that would delight today's process theologians and ecologists. They saw that earth's beauty is comprised of interactive relationships, diversity, and movement. The fourth century theologian, Macrina, offered her observation:

> We see the universal harmony in the wondrous sky and on the wondrous earth; how elements essentially opposed to each other are all woven together in an ineffable union to serve one common end, each contributing its particular force to maintain the whole . . . the heat of the sun, for instance, descending in the rays, while the bodies which possess weight are lifted by becoming rarefied in vapor, so that water contrary to its nature ascends . . . how too that fire of the firmament so penetrates the earth that even its abysses feel the heat; how the moisture of the rain infused into the soil generates, one though it be by nature, myriads.[2]

Pseudo-Dionysius echoed her sentiments a century later, writing of the love formed in "the innate togetherness of everything . . . the intermingling of everything . . . the unceasing emergence of things . . . traveling in an endless circle through the Good, from the Good, in the Good and to the Good."

This ancient Christian understanding of the earth as an interactive community of life, blessed and permeated by the Spirit of God, shines through in the pope's encyclical. Though he does not discuss the paradise spirituality of early Christianity (and therefore neglects some teachings and insights that are worthy of further development), the pope takes care to connect his earth-loving assertions with a multitude of Christian voices from diverse cultures around the globe as well as those of people of other faiths and no-faith, along with the testimony of the scientific community. He lifts up the teachings of the Catechism, "God wills the interdependence of creatures. The sun and the moon, the cedar and the little flower, the eagle and the sparrow: the spectacle of their countless diversities and inequalities tells us that no creature is self-sufficient. Creatures exist only in dependence on each other, to complete each other, in the service of each other" (86). He approvingly quotes Ecumenical Patriarch Bartholomew, whose perspective as a present-day Eastern Christian clearly carries forward the ancient Christian understanding of the earth as holy ground. Bartholomew writes that we are called "to accept the world as a sacrament of communion . . . the divine and the human meet in the slightest detail in the seamless garment of God's creation, in the last speck of dust of our planet" (9). The pope notes that the bishops of Japan affirm the inherent worth of all creatures—made not for human use, but to be of value in themselves: "To sense each creature singing the hymn of its existence is to live joyfully in God's love and hope" (85). This spiritual awareness leads the bishops of Brazil to call for the cultivation of "ecological virtues" so humanity can relate rightly to "the Spirit of life [which] dwells in every living creature" (88).

The theological and spiritual grounding present in the pope's encyclical establishes anew the ancient foundation of Christian faith—love for the world, respect for the interdependence of all life, humble acceptance of human responsibility and power to care for the gifts of creation and assure their just sharing for the well-being of all, rejection of the misplaced notion that the earth belongs to human beings who have the right to rule over it, affirmation that biodiversity is a sign of God's creativity and presence, and respect that all life forms are of intrinsic—not utilitarian—value.

Taken as a whole, the pope's clarification of Christianity is in sharp contrast to the dominant and dominating economic practices in which most of humanity is now implicated and on which, it seems, our way of life depends. These practices assume a very different set of core values: that earth is of utilitarian value, that human nature is defined by individual self-interest, that survival is a competition, that limits on consumption threaten economic growth, and that economic growth is the most important end to be served. A more dramatic conflict of values is hard to imagine, and it is not surprising therefore that those who put their faith in current economic practices are raising an outcry of opposition to the pope, suggesting that the pope has overstepped his bounds. He should only be concerned with "spiritual" matters, they declare. Ironically, the pope's opponents want Christianity to be other-worldly! But it is not. As Francis has so eloquently re-established, Christianity calls its proponents to love this world that God loves and to love all creatures as our neighbors with whom we are bound in interdependent life. Paradise present here and now is a blessing, a holy gift and a sacred trust—not only for ourselves but for all creatures and for generations to come.

God's paradise and human empires

"It's not an Empire, it's a planet"—reads a popular bumper sticker. Ancient Christians understood that their view of this world as God's paradise countered the claim of the Roman Empire that the empire was the source of peace, justice, and abundance for all. Christian teaching— like prophetic Judaism—asserted a counter-imperial faith in a source of life that did not exploit human labor and land, oppress resistant cultures and communities, wage wars for control of territories, or use violence to subjugate and control. The ethics of paradise required the practice of nonviolence, generosity, and mutual assistance—understanding that all are dependent upon the abundance of the community of life and must engage in life-sustaining acts of interactive interdependence: As Ephrem of Syria explained:

> The inhabitants of the world fill in the common need
>   from the common excess.
> We should rejoice in this need on that part of us all . . .

Our need for everything binds us with a love for
 everything.
One person falls sick—and so another can visit and help him;
One person starves—and so another can provide him with
 food and give him life;
One person does something stupid—but he can be
 instructed by another and thereby grow.[3]

The global economic empire that dominates today is failing profoundly to support this kind of life-sustaining interdependence. Instead,
as the pope so vividly describes, humanity's exploitation of earth's ecosystems is inextricably bound up with patterns that harm the poor, intensify
the widening gap between those who have much more than enough and
those struggling for life. The pope refuses to separate love for the earth
from neighbor love and exposes how significantly the two are linked.
He writes,

> A sense of deep communion with the rest of nature cannot be
> real if our hearts lack tenderness, compassion and concern for
> our fellow human beings. It is clearly inconsistent to combat
> trafficking in endangered species while remaining completely
> indifferent to human trafficking, unconcerned about the
> poor, or undertaking to destroy another human being deemed
> unwanted. This compromises the very meaning of our struggle
> for the sake of the environment. . . . Everything is connected.
> Concern for the environment thus needs to be joined to a
> sincere love for our fellow human beings and an unwavering
> commitment to resolving the problems of society. (91)

Here is where the wisdom of ancient Christians may be most helpful. They understood religious community to be the training ground
and sustaining context for resistance to the exploitations and injustices
of empire. Today, we face the daunting challenging of finding ways to
extricate ourselves from the systemic structures of evil that are destroying the planet's life-systems. Entangled in unsustainable ways of life,
poisoned by the performance of values so contrary to our spiritual and
ethical traditions, how do we find liberation from the false world view
implicit in the economic empire that dominates our lives?

Toward an eco-ecclesiology

The two thousand or so Earth activists, scholars, artists, and religious leaders who gathered in Claremont in June 2015 sought to bring their best thinking to bear on the call to "Seize an Alternative" and lay the foundations for an ecological civilization. In the context of that global gathering, with the values of process philosophy guiding our efforts, our working group on "Reclaiming Love for Paradise Here and Now" sketched out some ideas for an eco-ecclesiology, inspired by the paradise spirituality of ancient Christianity.

Our work included a series of questions worthy of reflection:

1. Given the threats to sustainable life posed by the intertwined structural evils of ecological exploitation and economic injustice, what resources from Christianity's first millennium might hold potential to be helpful and life-saving now?

2. How might we creatively adapt these resources to forge in our cultural settings an alternative ecclesiology for a just and sustainable ecological civilization?

3. Where and how do we detect the toxic legacies of sanctified violence in present patterns of ecological exploitation and economic injustice? What frameworks do we see emerging in diverse communities, congregations, and cultural contexts that are life-giving, resistant spiritual alternatives to these toxic legacies?

4. How do human beings become what Earth needs us to be—resilient, responsible, loving, restorative, and life-sustaining participants in "this present paradise," a living, inter-dependent web of life torn by legacies of trauma and injustice and permeated by the divine presence of ongoing creativity and love?

5. How might a transformed approach to ritual, baptism, and Eucharist strengthen a spirituality of responsive love for this world, here and now?

6. How might contemporary religious communities orient themselves to discerning ethical and spiritual guidance arising from the Earth itself?

7. Taking seriously that a culture's "read" of the natural world is shaped by its religious, philosophical, spiritual, and moral frameworks, what hermeneutical approaches to "nature"—including ourselves as part of nature—might be advisable practices for an eco-justice ecclesiology?

8. How might we draw on the sacred scriptural traditions in the Hebrew Bible to relate to the natural world as a source of ethical imperative, ultimate concern, and wisdom?

9. What practices in sacred spaces and places attune us more effectively to the presence of paradise here and now and nourish our vocation to live rightly as citizens of paradise?

10. What acts of creative resistance and recovery are needed to counter life-harming systems and environments, especially with respect to the visual worlds we create, as well as the sacred gathering and living places we construct?

11. How might the mission and purpose be defined for an eco-ecclesiastical community? What might be the spiritual grounding, structure, rituals, spiritual practices, system of decision-making, and leadership, etc.?

Eco-ecclesiology envisions religious communities that, like the ancient Christian church, train and sustain human beings in life-giving and life-sustaining ways of being in right relationship with one another and with the planet. Eco-ecclesiology embraces the power and possibility of integrative ecological spiritual communities as communities of resistance to the dominant "empire" and tangible manifestations of abundant life, Eco-ecclesiology is experienced in practices that nourish joy in the present gifts of paradise. It recognizes how much is enough, respects limits, exorcises our souls from the toxins of alienating consumerist values, defends life-systems and at-risk communities and cultures from harm, and engages in actions of repair and renewal where eco-systems and lives are being profoundly damaged.

Eco-ecclesiology recognizes that individual ethics and efforts are not sufficient. We need transformed and tangible experiences of life together grounded in the values of interdependence, reverence for the

Earth, commitment to the flourishing of the whole human family and all life forms. Eco-communities, spiritually grounded in integrative, holistic and transformative practices, are one way to move towards an eco-civilization.

Working-group participants, noted by Sheri Prud'homme, lifted up these thoughts:

1. Religious community can be a training ground for people to negotiate change and loss and to experience a foretaste of new, sustainable ways of living.

2. Churches are native plants, struggling to survive in an environment filled with invasive species. Resistance matters.

3. The Church fulfills its purpose of promising abundant life for people and for our communities, by creating ways for people to:

    a) Dwell together in a weekly space and place that is an environment of beauty, with good things for the eyes and ears and mouth—music, flowers, simple good food.

    b) Partake in rituals that honor the goodness of life's blessings, mourn loss, grapple with difficulties.

    c) Foster affection and friendship.

    d.) Come together to face together what is happening in their lives and in the world that is depleting or harming life.

    e) Learn the spiritual practices and spiritual wisdom of life-sustaining and life-honoring traditions.

    f) Open to the wellsprings of saving grace—however those wellsprings may be known, named, and accessed (God, Jesus, Spirit, Spirit of Life, etc.).

    g) Engage in small groups on a weekly basis to ask: How is it with your soul? What are you thankful for? What are you grieving? What do you see happening in the world and in our community that is harming life? What are the structural evils that are impinging on us and how do we resist them?

h) Develop capacities to see through the guises that structural evil wears in our lives and world and develop approaches to resist—or share wisdom on how to resist or re-orient.

i) Learn spiritual disciplines and practices to recover from being addicted to consumerism.

j) Join one another in community gardening, feasting together on good food grown together.

k) Bring the values learned at church into workplaces and vocations—connecting church with world through the work people are doing in their daily lives.

The simplicity of this vision is part of its strength. "Simplify, simplify, simplify!" Thoreau implored. This simplicity—like that of St. Francis—is far from innocent, naïve, or powerless. It has a gentle force, like the greening energy of earth itself. Its potential impact can be measured in the amount of opposition it generates. Jesus was crucified because, as a prophet of paradise, his ways of healing, teaching, and loving threatened a mighty empire. Opposition is incidental, however. What matters is persistence in the ways of abundant life.

Pope Francis has urgently called the global community to this persistence. For Christians, Jesus is the model; religious community is the path; the earth itself is a blessing; and the spirit of life is celebrated as at work in all things, offering the possibility of creation's renewal. Christianity has no exclusive claim on the wisdom and ethical energy needed now. Rather it has a set of values, traditions, spiritual understandings, and practices that can contribute to the global common good. As Ephrem noted fifteen centuries ago,

> Our need for everything binds us with a love for
>   everything . . .
> In this way the world can recover;
> Tens of thousands of hidden ways are to be found,
> Ready to assist us.[4]

Now is the time to embrace this wisdom with fierce devotion.

Endnotes

1. Ephrem, *Saint Ephrem: Hymns on Paradise,* trans. Sebastian Brock (Crestwood, NY: St.Vladimir's Seminary Press, 1990. 109-10.

2. Macrina, "On the Soul and the Resurrection," in Amy Oden, ed., *In Her Words: Women's Writings in the History of Christian Thought* (Nashville, TN: Abingdon Press, 1994) 50.

3. Ephrem, *Heresies* 10:9, quoted in S. Brock, *Luminous Eyes,* 166.

4. Ephrem, *Letter to Hypatius,* quoted in S. Brock, *Luminous Eye,* 167.

PART
FIVE

Multi-Faith,
Multi-Cultural Responses

Indigenous Wisdom and Pope Francis' Encyclical Letter

Chris Daniels

When I first heard that Pope Francis was issuing an encyclical on the environment and ecology I was hopeful and excited that such an influential person was taking a public stand on arguably one of the most important, and certainly the most critical issues humanity and the world has ever faced. When content of his letter was leaked just prior to the official release I was even more hopeful, both by the content I was able to access, and the obvious compassion and commitment it portrayed. But it wasn't until I read the full document that the scope of his knowledge, understanding, and compassion was revealed. At that point I came to believe that this letter in its entirety is a "must read" for anyone concerned with environmental issues, whether Christian or not. The sheer breadth of his knowledge and understanding of the moral, social, economic, political, religious, and scientific issues enables him to drive home a message on the urgency of action if humanity and the world are going to survive this crisis.

In as much as this encyclical can be read as a comprehensive way of gaining information on the breadth of issues involved, it is ultimately, and rightly, a call to moral action. It is a prescription on the ethical responsibility we, as human beings, have toward all aspects of the environment, and how we have to change our perspective in order to survive. We cannot continue to believe that the mere application of more technology will solve the problems that technology started in the first place (60). Expecting these problems to disappear by simply expanding the materialistic and mechanistic practices and methodologies that led to the current crisis will not get us out of it. We need to move away from an amoral paradigm of unchecked consumerism and technological advancement based solely on personal and corporate profit that does not take into account the ethical responsibility we have to all worldly creatures, including humans, as well as all of creation, and ultimately to the divine.

In this document Pope Francis also acknowledges the values and community awareness that he feels are vital in moving forward toward a solution; those values that the world's Indigenous cultures exemplify to this day in spite of the violence and oppression they have suffered. He recognizes how local individuals and groups, including aboriginal communities, have a "greater sense of responsibility, a strong sense of community, a readiness to protect others, a spirit of creativity and a deep love for the land" (179). They are also, he says, "concerned about what they will eventually leave to their children and grandchildren." These characteristics are sadly lacking in those that seek to exploit the world's natural resources for personal and corporate profit, but are "deeply rooted in indigenous peoples." Pope Francis stresses that aboriginal communities should be the principle dialogue partners when mainstream society's activities impact the environment:

> They are not merely one minority among others, but should be the principle dialogue partners, especially when large projects affecting their land are proposed. For them, land is not a commodity, but rather a gift from God and from their ancestors who rest there, a sacred space with which they need to interact if they are to maintain their identity and values. When they remain on their land, they themselves care for it best. (146)

These words illustrate the pope's understanding of indigenous peoples' deep connection and relationship to land, as well as how that connection, and the sacred ceremonies that accompany and maintain it, are vital to their identity creation, both personally and communally. They certainly have proven, over tens of thousands of years, that when left to their own devices they care for the land best, and we have much to learn from their wisdom.

So, in spite of Christianity's past historical record that includes its active participation in the destruction of indigenous cultures, languages, communities, and both personal and communal identity, as well as the unchecked exploitation of the natural world, Pope Francis, through this letter, envisions moving forward in a way that recognizes the many misinterpretations of biblical teachings that in the past have justified destructive hegemonic attitudes of dominion (66-67). He promotes a vision of the world, God, and the best path forward toward an ecological civilization, that I believe parallels the Indigenous worldview and wisdom that the church previously sought to eradicate. As cynical and hypocritical as that might sound, I find it profoundly hopeful and inspirational.

The balance of this short response, which I hope to expand on in the future, will concentrate on a few of these parallels and how adopting such wisdom may help mitigate the severe consequences of our previous actions that we must now deal with. Not being Indigenous or aboriginal myself I do not presume that I can speak for, or speak *from* an Indigenous perspective, but I can point out what I believe are similarities to what aboriginal scholars, elders, and leaders have identified as their ways of knowing and understanding both the world and the divine. These similarities, explicitly stated by Pope Francis, include that:

1. Everything is related and interrelated, and these relationships constitute reality as an integral whole including ourselves, the natural world, and the divine;

2. The "common good" includes and extends to future generations;

3. If we truly understand and feel these first two truths it will deeply affect our choices and determine our behaviour;

4. We have lost what it means to be "human" in relationship with the natural world and must reconnect with the land to rekindle those relationships;

5. Because everything is related there is reciprocal responsibility to all aspects of creation;

6. Everything in creation has intrinsic value in and of itself, regardless of whatever instrumental value it may or may not have;

7. An "ecological approach becomes a social approach" thereby requiring adequate responses to instances of social injustice that take into account both "the cry of the earth and the cry of the poor"; and

8. The divine mystery (God) is present in all aspects of creation, as all creation is present in it, and Creation is therefore deserving of love, respect ,and reverence for its own sake.

Pope Francis quotes a number of previous popes and patriarchs when establishing his position that humans, the natural world, and God are intrinsically interwoven, including Pope Benedict who stated that "the world cannot be analyzed by isolating only one of its aspects since the book of nature is one and indivisible" (6), and Patriarch Bartholomew who said "it is our humble conviction that the divine and the human meet in the slightest detail in the seamless garment of God's creation, in the last speck of dust of our planet" (9). Throughout the letter Francis reiterates this fundamental understanding with such comments as "Because all creatures are connected, each must be cherished with love and respect, for all of us as living creatures are dependent on one another" (42), "Creatures exist only in dependence of each other to complete each other, in the service of each other" (86), and "our relationship with the environment can never by isolated from our relationship with others and with God" (119). However, his most passionate and poetic comments are when he is referring to the writings of his namesake, Francis of Assisi, who speaks of the natural world in kinship terms and "would call creatures, no matter how small, by the name of 'brother' and 'sister'" (11), such as "Brother Sun," "Sister Moon," "Brother Wind," and "Sister Water." This appears to be how the pope is suggesting we fundamentally conceive of our relationship with God and the world.

As far as aboriginal scholars and leaders, such as E. Richard Atleo, Shawn Wilson, Black Elk, Vine Deloria Jr., and Cree Elder Pauline (Fishwoman) Johnson are concerned, this relational way of understanding the world and the divine is primordially foundational to all other aspects of Indigenous belief and practice. Atleo speaks of *tsawalk*, or the oneness of all creation (Atleo, *Tsawalk*); Wilson states that we *are* the relationships that we hold and are part of (Wilson 80); Lakota Elder Black Elk says "The chief proposition of the universe is relationality" (Atleo, *Tsawalk* 30); Vine Deloria Jr. says a central tenet of Native worldviews is that: "everything in the natural world has relationships with every other thing and the total set of relationships makes up the natural world as we experience it" (Deloria 34), and Fishwoman says "We are human beings on this planet and we are the two legged, but everything out there—we acknowledge that they are part of us, part of our life, part of who we are, and we are part of them"(Daniels 120).

From statements such as these I would argue that a relational way of understanding reality forms the basis of most, if not all, Indigenous worldviews; it is a perspective that permeates beliefs, practices, and identity creation. Therefore, as it was for St. Francis of Assisi, all of creation is thought of in kinship terms because we truly are related. Pope Francis points out throughout his letter that because of such relatedness we have a responsibility to all creation in the same way we do for family and "if we feel intimately united to all that exists, then sobriety and care will well up spontaneously" (11). This responsibility, as pointed out earlier, also extends into future generations and what is to be left as a legacy. These sentiments go to the heart of what North American First Nations' mean when they say "We are all related," and that no decisions can be made without taking into account "the seven generations that come before and the seven generations that come after." If we were to truly understand and embody this wisdom it would not only change our decisions, but the whole decision making process. As the pope says "Such a conviction [of relatedness] cannot be written off as naïve romanticism, for it affects the choices which govern our behaviour" (11).

This perspective of interconnectedness and relational responsibility extrapolates to all the other points made earlier. Once the world is understood as constituted by relationships, which includes the divine, it follows that everything in creation has intrinsic moral value, not just the instrumental value that past biblical interpretations came to conclude, which conclusion forms the basis for much of the exploitation of natural resources with a disregard for any sense of moral responsibility. The pope states "It is not enough, however, to think of different species merely as potential 'resources' to be exploited, while overlooking the fact that they have value in themselves" (33). Because of this universal intrinsic value everything in creation is owed respect and moral consideration. It also becomes obvious that social justice for one must be social justice for all. A truly ecological approach has to include justice for humans as well as the environment. We cannot think in terms of saving one aspect of creation, such as endangered species or environmental habitats, without also considering those humans who have been most oppressed and taken advantage of. Often, because those same people are also those living closest to the land, such considerations are one and the same. Recognition and reconciliation for what has been done in the past and is still being done today to our most vulnerable communities, particularly to our aboriginal peoples, cannot be separated from questions of environmental justice and responsibility in an interconnected world. Francis says:

> Disregard for the duty to cultivate and maintain a proper relationship with my neighbour, for whose care and custody I am responsible, ruins my relationship with my own self, with others, with God and with the earth. When all these relationships are neglected, when justice no longer dwells in the land, the Bible tells us that life itself is endangered. . . . These ancient stories, full of symbolism, bear witness to a conviction which we today share, that everything is interconnected, and that genuine care for our own lives and our relationships with nature is inseparable from fraternity, justice, and faithfulness to others. (70)

In a world constituted by relationships that includes the divine, such as is understood in most, if not all Indigenous cultures, the great mystery is typically understood panentheistically; a view in which God is in the world and the world is in God, thus forming an intrinsic point of interconnection and relatedness that imbues sacredness and value to all things. For me, this vision of God is one of the boldest and most courageous religious positions Pope Francis takes in this document. He clearly states that God can be found as an integral aspect of creation, rather than the ontological separateness of creation and Creator that is so often found in Western religious thought; that "soil, water, mountains: everything is, as it were, a caress of God" (84). And more clearly:

> The universe unfolds in God, who fills it completely. Hence, there is a mystical meaning to be found in a leaf, in a mountain trail, in a dew drop, in a poor person's face. The ideal is not only to pass from the exterior to the interior to discover the action of God in the soul, but also to discover God in all things. (233)

With the divine included in such relational thinking, religious imperatives and moral responsibilities coincide. One's ethical responsibility to creation, including other human beings, is interlinked with one's religious obligations to the divine. Actions toward one constitute actions toward the other. Sins against one are sins against the other. All decisions and actions, no matter how large or small, affect all others. Francis says, "Nothing in this world is indifferent to us" (3), and "Our relationship with the environment can never be isolated from our relationship with others and with God" (119).

As I stated earlier, and is clearly illustrated by such comments, there is no doubt that this encyclical is a call for moral action. It is a plea to put a sense of ethical responsibility toward all of creation back into our decision-making process in all aspects of human social life, whether economic, political, technological, religious, or personal. This recognition of shared responsibility and connectedness can manifest in something as small as taking seriously a personal commitment to recycle and reuse whenever possible and much needed water conservation, or something as large as corporate responsibility toward the environment and its inhabitants, both human and nonhuman.

With such strong parallels between the position he is taking and the Indigenous perspective, it seems clear to me that Pope Francis, however unknowingly, is calling for what Okanagan scholar Jeannette Armstrong has termed the "re-Indigenization" of humanity, and I have elsewhere called "becoming Indigenous." In this context "Indigeneity" is understood as a social rather than racial or political paradigm in that it is a way of living, respecting, and connecting with the land, and through the land, the rest of creation and the divine. It is also an acknowledgement that indigeneity in that sense is something shared by all people's ancestors and can therefore be rekindled by all of us. It is a way of understanding the world as constituted by relationships that must be respected and maintained in order to remember what it means to be authentically human. It is also a reminder that bringing a sense of moral responsibility toward all aspects of creation, both present and future, into the decision making process may be our only hope of surviving the crisis we have created. What I am suggesting is that any move toward an ecological civilization based on the alternative perspectives and moral actions suggested by the pope can be considered a step toward becoming more Indigenous.

This is the wisdom our indigenous peoples have been telling us for hundreds of years, and that our own indigenous ancestors knew and lived by. We just haven't been listening carefully enough or taking it seriously. Hopefully, now, with someone like Pope Francis bringing it to our attention, we may begin to.

Works cited

Atleo, E. Richard. *Tsawalk*. Vancouver: UBC Press, 2004.

Daniels, Jaki. *The Medicine Path: A Return to the Healing Ways of Our Indigenous Ancestors*. Calgary: Hearthlight Publishing, 2014.

Deloria Jr, Vine. *Spirit and Reason*. Golden, Colorado: Fulcrum Publishing, 1999.

Wilson, Shawn. *Research Is Ceremony: Indigenous Research Methods*. Halifax: Fernwood Publishing, 2008.

Reflections on *Laudato Si'* and the Debt to Ecology, Culture, and Society

Toni M. Bond Leonard

Pope Francis' encyclical on climate change offers humanity profound insights on what it will take to create solutions to our current ecological crisis. Many process philosophers and theologians have noted the important parallels between *Laudato si'* and the process concepts of becoming and interrelatedness. *Laudato si'* begins by referencing Saint Francis of Assisi and the interrelatedness of humans to the earth.

Traditional African spirituality and wisdom cultures have long understood the unique connection to, and relationship with, nature and the divine. Ecowomanist activist-scholar and author Layli Phillips writes that what is needed is "a social change perspective based on a holistic perception of creation encompassing humans and all living organism plus the nonliving environment and the spirit world."[1] She writes that a healing framework is needed, one that honors a collective human-environmental-spiritual superorganism through intentional social and environmental rebalancing as well as the spiritualization of human practices.

Like process thought and ecowomanism, forms of traditional African spirituality and wisdom acknowledge the interconnectedness of the earth, humans, and the spirit world, but also recognize how human greed and mass consumption have collectively contributed to the degradation of the environment. Pope Francis' encyclical affirms the voices of environmentalists who continue to warn us about climate change, water privatization, deforestation, etc. He also affirms process thinkers who insist that the planet's future sustainability is dependent upon humans adopting a new ecological consciousness that recognizes the interrelationship between all human and nonhuman forms of life. Pope Francis' encyclical challenges humans to rethink not only their relationship to the earth, but to each other. Vandana Shiva lifts up Pope Francis' use of the phrase "integral ecology," which recognizes the inter-relatedness of society and culture, ecology, and economics.[2] Certainly the pope's manifesto delivers a message of love and compassion, as it also calls for a renewed relationship between humanity and nature. However, it resonates just a bit less loudly for this black womanist who walks in a continued double-consciousness of the historical roots of 1) Christianity and the transatlantic slave trade and 2) the devaluation of traditional African spirituality and wisdom through colonization and the coloniality of power.

Traditional African spirituality and the environment

Forms of traditional African spirituality like Ifá are grounded in an ecological and spiritual framework of maintaining the human-environ-mental-spiritual balance. The spiritual foundation of Ifá rests on three pillars: the Orisha, who represent aspects of nature; ancestral worship, the primary channel through which knowledge and wisdom are gained and a way to honor the departed; and divination, a systematized way to foresee the future to divine one's path and destiny.[3]

Like ecowomanism, the natured-based aspects of Ifá are closely tied to precepts of communality and relationality. For example, two tenets of Ifá are that one must never initiate harm to another human being or to the universe and that the spiritual, physical, mental, and emotional realms of our existence must all work together in harmony and bal-ance. At the heart of the Ifá tradition is the belief that Oludumare, the Supreme Being, is in all things. Oludumare is the essence of all living and inanimate things, thus, there is no separation between human beings, nature, and the earth.

Ifá recognizes the interconnectedness and interdependence of all existence through Oludumare as the life force. As humans are connected to and dependent upon each other, there is a corresponding connection between even the rock, water, or tree, as all forms of existence, human, nonhuman, and matter have the common thread of the life force of Oludumare. This universal view of interdependence and relationality upholds a broader perspective of the divinity of all forms of existence and supports the tenet of not committing acts that would harm the universe.

The term Orisha combines aspects of the human consciousness with divine consciousness.[4] The Yoruba word "Ori" means the "human consciousness embedded in human essence, and the word 'sha' expresses the ultimate potentiality of that consciousness to enter into or assimilate itself into the divine consciousness."[5] There are eight primary Orishas, with each Orisha representing some aspect of the universe and life force. Oludumare oversees the power of each of the Orishas, as they represent the various divine elements of the Supreme Being. The Orishas are personifications of Oludumare. Through their nature-based attributes they serve as a "vehicle to God-consciousness."[6] This God-consciousness is central to the understanding of the delicate balance of the universe and human beings' role in maintaining that harmony.

The pope's encyclical references respect and special care for indigenous communities and their cultures, highlighting the important fact that indigenous cultures already comprehend the delicate balance between humans and nature, understanding that nature is, in fact, divine. Yet, the pope makes no direct reference to the divine wisdom that was suppressed in the African continent through colonialism and the labeling of traditional practitioners and healers as backwards or witch doctors. This repression continues as both science and modernity have used academic and philosophical knowledge to invalidate anything tangentially related to traditional forms of knowledge and wisdom.

We cannot move forward as if the past has not happened and now we wish to save the planet. Creating a sustainable planet must include social, economic, and political redress for the historical atrocities that resulted in stolen land, devastated economies, and suppressed cultures. This suppression has worked to the benefit of greedy, globalizing multinationals in their efforts to keep people from being connected to their land in a meaningful way. Black womanist theologian Karen Baker-Fletcher points out that the forced separation from the African continent of Black people disconnected them from their relationship to the land.[7] She further posits that this separation has led to the "nihilism and despair in black communities."[8] How can we really hope to create a sustainable planet that values all forms of life and cultures when there has been no restitution to the ancestors of the humans stolen from one part of the world and taken to create economic wealth and prosperity in another part the world? Colonizers have been exploiters of the planet and, through the enslavement of Africans, assumed the role as masters of both humans and nonhumans. Not only must those who have raped and pillaged lands and humans "repent," but there must be restitution, reciprocity, and reconciliation if there is to be an authentic effort to achieve balance and harmony with the planet.

Sharing and sacrificing: toward the common good

Laudato si' calls upon humans to engage in a spirit of sharing and to replace consumption with sacrifice. Pope Francis makes reference to philanthropic efforts that lack consistency and to the concentration of wealth in privileged sectors of society. Sacrifice by the poor looks very different from sacrifice by the affluent. Pope Francis notes that the "climate is a common good, belonging to all and meant for all" (23). The common good of all means that the privileged few must no longer be allowed to sustain themselves upon the backs of the impoverished multitudes. The debt owed to the poor and oppressed needs to be repaid in full, not partially. The rights of poor people to live a life consistent with their inalienable dignity means access to food, shelter, health care, work, and safety, all of which are needed in order to fulfill the grave social debt owed to poor people and the planet. Our world cannot in good conscience ask those among us living in poverty to sacrifice anything else. Rather, realizing the common good of all means that the spirit of sharing and sacrifice can only be genuine when the ones being asked to share and sacrifice are not those who already live off a meager subsistence.

Threads of denying women bodily self-determination

I would be remiss if I did not reflect on paragraph 23, which contains Pope Francis' comment that abortion is incompatible with a concern for the protection of nature. It is a misrepresentation of the realities of women's lives when we apply a reductionist lens to the issue of women's bodily integrity and self-determination. Unintended pregnancies cannot be reduced to merely being "uncomfortable or inconvenient" as Pope Francis notes. Rather, the larger discussion must be about the lack of access to women-controlled methods of family planning that empower women to space their pregnancies. Women, especially poor women of color, are caught in a quagmire between population control advocates who continue to blame them for the worldwide population explosion and anti-choice advocates who not only want to deny them access to safe abortion services, but also the means by which to control their fertility through birth control and comprehensive reproductive and sexuality education. The World Health Organization reported that 4.6 million (74 percent of all under-five deaths) occurred within the first year of life in 2013.[9] If we are truly to embrace the cultures and conditions of peoples' lives, then we cannot overlook the anti-choice sentiment of this particular section of the encyclical and how it disaffirms women's self-determination, especially that of women in developing countries who are at higher risk of infant and maternal mortality and morbidity. Instead, what is needed is a reproductive justice analysis that affirms a woman's moral capacity to make ethical decisions about reproduction that are in her best interest, that of her family, and the community in which she lives. We cannot separate the life of the human embryo from that of the woman. The collective common good must also acknowledge what is unethical about forcing a woman to bring forth a child with no social or economic supports.

Endnotes

1. Layli Phillips, "Veganism and Ecowomanism," in *Sistah Vegan: Black Female Vegans Speak on Food, Identity, Health, and Society,* ed. A. Breeze Harper (Lantern Books, 2010), 8.

2. Vandana Shiva, "Shiva on Francis's Manifesto," *Pando Populus,* 22 June

2015 <http://www.pandopopulus.com/shiva-on-franciss-manifesto/>. Accessed July 8, 2015.

3. Toni Bond Leonard, "The Middle Way and Way of the Orishas A Comparative Study of Buddhism and Ifá" (unpublished paper, Claremont School of Theology, 2014), 5.

4. Baba Ifa Karade, *The Handbook of Yoruba Religious Concepts* (Boston: WeiserBooks, 1994), 23.

5. Ibid.

6. Ibid., 28.

7. Karen Baker-Fletcher, *Sisters of Dust, Sisters of Spirit: Womanist Wordings on God and Creation* (Minneapolis: Augsburg Fortress, 1998), 53.

8. Ibid.

9. World Health Organization, Infant Mortality, 2015. <http://www.who.int/gho/child_health/mortality/neonatal_infant_text/en/>. Accessed July 9, 2015.

Hope Lies in Change

Zhihe Wang & Meijun Fan

The message Pope Francis delivers is very profound and also encouraging. To Chinese eyes, that the pope casts his hopes in terms of "integral ecology" seems very much like what the Chinese have been calling "ecological civilization," which has become very popular in China today. This idea was first officially proposed by the Chinese government at the 17th Congress of the Communist Party of China. The goal is to form "an energy and resource efficient, environment friendly structure of industries, pattern of growth, and mode of consumption."[1]

This concept reflects an important change in the party's understanding of development. Rather than emphasizing economic construction as the core of development, as it did in the past, the party authorities have come to realize that sustainable development must be based on an understanding of an intertwined relationship between humanity and nature. At the 18th Congress, held from Nov. 8-14, 2012, President Hu Jintao mentioned "Ecological Civilization" fifteen times in his report. The Congress even wrote ecological civilization construction into the CPC constitution for the first time. Hu said, "We must give high priority to making an ecological civilization, work hard to build a beautiful country, and achieve lasting and sustainable development of the Chinese nation."[2] Hu gave ecological civilization a prominent position by incorporating it into the country's overall development plan together with economic, political, cultural, and social progress. In his report, Hu called for efforts to keep more farmland for farmers and leave to future generations a beautiful homeland with green fields, clean water, and a blue sky. Not long ago, Chinese President Xi Jinping, also general secretary of Chinese Communist Party, stressed that "We should never judge a cadre simply by the growth of gross domestic product (GDP)."[3] What he said signaled an intention: The authorities are determined to shake off GDP obsession in promoting officials. This is a very important change, given China's political environment, which will greatly help turn the scales in favor of ecological civilization. At an important meeting held on July 2, 2015, Xi emphasizes that "the officials who have harmed ecological environment will be prosecuted" and bear lifelong consequences for their actions.[4] It is apparent that this is the alternative that conference goers were urged to "seize" at the June 2015 gathering in Claremont.

We notice that the pope is critical of many features of modernity and what it calls "progress," but he does not call for wholesale rejection. It is safe to say that his hope is for what we have been calling a "Second Enlightenment," which can also be called a postmodern Enlightenment, because it is not a complete rejection of the modern Enlightenment but an integration of "many of its greatest achievements."[5]

The core value is respect for others. But "others" refers not only to other people, other nations, and other countries, but also to the non-human community.

1) The imperialistic attitude toward nature

The inperialistic attitude is disrespectful toward nature. Starting from an anthropocentric stance, this attitude treats nature as an object to be conquered, manipulated, dominated, and exploited by humankind. Nature was treated as a slave under the imperialistic attitude. This attitude is closely related to the disrespect for women, because both nature and women are seen by the Western culture as "irrational, uncertain, hard to control, fuzzy."[6] Therefore, it is a "mission impossible" to liberate women from men without fighting against the imperialistic attitude toward nature.

2) The nihilistic attitude toward tradition and the past

The nihilistic attitude toward tradition and the past refers to a radical rupture with tradition and the past. In Europe, the past was treated as "dark ages." In China, tradition, the past, was treated as trash that should be totally and completely abandoned. "Down with Confucianism" was the most famous slogan of the modernizers. Such a radical rupture with tradition made us cut off the intrinsic link to our own tradition, making us abandon a lot of excellent spiritual resources in our tradition such as "respect for the heaven and awe for the Dao" and "harmony with difference."

Also, it is the nihilistic attitude that causes the loss of faith or values crisis in China today. Because of the absence of faith in any divinity, it is very easy for people to treat something secular as the object of worship, such as science or money. That explains why scientism and the worship of money are so widespread in China and in the West as well.

3) The contemptuous attitude toward farmers and peasants

This attitude is closely related to the two attitudes above. "Land" is a synonym for "nature," and farmers and peasants are the persons who are closest to the land. Therefore, contempt toward farmers and peasants constitutes an important component of the First Enlightenment. Farmers, being conceived as "backward," have been looked down upon by modern society.

In China, peasants have been a main target of attack. They have been treated as "stupid, narrow minded" and deemed to be a stumbling block to the progress of Chinese society. They have been treated as those who need to be enlightened. Likewise, organic farming means "backward" and "poverty." Thus, it is no wonder that it has been suppressed. This to a large extent explains why small farms have been declining in both the West and China.

4) Worship of science

Science is worshipped by first Enlightenment thinkers. Science was asserted by them as the only correct and valid way to know the universe. All other ways to know the universe, such as religious, artistic, intuitional, and emotional were viewed as unscientific; therefore, they should be suppressed and demolished. In this sense they were committed to scientism or science chauvinism. According to Li Yusheng, scientists in China deeply believed that truth was on their side and the progress of China would totally rely on them. "I believe in science, therefore, I am superior to you both mentally and morally."[7] Most scientists held such an arrogant attitude toward their adversaries when they debated with them. Chen Duxiu, one of the leading Enlightenment thinkers in China, claimed that only science and democracy could save China from "all dark sides including political, moral, academic, thought Levels."[8]

There is little doubt that science has made a great contribution to promoting human civilization. However, it is very dangerous to put science as an object of worship. It is this worship that makes people both in China and the West neglect the limits of science. In fact, the Western science that Enlightenment thinkers worshiped was based on Newtonian physics, characterized by mechanism and reductionism. While this has been very successful in many fields, it went wrong in others in crucial respects.[9] The world was viewed as a machine, with nature "a dull affair, soundless, scentless, colorless."[10] In Max Weber's phrase, the world is disenchanted by modern science. According to Ulrich Beck, it is this science that constituted "a potential cause of civilization-induced mass immiseration."[11]

5) The worship of reason

Closely related to the worship of science, is the worship of Reason. The first Enlightenment has been regarded as an "Age of Reason," because "Reason becomes the unifying and central point of the century, expressing all that it longs and strives for, and all that it achieves."[12] Enlightenment thinkers believed that Reason, especially "pure reason" which is "untainted by emotion, sensate knowledge, social constructions, and noncognitive awareness,"[13] was the driver of progress and could build a brand new civilization.

However, history has shown that Reason with a pure pedigree not only failed to improve the human condition but also failed to solve the problems of the oppression of women and of Blacks. Reason did not keep its promise to bring us a beautiful new world. In contrast, it has brought us a fragmented world that is facing a serious crisis. All of these results are closely related to the weaknesses of reason. One of the weaknesses of reason, in my opinion, is its lack of a moral dimension. It separates itself from value. Reason has become limited to instrumental reason, which oppresses anything irrational. It is both player and judge. In this sense, it is a dictator.

The second shortcoming of modern reason is its compartmentalization. Reason has various forms such as social reason, political reason, economic reason, technical reason, functional reason; each of them dominates one part of human life. The dominance of these "reasons" can be viewed as "the defining feature of modern industrial society."[14] However, there is no longer any "reason" that perceives human society as an organic whole and considers its long-term development. Modern reason is good at calculating precisely, but lacks any integrative, far-reaching perspective.

Closely related to above, the third shortcoming of modern reason is its individualism, which assumes selfishness as the only drive of human activities.

Rational people only care about maximizing their interest and have no interest in taking into account the consequences of their actions for others.

6) The one-dimensional understanding of freedom

Freedom was a ubiquitous slogan of the Enlightenment. It played a very positive role in encouraging people to fight against the oppression of feudal tyranny. However, the concept of freedom that Enlightenment thinkers promoted has its limits, which unfortunately have been ignored. Briefly speaking, freedom was understood abstractly by Enlightenment thinkers; that is, they understood freedom from a merely individualistic perspective. They not only referred freedom to freedom from others but also equated freedom with absolute freedom, without any constraints. These limitations of the first Enlightenment share responsibility for the current crisis—ecological, social, and spiritual. In order to survive these crises, a second Enlightenment is called for.

The second Enlightenment is a transcendence of the first enlightenment. Although it is not an easy task to summarize the defining features of the second Enlightenment, we offer to sum them up under the following six aspects. (1) It goes beyond anthropocentrism and promotes ecological awareness. (2) It goes beyond discrimination against women, and it calls for honoring farmers. (3) It goes beyond both West-Centrism and East-Centrism and promotes complementary awareness. (4) It challenges homogenizing thinking and appreciates the beauty of diversity and plurality. (5) It goes beyond a "one-dimensioned view of freedom" and toward a deeper freedom with responsibility. (6) It goes beyond instrumental reason and calls for an aesthetic wisdom

There is little doubt that ecological civilization badly needs such a Second Enlightenment because it is impossible to create a new civilization apart from fundamentally changing people's mindsets. While modernity is still powerful in China, fortunately, more and more Chinese have realized that another alternative is possible. This is partly due to the efforts of process thinkers and constructive postmodern thinkers.

In a survey conducted by the People's Forum Poll Research Center, a national-level survey center, about "The Most Valuable Theoretical Point of View in 2012," the view of Yijie Tang was selected as the best analysis. Tang is one of the leading philosophers in China and teaches at Peking University. He described the situation in China as follows.

> At the end of the last century, Constructive Postmodernism, based on process philosophy, proposed integrating the achievements of the First Enlightenment and postmodernism, and called for the Second Enlightenment. The two broadly influential movements in China today are: 1) "The zeal for traditional culture" and 2) "Constructive Postmodernism." If these two trends can be combined organically under the guidance of Marxism, they can not only take root in China, but further develop in a way that in future, with comparative ease, China can complete its "First Enlightenment" in realizing its modernization, enter into the "Second Enlightenment" very quickly, and become the standard-bearer of a postmodern society.[15]

Although creating an ecological civilization has become the consensus of the whole of China, the path to ecological civilization holds perilous twists and turns given China's present complex situation. Huge population, limited natural resources, economic inertia inherent in diverging from a development model focusing only on GDP, and resistance from vested interest groups all present major challenges to change. But we agree with John Cobb's prediction: "China is the place most likely to achieve ecological civilization."[16]

The reason is that China is a nation of process thinking that understands the universe "in terms of processes rather than things, in modes of change rather than fixed stabilities."[17] Chinese not only have faith in a dynamic harmony of nature and humankind, but also have faith in change and transformation. In ancient Chinese, the opposite of the word "poor" is not rich, but change. And *Yi Jing (The Book of Changes),* says, "Poor leads to changes, changes in turn lead to finding a way out, and in turn *enable sustainability.*" This ancient wisdom would guide the Chinese people toward the "integral ecology" the pope proposes and the Second Enlightenment and ecological civilization toward which it is now directed.

Endnotes

1. Hu Jintao's report at 17th Party Congress. <http://www.china.com.cn/17da/2007-10/24/content_9119449_4.htm>.

2. <http://v.china.com.cn/18da/2012-11/11/content_27074139.htm>.

3. <http://news.xinhuanet.com/world/2013-10/07/c_117609149.htm>.

4. <http://news.china.com.cn/2015-07/02/content_35959561.htm>.

5. Thomas Altizer, "A Holistic, Un-alienated Theologian," in *John Cobb's Theology in Process,* ed. David Griffin & Thomas Altizer (Philadelphia: Westminster Press, 1977), 3.

6. Andrew Dobson, *Green Political Thought* (London & New York: Routlege, 1995), 192.

7. Lin Yusheng, "The Rise of Scientism in China since May 4th." *Science Times,* 7 June 2006.

8. Duxiu Chen, "Defense of *New Youth.*" *New Youth.* 1919, Vol. No.1.

9. Charlene Spretnak, *The Resurgence of the Real* (New York: Routledge, 1999), 21.

10. Alfred NorthWhitehead, *Science and Modern World*, 1925 (New York: The Free Press, 1967), 54.

11. Ulrich Beck, *Ecological Enlightenment* (New Jersey: Humanities Press, 1995), 50.

12. Ernst Cassirer, *The Philosophy of the Enlightenment* (Princeton NJ: Princeton University Press, 1951), 5.

13. Charlene Spretnak, *The Resurgence,* 220.

14. Water F. Baber & Robert V. Bartlett, *Deliberative Environmental Politics: Democracy and Ecological Rationality* (London: MIT Press, 2005), 19.

15. Yijie Tang, "The Enlightenment and its Difficult Journey in China," *Wen Hui Bao,* 14 November 2011 <http://theory.people.com.cn/n/2013/0110/c49165-20158762.html>.

16. Junxian Liu, "China is the Place Most Likely to Achieve Ecological Civilization—An Interview with Constructive Postmodern Thinker John Cobb," *Journal of China Executive Leadership Academy Pudong* 3 (2010).

17. Jan B.F.N. Engberts, "Immanent Transcendence in Chinese and Western Process Thinking" *Philosophy Study* 6 (2012): 377-83.

Constructing LOHO Communities with Confucian Wisdom

Liao Xiaoyi (Sheri Liao)

I rejoice that Pope Francis can find in the Christian tradition the basis for developing "integral ecology" and is calling the world to do so. What he seeks is much the same as what in China we call "ecological civilization." I have been working for this for many years. I am quite sure that an integral ecology arises best out of rural villages inhabited by farmers who live close to the land. In China this can best be developed on a Confucian basis.

I have just come from a village in China, where my team and I are constructing LOHO communities with Confucian wisdom, which can be expressed in two Chinese characters, one is "Le" (乐), another is "He" (和). LOHO (**Life Of HarmOny**) connects with the fountainhead of traditional Chinese culture at one end and walks into common people's lives at the other end.

The core ideas of LOHO include difference, complementation, mutualistic symbiosis, embodied as respect, communication, and inclusiveness. Taoism holds, "'He' (和) is commonsense; being aware of 'He' (和) is knowing righteousness." Confucianism states: "'He' (和) is the highest Tao in the world." Contemporary people say: ordinary people feel happy; the society is in harmony; and happiness exists in the harmonious relationship of Heaven, Earth, and human beings.

The universal value in it is how to rebuild the relationship with other people, with the earth and with one's self. To put it in five aspects, it is to actualize the harmony between individuals and groups by governing in the sense of LOHO, to actualize the harmony between things and persons by living in LOHO communities, to actualize the harmony between emotion and intelligence by observing LOHO rituals and righteousness, to actualize the harmony between justice and benefit by living in the LOHO perspective, and to actualize the harmony between body and mind by keeping healthy in the sense of LOHO. The five aspects can go in balance in a system in which they mutually reinforce each other.

I can't agree with Professor Cobb more on this viewpoint: we are standing here not to restore the environmental problems here and there but to lay a foundation for the shared sustainable development of human beings, that is, for an ecological civilization. Each of us shares the responsibility for exploring a path to the new ecological civilization.

As an ordinary Chinese citizen, I have been searching for such a path for 40 years.

Forty years ago, I, aged twenty, was a student of the Philosophy Department in Sichuan University, in which I became a teacher after graduation, working there for five years teaching undergraduates philosophy. My ideal then was to become a philosopher, one who was at home with Western philosophy, so in those eight years, three years of a college student majoring in philosophy and five years staying in the same place as a teacher of philosophy, I was sedulously infatuated with Western philosophy and fascinated by such thinkers as Kant, Hegel, and Heidegger.

Eight years later, I felt it was not enough for us just to study their philosophical thinking; we needed to study how to employ this philosophical thinking in the work of modernization. So I've managed to study further in the Philosophy Department of Zhongshan University as a postgraduate for three years and conduct research in the Chinese Academy of Social Sciences for five years, focusing on Western modernization. I wanted to figure out how China could walk onto the path of the Western modernization. However, in the process of this research, I found a problem; that is, the Western world has encountered environmental problems, global environmental disasters that might destroy human life.

It was possible that the consequence of our laborious work might be that we human beings have no future. What should we do? Again I turned to the West for help to learn how it protects the environment.

Thereafter, I spent a third eight years seriously learning and practicing the Western model of environmental protection. At that time, I was strongly confident that there would be hope as long as we followed the Western road of environmental protection. Thereupon, I should say I fulfilled my first aspiration; that is, I managed to go to the United States as a visiting scholar, majoring in international environmental politics, and to get in touch with a few nongovernmental organizations. At one point I was involved in New York, in the preparation for the World Conference on Women. Nongovernmental organizations from many countries such as Brazil, India, and Kenya, were involved, but none were from China. I went there to make a documentary—*Daughter of the Earth*. People saw me as a rare species when I arrived there, believing I was a Japanese or Korean instead of a Chinese, for no Chinese individuals or civil organizations were working to protect the environment. This so greatly upset me that I returned to Beijing 20 years ago, in 1995, and made my 2nd dream true in March 1996; that is, I managed to found a Chinese non-governmental organization of environmental protection—Global Village of Beijing Environmental Culture Center.

With the establishment of the Global Village, I threw myself into doing three green things: green media, green community, and green life. (1) **Green media.** For five years we produced a 10-minute TV program—*Green Time*—in CCTV-7 starting at 6:15 every Saturday. We went on with the work on green media. (2) **Green community.** We thought, regardless of their jobs and titles, people lived in communities, and if environmental protection could be conducted in communities, it could reach and involve every individual. So we began to try building green communities. We also promoted the construction of green communities in Beijing. (3) **Green life.** We thought we should choose an environment-friendly lifestyle and so organized many activities of green life, including China Action on the Earth Day of 2000.

As a follower of Western environmental protection, I was also accepted by the field of environmental protection in the West. In 2000,

I was invited to Norway to receive the Sophie Prize, an international environmental award, which is given to one individual or organization per year, and which was given to a Chinese citizen in 2000.

It was on this occasion that I felt stimulated and upset again, for when I was asked by the Sophie Foundation to talk about Chinese culture, including Buddhism, Taoism, and Confucianism, I could tell little. They had even invited some actors from a Peking opera theatre to perform there. They expected to find some new ideas as to how to handle the big environmental issues from a Chinese like me. This made me feel deeply guilty and ashamed. Although I was Chinese, I knew little about Chinese culture.

I read the confusion they felt about Western environmental protections from their expectations for Chinese culture, and this made me confused, too. When I was shooting a film on *The Journey of Global Environmental Protection* in Europe, at a recycling station, I met a fashionable young woman, an environmentalist as she claimed, who would go to collect garbage in the recycling stations every one or two months. But when she opened her heavy sack, I saw many items good enough for her to open a boutique. How much time could we have to care about our bodies and souls if we take environmental protection only as material consumption? Was it the future of environmental protection if we turn ourselves into a machine of consuming, producing, and recycling material items? How much capacity does nature have to support a lifestyle like ours? How many resources have we exhausted to pursue for material comfort? Were we happy? Were we healthy? What on earth was the aim of development? What on earth was the meaning of life? What should we Chinese do, when the Western world expected to discover the wisdom of the East from which they could find a solution to the contradiction between human's infinite desire to develop and the finite resources of nature, and when they were persistent in protecting the environment in a fragmentary manner by depending solely on technological investment without changing their lifestyles or taking responsibility?

It was in the process of this exploration that I encountered process philosophy and constructive postmodernism, from which I managed to find answers to many of my puzzles. Whitehead has given me what Kant and Heidegger failed to offer. On page 7 of his *Process and Reality,* Whitehead explicitly stated that his *philosophy of organism seemed* to approximate more to some strains of Chinese thought (than to Western Asiatic, or European, thought).

As a reflection on and rectification of the modernism that abuses technology in a fragmentary, potent, and excessive manner, process philosophy and constructive postmodernism lay stress on wholeness, differentiation, and the organic way of thinking, and propose a mode of existence with ecological economy, organic farming, natural health, ecological architecture, spiritual arts, and simple living, which are consistent with the surviving wisdom that has supported Chinese civilization for five thousand years. Derived from ancient Chinese wisdom, LOHO is coincident with the thought of process philosophy and constructive postmodernism.

What touches me more deeply is that Dr. Cobb, Dr. Griffin, and other leading figures of the constructive postmodern community favor traditional Chinese culture and are optimistic about China's potential. They hold great expectations of China and view China as the hope of ecological civilization. I feel honored to have received the first "John Cobb Common Good Award" in 2007. This prompted me to go further on my journey to seek the roots of Chinese culture. I started to work hard at the study of ancient Chinese civilization: Buddhism, in which all living beings are considered equal; Confucianism, upholding such virtues as humanity, justice, propriety, and wisdom; and Taoism, which advocates following and learning from nature. There is one thing held in common by all these traditions—seeking harmony: the harmony between heart and brain, the harmony between body and mind, the harmony between justice and benefit, the harmony between individual and group, and the harmony between things and persons. I feel I have found the answers to my puzzles when I returned to our traditional life wisdom that has lasted for thousands of years.

How can we cultivate ourselves according to these ideals? How can we restrict our desires and transform them to what is referred to as the "capacity of the mind" that can bring us health and to the "capacity of the body" ("Qi" as it is called) that can bring us happiness? How can these help individuals obtain happiness from their families, parents, and friends? All these help me come up with my realization of the Chinese-style of environmental protection: it is not merely an idea but also a wisdom and operational technology.

However, where can we see and touch such culture under the impact of the global wave of urbanization and industrialization? I've found hope in the rural areas of China, based on my years-long investigation in villages, and after making the long documentary of the rural areas of nine nationalities in China, such as Han, Zang (Tibetan), Mongolia, Miao, Dong. There still exists the philosophy characterized by differences, complementation, and mutualistic symbiosis. There still are villages that have managed to survive. In many developed countries, there are farms without rural communities; there are farm workers without farmer culture; there is agriculture without agronomic skills. There are villages in China with ecological systems that are not yet altogether covered by concrete; where native culture has not yet been desolated. Therefore, there still are possibilities to establish a complex ecosystem composed of dwellings, industries, health-keeping, native culture, and self-consistency of the rural communities.

What comes next is how to transform the traditional rural wisdom into the modern modes of rural construction, and how to create actual examples of LOHO villages. In 2008, when I was 54 years old, my Global Village team and I walked into a disaster-hit area and conducted an experiment: constructing a LOHO community together with the local government and villagers. By "constructing a 'Le He' community", we meant to participate jointly, share governance, build eco-houses, undertake eco-industries, protect environment, preserve people's health, and constitute a eco-village. We attempted to make true the five LOHO ideals in a mountain village at an altitude of 1300 meters with steep mountain paths. It was on such a path that I received a phone-call, inviting me to receive an international award—"Global Citizen Award" given by the Clinton Foundation.

I figured that it might be a bit different this time if I wore a cheongsam when receiving the award on the podium, compared with the last time when I had been in a Western-styled suit. I was no longer a simple follower; I was a disseminator, inheriting and disseminating Chinese wisdom. I felt that I got responses from the world on the spot when I delivered the concept of the three capacities and our attempts to integrate the body, spirit, and the abstinence from desires into environmental protection. Three times Clinton expressed to me that he was startled by my address about Chinese wisdom.

A week later, I returned to Dapingshan, took off my cheongsam, put on my working clothes, and went on building eco-houses and eco-farms together with the villagers. The following 8 years was the time when the social-work team of the Global Village, together with the local government and villagers, kept improving the LOHO idea and the LOHO mode.

You know? According to the measurement done by our architect academician, an eco-house we build can conserve energy and reduce carbon emissions by 60%; according to the data provided by the Food and Agriculture Organization of the United Nations, the transformation from oil agriculture to ecological agriculture can reduce coal-burning by 80%. This is the way we need to conduct environmental protection; the hope lies only in a holistic world view and a systematical plan to live sustainably and well.

LOHO became more and more acknowledged and accepted by the society and government. Our Daping LOHO community was given the Most Influential Award of the China Charity Award issued by the Ministry of Civil Affairs of China. In 2010, as a social work organization, a team of the Beijing Global Village went to my home village, Wuxi, Chongqing, where I was born, to offer technological service for constructing a LOHO community by collaborating with the local government, focusing on the service for the left-home group. In 2013, we were invited by the Changsha County Government to build LOHO villages in three villages and then in 25 villages a year later and then in over 200 villages of the whole county in 2015, from which we see the hope of starting the Chinese-style environmental protection from the grass roots in China.

In 2014, we went to Qufu, Shangdong, the birthplace of Confucius, where we saw the power of environmental protection within the traditional culture itself. This is our Academy Village, an experimental village. They chose to use this area to construct an experimental eco-farm, in which there is a food education workshop where villagers take out their farm tools to have an exhibition; children can role-play the story of the Chinese cabbage; people can talk about the harm that chemical pesticides can do to the human body and to the fields. There is a school focusing on studies of Chinese traditional culture and ancient civilization, where our social workers give lectures to the villagers on such virtues as "humanity, justice, propriety, wisdom, honesty; as well as diligence, goodness, fairness, introspection, and harmony". Here, the villagers are learning to sing *Great Harmony*, when Great Tao prevails, the whole world is but one community. Here, children accompanied by their mothers are reading *Hsiao Ching* (*The Classic of Filial Piety*), learning to observe filial piety to those who accompany them in their daily life. Thanks to the environmental education and the increase of their environmental awareness, villagers have learned to sort out for recycling the waste plastics that they used to burn. Here, they are holding garbage cans, not red lanterns. Everyone who promises to classify garbage and sort out plastic trash can receive a garbage can after signing. They start their journey of environmental protection in a festive atmosphere. Children and adults alike take part in the journey, sharing the responsibility of garbage recycling. After changing the habit of ignoring the garbage issue, every household takes turns to manage the cleaning and other activities of environmental protection. Garbage treatment, a thorny problem in other rural areas, is a piece of cake in LOHO communities.

In order to plant more trees in the limited space, some villagers contributed their water vats, sawed them into two halves, filled in enough soil and planted trees there. Everyone volunteered to water public green land. By arousing their inherent potential and primitive wisdom in respecting nature and cherishing resources, it is possible for our villagers and villages to take public welfare into consideration and respect and follow the way of nature. A good case in point is observing the solar terms. In every solar term, we gather to perform with our bodies and understand the wisdom and power in them, practice a set of Qigong, learn a principle about life, and cook a meal; we learn together and integrate with each other physically, emotionally, mentall, and spiritually. This is how propriety is observed in our Shuyuan Village and Yaozhuang Village.

About forty people are "Le He Representatives," volunteers organized at the level of villager group to constitute a mutual benefit association, which integrates the function of the village committee and the village Party branch into the natural village. Rather than receiving top-down rules and regulations from the upper levels of the government, they discuss and work out their own detailed village rules and regulations, which can be observed in their daily life. They show the theater, renovated and decorated from a shanty in the village, in which villagers began to put on self-composed plays reflecting their own life. This drama shows how the mutual benefit association mediates and eventually helps settle the conflicts between mother and daughter-in-law. They have played it many times, and each time when they perform, both the performers and the audiences are moved to tears.

Now comes a question: who offers financial support for these activities? The villagers themselves, following the examples of the representatives of the mutual benefit association, donate money for their shared cause. Look, this 80-year old woman is also donating. One yuan is ok, and ten yuan can also do. What's important here is not how much one contributes but that everyone donates for the common fund that is to benefit everyone. Therefore, I hope to set up a village fund that will flow directly to the most elementary level of the village, to the mutual benefit association, and to the individual villagers. The construction of the LOHO communities needs the participation of many warm-hearted people, especially college graduates, to be social workers to contribute in the following social work: social surveys, social organizations, social activities, social education, social publicity, and social records. The history needs to be recorded; people's feet need to be rooted; individuals need to be gathered; lectures need to be given; things need to be done, and beauty needs to be publicized! We hope more people can join us to work as professional social workers or volunteers, to help keep our villages, preserve our roots, and pursue a new path of urbanization on the basis of the construction of rural areas.

How can we handle the problems resulting in environmental and social recessions? Just as Pando can reveal both hope and direction, so in our case will the unity, if it can become a common sense of the villagers, make our villages powerful. Despite its seemingly separated phenomena, the roots of Pando are inherently and organically interconnected. We can see promising hope if we make use of this sense of organic wholeness to adjust ourselves.

While facing the various crises of modernization and industrialization today, words are important, but actions speak louder than words, and directions further outweigh actions. Selecting one's worldview is a matter of life and death for human beings. All the existing problems— the split and estrangement of body and mind, of things and persons, of heart and brain, of justice and benefit, and of individuals and groups— result from a split way of thinking that human employs with regard to the environmental issue. Just as Professor Cobb puts, "We can't change our way of acting without altering our way of thinking. We can't apply views resulting in the environmental and social recessions to solve them."

To face the crises, we need traditional Eastern wisdom to help us construct a world community with a co-governed society, all-win economy, shared values, mutually valued life, and coexisting environment. We need countries throughout the world to promote the establishment of the world community with shared destiny through cultural communications and actions of the communities: i.e., to strengthen contacts, respect one another, inter-depend on one another, and pursue common well-being. The idea of LOHO and the practice of the LOHO communities is a vigorous response to the call of building such a community.

If we depict the LOHO communities in the Chinese way of thinking about environmental protection, we can see LOHO inhabitation involves ecological dwellings, garbage sorting, water-resource protection, and diversity of renewable energy resources. How can the material level of energy come true? It's necessary to construct a society, to build an organism in which the government, society, and enterprises interconnect, mutually benefit, and co-exist. Hence out of ecological agriculture we can draw many renewable industries, such as the pension industries, health-keeping industries, novel education industries, in which MOOC can find a place in China's rural areas as Professor Tang Min says. We can actualize the idea of health-keeping in a wider sense: with someone responsible for villagers' health in the villages, with the publicity of the culture of Chinese medicine, most important of which is to nourish our hearts. In the LOHO idea, it is of vital importance that our hearts be "self-reliant, mutually-assistant, and public-interest," keep the sense of fair play, cultivate public spirit, act with conscientiousness, keep genuineness, foster compassion, and nourish wisdom.

Let's share the beauty of the LOHO flower: "One flower fragrant out of five pistils or stamens, its rootstock growing strongly out of deep-rooted loams, leafy and colorful for being raised by all, attractive to bees and butterflies sweet around all."

What is needed is neither complaints, nor waiting, nor despair, but more thinkers and action-takers who can bring new hope for ecological civilization! An alternative civilization, an ecological civilization, is possible.

A Hindu Response

Rita D. Sherma

In the preamble to Pope Francis' encyclical on ecological action for amelioration of the condition of the earth, he writes: "This sister [the earth] now cries out to us because of the harm we have inflicted on her by our irresponsible use and abuse of the goods with which God has endowed her. We have come to see ourselves as her lords and masters, entitled to plunder her at will. The violence present in our hearts...is also reflected in the symptoms of sickness evident in the soil, in the water, in the air and in all forms of life. This is why the earth herself, burdened and laid waste, is among the most abandoned and maltreated of our poor; she 'groans in travail' (Rom 8:22). We have forgotten that we ourselves are dust of the earth (cf. Gen 2:7); our very bodies are made up of *her elements*, we breathe her air and we receive life and refreshment from *her waters*"[1] (2, italics mine).

Such words speak deeply to the Hindu sensibility honed by five thousand years of communion with the natural world, considered not as a lower realm over which humans have been given "dominion," but the physical manifestation of the Divine—metaphorically, the body of God. "Her elements" are evoked in prayer and worship over and over again. They are acknowledged to be the material of our embodiment and the ligaments that connect us to the rest of nature. We think of her not as "sister" but as "mother," and early Vedic hymns express pain at the thought of tilling the soil and forcing a weapon in the heart of our "mother." Conceptual resources for ecology in Hindu thought and practice abound. From the foundational philosophical principle of Brahman, the all-pervasive ultimate reality of the Upanishads that evinces what I have referred to elsewhere as "radical divine immanence," to the common practice marriage performed for trees, sacred groves, the inclusion of animals in sacred literature, ancient ascetic observances that leave almost no footprint upon the earth, and diverse pious observances for the remembrance of the preciousness of land, waterways, mountains, forests, and other living creatures.

The question that comes to mind, in view of the rich ecological resources inherent in Hindu thought and praxis, is why is India so polluted? First, India is a rigidly secular industrial nation where the ancient wisdom traditions of her past have been nearly swept into the dustbin of history. Historically, centuries of European colonization and decades of cultural and intellectual domination by the West have removed most traces of reverence for the ecological wisdom embedded in the scriptures of the ancient Vedic people. Where these principles and practices exist are in remote places and in rural areas—not in the corridors of power, whether intellectual, economic, or political. The search for material prosperity and the uncritical race towards to the highest technological knowledge has great cachet in the emerging nations that feel the desperate need to "catch up" to the West in economic terms. Pope Francis alludes to this disparity and imbalance:

> The foreign debt of poor countries has become a way of controlling them, yet this is not the case where ecological debt is concerned. In different ways, developing countries, where the most important reserves of the biosphere are found, continue to fuel the development of richer countries at the cost of their own present and future. The land of the southern poor is rich…yet access to ownership of goods and resources for meeting vital needs is inhibited by a system of commercial relations and ownership which is structurally perverse. The developed countries ought to help pay this debt by significantly limiting their consumption of non-renewable energy and by assisting poorer countries to support policies and programmes of sustainable development. (52)

Pope Francis' estimation is all the more poignant when one recalls that India's pre-colonial civilization and economy was highly advanced for its time. Estimates for the pre-colonial combined GDP of China and India in the 17th century range from 60 to 70 percent of world GDP.[2]

Laudato si' is a commendable effort: It covers a lot of conceptual territory, it offers many valuable insights, and will, hopefully, bring faith back to the table in the search for ways and means of saving what remains of our natural world. Nevertheless, a critical reading reveals a number of blind spots. Pope Francis speaks movingly about the injustice of anthropocentrism that is the foundation of the ecological disaster. However, he refrains from speaking of the injustice of androcentrism that is the cause of the near absence of one half of the human species from leadership in religion, politics, and economics. He mentions the need for dialogue with partners of different cultures, fields, and faiths as all humans are in possession of intellectual and cultural resources that may help ameliorate the ecological crisis. But he does not mention any examples of such conceptual or practical resources, or the faiths that may possess them. Nor is there any acknowledgement of the role that culturally insensitive evangelization of indigenous people by the Church that he leads has played, historically, in the death of cultural resources for environmentally-sound thought and practice. Pope Francis has laid out a number of excellent suggestions which, if adopted, would undoubtedly help environmental protection efforts. Yet, the key role in ecological devastation played by the explosive population growth of the human species, testified to by every bit of demographic data available, is dismissed as insignificant in the face of the unprecedented levels of consumption and luxurious lifestyles adopted by a small fraction of humanity. The encyclical, despite these lacunae, is a historically significant document and, inspired as it is by Saint Francis of Assisi, possesses a lyrical, almost mystical sense that, if understood and appreciated, may change the consciousness of many towards reverence and love for the natural world, without which, we are unlikely to save what remains of it.

The fabric of Hindu thought, from its inception, has contained strands which have been informed by a deep reverence for, and profound intimacy with, the natural world. There are numerous passages in the vast corpus of Hindu scripture that reflect a sense of attunement with the rhythms of nature that echo the sage's awe and wonder at the majesty and power of the elemental world, and evince a concern about human pollution of the air and of bodies of water. There are also elements in the Hindu worldview that reflect an organic perspective and resonate with the insights of modern ecological consciousness. Nevertheless, conceptual resources—no matter how supportive of an ecological worldview—do not add up to an overarching ecological meta-theology or philosophy. Perhaps it for this reason that Advaita Vedanta has been repeatedly drawn upon to provide the foundation of an ecological philosophy. Yet, without a careful re-envisoning and re-application, no philosophy/theology that arose in the ancient past can be expected to provide a prescription for the specific problems of sustainability of the current, technological era.

Such a re-envisioning, however, begins with a recollection of the resources that lie in texts and traditions, awaiting a new appreciation and application. The Vedas, the earliest texts of Hindu culture, record the worship of the elemental powers and phenomena of the natural world. The people of the early Vedic era had a sense of reciprocity with the earth and the elements of renewal and destruction (the winds, fire, water), which were deified but accorded a symbiotic status. The cosmic forces needed human devotion as much as humans needed the munificence of the forces in return. The gods of nature, who were the divinized forces of the natural world, were nurtured and rejuvenated by the gratitude and worship accorded them by the ritual of the Vedic sacrifice; they in turn were able to bestow blessings on the cosmos. The visualization of elemental forces as divine beings, invoked through prayers and offerings, created a locus of power which then could be channeled productively for the welfare of the world. Humans, in this worldview, did not see themselves as separate and divorced from the rest of the cosmos. Humans, animals, plant life, the sun, the moon, stars, and indeed the entire cosmos were seen as one continuum, where humans, as participants in the cosmic drama, had a special obligation to support the divine powers and phenomena that give rise to life on earth.

The processes of ritual serve to 1) create space for the envisioning of the elemental powers in divinized form; 2) provide the necessary environment in which to offer recognition, homage, and gratitude to the powers of nature through the offering of things of value (sacrifice); 3) the evocation of an inner conviction that the revivification and supplication of the divine forces will bring forth blessings and plenitude for self, and the world. The Vedas exalt the wonders of nature and regard the earth (Prithivi), and the major rivers (Ganga, Yamuna, Sarasvati, and Sindhu) as goddesses. In the *Atharva Veda*, the earth is eulogized as the lavish bestower of all wealth, but she is also the mother who deserves our respect and protection: "The earth is the mother, and I the son of the earth!" AV (12:12) Another passage reflects a deep concern for her well-being, and a sense of responsibility for her care and preservation: "What, O earth, I dig out of thee, quickly may that grow again: may I not, O pure one, pierce thy vital spot, not thy heart!" (12:35). This sentiment is echoed again in the following passage from the AV, which expresses a recognition of earth's bounty as well as an assurance of protection from harm due to human settlement:

> Thy snowy mountain heights, and thy forests, O earth, shall be kind to us! the brown, the black, the red, the multi-colored, the firm earth, that is protected by Indra, *I have settled upon, [but] not suppressed, not slain, not wounded.* AV (12:11) [italics mine]

Plants and trees were also experienced as particularly animated by the power of divine presence. Plants and foliage materials used for medicinal or ritual purposes were offered prayers. When a tree was cut down, a blade of grass was placed and sacrificial butter was poured on the remaining tree-stump with the following prayer: "Lord of the Forest, grow with hundred branches; may (you) grow with a thousand branches."[3]

A vision of the noumenal as fully present in the phenomenal, and not just in the oversoul (paramatma), is fundamental to an ecologically oriented theology. The nascent idea of a foundational unity glimpsed in the Vedas ripens to full maturity in the Upaniṣads. Although the Upaniṣads reflect a diversity of authorship and therefore embody a variety of teachings, the unifying thread of the non-dualistic doctrine of Brahman runs through the texts. This doctrine asserts that there exists a conscious, underlying reality called Brahman that pervades this universe of forms.

Brahman is beyond form, attributes, personality, and any other limiting characteristic, and exists in all beings in the form of the higher self (atman) and consciousness. The religious aim in the Upaniṣads revolves around the nucleus of liberation (mokṣa) from this world of forms and flux. Liberation consists in the realization of the identity of the higher self (atman) with the Supreme Identity (Brahman). Mokṣa is first conceived as the ultimate aim of religious endeavor and ascetic disciplines; meditational techniques, and renunciation of the material possessions are advocated as integral to a methodology of liberation.

Although by the time of the Upaniṣads, there is a shift in emphasis from the temporal order to that which is eternal, various Upaniṣadic texts reveal a perspective deeply respectful of the natural world and conscious of a continuum between the human and nonhuman realms.

The *Chāndogyopaniṣad* 6.8.7 proclaims "that which is the subtle essence [the source of all] this whole world has for its self." The text (Ch U 6.11.1) then goes on to describe a tree as having such a self—as a sentient being, infused with consciousness, capable of pain and joy. Contemporary botany suggests that trees experience sensations and react biochemically. A theology of identification of the sacred presence within, with the divine presence in all things is powerfully articulated in these verses from the īśopaniṣad:

> And he who sees all beings in his own self and his own self in all beings, does not feel any aversion by reason of such a view. (IU verse 6)

> When, to one who knows, all beings have become one with his own self, then what delusion and what sorrow can [come] to such a one who has seen Unity? (IU verse 7)

Western scholars such as J. Baird Callicott assert that this perception of the oneness of nature in the Brahman doctrine seems to obliterate the individuality of the various elements of the natural world. Yet, a careful reading of the Upaniṣads indicates otherwise. S. Radhakrishnan's comments on IU verses 6 posit that "unity is the basis of multiplicity and upholds the multiplicity" and *that the Supreme is both Being, and Becoming*—both the One essence and the Manifold phenomena of the universe. Interpreting Arne Naess's Vedanta-inspired eco-philosophy, known as Deep Ecology, Australian ecologist Warwick Fox also notes that "The realization that we and all other entities are aspects of a single unfolding reality—that 'life is fundamentally one' —does not mean that all multiplicity and diversity is reduced to a homogenous mush."[4]

Many Hindu texts reflect a lack of a hierarchical dualistic distinction between humans and others in the chain of being—viewing sentient beings as others on the Path of Life. In the Śrīmad BhāgavatamI:3:5, the Lord says of Himself:

> This form is the source and the indestructible seed of multifarious Incarnations within the universe, and from the particle and portion of this form, various sentient forms, such as divine beings, animals, human beings and more, are created.

The *Manusmṛti* VI:65 states: "Through the deepest contemplation let [the sage] recognize the subtle nature of the Supreme, and its presence in all sentient beings, from the highest to the lowest." The understanding is that nonhuman forms of life are not soulless creatures on the margins of a creation over which "man" has been given dominion but, rather, ensouled beings on a journey of consciousness all their own. For those on the path to liberation, the highest goal in the Hindu tradition, the realization that different forms of life are but various stages of the evolution of the One Self (atman) towards ultimate union with the Divine, is one of the first steps on the road to enlightenment. This sense of connection to others on the chain of being is amply attested to by the close connection of puranic deities with various animals. Examples include Rama's ubiquitous attendant Hanuman (the monkey deity who is popular as the exemplar of sublime devotion); the association of Krishna with cows in the pastoral Vrindavan; as well as the mounts (living vehicles) of the different deities. This is further strengthened by the existence of zoomorphic deities such the ubiquitous Ganesh, or the goddess Vindhyavasini. Perhaps the most lucid illustration of Hindu reverence for animal life is the doctrine of the incarnation of Vishnu. Viewed as the vision of God by many Hindus, Vishnu's incarnations (ten or more, depending on the source) include the kings Rama and Krishna, as well as several nonhuman species such as a fish, a tortoise, a boar, and a man-lion reflecting an evolution of consciousness. *Thus, other forms of life are seen as part of a holarchical, not hierarchical, chain of consciousness (more on this distinction later)*. It follows, therefore, animal and plant life are always worthy of our empathy and, at times, of our reverence as embodiments of the Divine.

This sense of respect for other species is best illustrated by the doctrine of *ahiṃsā*. Usually interpreted as non-injury to all living things, *ahiṃsā* figures prominently in the lists of moral virtues found in both texts that lay out the framework of spiritual practice for the renouncer and those that provide the guidelines of ethical behavior for the householders. With the emergence of the concept of atman, and the possibility of release from the cycle of rebirth, and the fetters of embodied life, renunciation came to be seen as the key to liberation. There was a corollary rise in the importance of the doctrine of *ahiṃsā* as a virtue to be cultivated on the renunciatory path. It became the first step on the ascetic journey. The *Bṛhat Saṃnyāsa Upaniṣad* goes even further, and suggests that an ascetic should always work for the welfare of all creatures because of their ongoing suffering (II.271). The Yoga System of Patanjali (c.100 C.E.), arguably the leading ascetic school of thought in Hinduism, affirms ahiṃssā as a foundation and rationale for right action (*Yoga Sutra* ii.30, and Vyasa's commentary on the same).

Hindu ethics holds four aims to be the valid goals (the Puruṣārtha) of human life. These are ethical and dutiful conduct (dharma), enjoyment of material well-being (ārtha); the cultivation of sensory, emotional, and aesthetic refinement (kāma); and spiritual liberation (mokṣa). The inclusion of material wellbeing in this list is instructive, for the consensus of the Hindu tradition holds that it, alone among the four, is of instrumental value, while the other three aims are of intrinsic value. The word dharma is derived from the root dhr, "to hold in place, or sustain." Dharmic action is that which sustains the world order. The perception of the fluidity of boundaries between the human and natural is further developed in the later legal and ethical treatises (Dharmaśāstra) in terms of moral codes of conduct which deal not only with relationships between humans but also with the nonhuman world. Dharma is inextricably linked to the sacralization tradition; the world must be properly maintained because it is, indeed, of ultimate value. Concern for the welfare of animals is visible in many of the injunctions and prohibitions; even a king is prohibited from cutting or damaging flowering or fruit trees, unless necessary for cultivation (Vāsiṣṭha Dharmaśāstra 19.11-12).

Since dharma is the maintenance of harmonious and healthy cosmic order, and since there is an organic continuity between realms in that order, it stands to reason that the devastation of earth is adharma (anti-dharma). The great epic poem *Mahābhārata*(M.B. 12.110.11) reminds us that the term dharma is rooted in the notion of "upholding" or "sustaining" because it is dharmic action in the world that allows for the sustenance of all creatures (prajā) according to their natural order. In reference to the perspective evoked by this passage, many Hindu practitioners feel that the traditional Hindu notion of dharma is naturally extendible to include the modern notion of ecological order and balance, because it is eco-systemic order and healthy functioning that is the foundation of the earth and sustains all life.

In a world run by corporate rapaciousness and the successful imposition of a marketing monoculture on the entire human community, are these unique principles, practices, and philosophies—that have informed a civilization for over five millennia—of any importance? Pope Francis helps us to see that yes, indeed, they are of critical importance. He speaks of the need to recognize the value of "Cultural Ecology" in preventing the complete destruction of our "common home," the biosphere:

> Together with the patrimony of nature, there is also an historic, artistic and cultural patrimony which is likewise under threat. This patrimony is a part of the shared identity of each place and a foundation upon which to build a habitable city. It is not a matter of tearing down and building new cities, supposedly more respectful of the environment yet not always more attractive to live in. Rather, there is a need to incorporate the history, culture and architecture of each place, thus reserving its original identity. Ecology, then, also involves protecting the cultural treasures of humanity in the broadest sense. More specifically, it calls for greater attention to local cultureswhen studying environmental problems, favouring a dialogue between scientific-technicallanguage and the language of the people. Culture is more than what we have inherited from the past; it is

also, and above all, a living, dynamic and participatory present reality, which cannot be excluded as we rethink the relationship between human beings and the environment. (143)

I couldn't agree more!

Endnotes

1. <http://w2.vatican.va/content/francesco/en/encyclicals/documents/papa-francesco_20150524_enciclica-laudato-si.pdf>.

2. Sean Harkin, "Will China Really Dominate"? *World Finance* (19 April 2012).

3. Rig Veda 1: 90, 7:34, 23, as cited in Hermann Oldenberg, *The Religion of the Veda,* trans. Shridhar B. Shrotri (Delhi: Motilal Benarsidass, 1988), 128-29.

4. Warwick Fox, *Towards a Transpersonal Ecology: Developing New Foundations for Environmentalism* (Boston: Shambala, 1990), 232.

Catholic and Buddhist Perspectives

Lourdes Argüelles & Anne Rivero

We are very grateful to His Holiness Pope Francis for partially reinterpreting and marshaling the full weight of the powerful social teachings of his Church in order to issue a rejection of the theology and practices of human dominion which have so greatly contributed to the devastation of the Earth and her creatures. In *Laudato si'* (Praise Be to You), the papal encyclical on "Care for our Own Home," the pope at a critical time in human history gives the world much more than a message purportedly only of interest to the Catholic faithful and a few others.

Those who read the 190 pages of the papal message may be surprised at its overarching nature, depth, and thoroughness. It contains much food for thought, debate, and ideas for action for scientists, politicians, activists, and all people of good will. The encyclical is also an important message of both warning and support for religious and spiritual leaders around the world. One religious leader who undoubtedly will feel supported by the pope is the spiritual head of our Tibetan Buddhist tradition, His Holiness the 14th Dalai Lama of Tibet. The Dalai Lama, who has been pressing the ecological alarm button for some time now, is a living witness to the systematic environmental devastation of his country and its unfortunate planetary consequences. Because he is well known for his optimistic tendencies and his avoidance of extreme comments, many people were indeed surprised and even annoyed when decades ago he began making such ominous statements as, "You see, one day we might find that all living things on this planet, including human beings, are doomed" (Dalai Lama, Rio Summit, 1992).

In this brief essay, due to time and space constraints, we will limit our comments to some similarities and differences between the spiritual ecological elements of Catholic and Buddhist traditions and how these shape what it means to be "caring for our common home." We will also address two areas of concern that we believe were not adequately or fully addressed in the encyclical and which represent differences that exist between the pope's thinking and that of many Buddhist scholars and practitioners including ourselves. It is also in these areas where Buddhism may have some practical guidelines to offer for addressing our ecological crisis.

Spiritual ecological elements

Pope Francis is a spiritual ecologist. He recognizes the considerable relevance of religions and spiritualities in identifying and responding to the origins of planetary suffering, and he has not been hesitant to address the spiritual poverty of humankind. Spiritual ecologists view our current environmental crisis as far more than merely a social, economic, political, governmental, legal, scientific, or technological matter, and see it ultimately as a much deeper cultural, moral, ethical, and spiritual crisis. They note that a substantial number of individuals, organizations, and communities, even those that are religiously oriented, are often unwilling or unable to intelligently formulate and answer questions that are key to our planetary survival such as "What is and what should be the place of humans in nature?" and "What should humans do to heal the Earth and neutralize the suffering of her inhabitants?" They are also unwilling or unable to live in a way that protects and restores the planet and ensures that their descendants and fellow human species inherit a livable home.

The pope sees his encyclical pronouncements as a partial remedy to the above situation. He understands that in most traditional teachings of theology there is hardly any place for ecology and that, to make matters worse, theology departments are gradually disappearing from institutions of higher learning in overdeveloped societies. Thus, he devotes an entire chapter (Chapter 2) to illustrating the profound ecological implications of the Christian doctrine of Creation including the closely intertwined relationships of Christians with God, with their neighbors, and with the Earth herself. In short, he rediscovers for the Christian faithful a spiritual ecology that has been forgotten for some time yet which remains deeply embedded in scripture. In this spiritual ecology God entrusts the protection and healing of God's creation to human beings and through the example of Jesus and his followers nudges them to struggle against the exploitation of the Earth's bounty, to walk lightly on the Earth, and to attend preferentially to the concerns of those bound to suffer the most from environmental catastrophe, the poor.

The various Buddhist traditions also have a strong spiritual ecological orientation. The Buddha's life was intimately associated with nature, especially with trees. More than 200 of the regulations for Buddhist monks in the *Vinaya* (monastic code) are ecologically relevant. In some Buddhist traditions lay practitioners are not supposed to disturb plants and animals within temple complexes. However, as Buddhism has been secularized and presented more as a series of self-help methods than a spiritual practice, the complex ecological elements of the *Buddhadharma* (teachings of the Buddha) are being neglected by many teachers and practitioners alike.

However, a number of contemporary Buddhist scholar-activists such as Sulak Sivaraksa, David Loy, Joan Halifax, David Brazier, Stephanie Kaza, and Bhikku Bodhi, have sought to reclaim the ecological elements of Buddhism. Loy and Bikkhu Bodhi, for example, have related our spiritual poverty and its consequent ecological fallout to three mental factors or "afflictive emotions" which are universally understood in basic Buddhist teachings to keep us prisoners in *samsara* or the world of suffering. These three are, specifically, greed, hatred, and delusion/ignorance. In the context of the eco-crisis, they point out that greed can be seen as responsible for ravaging the finite resources of the Earth and contaminating her with toxic waste. Hatred can be seen as responsible not only for wars but for all types of violence including environmental violence. Delusion/ignorance can be thought of as the main cause for the denial of the reality of the environmental devastation that threatens us all even in the face of incontrovertible scientific evidence.

Thus, not surprisingly, the focus of much Buddhist environmental activism has been on encouraging the serious practitioner to engage in intense mind training practices as a prerequisite for, or simultaneous with, ecologically oriented action. These practices help individuals to realize the fundamental interrelatedness and interdependence of all that lives. They differ, though, from the Catholic traditional spiritual teachings and practices in that they do not guide the practitioner to establish a preferential option for those most harshly affected, the poor. However, many Buddhists who direct or work in relief and other nonprofit organizations do prioritize helping the potential victims and survivors of environmental racism or classism, though the welfare of those who abuse them also remains a concern. Buddhist teachings always remind us that "our worst enemies are our best teachers" and thus deserve our gratitude and help even when we must stand up against their actions.

Both Buddhist and Christian spiritual ecological traditions emphasize the urgent need to protect and heal our common home though they may differ on the reasons for doing so. As a spiritual ecologist Pope Francis is an heir of the legendary medieval and radical mystic Saint Francis of Assisi. Like his chosen namesake, the pope sees divinity everywhere throughout the Earth and the cosmos. The liberation theologian Leonardo Boff has described the Franciscan legacy as one that celebrates the fact that "this world is not mute, not lifeless, not empty; it speaks and is full of movement, love, purpose, and beckonings from the Divinity. It can be a place for encountering God and God's spirit, through the world itself, its energies, its profusion of sound, color, and movement. The Sacred dwells in it. It is God's extended body" (Boff 1997). It is from this extended body of Creation which is now under threat that the good pope crafted his powerful message.

Because we practice within a nontheistic religious tradition, unlike the pope, Buddhists are not necessarily motivated to defend and heal creation for its inherent value. Based on our understanding of Karmic Theory (Traleg 2015), we see worlds such as our Earth as being born and dying incessantly and in relatively rapid succession due to the collective karma of its inhabitants. These worlds are constantly emerging, growing, flourishing, decaying, and dying only to be born again. Thus, our moral commitment to defend and heal our common home arises from our obligation to further the well-being and ease the suffering of ourselves and other living beings. That commitment is not born, as in the case of Christian understanding, from a decree of protection emanating from a Creator God. Though many Buddhists do not deny the mysterious nature of creation and the possible existence of a creative intelligence, for the most part we craft our urgent ecological messages based on standard Buddhist sutric teachings. These posit that it is we ourselves, through our own efforts infused with the blessings of those who have already achieved enlightenment, that can overcome the detrimental forces of greed, hatred, and delusion and thereby end suffering.

We now turn to some similarities and differences between Christian and Buddhist spiritual ecological thinking as expressed in two areas of ecological significance and concern. Let us look at human population numbers and the animals we eat. It is in these areas that we believe that the Buddhist traditions have some effective traditional and contemporary practical guidelines for positive attitudinal and behavior change.

Population numbers

The 7 billion plus human population level of the planet is rapidly soaring at the rate of 1.14% per year, and is estimated to reach 9 billion by 2042. The negative planetary impact of this increasing number of people is of great concern. If human population levels continue to rise at the current rate, the Earth will be plunged into an ecological crisis from which it will be difficult, if not impossible, for her to recover. As our numbers continue to grow, even if a large portion of the populations of overdeveloped societies were willing to adopt a lifestyle of voluntary simplicity (a highly unlikely scenario) we will continue to increase our need for the finite resources of water, food, land, transport, and energy.

Buddhists and Catholics have traditionally and currently been guided by the hierarchies of each of their respective religions and their own scriptures to live within two very different types of reproductive cultures. The differences between these two cultures have now become more important in light of the ecological crisis, and in the context of this papal encyclical have also become more stark.

In a recent article entitled "Laudato Si Should Have Lifted the Ban on Contraception" in the *National Catholic Reporter* (June 24, 2015), the author expresses a strong concern that Pope Francis is still not ready to use the term "overpopulation" and to revoke his Church's ban on contraception when exponentially increasing population has been shown to be a major contributor to environmental destruction and personal suffering. The pope, like many in the earthly population, argues that the world does not need a lower birth rate. He proposes, rather, that we need to focus on insuring a better food and water distribution system, develop a means for a legitimate redistribution of wealth, improve agricultural and other production technologies, and decrease rampant consumerism worldwide in order to avoid environmental catastrophe. In addressing the topic of population the pope seems to have overlooked the suffering of many women and families who struggle with hunger and deprivation, especially in poor countries. Such suffering has been exacerbated by a lack of access to birth control services, a lack of access which is directly traceable in many countries, such as the Philippines, to the pro-natalist policies of the Roman Catholic Church.

Had the pope been willing to acknowledge in his encyclical the danger of soaring human population levels and accordingly agree to change Catholic teachings on birth control, he would not have broken new ground. More than fifty years ago, a birth control commission appointed by Pope John XXIII, overwhelmingly voted to rescind the ban on artificial contraception. After the death of Pope John XXIII, his successor, Pope Paul VI, refused to accept the decision of the commission.

Buddhism's attitudes and behaviors related to fertility, procreation, and family life are worth examining if we are to begin, as we must, seeking to reduce population numbers by voluntary means in the face of our eco-crisis. These attitudes and behaviors are different from those of many religious traditions, including Catholicism which has often been seen, at least in preaching and in parish life, as encouraging every additional birth and within which those who remain childless may be looked down upon.

Ancient Buddhist scriptures as well as more contemporary Buddhist teachings have routinely emphasized the need to control sexual desires and behaviors, behaviors that often lead to unwanted pregnancies and births and to much suffering. On the one hand, these teachings about the need to control and contain sexual excesses are similar in Buddhism and Catholicism. On the other hand, there is a difference between the two faiths in that Buddhists have tended to encourage people to move away from being family focused and from rampant pro-natalism. The reasoning behind this approach is profoundly spiritual and ethical and based on concern for the well-being of self and all other living beings.

Thus, unlike the pope, the Dalai Lama has assumed leadership in clarifying for Buddhist practitioners that though Buddhism considers human life to be precious and that he believes, as do most Buddhists, that countless beings are searching for human bodies in which to be reborn at any one time, this does not mean that human population numbers on this Earth should not be controlled for the benefit of all beings. He has also emphasized that abortion in all the Buddhist traditions is unacceptable except in a very limited number of circumstances. Thus, he has encouraged the control of population numbers through easy access to non-life threatening contraception methods and to family planning.

It is also notable that a large number of Buddhists live and support non-reproductive lifestyles as well as the moral legitimacy of not reproducing. This is reflected in the strength of the Buddhist monastic tradition with its emphasis on celibacy and voluntary simplicity, which is seen as an ideal life choice in Buddhist communities around the world. In contrast, monastic lifestyle choices have been sharply on the decline in Catholic populations and some other traditions, while maintaining a normative and even a preferred choice in Buddhist traditions.

Recently, however, there has been a promising re-elaboration of western monastic legacies and a recognition of their importance for our world today. Members of the "New Monasticism" movement (McEntee & Bucko 2015), in their quest for simplicity and a spiritually based life seem to be weighing the costs and benefits of procreation in this time of ecological crisis.

The animals we eat

We mentioned before that Pope Francis is an heir to Saint Francis of Assisi, the patron saint of animals. We feel that, as such, he fell short in his encyclical in failing to advocate for the well-being of the most vulnerable creatures on Earth, particularly but not exclusively for those destined for the slaughterhouse. Though indeed critical of factory farming methods for the suffering they bring about, the pope did not choose to actively encourage the faithful to engage in compassionate or plant-based eating. Like leaders in many other religious traditions, the pope has shied away from the important topics of vegetarianism and veganism, perhaps for fear of dramatically antagonizing his followers. This stance is taken in spite of the ancient legacy of the Desert Fathers and Mothers and the fact that many contemporary Catholics and other Christians are already vegetarians. There are also (nonCatholic) Christian denominations that have rejected animal eating for spiritual/ethical reasons with the resultant consequence of considerable health and longevity benefits.

It is well known that the overall effect of consistent meat and dairy eating is having a devastating ecological impact. Here we quote some statistics published recently in an article entitled "Are you Willing to Change your Diet?" in the *National Catholic Reporter* (July 3, 2015): "Animal agriculture is responsible for 18% of greenhouse gas emissions, more than the combined exhaust from all transportation." "Methane from livestock has a global warming power 86 times that of carbon dioxide." "Approximately 2500 gallons of water are needed to produce one pound of beef." "1.5 acres can produce 37,000 pounds of plant-based food. 1.5 acres can produce 375 pounds of meat." "One dairy cow produces approximately 120 pounds of waste every day." "Animal agriculture is responsible for up to 97% of Brazilian Amazon rainforest destruction." "Eighty-two percent of starving children reside in nations where livestock animals are fed." "Animal agriculture is the leading cause of species extinction, ocean dead zones, water pollution, and habitat destruction." Enough said. It is clear that not all Catholics agree with the pope in his non-objection to meat-based dietary practices.

Buddhists of some traditions, including the Tibetan lineages, do not fare much better in this area of concern in spite of their professed love and compassion for all that lives. Many persist in inflicting animal suffering and causing environmental damage through their meat eating practices in spite of the many non-meat eating options in the contemporary overdeveloped world, even for the poor.

Contemporary Buddhists recognize that Buddhist perspectives on meat eating have a long and complex history. Though the First Precept that we take as Buddhist practitioners admonishes us to refrain from killing, we are sometimes told that meat eating is not to be regarded as an example of killing and thus is not specifically forbidden in the scriptures. One notable exception is the Lankavatara Sutra, which takes a strong position in favor of vegetarianism. However, in the Telovada Jataka the Buddha himself directly criticizes a Jaina ascetic who ridicules him for accepting food with meat. The Buddha affirms that his monastic code is designed to allow his monks to eat whatever food is customary to eat in any place or country so that it can be done without the indulgence of the appetite or evil desire. Monks are permitted to eat whatever is offered to them.

Buddhists today, given the availability of a large variety of non-animal based foods and other products, identify the suffering of non-human sentient beings caused by humans as an important spiritual and moral issue and have begun to take action. For example, Tibetan Buddhist lama Chatral Rinpoche in the East and Zen master Nhat Hanh in the West have recommended to the large number of their personal students that they become vegetarians and animal welfare advocates. In fact, Chatral Rinpoche *demands* that his students be vegetarian. Thich Nhat Hanh (2008) said, "By eating meat we share the responsibility for climate change, the destruction of our forests, and the poisoning of our water. By the simple act of becoming vegetarian we will make a difference in the health of our planet." These leading teachers routinely challenge the rationalizations that support meat and dairy eating lifestyles and have created temples and Dharma Centers that are leather and meat free and where not even the most humble bug is purposefully killed.

Going beyond the motivation to protect the animals we eat, Joanna Macy, a lay Buddhist teacher, has developed a practice that became popular two decades ago in colleges and universities and in Dharma Centers. Macy's practice of *The Council of All Beings* was developed to help participants reconnect with other many other species beyond those which we use for food and other products. The practice has been found to facilitate a deeper feeling of respect, caring, and compassion for the interconnectedness and interdependence of all living beings. The 900-year-old Tibetan Buddhist practice of *Tonglen* (sending and taking) has become widely practiced among modern Tibetan Buddhists who often utilize it to take in the suffering of other species into their own hearts. Both practices of the *Council* and of *Tonglen* are based on the understanding that meaningful change toward ecological sensitivity and environmentally beneficial behaviors can only come about as part of a more comprehensive program of developing higher states of contemplative and meditative awareness. They parallel in some ways various promising emerging practices in Catholic settings such as the ecological reinterpretation of the Ignatian Examen practice.

In sum we can say that because of the similarities, and in spite of the differences, between *Laudato si'* and the Buddhist teachings and practices that inform the lives of many, Pope Francis is and will remain a source of wisdom and solace in the context of our current eco-crisis. He will continue to be an inspirational guide to Catholics, Buddhists, and members of other faith traditions seeking to develop effective ecological ethics and practices based in ancient wisdom traditions and in modern science.

May all beings benefit.

References

Leonardo Boff, "All the Cardinal Ecological Virtues: St. Francis of Assisi." In *Cry of the Earth, Cry of the Poor* (Maryknoll: Orbis Books, 1997), 203-20.

Dalai Lama. Accessed July 6, 2015. <www.dalailama.com/messages/ environment/address-at-rio>.

Colman Mc Carthy, "Are You Willing to Change Your Diet," *National Catholic Reporter,* July 3-16, 2015, 29.

Jamie Manson, "Laudato Si" Should Have Lifted the Ban on Contraception, *National Catholic Reporter,* 24 June 2015, 53.

Rory McEntee & Adam Bucko, *The New Monasticism* (Maryknoll: Orbis 2015).

Thich Nhat Hanh, *The World We Have: A Buddhist Approach to Peace and Ecology.* (Berkeley: Parallax Press, 2008).

Traleg Kyabgon, *What is Karma, What it Isn't, Why it Matters* (Berkeley: Shambhala Press, 2015), 7.

Walk Not Exultantly Upon the Earth: An Islamic Response

Joseph E. B. Lumbard

Laudato si' ("Praised be You"), is a clarion call to all of humanity. The ecological crisis is not simply a moral issue. It is the ethical issue of our time. Given the utter failure of political leaders to address the rapid environmental degradation that threatens all ways of life, it is clear, as Pope Francis observes, that the need for sustainable solutions is "a summons to profound interior conversion" (158). Such a conversion demands dramatic change not only in how we conceptualize the environment but also in how we interact with each other, and in how we serve God.

Pope Francis' address "to every living person on this planet" (4), combined with his call to respect the quality of life "within the world of symbols and customs proper to each human group" (109), opens to an important and necessary opportunity for interfaith climate action. Given the depth and breadth of the crisis that confronts humanity, we have no choice but to mine the riches of all the world's traditions to find alternative ecological paradigms and new solutions to environmental degradation. As the encyclical states, "We need a conversation which includes everyone, since the environmental challenge we are undergoing and its human roots, concern and affect us all" (12).

According to the latest results from the Pew Research Center, by 2050, 29.7% of the world population will be Muslim and 31.4% will be Christian.[1] As they will comprise over 60% of the world's population, Muslims and Christians have no choice but to come together to work for the common cause of humanity in confronting the unprecedented challenge posed by climate change. Moreover, to take root in humanity any sustainable ecological worldview must incorporate and address the teachings that much of humanity seeks to follow. This requires that we question the underlying premises of the modern secular civilization whose paradigms and processes have led to the environmental crisis. As Pope Francis observes, "there is a growing awareness that science and technological progress cannot be equated with the progress of humanity" (85). Indeed the reductionist epistemological paradigm that now dictates the implementation of technology has imposed a model of reality that leads to the degradation of both the natural environment and the human soul. In the words of one contemporary Muslim commentator, "the environmental crisis is an outward reflection of the inward crisis of modern day humanity."[2] We are thus in need of new paradigms that provide a more holistic view of nature and an attendant ethical framework which will allow us to implement the solutions that the science deriving from such paradigms would provide. As his holiness writes, "Our difficulty in taking up this challenge seriously has much to do with an ethical and cultural decline which has accompanied the deterioration of the environment" (120).

To establish alternative ecological paradigms and reinvigorate our collective ethical frameworks we must turn to those traditions that have guided much of humanity over the millennia. These traditions are in fact essential for recovering a holistic relationship with nature in which God, humanity, and nature are in harmony. As Seyyed Hossein Nasr observed almost fifty years ago,

> If a day were to come when Christianity, rather than trying to convert the followers of Oriental religions, should also try to understand them and enter into an intellectual dialogue with them then Oriental metaphysics, which is also in its essence the *philosophia perennis,* as well as the cosmological doctrines of the Oriental traditions (which could also be referred to as *cosmologia*

perennis), could act as a cause and occasion for recollection of elements forgotten in the Christian tradition. They could aid in restoring a spiritual vision of nature that would be able to provide the background for the sciences.[3]

Among the world scriptures, the Quran provides a unique resource for building an ecological paradigm. Grounded in the Abrahamic tradition, it presents a harmonious view of nature reminiscent of the Far Eastern or Indigenous traditions. In the Quran, *whatsoever is in the heavens and whatsoever is on the earth glorifies God* (Q 59:1; 61:1; 62:1; 64:1), *the stars and the trees prostrate* (Q 55:6), the *thunder hymns His praise* (Q 13:13), and *unto God prostrates whosoever is in the heavens and whosoever is on the earth, the sun, the moon, the stars, the mountains, the trees, and the beasts* (Q 22:18; cf. Q 13:15). In these and many other verses, the whole of creation is presented as a Divine symphony, for *there is no thing, save that it hymns His praise, though you do not understand their praise* (Q 17:44).

The extinction of species and the eradication of pristine environments is a direct result of our failure to hear and understand the praise they sing. The destruction of each is like the removal of a section from this orchestra of which we are all a part. From a Quranic perspective, *there is no creature that crawls upon the earth, nor bird that flies upon its wings, but that they are communities like yourselves* (Q 6:38). As communities, all living creatures have inherent rights. For this reason Islamic law has always recognized the rights of animals, water, and even trees.[4] When any species is rendered extinct or their habitats are compromised through the withering touch of humanity, we eliminate entire communities from the face of the earth. We commit ecocide.

To avoid violating the rights of other communities, the Quran enjoins humanity *to walk not exultantly upon the earth* (Q 17:63) and to view the whole of nature as signs of God: *And whatsoever He created for you on the earth of diverse colors—truly in this is a sign for a people who reflect* (Q 16:13). From a Quranic perspective, nothing exists but that it is a means whereby we can better understand and witness the glory of the Divine. A bird,[5] the trees, the stars,[6] the change from night to day[7]—God is present in each of these. Every part of creation, no matter how big or small, is like a word or letter in an ongoing revelation. God employs all aspects of creation to help human beings better understand the Divine, their own selves, and the cosmos. Indicating the importance of all aspects of creation, God says in Q 2:26, *Truly God is not ashamed to set forth a parable of a gnat or something smaller. As for those who believe, they know it is the truth from their Lord, and as for those who disbelieve, they say, "What did God mean by this parable?"*

Given this understanding of creation as a continuous message, the Quran enjoins us to reflect upon the natural world and recalls the wonders of creation as a means of reminding the reader or listener of God. As Martin Lings has expressed it, "It as if God's final revelation allows God's first revelation to speak through it."[8] As they convey God's wisdom to us, the heavens and the earth are filled with *signs for believers* (Q 6:99; 15:77; 16:79; 27:86; 29:24, 44; 30:37; 39:52), *signs for a people who reflect* (Q 13:3; 30:21; 39:42; 45:13; cf. 10:24), *signs for a people who hear* (Q 10:67; 16:65; 30:23), *signs for those who know* (Q 30:22), *signs for a people who understand* (Q 2:164; 13:4; 16:12, 67; 30:24; 45:5), *signs for a people who are reverent* (Q 10:6), *signs for those possessed of intelligence* (Q 20:54, 128), *signs for the possessors of intellect* (Q 3:190), *signs for those who possess insight* (Q 3:13), and *signs for a people who are certain* (Q 45:4; cf. 51:20). These recurring injunctions make it clear that when sound in heart and mind, the human being is able to reflect upon the world of nature in a manner that increases faith, knowledge and understanding. In this vein, the Quran says in another oft-cited verse:

> *We shall show them Our signs upon the horizons and within them-selves till it becomes clear to them that it is the truth* (Q 41:53).[9]

When we fail to contemplate the signs of God on the horizons and within ourselves and to hear their praise, we are among those regarding whom God asks rhetorically, *who does greater wrong than one who has been reminded of the signs of his Lord, then turns away from them?* (Q 18:57; 32:22); and in another verse, *Who does greater wrong than one who denies the signs of God and turns away from them?* (Q 6:157). Given the state of the natural environment today, and our having begun what some refer to as "the sixth extinction,"[10] one cannot but conclude that we have indeed turned away from, and forgotten how to reflect upon, the signs of God in the natural order. From a Quranic perspective, corruption of the earth is the inevitable result of such turning away from God and His signs: *And when he turns away he endeavors on the earth to work corruption therein, and to destroy tillage and offspring, but God loves not corruption* (Q 2:205).

Numerous scientific studies indicate that the balance of the world's ecosystems has been corrupted by our irresponsible and excessive consumption. From one perspective it is this very balance that God enjoins mankind to maintain in Q 55:7-9: *Heaven He has raised and the Balance He has set, that you transgress not in the Balance. So set right the measure and fall not short in the Balance.* In another passage, the Prophet Shuʿayb[12] enjoins his tribe, *"O my people! Observe fully the measure and the Balance with justice and diminish not people's goods, and behave not wickedly on the earth, working corruption"* (Q 11:85). As Seyyed Hossein Nasr observes, in Islamic thought the Balance, or *mīzān*, referred to in the Quran, "is associated with the balance of the Universe itself through that Divine Wisdom which preserves everything in its place and has created everything according to a just measure so that the term becomes closely associated with the order prevalent in nature."[13]

From a Quranic perspective, God has established the Balance and Harmony of nature and *made beautiful all that He created* (Q 32:7). The position of human beings as vicegerents of God then makes us responsible for observing and maintaining the Balance that God has set aright.[14] But having failed to do so, human beings have come to work corruption. As a result the signs that we witness in the created order today speak to us not only of God's glory, but also of the imbalance that our own corruption (*fasād*) has wrought. Of such corruption the Quran states, *Corruption has appeared on land and sea because of that which men's hands have wrought, so that He may let them taste some of that which they have done, that haply they might return* (Q 30:41).

For Muslims and Christians, the place of human beings is not to subdue the earth. It is to hear the patterns already established within nature and live in harmony with them, had we but eyes to see and ears to hear. In both Christianity and Islam, human beings are presented as stewards of the earth. In the Quran, this responsibility is both an honor and a trial. Verse 6:165 states, *God it is Who appointed you stewards upon the earth and raised some of you by degrees above others, that He may try you in that which He has given you.* From this perspective, being stewards of nature is a test to see how we respond to the gifts that God has bestowed upon us. It is about our responsibility toward God, not our dominion over creation. Neither the Bible nor the Quran has any place for what Pope Francis calls "a tyrannical anthropocentrism unconcerned for other creatures" (50). We will thus be held accountable for the degree to which we have carried out our function as stewards and vicegerents. As the Prophet Muhammad is reported to have said, "The world is a green and pleasant thing. God has made you stewards of it, and looks at how you behave."

Given the state of the environmental crisis and the alarming increase in environmental degradation, one cannot but conclude that contemporary humanity has failed this test. The world and our children can no longer afford the consequences of our behavior. In our rapacious approach to nature, we have failed to reflect upon and understand God's signs and thus become like those of whom the Quran says, *they have hearts with which they understand not; they have eyes with which they see not; and they have ears with which they hear not* (7:179).

By drawing upon the shared teachings of our traditions, humanity can again learn to honor the immutable rights of rivers, animals, and trees. By bearing witness to our own transgressions, we can reverse our course and ensure that the rights of God's creation prevail over the transient interests of corporations. We have no choice but to take this direction and to work with one another. Let us hope that by virtue of having tasted some of the corruption we have wrought, we might turn again to reflect upon God's signs. The papal encyclical provides an opportunity for the people of the world's faith traditions to open our hearts to one another and to the plea of Mother Nature. For her fate and that of all generations will be determined by the decisions of our generation. It is indeed time that people of all faiths unite and in the words of Martin Luther King, "rededicate ourselves to the long and bitter, but beautiful, struggle for a new world."

Endnotes

1. "The Future of World Religions: Population Growth Projections, 2010-2050." <http://www.pewforum.org/2015/04/02/religious-projections-2010-2050/>.

2. Munjed Murad, "Inner and Outer Nature: An Islamic Perspective on the Environmental Crisis," *Islam & Science*, Vol. 10. No. 2 (Winter 2012), 119.

3. Seyyed Hossein Nasr, *The Encounter of Man and Nature: The Spiritual Crisis of Modern Man* (London: Allen & Unwin, 1968), 99.

4. For a discussion of Islamic environmental law, see Othman Abd ar-Rahman Llewellyn, "The Basis for a Discipline of Islamic Environmental Law," in *Islam and Ecology, A Bestowed Trust*, ed. Richard C. Folz, Frederick M. Denny, and Azizan Baharuddin (Cambridge, MA: Center for the Study of World Religions, Harvard Divinity School, 2003), 249-80.

5. *Have they not considered the birds above them, spreading and folding up [their wings]? None holds them save the Compassionate. Truly He sees all things* (Q 67:19); *Have they not considered the birds, made subservient, in midair? None holds them save God. Truly in that are signs for a people who believe* (Q 16:79).

6. *And the stars and the trees prostrate* (Q 55:6). Trees are used in symbolic manner throughout the Quran, as in 14:24–25: *Hast thou not considered how God sets forth a parable? A good word is as a good tree: its roots firm and its branches in the sky. It brings forth fruit in every season, by the leave of its Lord. And God sets forth parables for mankind, that haply they may remember.*

7. *Among His signs are the night and the day, the sun and the moon* (Q 41:37); *Hast thou not considered that God makes the night pass into the day and makes the day pass into the night, and that He made the sun and the moon subservient* (Q 31:29; cf. 16:12; 35:13; 39:5).

8. Martin Lings, *What is Sufism?* (London: Allen & Unwin, 1981), 23.

9. This verse is subject to multiple interpretations. The antecedent of the pronoun *it* (*hu*) in *it is the truth* is ambiguous. It could be seen as a reference to an unstated "everything," meaning all of creation, both macrocosmic and microcosmic, or to God, in which case it would be rendered "that He is the Truth." See Joseph E. B. Lumbard, "Commentary

on *Sūrat Fū""ilat*," in *The Study Quran*, ed. S. H. Nasr, Caner Dagli, Maria Dakake, Joseph Lumbard, and Mohammed Rustom (San Franciso, HarperOne, 2015), 1170.

10. For the most recent study, see Gerardo Ceballos, Ehrlich, Barnosky, García, Pringle and Palmer, "Accelerated modern human–induced species losses: Entering the sixth mass extinction." <http://advances.sciencemag.org/content/1/5/e1400253.full>.

11. The Prophet Shu'ayb, who was sent to preach to the people of Midian, is considered by most Quranic commentators to be the biblical Jethro, the father-in-law of Moses.

12. S. H. Nasr, *Religion and the Order of Nature* (New York: Oxford University Press, 1996), 128.

13. See e.g. Q 7:56: *And work not corruption upon the earth after it has been set aright, but call upon Him in fear and in hope*, and Q 7:85: *So observe fully the measure and the balance and diminish not people's goods, nor work corruption upon the earth after it has been set aright. That is better for you, if you are believers.*

Back from Quantity to Quality, from Appearance to Reality?

Denys Zhadiaiev

From the beginning of the industrial era up to the present time, after a long battle in which nations pretended to be faster, know more, and achieve more, humanity has apparently came full circle. A circle is a geometrical figure, and it can be contrary to quantity, which is a number. The encyclical letter *Laudato si'* is that point at which the acceleration of the drawn line turns into something completely different: the circle (integrity, coherence, quality instead of quantity, rest instead of rush).

I find the encyclical written in organic philosophical language, where the notion of actuality dominates the traditional Christian concept of eternity: the category of time is more appreciated than space, process is considered more effective than positions. The category of transcendence is modulated and can be compared to long-term goals that are conditioned by the future generations that succeed us here on earth, not somewhere in the sky.

Theories are like species—some of them thrive and survive, and some of them achieve their immortality only in outdated textbooks. I particularly appreciate the fact that the Roman Catholic Church with all its many members, in comparison to other Christian religions, does not pretend to play the role of "genus" for other religious communities and wisely takes into account what happens in the real world—this Sister of the Lord and our Mother, as Holy Father Francis puts it—trying to remind us that we all are servants, not lords.

As a philosopher by training (re-thinking this title I have to admit it sounds as weird as "professional believer," "qualified brother," etc.), I also have to admit that ecological civilization is the problem of certain worldview, and, though I am not Catholic, I agree with the first lines of the letter, wherein the pope quotes Saint Francis of Assisi: "integral ecology calls for openness to categories which transcend the language of mathematics and biology" (11). To be sure, numbers, figures, and charts are important scientific data, yet they are only the quantitative side of our understanding of the world, like the money that corporations put on one side of the scale, letting it outweigh the other side of the scale; namely, threatening statistics. Since René Descartes transformed qualities of geometrical figures to algebraic equations, the dominant paradigm of the market has reduced human beings to the amount of money they earn (trying to ignore their uniqueness and irrevocable nature), and the number of hours they work (trying to ignore what real ethical value their action can have).

Science has selected definite short-term goals while ethics deals with rather long-term aspirations. This long-term orientation is what Holy Father Francis want us to follow in opposition to local political will (184): "'time is greater than space' . . . we are always more effective when we generate processes rather than holding on to positions of power" (178). I do not believe that we will save our Mother Earth when all local politicians will be dethroned. It is rather about a spiritual revolution that can happen when we start to choose wisely, buy and consume in awareness of environmental issues. As Holy Father Francis writes, "the emptier a person's heart is, the more he or she needs things to buy, own and consume"(204).

The problem of ecology is more than a problem of nature. Well, should we continue selfishly to pollute the environment? We human beings and other animals will be extinct, but other types of organisms (rocks, sands, magma) will continue to exist over a longer period of time. So, we have to take into account that this environmental problem is a problem for human beings (and animals without which humankind

can scarcely flourish as a species). That is, the problem is anthropological. And this problem is ethical. In this regard, paragraph 202 reminds
us that it is we, human beings, who need to change. This unique point
of self-causation in the human is referred to in the history of philosophy many times, from different angles. For instance, Johann Gottlieb Fichte wrote that mighty rocks can come down and bury him or
waves of the ocean can sink him, but he is not afraid of them because
he courageously accepts his vocation, calling, destiny. In a nutshell,
human beings have a very unique ability to be aware that they cannot
change everything at will (even to marry or to divorce, etc.), but there
is nothing in the whole universe that can prevent them from thinking
differently. I particularly wonder why nature allowed us to be able to
refuse pleasure if we do not really want it. No natural force, government, or weapon can make a male procreate without his will. Nature
does not allow us to live forever, but it granted males the freedom to
choose celibacy. Can we just "force" ourselves to use less electricity, or
to eat no more than we need? True freedom and independence can be
achieved by means of this unique ability of self-causation, owing to
which any changes for a good cause only ever happened in history by
the intrinsic efforts of some courageous individuals.

Self-causation is not necessarily about self-restraint from everything
good. Try to recall how strong our instincts were when we were young.
Does strict self-restraint work? Once we accept celibacy we may end up
with another sin—pride in how advanced our spirituality seems to us.
Thus the spiritual path is narrow, for we can easily turn one virtue into
a sin, going from bad to worse. What is the answer then? "Christianity
does not reject matter" (235). We cannot suppress a tempest by means
of another tempest, yet we can just wait and have a rest, "thinkng that
we enjoy absolute power over our own bodies turns, often subtly, into
thinking that we enjoy absolute power over creation" (155).

Since Thomas Aquinas the Catholic Church accepts that matter
is one of the levels where universals exist. An example of service that
we can learn from the Catholic Church is its loyalty to actuality. For
example, initially the eco-problem started from reading the Bible as law,
according to which every animal and plant was created from "nothing"

and granted by God to humans for their own purposes (Genesis 1, 2). Then, that "nothing" was considered "something," that is to say, as matter. What we face now is that this "lowest type of being" is not chaotic and subordinate but a special kind of order in terms of which we have to order our thoughts and improve our understanding of the world: "There is the recognition that God created the world, writing into it an order and a dynamism that human beings have no right to ignore" (221). Here I have to admit that the church not only meets science but respects philosophy. This is a sign of the vitality of religion (like in China where Confucianism flourished with a totally different religion, Taoism, owing to their philosophic and non-dogmatic roots). This encyclical is a sign that the Catholic Church is less about teaching belief in a particular confession than in teaching belief in God. (We see the former when some denominations so "deeply love" God that they denounce others with a different experience of reading the Bible.) And in this way the Catholic Church might possibly unite humanity under the banner of actuality (the world we share) more effectively than under the potential salvation granted by a particular Church as if it had monopoly on relationships with God.

Special attention has been paid to the notion of balance by Father Francis (224-25). Environmental education "seeks to restore the various levels of ecological equilibrium, establishing harmony within ourselves, with others, with nature and other living creatures, and with God" (210). Taking into account the conceptual style of the encyclical, based on concepts of time and self-causation, the pope's address is not only about extensive development (harmony with others, with nature), but it also concerns individual growth (harmony with ourselves). This means, in my opinion, that all the problems human beings ever face come when we consume energy not by transforming it into something higher than we are (even plants which produce oxygen and food for animals transcend themselves in this way). Balance or equilibrium actually cannot be distorted. Once any species tries to distort it, nature fights back. If people take more than they give, they will become afraid of natural processes like physical death. If we consume energy without transforming it for the benefits of others (in forms of art, science, philosophy, sports etc) we naturally end up with social and personal conflicts. There are a lot more conflicts in families where parents think about themselves and not about the future of their children; there are a lot more quarrels where colleagues feign cooperation in their work and fail to pursue real social values. Governments that cannot value purposiveness in an individual's nature can find nothing better in order to control society than to threaten it, to deprive individuals of their freedom and creativity, and force them to expand spatially (conquer other nations and proclaim how "great" they are). When political leaders are unable to govern for good causes (transform energy that they take from society in the form of comfort, "freedom," and salary), they artificially try to establish and impose their importance as the so-called "defender" or "conqueror" and try to find enemies in their surroundings. Their fear of people leads them to threaten local communities and other areas. This is how the *circle* of being works when leaders think they can turn it into the line of their own personal progress.

Only the mental myopia of the industrial era offered a one-way paradigm: "just take and consume!" Human beings, like nature itself, are far more complex: behind stomach (economy, K. Marx) and other physical aspects (libido, S. Freud) human creatures have ideals, hopes, subjective aim, and subjective form that are parts of the balance and equilibrium as well.

Trying to think through the idea of balance, we have to admit that "consumer era" becomes outdated due to the fact that it is not enough for human beings to live in the most developed country because we are not defined just by the things we possess but by relationships. If you live in the most developed country but cannot agree with someone in your surroundings or even want to live with them, the best way for you is to move to another country, to other people who share the same ideas. Our true motherland is not defined by territory (we are not vegetables) but by others who have a comparatively similar point of view or world outlook to your understanding of reality. It is not even defined by language since once you have misunderstood or voluntarily disregarded others you will learn another language for nothing, be it German, Ukrainian, or even Chinese. But, how can you move somewhere if the rest of the world is poor and potentially dangerous for you? Even if you earn and spend each month the same amount of money as other people earn for years, but you have no choice except to agree with unjust decisions you may end up being mentally damaged because the superiority of the country where you live has bribed you and you are unable to live a truly human life. That is why eco-civilisation must suppose overcoming a big gap between developed and developing countries. Speaking to people from different countries has a healing effect because human beings realize their involvement with all humankind, and independence from a particular person might not always be good and sincere.

One very important outcome from this notion of balance in light of politics and consumerism has been made by the pope in his letter. In my reading of this encyclical, I find some cautions and warnings about obsession with a consumerist lifestyle: "when few people are capable of maintaining it, can only lead to violence and mutual destruction" (206).

Consider the beginning of World War II. Industrialization provided new workplaces for thousands of citizens, yet a lot more hands were free from constant labor in the fields, in the mines, due to new machinery intervention. People had electricity, oil, clothes, and . . . free time. How to control a population if people can use that time to develop their talents, communicate? Unfortunately, perhaps politicians of that time found nothing better than war that could provide 100% emmployment. I can be mistaken in my opinion of the real causes of World War II, but why were prisoners of war who voluntarily returned to their mother-land (my grandfather was among them) forced to go to other camps in their land (USSR after WWII)? Again, why did some countries experience genocide in circumstances wherein it can be avoided (e.g., the Ukrainian Genocide Famine 1932-1933)? The answer is obvious: politicians become afraid when people have free time. This is why the pope's words are very important when he says that "We need to strengthen the conviction that we are one single human family. There are no frontiers or barriers, political or social, behind which we can hide, still less is there room for the globalization of indifference" (52).

Now, let us ask what can occupy us in our free time. Programming? No, we have almost everything we need from IT. Space technologies?

Good idea, but we have problems on Earth which we do not want to solve. So-called exact science? Well, we cannot perceive more than our body affords us, and theories are merely mediated by other tools that cannot provide a picture without turning into a mere game of symbols that scientists proclaim as their calling (Adorno). Medicine? Economics? How long can we develop our comfort relying on a theory of economics (which, actually, fails from the beginning in its cardinal and ordinal approaches towards a theory of consumption)? How can our smart phones be improved, and do they certify that we are a civilized society when 1 billion of the population still works for 1 USD per day?

Unnecessary applications and media products are a sign that humans are not able to spend their time properly, that we want to avoid thinking about how to live in harmony with self and others. Instead, we become prone to "mental pollution." Thus, again, the problem of ecology is rooted in our mentality, and until we care properly for the "oikos" in our world outlook, we might wish to avoid creating problems with other creatures: "True wisdom, as the fruit of self-examination, dialogue and generous encounter between persons is not acquired by a mere accumulation of data which eventually leads to overload and confusion, a sort of mental pollution" (47) "Today, however, we have to realize that a true ecological approach *always* becomes a social approach; it must integrate questions of justice in debates on the environment, so as to hear *both the cry of the earth and the cry of the poor*" (49).

The bottom-line is: If we are unable to find a higher purpose by means of which we could transcend ourselves for other generations, then we have to produce and consume no more than what is necessary. Otherwise inexorable laws of nature or internal conflicts in our society will require us to pay the price of a reduced population. But "peace . . . is much more than the absence of war" (164). And the only cure, as it seems, is self-causation and creativity instead of production; *good will* instead of so-called *professionalism*.

To paraphrase Aristotle (who said that the state exists for individuals, not individuals for the state) we have to say that theories, like species, exist for humans, and no human should exist only to serve theories because theory itself is grounded in a certain purpose. And what kind of purpose we choose to follow is a *philosophical*, not scientific task to solve.

As Holy Father Francis puts it, to develop technologies is not bad (since it is in accordance with an individual's creativity, dignity, quality of life etc.). What is not good is when creativity is conditioned by profit for some minority in power (187).

The importance of religious figures lies in their role as moderators between two opposite political opinions. Sometimes, when two leaders are unable to come to terms, the only effective method is to show them how many people exist beyond their personal ambitions, and that their political (rather economical, to be honest) interests may represent only one tiny thing in light of long-term life: "the Church has no reason to offer a definitive opinion; she knows that honest debate must be encouraged among experts, while respecting divergent views" (61).

Again, from a philosophical point of view, I find this message from Holy Father Francis to be an invitation or offer to live a qualitatively different life in our century; we have to value our free time in the real world instead of stressful competition for the sake of consumption of things that rather have *appearance* than real value. *The primary task in the 21st eco-century is to **learn** how to live properly **qualitatively different** life, **not** to be enslaved by possession or the **multiplicity** of things.*

Some reporters admire how "great" politicians of the 20th century cope without sleep. New generations may wonder: would we have had fewer problems if responsible persons *did* sleep well? It is not a "Big Sleep" that I am offering here; rather it is *healthy nap* that prevents further mental diseases. Temporary chaos on the mental pole naturally cures order on the physical one. "Rest opens our eyes to the larger picture and gives us renewed sensitivity to the rights of others" (237).

Ironically, the dominant category of "appearance" (TV shows, glossy pictures, etc. that caused the crazy rat races of the 20th century) turned humanity into deep sleep where happiness is misplaced by the concept of success. Now we have to stop and be ready for a "reality" that might not be as pleasant as a dream is, but where relationships between events are not that ephemeral.

An Interreligious Response: Are We at the Tipping Point?

William Lesher

Are we approaching the Tipping Point in the ecological crisis? Is the papal encyclical *Laudato si'; mi' Signore (Praise be to you, my Lord)* that added bit of weight needed to send resistance to the climate-crisis plummeting? Now, will support grow for what the pope called "integral ecology" and for what was called "ecological civilization" at the June 2015 Claremont conference, not only among Catholic Christians but among people of all faiths and people of no faith, among the young and the old, from all walks of life and everywhere in the world? Probably not. These are questions that history will answer, of course. But for those of us who have pressed for, watched for, and prayed for a "breakthrough" of authoritative, worldwide inspiration to consolidate, challenge, and catalyze the global interfaith ecological movement, Pope Francis' eagerly awaited encyclical feels like it might be just such an event.

At the Claremont conference, I co-chaired one of the many small group tracks with Joseph Prabhu and Christopher Ives called "Re-imagining and Mobilizing Religious Traditions in Response to the Eco-crisis." At one point in this interfaith discussion with about 20 participants, I became aware that there were only two of us in the room from a Christian tradition. Yet the group was vigorously discussing, with great anticipation, the release of the papal encyclical ten days hence. It was obvious that for this sampling of interfaith, environmental activists, there was great expectation for what the pope's initiative would do to give new impetus to the whole interfaith climate movement. One of the participants told about an interfaith calendar of workshops, mass gatherings, and marches called "The Road to Paris," aimed at enlisting the full capacity of the interfaith world to influence the United Nations environment conference in December 2015. The release of the papal encyclical, *Laudato si'*, was the major happening that would be the kick-off of the whole ambitious endeavor.

As the Interfaith community becomes familiar with this remarkable document over the summer months, it is my judgment that they will not be disappointed. I think "Praise Be, To You My Lord," will inspire a wide swath of the global interfaith community to connect the links between faith and the deteriorating environment. It will set an agenda for many intra- and interreligious dialogues around the world, and it will draw out people of faith, spirit, and commitment to join local, national, and international movements seeking short- and long-term strategies to address the urgent eco-crisis.

In this brief article I want to share some of my initial responses to the pope's encyclical from my current viewpoint as an interreligious participant and observer. Specifically, I will comment on five elements that I consider to be strengths of this document.

The first is the inclusive nature of its address. In the introductory paragraphs, the pope writes, "I wish to address every person living on this planet. . . . In this Encyclical, I would like to enter into dialogue with all people about our common home" (3). This is unquestionably an unusual approach for the head of a major religious community. It may even be unique in the annals of interreligious declarations. As one reads on, it is clear that all humankind and even all life forms, the animals and the plants with whom we share the planet, are the audience for these words. Throughout the document the inherent unity of all aspects of the creation is echoed and presumed.

One can hope that the interreligious world will feel addressed by this prophetic, carefully researched call to a profound transformation of human and social behavior for the sake of our common home. And then ask: how can our faith tradition play its best role? Initial interreligious responses are encouraging. The major international interfaith organizations have enthusiastically welcomed the pope's encyclical. Hopefully this will stimulate the leadership of individual religious traditions around the world to take the pope's message personally and accept his collegial invitation to dialogue with him and with one another, seriously and urgently about the role of the religions in responding to the eco-crisis.

The second strength of *Praise Be*, from my interfaith perspective, is its literary accessibility. I am not an expert on papal encyclicals, to be sure, but this document with its imposing title is disarmingly easy and interesting to read. It is not a document couched in theological doctrine. Throughout, the warm, human personality of the Francis we are coming to know shines through. The language is clear and straightforward. At points he uses personal references to his own experience as illustrations. Even the more technical sections where the pope describes the science behind environmental degradation and later, when he writes directly about political obstacles, the role of market forces and carbon credits, his language is direct and uncomplicated. It is clear that he wants to communicate with us all. At times, I felt as if the English version were written specifically for Americans, given the language structure and idioms employed. It is a Catholic document from the leader of the largest global religion yet it contains little exclusive Catholic jargon. It is a good example of how best to communicate with the larger interreligious community and with all people on the planet.

A third strength of the encyclical is that it models a methodology for dealing with contentious issues in interfaith circles and with the larger human community. Throughout, the encyclical is an invitation to dialogue. The pope lays out strong positions on many disputed issues in the climate crisis discussion including: the human responsibility for the degradation of the environment; the immorality of consumerism and unbridled capitalism driven by profit motives; and the ineffective response of political structures especially when dominated by economic considerations. Then the pope writes, "There are certain environmental issues where it is not easy to achieve a broad consensus. Here I would state once more that the Church does not presume to settle scientific questions or to replace politics. But I am concerned to encourage an honest and open debate so that particular interests or ideologies will not prejudice the common good" (188). The strong stands articulated in the encyclical make it clear that while the pope does not expect the Church (or presumably any other religion) to "settle scientific questions or replace politics," he does presume that the Church, along with other religious communities, will have a prominent place at the table. One of the several roles the interreligious community might play is to support and echo this concern that as the discussions unfold and actions are taken in international, national and especially local venues, all the interests are represented and all the voices are heard.

A fourth, and very welcome strength of this encyclical, is that it sets an agenda for an urgent, fruitful, interreligious dialogue at many levels around the world. Again, the friendly, collegial, accessible way the pope has written makes this far-reaching use of the document possible. One can hope that interfaith leaders around the world are already planning how to unpack this document in local, regional, and international settings. What an ideal way to stimulate awareness and participation in the buildup to the December 2015 United Nations meetings on the eco-crisis. One can also hope that leaders of the many other religious and spiritual communities around the world are hearing that this personal, heartfelt appeal from the pope is addressed to them; that they will not receive it defensively but openly and graciously; that they will study it in the warm, concerned spirit in which it is written; and that it will move them to think about their own analysis of the global eco-crisis and how their faith community has and is and could respond in the future. In a best-case scenario, religious leaders will take this as a chance to do for their followers and for the whole human community what the pope has done. Where does *Praise Be* reflect a general ecumenical consensus among the world's religions? Where do others see the world differently and what is their call to their constituents and to us all about human life styles in the light of environmental degradation? This is obviously a highly optimistic possibility, yet, given the severity of the circumstances and the maturing of the interreligious movement in some places in the world, one could hope that this response will come from some quarters.

Fifth, this is a courageous document. The pope delivers a forceful critique of the effect of the unsustainable, consumer-dominated lifestyles of first-world people. In another section he carefully reasons how the idea of "unlimited growth so attractive to economists, financiers and experts in technology…is based on the lie that there is an infinite supply of the earth's good and this leads to the planet being squeezed dry beyond every limit" (106). Hard-hitting assertions like these found throughout the document have already thrown up formidable walls of resistance especially in conservative circles in the West. The pope's analysis is on a collision course with a host of ideas that are sacrosanct in some quarters including: the predominance of the human species over all other creatures and a form of patriotism or national pride that sees one's own nation as superior to others with permission to exploit an unequal amount of the world's resources. Again, when the encyclical is read in its entirety, it is clear throughout the document that the pope is inviting a vigorous global dialogue about an issue that is at the heart of our human unity, which is to say, our human survival. This is how he sees it. How do others see it?

Hopefully, many brave, concerned, and thoughtful people will accept the invitation and participate in a many faceted dialogue on the future of what the pope reminds us is "our common home." But many will not. Already the negative responses have overwhelmed the positive reactions in the popular press. *Laudato si'* will need defending by religious and spiritual communities around the world in general and by the interreligious communities in particular. On the one hand, critics will need to be challenged to put their criticism in a way that presents alternative points of view. On the other hand, there are many places where a document of this kind will simply be met with indifference, in which case it will be the task of the interfaith communities to promote its consideration as a means of initialing a critical discussion of these vital common issues.

A few additional observations are in order.

As many have noted, the pope has succeeded in making the environmental crisis not only a scientific or a political issue. *Praise Be* has made it a moral issue. I was surprised to hear the Legal Counsel of the city of Los Angeles echo and affirm these very words in a presentation of how LA will address carbon issues. Working to build an ecological life style, or as the pope says, teaching "ecological citizenship," is what it means to be a "good person." It is interesting for non-Catholic readers of the encyclical to remember that this document now becomes a part of Catholic social teaching.

The encyclical also builds a direct interactive bond between the eco-crisis and the plight of the poor, a special concern of this pope. The pope's own words here, where he undoubtedly is speaking from experience, make the point that care of the earth and of the poor must go together.

> The human environment and the natural environment deteri- orate together.... In fact, the deterioration of the environment and of society affects the most vulnerable people on the planet: For example, ...water pollution particularly affects the poor who cannot buy bottled water; and rises in the sea level mainly affect impoverished coastal populations who have nowhere else to go. The impact of present imbalances is also seen in the pre- mature death of many of the poor, in conflicts sparked by the shortage of resources, and in any number of other problems which are insufficiently represented on global agendas. (48).

Finally, from my personal perspective I wish the pope could have found a way to make this historic appeal an interreligious happening. One can only wonder what the impact would be if a document similar to this encyclical, addressed to all the people of the world, had come from the pope, together with the Dali Lama and a representative group of leaders of the world's religions. Unfortunately such a wish is unre- alistic given the present stage of interreligious development. The next best thing will be for people the world over to seize this chance the pope has provided to launch the urgent dialogue he is pleading for. It would be an extraordinary response, indeed, if people of faith and spirit and goodwill and those concerned for our common human home would hear the pope's call, and engage in discussing, debating, and deciding about these critical human issues. Many people will dismiss notions like this as naive and impossible. Yet these are extraordinary times that have the capacity to provoke surpassing and uncharacteristic actions—like the pope has demonstrated in issuing *Laudato si'* to the world.

PART

SIX

Philosophy

At the Bedside of Mother Earth

Bonnie Tarwater

June is bustin' out all over
All over the meader and the hill
Flowers bustin' out on bushes
And the roughen river pushes
Ev'ry little wheel that wheels beside the mill

~Rogers and Hammerstein, *Carousel*

The last few days of June 2015, I found myself humming this tune. "That is odd," I thought to myself. "What in heaven's name made that obscure song pop into my head?"

It came to me in a flash: June 2015 was the month that "busted out all over" in global consciousness-raising, not only for me but for Gaia, *anima mundi* (the soul of the world), planet earth, or—as Pope Francis tenderly refers to her as "our Sister, our Mother."

The nightmare that is climate change and our current ecological crisis are so horrifying that many of us have gone into denial and paralysis. Scientists who study the history of the earth tell us that we are in the sixth mass extinction of life on earth, but this one (unlike the first five mass extinctions) has not been brought on by an asteroid or other natural event; it has been brought on by us—humans. "Our sister and our mother," the earth, is a living, breathing organism, and she is sick with a fever called climate change that keeps rising. If the earth was a human body, or if the human family were one body, she would be in intensive care in a hospital, and a chaplain would be called. Just as we watch human organs begin to fail and shut down in a dying human, we are witnessing animals and plant species become extinct daily, and millions of our brothers, fathers, sisters, and mothers suffer from disasters, poverty, and violence.

June 2015, however, brought several extraordinary caregivers to our mother's bedside.

On June 18, 2015, many of us read Pope Francis encyclical titled "*Laudato si'* Praise be to you—On Care for Our Common Home." It is the first encyclical on the environment in the history of the Roman Catholic Church, and it comes just in the nick of time. I have a sense of relief similar to the relief I feel when a religious person comes to pray at the bedside of a seriously sick loved one.

This encyclical is not just about the environment; it is also about people. It is a bold statement about the moral bankruptcy that enables us to put profits above the common good. In the tradition of biblical prophets, the encyclical shouts:

> We have to realize that a true ecological approach always becomes a social approach; it must integrate questions of justice in debates on the environment, so as to hear both the cry of the earth and the cry of the poor. (49)

Not just the earth but our human family is sick and crying out in pain, for we are not separate. We are one body. Prophet Francis calls us to a "global ecological conversion." He ends the encyclical with prayer. Thank you, Pope Francis. Thank you for coming just in the nick of time and praying for us, and thank you for your spiritual leadership. I will pray for you and support you in any way I can.

Crisis brings the invitation for radical consciousness-raising or a "bustin' out all over" of old ways of thinking and behaving. This new "Green Pope" is the moral, spiritual, and religious leader for 1.2 billion Roman Catholics. In theory, his message to them could lead the Catholic Church to begin immediate raising of consciousness as they work *en masse* for "global ecological conversion." There has never been an institution like the Catholic Church with its massive ability to effect change.

Already Jesuit universities and high schools around the world have begun teaching about the environmental crisis. With this astoundingly passionate theological proclamation of the duty to protect God's creation, the Green Pope has begun "bustin' out all over" in consciousness-raising in the Catholic Church. He does not however, just address Roman Catholic bishops, or even just the laity:

> Now, faced as we are with global environmental deterioration, I wish to address every person living on this planet. . . . In this Encyclical, I would like to enter into dialogue with all people about our common home. (3)

If anybody can write a letter to the seven billion human souls in our human family, knowing it will be read by a significant number of us, it is Pope Francis.

Earlier in June 2015, a mere two thousand of us participated in "Seizing an Alternative," the largest transdisciplinary conference ever held on behalf of the planet. The architect of this conference was Dr. John B. Cobb, Jr., who is considered to be one of the most important North American theologians of the 20th and 21st centuries. It was organized by the Center for Process Studies at the Claremont School of Theology. It was the Tenth in the series of International Whitehead Conferences sponsored by the International Process Network. Whitehead's "process" philosophy provides the radical vision that shapes the work of the Center and the Network. As if we really were one human family, people from many different backgrounds, worldviews, and cultures gathered in unity at the bedside of "our Sister and our Mother." This is the natural response the world over when someone in a family is sick Sitting at this bedside calls for the unity of science and religion and of the various religious traditions. Whitehead's philosophy provides grounds for this unity.

Unfortunately, our modern scientific era has often led us to go against our natural intuitive human responses. Specialization in education, for example, has not fostered the academic disciplines to gather round the bedside of any of our social ills. Instead, they have stayed in their own rooms like antisocial teenagers who can't be bothered with a sick relative. The ill effects are countless and include the promotion of "value free" education and the inability to see the big picture. We have focused on smaller and smaller pieces of information, and everyone has suffered the pain of alienation, isolation, loneliness, and meaninglessness. Information is obviously not all that is needed at the bedside of sick loved ones. We need the invisible non-rational stuff that religious people represent. We need soulful love and the wisdom and life experience elders bring.

Hosting a transdisciplinary conference and inviting scientists and theologians, philosophers, social activists, artists, and economists to come together for the sake of the environment is radical in and of itself. As the Hebrews wandered in the desert for forty years, Moses could not get his people to stop thinking like slaves. Similarly, for forty-five years since the first Earth Day, Cobb and his colleagues have not been able to galvanize the academic community to oppose the greed and over-consumption that are wrecking the environment. The "value free" ideal for education leaves unchallenged the capitalist values that now shape education itself as well as the destructive culture in which it occurs.

Not only was "Seizing an Alternative" transdisciplinary, it was international and showcased leaders who represented millions of people. Keynote speakers included Dr. Vandana Shiva, a Hindu, physicist, and major leader in the ecology movement in India; and Sheri Liao, a Chinese environmental activist. If it is true that the pope has the ears of 1.2 billion Catholics around the globe; and Dr. Cobb and Sheri Liao have the ears of 1.4 billion people in China; and Vandana Shiva has access to the ears of 828 million Hindus in India, perhaps we can look to former U.S. Senator Everett Dirksen from Illinois for hope as he was reported to have said: "A billion here, a billion there, pretty soon it adds up."

The Claremont conference was also the Ninth in a series of conferences held annually by the Institute for Postmodern Development of China. This is a spin-off of the Center for Process Studies and has created such interest in China that twenty-six universities there have established their own Centers for Process Studies. The conferences are all on "Ecological Civilization," the term that has now been used for more than a decade in China to name what the pope calls "integral ecology." The Chinese government is committed to the goal of ecological civilization as the pope seeks to dedicate the Roman Catholic Church to the goal of integral ecology. More than a hundred came from China to take part in the conference. China has been dealing with this challenge for years and may have something to teach the rest of us. The Chinese have often found that Whitehead's philosophy helps them renew their traditional values without blocking their appropriation of science and technology.

When the Reverend Jorge Mario Bergoglio, Archbishop of Buenos Aires, was elected pope, he was asked, "By what name shall you be called?" His answer was auspicious: He took Francis as his name. His words about St. Francis in the encyclical encourage mystical Christian contemplation:

> Francis helps us to see that an integral ecology calls for openness to categories which transcend the language of mathematics and biology, and take us to the heart of what it is to be human. Just as happens when we fall in love with someone, whenever he would gaze at the sun, the moon or the smallest of animals, he burst into song, drawing all other creatures into his praise. He communed with all creation, even preaching to the flowers, inviting them "to praise the Lord, just as if they were endowed with reason". His response to the world around him was so much more than intellectual appreciation or economic calculus, for to him each and every creature was a sister united to him by bonds of affection. That is why he felt called to care for all that exists. His disciple Saint Bonaventure tells us that, "from a reflection on the primary source of all things, filled with even more abundant piety, he would call creatures, no matter how small, by the name of 'brother' or 'sister.'" Such a conviction cannot be written off as naive romanticism, for it affects the choices which determine our behavior. If we approach nature and the environment without this openness to awe and wonder, if we no longer speak the language of fraternity and beauty in our relationship with the world, our attitude will be that of masters, consumers, ruthless exploiters, unable to set limits on their immediate needs. By contrast, if we feel intimately united with all that exists, then sobriety and care will well up spontaneously. The poverty and austerity of Saint Francis were no mere veneer of asceticism, but something much more radical: a refusal to turn reality into an object simply to be used and controlled. (11, 12)

The pope was on a roll. On June 27, he invited Naomi Klein to the Vatican. Her recent book, *This Changes Everything,* speaks with unquestionable moral force against the evils of capitalism—as if channeling Jesus himself. (Yep, *this* is what got me humming "June is bustin'out all over.")

The pope and Klein both articulate the horrific effects of environmental degradation on the poor and the war that capitalism is waging against the earth. A secular Jewish feminist standing in solidarity with Pope Francis about the corrupt economic systems that have empowered the fossil fuel companies to destroy our planet? I *am* bustin' out all over in *song,* not just humming!

> For poor countries, the priorities must be to eliminate extreme poverty and to promote the social development of their people. At the same time, they need to acknowledge the scandalous level of consumption in some privileged sectors of their population and to combat corruption more effectively. (172)

The pope says, "All it takes is one good person to restore hope!" (71). But in June 2015, I heard the voices of many good people and caretakers: Vandana Shiva, Sheri Liao, Naomi Klein, Pope Francis, Bill McKibben, John Cobb, all sharing the inconvenient truth that we are in an unprecedented global and human crisis, and we *have* to come together in radical new ways. Comments by Shiva and McKibben promoting nonviolent revolution and civil disobedience were music to my ears. Jesus did not seek directly to overthrow the Roman Empire.

But who is going to teach this non-violent revolution? Learning to love your enemies and studying non-violence and civil disobedience requires spiritual teachers that, historically, have always come from the religious community. The anti-slavery and civil rights movements here in the United States and the non-violent revolution against the powers of the British Empire were religious movements. Are our Christian churches in the United States up to teaching non-violence and civil disobedience? Are we as Christians committed to the difficult work of learning to love our "inner Koch bothers?"

Frankly, as a Christian parish minister, I have been discouraged in recent years. The events of June have inspired me to recommit to follow in the footsteps of Jesus and Mary Magdalene, St. Francis and St. Clare of Assisi. Something is "bustin' out all over" in me as I feel movement from paralysis to resolve and commitment.

As a feminist, I wish the pope had addressed the ways that patriarchy, power-over relationships, and the church's history of misogyny have all contributed to our ecological crisis. We have dishonored the divine feminine in religion and in patriarchal societies for thousands of years, and *this must be named and changed.* What we have done to women's bodies we have done to the earth. Pope Francis says this indirectly when he writes:

> This sister now cries out to us because of the harm we have inflicted on her by our irresponsible use and abuse of the goods with which God has endowed her ... we have forgotten that we ourselves are dust of the earth (Gen. 2:7); our very bodies are made up of her elements, we breathe her air and we receive life and refreshment from her waters. (2)

Is it synchronicity (two or more events with no apparent causal relationship that seem to be meaningfully related) that the ecological conference and the pope's encyclical occurred within days of each other? As Jesus says, "Whoever has ears to hear, let them hear" (Mark 4:9).

But it does not stop there. Naomi Klein was invited to the Vatican (my personal humming begins), and soon Pope Francis will be the first pope to address the U.S. Congress (on September 24, 2015). In December he will be at the United Nations climate summit in Paris. "June *is* bustin' out all over." I hope and pray that this bustin' momentum is the tipping point for the birth of a new consciousness-raising, for "a global ecological conversion" (5). It is past time we "seize an alternative."

There are not words enough to express my gratitude for all who are now at the bedside of our sick sister and mother. In my experience as a minister, there is something that happens in the invisible realm when I invite a family to join hands and pray around a sick relative in a hospital room. I do not understand it, but I have experienced it many times. Something indescribable but powerful and important occurs. Even the loved one who is in a coma seems to know when everyone has cared enough to gather round in prayer. It is past time that we come out of our teenage self-centered rooms of isolation and gather round the bedside and pray. Perhaps someone is pregnant in our prayer circle and will give birth to a symbolic divine child for a new era—not only for a global consciousness but for a cosmic consciousness.

Of all those who have ministered at the bedside, I want especially to thank Pope Francis and Cobb, prophets and spiritual high priests of astonishing moral courage, vision, and love. For me personally, "June is bustin' out all over" is about the joy and movement of the Holy Spirit, Pope Francis, and Cobb, who have made Christianity relevant for me again—and, I am guessing, for a few billion others of us.

I offer you and all God's creatures the prayer attributed to St. Francis of Assisi:

> Make me an instrument of your peace,
> Where there is hatred, let me sow love;
> where there is injury, pardon;
> where there is doubt, faith;
> where there is despair, hope
> where there is darkness, light
> where there is sadness, joy;
>
> O Divine Mother/Father, grant that I may not so much
>   seek to be consoled as to console;
> to be understood as to understand; to be loved as to love.
> For it is in giving that we receive;
> it is in pardoning that we are pardoned;
> and it is in dying that we are born to eternal life.

Some Reflections on *Laudato Si'*

Vern Visick

Laudato si' may turn out to be the most important statement of Roman Catholic social teaching since *Rerum novarum*, (1891), perhaps the most important such statement ever. *Rerum novarum* was largely concerned with the internal justice of a rising industrial society, especially the proper relationship between capital and labor, while *Laudato si'* has to do with a much larger and more basic question, namely, the justice of a fully developed industrial society in relation to the fate of life itself.

As a document with a practical end in mind, the encyclical is extremely timely, appearing, as it has, six months before the December 2015 Paris negotiations over climate change, and three months before Pope Francis's projected appearances before the United Nations, the U.S. Congress, and the Roman Catholic conference on the family. As Hannah Arendt has said, the right word at the right time IS action.

But the right word at the right time is also a matter of content, and on this front as well the encyclical shines.

For one thing, the encyclical strongly supports the scientific consensus on the impact of rising levels of CO_2 and other greenhouse gases on climate change. This is a politically important matter because of the attacks on climate science by climate science skeptics, so potent in the larger community.

For another, the encyclical brings forward, in a very compelling manner, the environmental concerns of previous popes, as well as similar concerns by bishops and church leaders from around the world, and sets them in the context of a well-thought-out biblical theology of the environment. Few reading this text will be able to avoid the judgment that concern for the environmental crisis, and especially its impact on the poor and marginal around the world, is not an optional matter for people of faith, but a necessity.

And finally, the encyclical places the responsibility for our decrepit state of affairs squarely where it belongs. He shows that the leading elements in our civilization have not only mismanaged the science, technology, and markets that characterize our civilization, (i.e., capitalism). But there is but also something deeper—an arrogant attitude of domination toward the creation, or even—as Francis suggests at one point—a desire to play God.

All of this is well taken, appropriate, and powerful, and it has been interesting to watch the public response to this encyclical in various sectors of the population. While watching the reaction unfold, however, it must be remembered that the pope has made some further suggestions about what ought to be done in the midst of the environmental crisis, and his comments deserve at least some brief attention.

Quite appropriate, in the midst of our confused and distracting situation, is Francis' assertion that what is needed now is action at the most general, corporate, political level as well as at the individual, local level.

Well taken is the pope's judgment that at the level of politics what will be happening at the Paris meetings in November and December will be of decisive importance for the future of the world, and that constructive efforts to limit the amount of CO_2 and other greenhouse gasses being put into the atmosphere need to be supported in as many ways as possible.

Also appropriate, over the longer run, is his judgment that the rich countries must now step up and begin to develop ways in which to repay their environmental debt to countries in the developing world, as is his suggestion that we need to work for reform at the national level in such matters as overcoming the financialization of our economic system.

Of special interest to environmentalists is Francis' negative judgment about the value of cap and trade programs that, in the European context at least, have proven to be ineffective and subject to corruption. But missing, as far as I can see, is any recognition of the virtues of a carbon fee and dividend system, a scheme that shows great promise in weaning us from fossil fuels and creating the conditions for a carbon-free energy system.

Also well taken is Francis' support for the value of "small steps" that might be taken toward environmental responsibility at the local, individual level. Such actions, he writes, are valid in themselves and are also to be valued because small steps can lead to larger, more extensive steps, later on.

Beyond responding in the immediate situation, however, Francis asserts that over the long run something deeper is needed, and that is a change of heart on environmental matters. We need an "ecological conversion," and the pope suggests that this might be brought about through the development of a new approach to technology, by a new educational effort, and finally, through traditional religious means.

Francis' suggestion about developing a new approach to technology involves the creation of what he calls "integral ecology," in which the controlling attitude typical of our practice of technology might be balanced with a contemplative, receptive attitude toward the natural world, a process that he feels might result in a more appropriate scientific, technological, and business practice.

Furthermore, Francis suggests that we need educational reform on two fronts: on the one hand, by encouraging a more active immersion in nature in such a way that the beauty of nature might increase our motivation to care for our injured sister (overcoming what some have called our "nature deficit" disorder) and, on the other hand, by encouraging the development of more ecologically responsible character traits and habits. Here, the pope shows himself to be a true son of the church and its Thomistic/Aristotelian emphasis on education.

But the pope, although a Jesuit, is a Franciscan by avocation and thus a fan not only of Thomas but also of Bonaventure. Thus his final suggestion is that an ecological conversion might be advanced by taking up the environmental issue in the context of Roman Catholic worship and liturgical life. Through a renewed relationship with God, Francis implies, a more meaningful ecological spirituality might be born, one that more adequately looks out for the welfare of the creation as well as that of the poor and marginal of our world. As John Shea, a Jesuit scientist responding to the encyclical said recently, "One does not simply read *Laudato si'*, one prays with it."[1]

One last comment, however, in relation to those of us reading the encyclical with philosophical questions in mind.

Anyone reading this encyclical will note the conspicuous absence of any references to utilitarian or pragmatic philosophers in the text of the document. Instead, there are numerous references to Thomas (Aristotelian) and to Bonaventure (a Platonist and Augustinian). What is going on here?

One clue might be the fact that in the 180 pages of text of this encyclical, one phrase is repeated at least 12 times: "everything is connected . . ." What is the meaning of the continuous refrain that "everything is connected"?

If one takes the sentence "everything is connected" seriously, it means at least the following: That nothing exists alone, in its owns right, but only in relationship—and that these relationships, therefore, must receive their due, or there will be trouble, and life will ultimately be endangered as a result.

The recognition of the ontological importance of relationship has many implications for the conduct of human life.

For example, in relation to the notion of human freedom, so important in American life, the fundamental importance of relationship means that a strictly negative doctrine of freedom, in which freedom is seen in the context of an increasing absence of restraints on one's behavior, is inadequate for the situation in which we find ourselves. For, if no one exists alone, but only in relationship, then freedom must have some positive content, namely what justice requires in each of the relationships that constitute our lives.

If the notion of freedom having content, which is the understanding of freedom in the classical tradition, makes any sense—and it makes more sense every day as the environmental crisis expands into every area of our lives—then the question must be raised: in an era in which human power has become a dominant element in the life of the planet, what is the positive content that freedom demands of us in our time? Given our historical situation, must we not make the judgment that freedom today demands a concern for, and response to, the welfare of the whole world and the multiplicity of its most significant relationships? In other words, shouldn't our orientation be toward what the Whiteheadians call "world loyalty," and our chief calling be to understand what such a loyalty might mean in our response to the contemporary world?

Endnotes

1. John Shea, *The Jesuit Post: Real Presence and the Living God* (2 July 2015), 1.

Local Change Agents and
General Perspective

Franz Riffert

Some call *Laudato si'* the groundbreaking first environmental encyclical; others argue it is another social encyclical, comparable in its
fundamental analysis to *Rerum novarum*. Such classifications, although
each of them is referring to an important aspect, do not, I think, reach
the truly revolutionary core of this text that addresses not only the Catholic world but "every person living on this planet" (3).

From a superficial quantitative glance at the English version of this
encyclical, one can find the words (inter)relate(d), (inter)relation(s), rela-
tionship(s), (inter)connect(ed), connection(s) about one hundred times.
Moreover, the importance of the concept of relationship is underscored
by a reference to the concept of a trinitarian God as a model of the
world: "The divine Persons are subsistent relations and the world, created
according to the divine model, is a web of relationships" (240). And
therefore "[o]ur efforts at education will be inadequate and ineffectual
unless we strive to promote a new way of thinking about human beings,
life, society and our relationship with nature" (215).

So the concept of "relationship" carries the argumentation of this
encyclical; but it goes beyond this heavy burden: it is the cornerstone of
an alternative world view. "The human person grows more, matures more
and is sanctified more to the extent that he or she enters into relationships

416

going out from themselves to live in communion with God, with others and with all creatures. In this way they make their own that trinitarian dynamism which God imprinted in them when they were created. Everything is interconnected, and this invites us to develop a spirituality of that global solidarity which flows from the mystery of the Trinity" (240.

This fundamental connectedness of all levels of reality seems to have been lost for many people living in an almost purely technology-driven culture. "To seek only technical remedy to each environmental problem which comes up is to separate what is in reality connected and to mask the true and deepest problems of the global system" (111).

At the same time "[m]odernity has been marked by an excessive anthropocentrism which today, under another guise, continues to stand in the way of shared understanding and of any effort to strengthen social bonds" (116). The combination of technical possibilities and excessive anthropocentrism has issued into a modern "Promethean vision of mastery over the world" (116).

In the light of this fatal development, Pope Francis calls for a conversion which issues into the development of "a number of attitudes which together foster a spirit of generous care, full of tenderness" (220).

I will focus on just two aspects of the pope's call for conversion and argue that these two aspects, despite their high demands are nevertheless realistic.

First, Pope Francis draws attention to the fact that local communities play an important role as carriers of change and should not be neglected:

> New processes taking shape cannot always fit into frameworks imported from outside; they need to be based in the local culture itself. [...] Merely technical solutions run the risk of addressing symptoms and not the more serious underlying problems. There is a need to respect the rights of peoples and cultures, and to appreciate that the development of social groups presupposes an historical process which takes place within a cultural context and demands the constant and active involvement of local people from *within their proper culture*. (144 italics in the text)

Sometimes, "while the existing world order proves powerless to assume its responsibilities, local individuals and groups can make a real difference" (179; see also 183).

For almost 200 years such calls for local activities, particularly when aiming at the sustainable self-management of common pool resources, seemed to be naïve due to the unquestioned paradigm of "the tragedy of the commons" (Lloyd 1833; Hardin 1968) in economic science. It was Elinor Ostrom (2010), the first female Nobel Prize laureate in economics, who challenged this long-standing prejudice of economy by gathering cases of successful self-management of diverse commons, such as fishing grounds and pasture and irrigation systems, from different parts of the world and combined them with field studies and laboratory experiments (for instance on communicative decision making). She was able to show that local communities cannot only successfully, i.e. in the first place sustainably, manage common pool resources, but they can do so more efficiently than central institutions (states) and free markets (private companies). Probably most important in this respect is that Ostrom (1990) was able to distill out of her multi-faceted work so-called core design principles which help local communities to organize in a way which makes sustainable success more probable. So the pope's reference to local communities as change agents today does not seem as naïve as it might have seemed.

Second, Pope Francis also laments the ongoing specialization within the technical culture:

> The specialization which belongs to technology makes it difficult to see the larger picture. The fragmentation of knowledge proves helpful for concrete applications, and yet it often leads to a loss of appreciation of the whole, for the relationships between things and for the broader horizon, which then becomes irrelevant. This very fact makes it hard to find adequate ways of solving the more complex problems of today's world, particularly those regarding the environment and the poor; these problems cannot be dealt with from a single perspective or from a single set of interests. A science which would offer solutions to the great issues would necessarily have to take into account the data generated by other fields of knowledge, including philosophy and social ethics; but this is difficult to acquire today. (110)

Alfred North Whitehead, one of the eminent metaphysicians of the 20th century and probably best known for his work in modern logic, has made the same point:

Another great fact confronting the modern world is the discovery of the method of training professionals, who specialize in particular regions of thought and thereby progressively add to the sum of knowledge within their respective limitations of subject. [...] The dangers of professionalism are great, particularly in our democratic societies. The directive force of reason is weakened. [...] In short, the specialized functions of the community are performed better and more progressively, but the generalized direction lacks vision. (1967, 196f)

Whitehead's answer to this problem was "to construct a system of ideas which brings the aesthetic, moral, and religious interests into relation with those concepts of the world which have their origin in the natural science" (1979, xii). Ilya Prigogine and Isabelle Stengers wrote that Whitehead's "extraordinary resoluteness to achieve a comprehensive consistency is truly fascinating. [...] Whitehead's cosmology is the so far most ambitious attempt of such a philosophy. [...] The point was to formulate a minimum of principles by which each and every physical existence—from stone to humans—could be characterized" (1981, 101ff translation FR; similar Bochenski 1951, 106).

Of course it is a very demanding task to develop such general and multi-disciplinary systems of thought and of course they are tentative and fallible: "In philosophical discussion, the merest hint of dogmatic certainty as to finality of statement is an exhibition of folly" (Whitehead 1979, xiv). The development of alternative general views is possible and Whitehead has even encouraged the development of such alternatives as a means of approaching the most comprehensible system of reality possible for finite human beings (Whitehead 1958, 65-90).

Here again Whitehead's position seems to come close to the one held by Pope Francis in *Laudato si'*: "

Viable future scenarios will have to be generated between these extremes [of a technological optimism on the one side and a technological pessimism on the other], since there is no one path to a solution. This makes a variety of proposals possible, all capable of entering into a dialogue with a view to developing comprehensive solutions. (60)

It should have become clear that *Laudato si'* is a document that calls for a radical change in moving our segregating scientific-techno-logical culture towards a culture of interrelationships. And Pope Francis leaves no doubt that such a culture of interrelatedness itself can only be brought about by interrelated activities such as communication: "I urgently appeal, then, for a new dialogue about how we are shaping the future of our planet. We need a conversation which includes everyone, since the environmental change we are undergoing, and its human roots, concern and affect us all" (14).

References

Bochenski, J. (1951). *Europäische Philosophie der Gegenwart [Contemporary European Philosophy]*. Bern: Francke.

Hardin, G. (1968). "The Tragedy of the Commons." *Science* 162, 3859, 1243-48. Also available online at: <http://www.geo.mtu.edu/~asmayer/rural_sustain/governance/Hardin%201968.pdf>. Accessed 07/07/2015.

Lloyd, W. F. (1833). *Two Lectures on the Checks to Population*. Oxford: Collingwood.

Ostrom, E. (1990). *Governing the Commons. The Evolution of Institutions for Collective Action*. Cambridge: Cambridge University Press.

Ostrom, E. (2009). "Beyond Markets and States: Polycentric Governance of Complex Economic Systems." *American Economic Review* 100 (3), 641-72. Also available online at: <http://bnp.binghamton.edu/wp-content/uploads/2011/06/Ostrom-2010-Polycentric-Governance.pdf>. Accessed 07/07/2015.

Prigogine, I. & Stengers, I. (1981). *Dialog mit der Natur [Dialogue with Nature]*. München: Piper.

Whitehead, A. N. (1958). *The Function of Reason*. Boston: Beacon Press.

Whitehead, A. N. (1967/1925.) *Science and the Modern World*. New York: Free Press.

Whitehead, A. N. (1978/1929.) *Process and Reality*. New York: Free Press.

Comments on *Laudato Si'*

Joseph A. Bracken, S.J.

Mary Evelyn Tucker, in her essay "Climate Change Brings Moral Change," notes that Pope Francis "encourages us to see the human economy as a subsystem of nature's economy, namely the dynamic interaction of life in ecosystems. Without a healthy natural ecology there is not a sustainable economy and vice-versa. They are inevitably interdependent." The underlying philosophical issue here, as I see it, is the proper relationship between the whole and its parts or members within an overall systems-oriented approach to physical reality. That is, systems, enduring well-organized groups of entities rather than individual entities as such, are the "building blocks" of physical reality. Admittedly, they cannot exist apart from the ongoing dynamic interrelationships among their constituent parts or members. Yet the system tends to outlast the individual entities that brought it into existence and, for the moment, keep it in existence. Sooner or later, these individual parts or members will be replaced by new parts or members but, in most cases, with the same basic mode of operation as before. A gradual change in the mode of operation of the system can indeed take place over time in virtue of changes in the dynamics of the ongoing relationships between the parts or members, especially in their dealing with an ever-changing external environment which is itself a vast system of ongoing interrelated sub-systems.

Whitehead's understanding of the ongoing reciprocal relation between societies and their constituent actual entities in *Process and Reality* admirably fits this generic description of systems and their constituent parts or members:

> The causal laws which dominate a social environment are the product of the defining characteristic of that society. But the society is only efficient through its individual members. Thus in a society, the members can only exist by reason of the laws which dominate the society, and the laws only come into being by reason of the analogous characters of the members of the society. (90-91)

Furthermore, Whitehead's notion of a "structured society" which includes subordinate societies and nexuses is likewise in accord with an overall systems-oriented approach to reality. For it allows for the coordination of ontologically independent societies of actual entities to bring about the emergence of a new higher-order society with a mode of operation distinct from the antecedent mode of operation of the subsocieties. Yet, while the subsocieties still retain their own basic mode of operation, that mode of operation is necessarily somewhat altered by reason of now being part of a higher-order social reality. A molecule is still a molecule within a cell, but the pattern of existence and activity of the molecule has to be adjusted to the independent workings of the cell and vice-versa. Whitehead's line of thought on the reality of structured societies within nature justifies, in my view, the contention of Pope Francis that the economic system has to work within the constraints of the broader ecological system governing the continued existence of life on this earth. If the economic system fails to work within these constraints, then it ultimately undercuts the basis for its own continued existence along with the continued well-being of the ecology of the planet.

Moreover, Whitehead's presupposition that the constituent parts or members of these societies or systems are actual entities, momentary self-constituting subjects of experience, is an effective guarantee that the system in question is not closed or fully deterministic in its mode of operation. That is, any system that is composed of individual entities with at least some measure of spontaneity in their self-constitution will necessarily be open-ended, not governed by universal laws or mathematical formulae which abstract from the concrete situation at hand in the effort to attain an unreal objectivity, often at the cost of considerable harm to those individual entities directly affected by those same universal laws or abstract mathematical formulae. Ontological reductionism, in other words, only seems to work within human thought-systems; it notably fails in describing the workings of actual life-systems in the world of nature. So the pope is correct in calling attention in the encyclical to the undifferentiated and one-dimensional character of modern technology insofar as it dehumanizes the relations of human beings to one another and strips the world of nature of its intrinsic meaning and value, apart from the purposes of those who seek to exploit its resources for self-centered reasons. Like everything else in life, technology is a two-edged sword that has to be used with caution lest it do more harm than good.

Finally, the long-term consequences of this surprising convergence of views between Whiteheadian metaphysics and papal teaching on the global economy are in my judgment twofold. First of all, it should remind Whiteheadians and other thinkers that are heavily influenced by the appeal to reason as the privileged answer to all life's problems that authority properly exercised can have an enormous impact on the thinking and behavior of people who only need the right kind of motivation to make significant changes in their customary way of life. That is, the appeal to reason, taken by itself, lacks the power to win over minds and hearts that a person in authority can command when he/she speaks with authority on matters of common concern not only to faithful followers but *urbi et orbi,* to well-intentioned people around the world.

Secondly, the papal insistence on the need to integrate concern for the needs of ordinary people with concern for the preservation of the environment within the workings of the present-day highly complex global economy should remind the admirers of classical Thomistic philosophy and theology that the latter worldview, even given its prominent place in the history of Western philosophy and theology, is not thereby a *philosophia perennis* suitable for use at all times and in all situations. Every human thought-system, however carefully articulated, is necessarily perspectival. Both in its metaphysical presuppositions and in its basic methodology or mode of operation, the system will reflect historical limitations that cannot be overcome simply by a process of tinkering with details so as to "save the appearances" of full conformity with physical reality. Sooner or later, a new thought-system, based on a new understanding of the world in which we live, will inevitably arise to supplement and thereby to enlarge the older world view, much in the same way that the Newtonian world view has been modified to accommodate insights from relativity theory and quantum mechanics even as it continues to function quite well within the world of common sense experience. Reality is too big to be fully encompassed within a single worldview, however impressive it may be in other respects.

References

Whitehead, A.N. *Process and Reality.* 1929. Corrected edition. Ed. D.W. Sherburne and D.R. Griffin. New York: The Free Press, 1978.

An Appeal to Build up an Ecological Civilization

Vesselin Petrov

It is not an overstatement to say that the papal encyclical *Laudato si'* is one of the most important events in our present epoch, because it points to the most pressing problem of our planet—the ecological crisis and the urgent necessity to find the right way for overcoming it. I shall express my attitude to the encyclical from three perspectives: first, as a Whiteheadian scholar who is worried about the present state and the future of our civilization; second, as a citizen belonging to Eastern Europe, and third, as Executive Director of the International Process Network. Of course, the expressed position from all these perspectives is directed to the same aim: the necessity to defend our civilization from an ecological and global crisis and to develop civilization toward a much better future.

In the introduction of his encyclical Pope Francis appeals for a new dialogue on how we are shaping the future of our planet, because there is an urgent challenge to protect our common home and to seek a sustainable and integral development (13-14). My response to that appeal as a citizen of our planet, a philosopher, and a Whiteheadian is that we should all actively participate in that dialogue. We need to reach an agreement about the next steps that are urgently needed to save our planet from ecological collapse and to develop it for a better future.

Let me note here the insight of Whitehead, expressed already in 1929 in *The Function of Reason*:

> The higher forms of life are actively engaged in modifying their environment. In the case of mankind this active attack on the environment is the most prominent fact in his existence. . . . (T)he explanation of this active attack on the environment is a three-fold urge: (i) to live, (ii) to live well, (iii) to live better. In fact the art of life is *first* to be alive, *secondly* to be alive in a satisfactory way, and *thirdly* to acquire an increase in satisfaction. (9)

Such satisfaction—and especially such an increase in satisfaction—cannot be achieved unless all the people in our planet work together to avoid ecological catastrophe. This, in turn, cannot happen without a dialogue about how we are shaping the future of our planet. That is why the appeal of Pope Francis is so important for all the people on our planet: equally for the believers belonging to different religions, as well as for nonbelievers.

There are many aspects of this dialogue which are important and which Pope Francis develops in some detail in his encyclical. In the present exposition I express an attitude only to some of them according to my humble abilities.

In the encyclical the pope stresses that simply reducing birth rates of the poor is not a just or adequate response to the problem of poverty or environmental degradation (50). Indeed, in fact, there are serious problems of population decline in many countries some of which are not so rich or are still developing. But this fact does not at all prevent the ecological problems in such countries. Let me give, as an example, my own country, Bulgaria. It belongs to the European Union, but it is one of the poorest countries in it. During the last 25 years its population has decreased by more than one million people, due, on the one hand, to migration, and on the other, to a decrease of the birth rate in the country. However, depopulation does not at all save Bulgaria from ecological problems such as pollution of the air in the big towns, the pollution of the soil, etc. In the globalized world in which we now live, the ecological crisis is a global one: it exists equally in countries with large or growing populations, and in others that are small or declining. The real solution of the ecological crisis is not a decrease of the population, but a radical change of the social order.

Pope Francis says that the roots of the ecological crisis are human. He emphasizes that at present a technocratic paradigm is dominant according to which unlimited growth is possible. All of us have to take into account that there is no infinite supply of the earth's goods (106). What should we do? The pope does not ask that humankind should stop technical development; he emphasizes instead that humans have to take into account that the earth's goods are limited. This means that changes are necessary in our human vision about civilization and its development, i.e. that we need "a bold cultural revolution" (114) that would lead to a revision of the present "modern anthropocentrism" (115). In this regard I would like again to emphasize the Whiteheadian position that supports biospheric deep ecology and non-anthropocentric deep ecology; process thinkers go beyond anthropocentrism and embrace a new conception of values.

Here we reach a very important point in the encyclical where Pope Francis says:

> When we speak of the 'environment,' what we really mean is a relationship between nature and the society which lives in it. Nature cannot be regarded as something separate from ourselves or as a mere setting in which we live. We are part of nature, included in it, and thus in constant interaction with it. . . . It is essential to seek comprehensive solutions that consider the interactions within natural systems themselves and with social systems. We are not faced with two separate crises, one environmental and the other social, but rather one complex crisis that is both social and environmental. Strategies for a solution demand an integrated approach to combating poverty, restoring dignity to the underprivileged, and at the same time protecting nature. (139)

The first part of this paragraph clearly reminds me of Whitehead's idea of a philosophy of organism. Whitehead says in his *magnum opus*, *Process and Reality*:

> The aim of the philosophy of organism is to express a coherent cosmology based upon the notions of 'system,' 'process,'

> 'creative advance into novelty,' . . . In the philosophy of organism it is held that the notion of 'organism' has two meanings, interconnected but intellectually separate, namely, the microscopic meaning and the macroscopic meaning. The microscopic meaning is concerned with the formal constitution of an actual occasion, considered as a process of realizing an individual unity of experience. The macroscopic meaning is concerned with the givenness of the actual world, considered as the stubborn fact which at once limits and provides opportunity for the actual occasion. (128-29)

The pope expresses this in simple words saying that "Nature cannot be regarded as something separate from ourselves or as a mere setting in which we live. We are part of nature, included in it and thus in constant interaction with it" (139). If we evaluate Pope Francis' thoughts from a philosophical point of view, I would say that he is definitely a process thinker. I would like especially to point here to the fact that the conviction is emphasized in the encyclical that everything in the world is intimately connected—a typical conviction for Whiteheadian process thought.

Besides, Francis speaks of an "integral ecology" that combines environmental (138-140), economic (141), social (142), and cultural (143) ecologies. It is very similar to what process philosophers and process theologians speak about—"ecological civilization." As a doyen of process thinkers, John B. Cobb, Jr., says, we need to open up discussion as to what an "ecological civilization" might mean. Our alienation from nature is very deep and it is the result of erroneous thinking about the natural environment.

> Some people suppose that an ecological civilization is simply a sustainable one. I mean more than that, and believe that sustainability can actually be realized only when the world changes at deep levels. ... *A truly ecological civilization is one in which human beings understand themselves as one species among others.* ... And at every step it will consider how that which contributes to sustainability can also contribute to personal enjoyment and social well being. (www.pandopopulus.com; italics mine)

Pope Francis speaks about "the common good" saying "Human ecology is inseparable from the notion of the common good, a central and unifying principle of social ethics" (156). An analogous thought we can find in Whitehead: "Morality of outlook is inseparably conjoined with generality of outlook. The antithesis between the general good and the individual interest can be abolished only when the individual is such that its interest is the general good, thus exemplifying the loss of the minor intensities in order to find them again with finer composition in a wider sweep on interest." (*Process and Reality* 15). In this way we can see again the actuality of process thought and its closeness to the concerns expressed in the papal encyclical.

Next Pope Francis pays attention to the lines of approach and action. In this regard he repeats the word "dialogue" many times emphasizing its significance and renewing his appeal in the introduction to the encyclical. This involves dialogue between religions that can work together for the common good. He says "the Church does not presume to settle scientific questions or to replace politics. But I am concerned to encourage an honest and open debate so that particular interests or ideologies will not prejudice the common good." (188). Francis himself gives an excellent example of a dialogue between religions united by the same concern, mentioning statements made by the Ecumenical Patriarch Bartholomew who—as the highest representative of the Orthodox Church—has said: "For human beings . . . to destroy the biological diversity of God's creation; for human beings to degrade the integrity of the earth by causing changes in its climate, by stripping the earth of its natural forests or destroying its wetlands; for human beings to contaminate the earth's waters, its land, its air, and its life—these are sins" (Address in Santa Barbara, California, 8 November 1997).

For me, as a citizen of an Eastern European country, it is an important fact that His Eminence, the Metropolitan of Pergamo, John Zizioulas, participated in the press conference devoted to the encyclical. He spoke as a representative of the Ecumenical Patriarch of the Orthodox Church and repeated Bartholomew's above-quoted words. Zizioulas reminded us that the Ecumenical Patriarchate already in 1989 drew the attention of the world community to the seriousness of the ecological problem. The issuing of *Laudato si'* is, therefore, an occasion of great joy and satisfaction for the Orthodox.

In his talk, John Zizioulas emphasized three related points: a) the theological significance of ecology; b) the spiritual dimension of the ecological problem, and c) the ecumenical significance of the encyclical. I hope that his will not be the only response of a high representative of the Orthodox Church, and that leaders from the other traditional Orthodox countries in Eastern Europe will soon join their authoritative voices to the appeal for a unity of the Churches in prayer for the environment.

Finally, in the encyclical *Laudato si'* Pope Francis expresses the need to develop new convictions, attitudes, and forms of life, including a new lifestyle. He stresses that this requires not only individual conversion but also community networks to solve the complex situation facing our world today.

In this regard I myself, as Executive Director of the International Process Network, feel an urgent need for that organization—as a network of organizations and individuals dedicated to supporting, generating, and disseminating an international discourse on the meaning and implications of process thought—to answer the appeal of the papal encyclical by including in the dialogue and organizing many events that will implement Pope Francis' appeal. It is remarkable that the 10th International Whitehead conference held in Claremont, California, on 4-7 June 2015 was focused on ecological problems at the center of which was the problem of how to build an ecological civilization. But it is not enough. After this conference and after the papal encyclical our International Process Network is not the same: it inevitably changes the focus of its activity, and all our plans for the future work are made through the prism of building up an ecological civilization. Analogous changes should occur also in the affiliating organizations that compose our global network. I am sure this focus will improve the International Process Network's activities, its visibility and its authority in the world.

References

Whitehead, A.N. *The Function of Reason.* 1929. Boston: Beacon Press, 1958.

___. *Process and Reality.* 1929. Corrected Edition. Ed. D.W. Sherburne and D.R. Griffin. New York: The Free Press, 1978.

Ecological Conversion:
The Plea for Sister Earth

Maria-Teresa Teixeira

*L*audato si' will probably be remembered in history as the ground-breaking document that changed, or could have changed, human destiny. At the beginning of the encyclical, Pope Francis, taking up one of his predecessors, John Paul II, emphasizes the need for "a global ecological *conversion*" (5); towards the end, he again writes about ecological conversion (216-21).

Francis addresses "every person living on this planet" (3). His message and his appeal to conversion are truly universal. But his call is not about religious conversion; it is rather about a change of heart, which is absolutely necessary if humanity is to continue being human.

Conversion is whole and unconditional. There is no halfway compromise towards conversion. It is a deep, sincere, and all-embracing engagement for the individual and for the whole human community. Francis call is for an interior and thorough conversion. "The ecological conversion needed to bring about lasting change is also a community conversion" (219). Ecological conversion should give rise to an irrevocable commitment to care "for our common home" and reconcile us with Creation.

Christians should be especially committed to this endeavour, but their behaviour is also the object of papal criticism: "It must be said that

431

some committed and prayerful Christians, with the excuse of realism and pragmatism, tend to ridicule expressions of concern for the environment. Others are passive; they choose not to change their habits and thus become inconsistent. So what they all need is an "ecological conversion" (217). Ecological conversion consists in a deep change of lifestyles, in new ways of production and consumption, and in revising our modes of exercising political, social and economic powers (5). It is the quest for a completely novel paradigm for our lives.

Ecological conversion will stem from an integral ecology. Most environmentalists have lost sight of the totality of the ecological problem because they do not take into consideration all aspects of reality. The problem needs a holistic and integral approach because we think in a fragmented way; that is why we often disregard the vastness and complexity of environmental problems. We neglect the "care for our common home."

Francis' encyclical proclaims an integral worldview. It is not only about climate change or environment. It proposes a new, comprehensive way of life, which is all-inclusive. He writes:

> Ecological culture cannot be reduced to a series of urgent and partial responses to the immediate problems of pollution, environmental decay and the depletion of natural resources. There needs to be a distinctive way of looking at things, a way of thinking, policies, an educational programme, a lifestyle and a spirituality which together generate resistance to the assault of the technocratic paradigm. (111)

Francis' idea of "integral ecology" ranks with "ecological conversion." He hails Saint Francis of Assisi as the example of integral ecology; he also points out that Saint Francis is admired and loved by both Christians and non-Christians, and he is the patron saint of ecologists. The figure of Saint Francis, too, has a universal vocation. And it can certainly set an example for ecological conversion.

Pope Francis emphasizes, for the first time, the importance of relationships as he refers to wholeness. He says, in particular, that Saint Francis can show us the inseparability of the "concern for nature, justice for the poor, commitment to society, and interior peace" (10.) The category of relation debuts with the category of integrity.

The first reference to integrity is made almost at the beginning of the encyclical. Reality should be taken in its entirety; single aspects give a distorted view of it. Our habitual fragmentary perspectives give us a biased and altered picture of reality. This is even more so when we consider nature. We have this habit of bifurcating nature, as the British philosopher, Alfred North Whitehead, pointed out (*The Concept of Nature*).

In this respect, Pope Francis also quotes his predecessor Benedict XVI: "The book of nature is one and indivisible" (6). This worldview, which is consonant with a well-balanced and integral natural harmony, shows that wholeness, complexity, and indivisibility are insurmountable characters of nature. Here, Francis alludes to an ancient philosophical tradition that finds the one in the many and the many in the one. Today, this old tradition is reinvented in process philosophy. Reality constitutes itself through creativity; the one emerges from the many, thus becoming a novel one, which is one again amongst the many. The one is a novel, synthetic unity, which, in spite of its complexity, is indivisible and becomes as an unbreakable whole.

However, the human mind, which usually proceeds in an over-intellectualized manner, breaks reality into disconnected parts, often into fragmented pieces. This operation is usually called analysis: it presupposes that the reduction of the world to disconnected pieces is a reasonable way of examining it; and also that all the disconnected bits can be re-assembled back again, without any loss of the integrity of the first entity that was subjected to analytic examination. But this kind of reversibility is merely intellectual. Any living being will not tolerate dismemberment and reassembly. The whole cannot be equated with the sum of its parts. Parts are not added on as the process of becoming proceeds. The process of becoming requires a deep integrity and unity that are unbreakable. Fragmentation leads to destruction and devastation.

> It cannot be emphasized enough how everything is interconnected. Time and space are not independent of one another, and not even atoms or subatomic particles can be considered in isolation. Just as the different aspects of the planet—physical, chemical and biological—are interrelated, so too living species are part of a network that we will never fully explore and understand. A good part of our genetic code is shared by many living

beings. It follows that the fragmentation of knowledge and the isolation of bits of information can actually become a form of ignorance, unless they are integrated into a broader vision of reality. . . . Nature cannot be regarded as something separate from ourselves or as a mere setting in which we live. We are part of nature, included in it and thus in constant interaction with it. (138-39)

The processes of nature are unitary and unifying. They establish a harmonious balance that favours sound growth and unveils the imperceptible and creative advance of nature. The vastness and complexity of nature cannot be turned into a few static, fragmentary entities, easily pinpointed and arbitrarily divided into parts. The fragmented knowledge of nature is actually lack of knowledge; knowledge of reality requires a comprehensive and holistic view. In this way, "[Saint] Francis helps us to see that an integral ecology calls for openness to categories which transcend the language of mathematics and biology, and take us to the heart of what it is to be human" (11).

Creation is a novel world of diversity emerging from an amazing web of relationships that creativity weaves into the interstices of the universe. Creativity and novelty are possible because of the unified, synthetic, overlapping complexity of nature. But our analytical mind ignores this creative and restless diversity, thus immobilizing everything it possibly can in order to examine it. This leads to a confusing grasp of the world and to an ethics that refuses its ontological foundations, thus perverting the human relationship with the natural world.

Modern technology and business completely disregard "the mysterious network of relations between things" (20), creating additional problems alongside the existing ones. As we lose sight of relationships we inevitably cause much harm to sister earth and to ourselves, because the degradation of nature is also the degradation of humanity. "Because all creatures are connected, each must be cherished with love and respect, for all of us as living creatures are dependent on one another" (42).

Interconnectedness is related to the care for sister earth. We are the custodians of the earth, the "stewards of all creation" (172), and in that capacity we should respect "the rhythms inscribed in nature by the hand of the Creator." (71) The rhythms of nature are akin to our rhythms. We should respect the *Sabbath*. In the same way, we should give the land a complete rest every seven years. (71) There should be "an apprehension of character permanently inherent in the nature of things. . . It is a character of permanent rightness . . . The harmony in the actual world is in conformity with character" (Whitehead, *Religion in the Making*, 61). The respect for the rhythms of nature recognizes the diversity of beings and the ontological dignity of every creature. Different rhythms of duration also permit the differentiation of creatures in their uniqueness and singularity, as the French philosopher Henri Bergson pointed out (*Matter and Memory*).

The complexity and interconnectedness of all the elements of reality emphasise the relational character of the world. The category of relationship could not be more emphasised by Pope Francis when he alludes to Saint Bonaventure who read "reality in a Trinitarian key" (239). He writes:

> The divine Persons are subsistent relations, and the world created according to the divine model, is a web of relationships. . . . This leads us not only to marvel at the manifold connections existing among creatures, but also to discover a key to our own fulfilment. The human person grows more, matures more and is sanctified more to the extent that he or she enters into relationships, going out from themselves to live in communion with God, with others and with all creatures. In this way, they make their own that Trinitarian dynamism which God imprinted in them when they were created. Everything is interconnected, and this invites us to develop a spirituality of that global solidarity which flows from the mystery of the Trinity. (240)

Francis' reading of the "Trinitarian key" has a marked ontological character that can also be found in process philosophy. The "mystery of one and the many" subtly reappears in the pope's encyclical providing heavy consistency to the edification of an integral ecology. He underlines the solidarity of every element of reality that can be included in a "general scheme of relationships providing the capacity that many objects can be welded into the real unity of one experience" (Whitehead *Process and Reality*, 67). Integral ecology requires the subsistent relationship between what we usually call "nature" and the human community. Nature should not be bifurcated: human beings are not separate from it; neither is nature "a mere setting in which we live" (139). The one emerges from and intermingles with the many in a true dynamic solidarity.

Everything is connected, and this connectedness will lead to the consideration of many different factors. Our present crisis is both environmental and social. We cannot address the different parts of the problem separately. Caring for nature and caring for society and for the individuals is one and the same thing. Each person, each organism, each ecosystem has an intrinsic value that must not be forgotten. We are bound to "make use" of these organisms and ecosystems in a sustainable way and to respect their integrity because they are not mere objects for our enjoyment. We depend on them, and they all have an ontological dignity of which we should be aware.

Integral ecology also includes "historic, artistic and cultural patrimony" (143). The cultural identity of people should not give way to the tearing down of old places, so that new cities are built, even if these new buildings are presented as being more consistent with the protection of the environment. Cultural diversity is as important as biological diversity, and it should not be erased or put at risk. "Culture is more than what we have inherited from the past; it is also, and above all, a living dynamic and participatory present reality, which cannot be excluded as we rethink the relationship between human beings and the environment" (143).

This is why it is so important to protect indigenous cultures and their traditions. Imposing our reckless ways of living on these cultures can be truly disastrous. "For them, land is not a commodity but rather a gift from God and from their ancestors who rest there, a sacred space with which they need to interact if they are to maintain their identity and values. When they remain on their land, they themselves care for it best" (146). The respect for the integrity of the earth is also the respect for human dignity; neither the earth nor human beings should be instrumentalized or manipulated at will. Taking land as a commodity, as is generally done in Western societies, greatly contributes to ecological abuses and to the denial of basic human rights.

Integral ecology is in alignment with the principle of the common good which should be "a summons to solidarity and a preferential option for the poorest of our brothers and sisters" (158). It extends to the destinies of future generations. Interconnectedness draws on the past, but it projects itself on to the future as well. It is an indivisible dynamics with immediate repercussions on the coming generations. "The Portuguese bishops have called upon us to acknowledge this obligation of justice: 'The environment is part of a logic of receptivity. It is on loan to each generation, which must then hand it on to the next. An integral ecology is marked by this broader vision'" (159.)

The earth is our common home. Sister earth is also mother earth: everything flows from it and is inextricably linked with it. We depend on earth to survive and we will ultimately go back to it. The interconnectedness of all elements of nature includes all human beings, all organisms and ecosystems. For "the book of nature is one and indivisible."

Pope Francis appeals for "a healthy relationship with Creation" (218) and for a deep ecological conversion, demanding an integral response and a full commitment of all people.

References

Bergson, Henri. *Matter and Memory.* 1912. Mineola, NY: Dover Publications, 2004.

Whitehead, A.N. *The Concept of Nature.* Cambridge: Cambridge UP, 1920.

___. *Religion in the Making.* 1925. New York: Fordham University Press, 1996.

___. *Process and Reality.* 1929. Corrected Edition. Ed. D.W. Sherburne and D.R. Griffin. New York: The Free Press, 1978.

PART

SEVEN

The Call Forward

"Go Thou and Do Likewise"

Philip Clayton

We need to strengthen the conviction that we are one single human family. There are no frontiers or barriers, political or social, behind which we can hide, still less is there room for the globalization of indifference. . . . These situations have caused sister earth, along with all the abandoned of our world, to cry out, pleading that we take another course. (Laudato si' 52-53)

It's an age when many feel powerless. As the immensity of the environmental crisis sinks in—melting ice caps, disappearing water tables, polluted rivers, and the rising carbon levels that no one seems able to cap—the sense of powerlessness has continued to grow. If the species as a whole cannot stem the deadly tide of consumption, what can any single person do? What can I do? Is it even worth trying?

With *"Laudato si', mi' Signore"*—"Praise be to you, my Lord"— Pope Francis begins his teaching on the environment, "On Care for Our Common Home." The opening words are taken from the canticle of his namesake, Francis of Assisi, who prays to "our Sister, Mother Earth, who sustains and governs us." Prayer closes the pope's document as well:

> O God of the poor,
> help us to rescue the abandoned and forgotten of this
>   earth,

so precious in your eyes.
Bring healing to our lives,
that we may protect the world and not prey on it,
that we may sow beauty, not pollution and destruction.

Laudato si' matters, first, because it signals what one person can do. For progressive people around the world, the Roman Catholic church over the last decades has not exactly stood out as the beacon of success. But almost from the beginning, Pope Francis has signaled that it would no longer be "business as usual" within the Church. The degree of change that he has brought about in less than two years is nothing short of unbelievable. To live with integrity, to speak the truth that you see, and to act prophetically in the ways that this truth demands—these steps are possible for all of us. If one in one hundred people acted with the courage and boldness in their particular sphere that Francis has evidenced in his, we could begin to put the brakes on climate change.

Laudato si' is a highly personal document in another sense as well. It is not shy about environmental science, politics and economics, philosophy, or Catholic doctrine for that matter. But its central message is not about any of these abstract topics. It is about selfishness and consumerism. The primary reason why the planetary system has been disrupted is that humans have taken far more for themselves than we needed, and we continue to choose our comfort and pleasure over the good of the whole. As much as the encyclical is a political and economic call to action, it is in the first place a moral critique:

> [E]conomic powers continue to justify the current global system where priority tends to be given to speculation and the pursuit of financial gain, which fail to take the context into account, let alone the effects on human dignity and the natural environment. Here we see how environmental deterioration and human and ethical degradation are closely linked. (56)

The words are directed as much to the middle classes in the developed nations as they are to the super-rich and the multinational corporations. We are meant to squirm as we read them.

This both/and nature of the encyclical is significant in the context of Catholic as well as Protestant theology. Because conservatives have been in the dominant positions of power over the last decades, the world has come to identify the Christian worldview with concerns about morality and sexual ethics, above all abortion, homosexuality, birth control, and celibacy. Like all oppositions, these vociferous voices have driven many spokespersons on the religious Left to focus exclusively on social and political issues.

Pope Francis argues that *both* perspectives are necessary. Government laws and interventions by themselves will not be sufficient until the majority of citizens in the developed nations recognize their own complicity in the global climate crisis. We who write these essays, and those who read them, are not innocent. Kant argues that actions are only permissible if the principles that underlie them are generalizable to all agents. Our lifestyle, our carbon footprint, does not pass the test. Francis offers his own version of the Kantian argument: "extreme and selective consumerism [is] an attempt to legitimize the present model of distribution, where a minority believes that it has the right to consume in a way which can never be universalized, since the planet could not even contain the waste products of such consumption" (50).

But the pope's response to religious conservatives is equally as devastating. The volume of their pronouncements on sexual ethics only highlights their silence on matters of economic injustice. We are the beneficiaries of a global economic system where the comfort of the wealthy comes at direct expense to the poor. The economic policies that produce these inequities do not lie outside the sphere of Christian concern; much less is our wealth of sign that God has blessed us and favored us above all others. Because Jesus directed his message preferentially to the poor, the oppressed, and the outcast, Christians are required to direct their attention to those on the bottom, the victims of economic injustice. It's not just that conservative Christians have put their primary attention in the wrong place; it's that they have been on the wrong side. As Francis writes in his closing prayer, "Enlighten those who possess power and money that they may avoid the sin of indifference, that they may love the common good, advance the weak, and care for this world in which we live" (246).

The ecological crisis is a moral issue, we saw, because it has much to do with what Francis calls the "ecological virtues" (88)—with how we actually live. It's a justice issue because the poor of the world—the people whose lifestyles have not created climate change—are already the first victims of polluted air, undrinkable water, desertification, and dying soil. North Americans saw this inequity up close and personal as we watched the devastation of Hurricane Katrina unfold on our television screens. Wealthy (mostly white) people made it safely out of New Orleans, while poor (mostly black) people suffered and died for days without assistance. The *Washington Post* recently (July 6, 2015) reported on the primary victims of the California drought: poor rural farmers and residents. Far more extensive suffering is occurring in sub-Saharan Africa, in India, and in fact across the global South as climate change continues its relentless destruction of their homes and their livelihoods.

To comprehend the depth of the inequity requires a synthetic perspective. The first step is to synthesize ecological science with a justice-based ethic: "Today . . . we have to realize that a true ecological approach always becomes a social approach; it must integrate questions of justice in debates on the environment, so as to hear both the cry of the earth and the cry of the poor" (49). But inevitably, the movement toward the broadest perspective brings us to metaphysics. Without some instance of Value that transcends the interests and desires of human agents in the here and now, all too many will adopt a "take what you can get" attitude. By contrast, life lived before a higher Value calls actors to self-limitation (*kenosis*): "If we acknowledge the value and the fragility of nature and, at the same time, our God-given abilities, we can finally leave behind the modern myth of unlimited material progress. A fragile world, entrusted by God to human care, challenges us to devise intelligent ways of directing, developing and limiting our power" (78).

Quickly the metaphysics circles back around to the world again: "The establishment of a legal framework which can set clear boundaries and ensure the protection of ecosystems has become indispensable; otherwise, the new power structures based on the techno-economic paradigm may overwhelm not only our politics but also freedom and justice" (53). Chapter 3 of the encyclical (101-36) details the human roots of the ecological crisis: technology, the globalization of the "technocratic paradigm," and the effects of modern anthropocentrism. Chapter 4 (137-62) defends an "integral ecology," expanding the ecological perspective to include its environmental, economic, social, and cultural dimensions, as well as "the ecology of daily life." All is driven by the principle of the common good, for in the end "human ecology is inseparable from the notion of the common good," which is the "central and unifying principle of social ethics" (156).

In short, Francis' first major social teaching is tightly argued yet poetic: scientifically informed, politically savvy, philosophically rich, and spiritually moving. Although it seeks to have interreligious appeal (see "Religions in Dialogue with Science," 199-201), it's also a deeply Catholic document. It's a sobering document, as is appropriate given the unprecedented global crisis we now face. But it is also a hopeful document: "Yet all is not lost. Human beings, while capable of the worst, are also capable of rising above themselves" (205).

In the end, the encyclical is groundbreaking for multiple reasons. First, it correctly identifies climate change as simultaneously about morality and justice. Second, in order to respond to the climate crisis, it draws on the resources of both science and faith. Without science we would not be able to draw the links between human actions and the rapidly changing climate, and we would not be able to extrapolate the trends outward into the future. Because of science we know that an immediate leveling off of carbon emissions would still have global consequences that will persist for many centuries to come, whereas "business as usual" will produce a "Sixth Great Extinction" of up to 90% of the species that currently inhabit this planet.

Science tells us what will happen, but faith (religion) is far better at motivating action. We look to the Intergovernmental Panel on Climate Change (IPCC) to convey the scientific consensus on the causes and effects of climate change. We look elsewhere for moral insight and spiritual inspiration. The papal encyclical shows how powerful a religious tradition can be when it brings its full collection of moral and ethical resources to bear on the scientific data: "Soil, water, mountains: everything is, as it were, a caress of God" (84). The Abrahamic family of religions is not alone in this regard; Buddhist, Hindu, Jain, and Sikh motivations are equally as powerful, and the indigenous traditions of the world are perhaps unrivaled in their testimony that, when we lose or destroy our homeland, we have lost everything.

Finally, the encyclical is groundbreaking because of the urgency of its call to action, here and now. No small fixes, no fortunate break-throughs in technology will get us out of this mess; after all, it was tech-no-absolutism that got us here in the first place. Nothing less than an "ecological conversion" (216-21) will suffice. Religion and science must now join hands in an integral ecology that serves "the full development of humanity"(62)—and, I would add, all living things. One does not need to be Catholic to pray with Francis his closing prayer:

> Teach us to discover the worth of each thing,
> to be filled with awe and contemplation,
> to recognize that we are profoundly united
> with every creature
> as we journey towards your infinite light.

Contributors

JOHN B. COBB, JR. taught at the Claremont School of Theology from 1958 to 1990. Together with David Griffin he organized the Center for Process Studies, which hosted the "Seizing an Alternative" conference of which Cobb was the prime organizer. He has taught theology, which he defines as critical reflection on important questions from an intentionally Christian perspective. In his view, the reductionist and materialist world view associated with modern science shares responsibility for the global crisis. He has been especially critical of the application of this worldview in biology, in economics, and in the disciplinary organization of knowledge.

PAT PATTERSON, originally a Maryland farm girl, devoted nearly twenty years to educational work in Japan as a United Methodist missionary. Then she served in New York, supervising the work in Northeast Asia. She retired to Pilgrim Place, where she continued to work on issues of social justice and climate change. She also began serious writing of poetry. Selected as poet laureate both of the Pilgrim Place Centennial and the "Seizing an Alternative" conference, she dedicated the latest of her four books, *Awakening to Ecological Civilization,* to the conference and the Center for Process Studies.

BILL MCKIBBEN is the Schumann Distinguished Scholar in Environmental Studies at Middlebury College, Vermont. He is author of several important books on climate change and is a fellow of the American Academy of Arts and Sciences. Together with a few students he founded 350.org, and he has made it the first and most influential planet-wide, grassroots climate change movement. His devotion to the cause has led to many acts of nonviolent resistance and to repeated arrests. He is recipient of the Right Livelihood, Gandhi, and Thomas Merton awards. Foreign Policy named him to its inaugural list of the world's 100 most important global thinkers, and the Boston Globe said he was "probably America's most important environmentalist." He keynoted the "Seizing an Alternative" conference.

Section One

VANDANA SHIVA is a scientist, philosopher, feminist, author, environmentalist, and activist for bio-ethics, eco-feminism, and biodiversity. She has a BS in physics, an MA in the philosophy of science, and a PhD in nuclear physics. To oppose control of food and pharmaceuticals by agribusiness through patented, genetically engineered seeds, she founded the Research Foundation for Science, Technology, and Ecology. In 1991, she founded Navdanya, a national movement to protect the diversity of native seeds. Among her many honors is the Right Livelihood Award for her work in placing women and ecology at the center of the international development agenda. She was a plenary speaker at the "Seizing an Alternative" conference.

ROSEMARY RADFORD RUETHER is an internationally acclaimed church historian, theologian, writer, and teacher specializing in the area of women and religion. She has been a major voice in raising a feminist critique of the traditionally male field of Christian theology. Active beginning in the early 1960s in civil rights and peace movements and, later, in the feminist movement, Ruether is thoroughly Catholic and radically reformist in her scholarly approach to various topics essential to contemporary religious discussions. Now retired from her long-term post as Georgia Harkness Professor of Applied Theology at the Garrett-Evangelical Theological Seminary, she is the author of 36 books and over 600 articles on feminism, eco-feminism, the Bible, and Christianity.

HERMAN DALY, while Senior Economist in the Environment Department of the World Bank, helped develop guidelines for sustainable development. He is regarded as the creator of ecological economics and is co-founder of the journal, *Ecological Economics*. Before joining the World Bank, Daly taught at Louisiana State University. He received a Right Livelihood Award, the Heineken Prize for Environmental Science, the Sophie Prize (Norway), the Leontief Prize from the Global Development and Environment Institute, and the Blue Planet Prize of the Asahi Glass Foundation. He was chosen 2008 Man of the by *Adbusters* magazine. Although his health prevented his speaking at the "Seizing an Alternative" conference, a video of an interview was shown.

DAVID RAY GRIFFIN is Professor of Philosophy of Religion and Theology, Emeritus, Claremont School of Theology and Claremont Graduate University. He is co-founder and a co-director of the Center for Process Studies. He has published (as author or editor) 34 books, primarily in theology, philosophy, and philosophy of religion, with special emphasis on the problem of evil and the relation between science and religion. He edited a series of books on "constructive postmodernism," under which label process thought has gained a large following in China. After retiring, he became the leading scholar in the 9/11 truth movement. Recently he has turned his attention to climate change and published *Unprecedented: Can Civilization Survive the CO_2 Crisis?*

DANIEL A. DOMBROWSKI is Professor of Philosophy at Seattle University. He is the author of seventeen books and over a hundred articles in scholarly journals in philosophy, theology, classics, and literature. His latest book is *Contemporary Athletics and Ancient Greek Ideals* (University of Chicago Press, 2009). His main areas of intellectual interest are history of philosophy, philosophy of religion (from a process perspective), and ethics (especially animal rights issues). He is the editor of *Process Studies*. For the "Seizing an Alternative"conference, he organized the track on process philosophy and analytic philosophy.

ANTHONY MANOUSOS is a Quaker who has been deeply involved in the ministry of writing and publishing for his religious group. He has participated in many interfaith organizations, most notably, the Parliament of World Religions. He and his wife, Jill Shook, live in a home they have outfitted to exemplify living in harmony with creation. They have received recognition by the city of Pasadena for their dedication to demonstrating ways of saving the environment and caring for those living in the margins.

BRIAN G. HENNING is Professor of Philosophy and Environmental Studies at Gonzaga University in Spokane, Washington. He is a leader in the Whitehead Research Project and is the Executive Editor of the *Edinburgh Critical Edition of the Complete Works of Alfred North Whitehead*. He has co-edited *Beyond Metaphysics? Explorations in Alfred North Whitehead's Late Thought; Beyond Mechanism: Putting Life Back into Biology;* and *Thinking with Whitehead and American Pragmatists.* His 2005 book, *The Ethics of Creativity,* won the Findlay Book Prize from the Metaphysical Society of America. His most recent book is *Riders in the Storm: Ethics in the Age of Climate Change.*

HOLMES ROLSTON III is University Distinguished Professor of Philosophy at Colorado State University. He is best known for his contributions to environmental ethics and the relationship between science and religion. He holds degrees in physics and mathematics, Davidson College; ministry, Union Theological Seminary; theology, the University of Edinburgh; and philosophy of science, the University of Pittsburgh. He is ordained to the ministry of the Presbyterian Church (USA). Among other honors, Rolston won the 2003 Templeton Prize, awarded by Prince Philip in Buckingham Palace. He gave the Gifford Lectures, University of Edinburgh, 1997-1998.

HERMAN GREENE is President of the Center for Ecozoic Societies, Chapel Hill, North Carolina. He holds degrees in Spirituality and Sustainability, United Theological Seminary (Ohio); Law, University of North Carolina; Ministry, University of Chicago; and Political Science, Stanford University and University of Florida. He was Founding Executive Director of the International Process Network and serves on its board. He is on the advisory boards of the Center for Process Studies and the Institute for the Post-Modern Development of China. He practices corporate, tax, and securities law through Greene Law, PLLC. He helped organize a track on philosophy of law at the "Seizing an Alternative" conference.

ANDREW SUNG PARK is a Korean-American theologian who teaches at United Theological Seminary in Ohio. He studied at Claremont School of Theology and Graduate Theological Union in Berkeley. He was engaged in racial healing in the 1992 L.A. eruptions and published "Racial Conflict and Healing: An Asian-American Theological Perspective" (1996), receiving a Gustavus Myers Award. In later books he introduced the Korean concept of *han*, emotional pain. He works in interreligious, peace, ecological, and holistic healing movements. At the "Seizing an Alternative" conference, he organized the track on "The Quest for Wholeness: East and West."

IGNACIO CASTUERA has been active in liberation theology circles and in process thought activities for many years. He is an ordained clergyman in the United Methodist Church where he has served as pastor, district superintendent, social service agency administrator, and theology lecturer. He was an early leader in seeking full acceptance and equality for homosexuals and is now working with Compassionate Choices. The concerns addressed by *Laudato si'* have been in his radar since 1970. At the conference on "Seizing an Alternative" he both chaired the section on spirituality and gave a section plenary address.

JOSEPH PRABHU is Professor of Philosophy and Religion at California State University, Los Angeles. He is a writer and editor especially interested in Raimon Panikkar. He has been a Senior Fellow of the Center for the Study of World Religions at Harvard and the Martin Marty Center at Chicago, President of the International Society for Asian and Comparative Philosophy, 2008-2010, and Program Chair for the Melbourne Parliament of the World's Religions, 2009. He won the Outstanding Professor Award of CSULA for 2004-05 and the Lifetime Achievement Award from Soka Gakkai, USA. He co-chaired the track on "Revisioning the Religions" at the "Seizing an Alternative Conference."

JACOB J. ERICKSON is Instructor of Religion and Environmental Studies at St. Olaf College in Northfield, Minnesota, and "Ecotheologian in Residence" at Mercy Seat Lutheran Church in Minneapolis. He is completing his doctoral work in theological studies at Drew University with Catherine Keller. His dissertation, "A Theopoetics of the Earth:

Divinity in the Anthropocene," constructs a theology of resilience and conviviality in the wake of climate change.

SANDRA LUBARSKY chairs the Goodnight Family Department of Sustainable Development at Appalachian State University in North Carolina. She founded the masters program in sustainable communities at Northern Arizona University, one of the first such programs in the country. She studied religion at Claremont Graduate University and has written on interreligious dialogue, Jewish theology, process thought, sustainability and higher education, and aesthetics and sustainability. At the "Seizing and Alternative" conference she not only organized a track on "sustainable practice" and also gave one of the section plenary addresses.

Section Two

DAVID CARLSON is an adjunct professor at Iliff School of Theology. He recently received his PhD from the joint program in Religious and Theological Studies of the University of Denver and the Iliff School of Theology. His dissertation was on "Thinking with Heidegger: the Religon-Science-Theology Dimension." He is convener of the Ethics and Ecological Economics Forum of Denver.

JIM CONN is a retired United Methodist minister. He has had an outstanding ministry, primarily as founding pastor of The Church on Ocean Park. Conn's ministry involved participation in many social movements in Santa Monica, CA, where the church is located. He served as mayor of Santa Monica and continues to be active writing for *Capital & Main,* an Internet publication dealing with social change.

CAROLYN THOMPSON BROWN serves on the Board of Trustees of the Fetzer Institute, an operating foundation headquartered in Kalamazoo, Michigan. In July 2014 she retired from her position as director of the Office of Scholarly Programs and the John W. Kluge Center at the Library of Congress. She joined the Library of Congress in 1990 after serving as Associate Dean for the Humanities at Howard University.

She holds degrees from Cornell University in Asian Studies and Chinese Literature and a Ph.D. in Literature from American University.

THANDEKA is ordained as a minister in the Unitarian-Universalist Church. Currently she is visiting professor at Andover-Newton Theological Seminary. She was given the name, meaning "beloved," by Archbishop Desmond Tutu in 1984. She wrote her dissertation at Claremont on Schleiermacher and is author of *The Embodied Self: Schleiermacher's Solution to Kant's Problem of the Empirical Self.* Among her other writings is *Learning to be White: Money, Race and God in America.* She is also an award-winning TV producer.

CLIFF COBB is editor-in-chief of *The American Journal of Economics and Sociology.* He was the developer of the Index of Sustainable Economic Welfare and continued working on it as it morphed into the Genuine Progress Indicator. He has worked in a variety of roles with the Schalkenbach Foundation, dedicated to promotion of the ideas of Henry George. In that connection, he produced a feature-length documentary entitled "The End of Poverty?" He has been an advisor to the Institute for the Postmodern Development of China. His home is in Sacramento.

DAVID ONGOMBE is a professor at the Catholic University of Congo in Kinshasha. He is committed to making Christianity relevant and helpful to the Congolese people. His use of Whitehead is gaining official recognition. He has been named director of two centers: one on African religion and the other on Congolese Ecclesiastical Archives, which he plans to combine in one on "African History." At the conference on "Seizing an Alternative" he shared his efforts in using Whitehead to facilitate the Africanization of Christian thought.

SHERI D. KLING is a doctoral student in religion and process thought at Claremont School of Theology and holds a master of theological studies from the Lutheran School of Theology at Chicago. Her research focuses on integrating process thought and Jungian dream work as a transformative spiritual practice to facilitate earth-friendly human flourishing and relatedness. She is a member of the American Academy of Religion and the International Positive Psychology Association, and is also an accomplished songwriter and recording artist. She chaired the section on the arts at the "Seizing an Alternative" conference.

ROGER S. GOTTLIEB is Professor of Philosophy at Worcester Polytechnic University. He has written and edited numerous books on environmental ethics, religious environmentalism, and the role of spirituality in this time of ecological crisis, most recently, *Political and Spiritual: Essays on Religion, Environment, Disability, and Justice*. At this time he is deeply concerned that when truly confronted with the desperate character of the global crisis, many people shut down and are unable to respond. At the "Seizing an Alternative" conference, he organized a track on "sustainable involvement."

JOHN QUIRING is Program Director at the Center for Process Studies in Claremont, California. He is responsible both for seminars and for conferences as well as visiting scholars. At Victor Valley College, Victorville, he teaches Introduction to Philosophy, Contemporary Moral Issues, and Philosophy of Religion. He is a co-organizer of the Society for the Study of Process Philosophies. At the "Seizing an Alternative" conference he organized a track on Whitehead's philosophy of religion and also chaired Section I.

BARBARA MURACA is an Italian who has studied and taught chiefly in Germany. She now teaches Environmental and Social Philosophy at Oregon State University and is co-director of the International Association of Environmental Philosophy. From 2011 to 2014, at the University of Jena, she was senior scientist in the Advanced Research Group 'Post-growth-societies'. In 2014 she was a member of the organizing committee of the 4th International Conference on Degrowth for Ecological Sustainability and Social Equity. Her most recent publication is "Décroissance: A Project for a Radical Transformation of Society", in: Environmental Values 22 (2013).

LILIA MARIANNO is a Brazilian educator who has distinguished herself in Biblical Studies in her country and elsewhere in Latin America. A member of the Baptist Church, she has branched out from theological schools to teach management and economics in State Universities. Recently she has become a living link between Process Thought and general education in Brazil and beyond. She organized a Brazilian delegation to the "Seizing an Alternative conference.

ANDY SHRADER is the Director of Environmental Affairs, Water Policy, and Sustainability for a Los Angeles City Councilmember. He is best known for: his work banning plastic bags in Los Angeles, the current proposed citywide efforts to reduce its methane footprint, and ongoing efforts at the Metropolitan Water District to protect the Endangered Species Act from short-sighted drought legislation.

RONALD P. PHIPPS was the founding Chairman of the U.S.-China Friendship Association of Seattle and was involved in the normalization of relations between the two countries. He has also worked with the United Nations Development Program, the WTO, Vietnam and South American Conferences on agriculture and ecology. He was the personal assistant to the former President of the American Philosophic Association, Henry S. Leonard, who for seven years had been Whitehead's personal assistant at Harvard. He writes on physics, cosmology, education, and development. He is also a photographer and a poet.

BOB HURD has served as a teacher, composer, and liturgist in various pastoral and academic settings. He currently teaches in the Graduate Pastoral Ministries Program of Santa Clara University, CA. His widely used liturgical music is published by OCP and is featured in numerous hymnals in the United States, Canada, Great Britain and Australia. He has a doctorate from De Paul University, Chicago. Bob lives in Claremont, CA, with his wife, Pia Moriarty, who has collaborated with him on much of his bilingual music. In 2010 he received NPM's Pastoral Musician of the Year award.

Section Three

CATHERINE KELLER is Professor of Constructive Theology at Drew University. Her theology, developed in many books, is literary, biblical, historical, cultural, postcolonial, postmodern, and process, among other things. She has kept theology alive in the broader intellectual discussion while maintaining an important role among professional theologians. Her most recent book is *Cloud of the Impossible: Negative Theology and Planetary Entanglement.* At the "Seizing an Alternative" conference" she both organized a track on gender, race, and class, and also gave a section plenary address.

MARY EVELYN TUCKER is a Senior Lecturer and Research Scholar at Yale University, where she teaches in a joint master's degree program between the School of Forestry and Environmental Studies and the Divinity School. Concern for the environmental crisis led her to organize, with her husband, John Grim, a series of ten conferences on World Religions and Ecology at the Center for the Study of World Religions at Harvard (1995-98). At a culminating conference at the United Nations in 1998, she and Grim founded the Forum on Religion and Ecology, now based at Yale. The most recent of their many books is *"Ecology and Religion."*

TINA CLARKE, a Certified Transition Trainer since 2008, has worked with over 120 Transition communities, given 42 of the official Transition weekend courses in the U.S. and Canada, and provided hundreds of Transition presentations. Prior to doing Transition work full-time, Tina had been a trainer, program director and consultant for 25 years, supporting leaders in over 400 local, national, regional and local organizations. Most recently she was a consultant with 350.org, the Massachusetts Municipal Association, and the Sustainability Institute.

RICK CLUGSTON was vice president of the Humane Society from 1989 to 2009 and led it to understand its mission in a global ecological context. He was also Executive Director of the Center for Respect of Life and Environment. From its inception he has played a major role in formulation and promotion of the Earth Charter, and from 1989 to the present he has participated in United Nations deliberations about sustainable development. He has worked closely with Religion and Ecology and many other organizations dealing with the ethical and spiritual issues related to the global crisis.

KARENNA GORE is director of the Union Forum at Union Theological Seminary. She studied at Harvard and earned a law degree at Columbia, and she is also an experienced journalist and attorney. She was Youth Outreach Chair for her father's 2000 presidential campaign and an official co-nominator at the Democratic Convention. She is the author of *Lighting the Way: Nine Women Who Shaped Modern America.*

RICK SMYRE is a futurist specializing in the areas of building "capacities for transformation" in local communities. He is president of the Center for Communities of the Future and is an architect in the new fields of "molecular leadership" and "community transformation." He is the past Chairman of the Board of the American Association of Retirement Communities and has been on the staff of the National Economic Development Institute. His work emphasizes innovative concepts, methods, and techniques in collaboration with a network of over 1000 individuals in forty-six states and six countries.

YOSHIHIKO WADA is Professor of Economics at Doshisha University in Kyoto. Globally he ranks as one of the most ecologically concerned professors in departments of economics. He studied at the University of British Columbia in Vancouver, Canada, with Mathis Wackernagel, the co-creator of the ecological footprint measure. He is the leading representative of Ecological Footprints in Japan and has contributed to the use of this measure there.

MICHAEL LERNER is the Rabbi of Beyt Tikkun Synagogue in Berkeley, California. He is also editor of the magazine *Tikkun* and the leader of the Society of Spiritual Progressives. In all of these he intimately connects the religious spirit and convictions to the critical analysis of current events. Everywhere he seeks justice as well as mercy. He offends some of his fellow Jews by criticizing some of Israel's policies, but he also criticizes those liberals who criticize Zionism itself. He articulates programs to heal many of the world's ills and promotes these programs aggressively. He now seizes on the pope's encyclical as a fresh occasion to promote ideas that he finds fully congruent with many of those of the pope.

STUART ALAN KAUFFMAN is an American medical doctor, theoretical biologist, and complex systems researcher who studies the origin of life on Earth. He became known through his association with the Santa

Fe Institute (a nonprofit research institute dedicated to the study of complex systems), where he was faculty in residence from 1986 to 1997, and through his work on models in various areas of biology. These included autocatalytic sets in origin of life research, gene regulatory networks in developmental biology, and fitness landscapes in evolutionary biology. His extraordinarily independent and creative thinking has led to his being invited to direct his attention to other fields of thought, such as economics.

Section Four

DAVID LEWIT has a PhD in Social Psychology. From his earlier experiences in academia in Michigan and Hawaii, he developed the creative suspicion that has made him remarkably effective in movements such as the World Social Forum and the Alliance for Democracy. He edited a paper for the Boston/Cambridge chapter of Alliance for Democracy that many found a rare source of reliable information. At the "Seizing an Alternative" Conference he organized a unique conversation about the economic changes now urgently needed.

TIMOTHY E. EASTMAN has more than 35 years of experience in research and consulting on plasma science and applications, space plasma physics, space weather, magnetospheric physics, environmental and basic energy sciences, public outreach and education, and philosophy. Dr. Eastman developed key foundations at NASA Headquarters and the National Science Foundation for major international and interagency projects. In 2009, he received the Creative Advance Award from the *International Process Network* for leadership in that scholarly community and multiple publications focused on process thought and natural science.

C. DEAN FREUDENBERGER is professor emeritus of Claremont School of Theology and Luther Theological Seminary. He has been a student and practitioner of agronomy and ethics throughout his forty-four year professional career. His years devoted to international agricultural development in Africa, Asia, and Latin America have provided him with a global perspective for addressing contemporary issues. He is the author of *Global Dust Bowl: Can We Stop the Destruction before It's Too Late* (1990), and *Food for Tomorrow?* (1984). In recent years, he has worked on agricultural policy in China.

DAVID FREUDENBERGER is senior lecturer at the Fenner School of Environmental Management at the Australian National University, Canberra. Prior appointments include research in wildlife ecology with the Commonwealth Science, Industrial Research Organization (CSIRO) and chief scientist for Greening Australia. His current research focuses on forest restoration. He received his PhD from the University of New England in Australia. At the "Seizing an Alternative" conference, he contributed to the track on agriculture.

MARCUS FORD has taught philosophy and environmental humanities at Eureka College, the University of Northern Arizona, and Appalachian State University. He is the author of *Beyond the Modern University: Toward a Constructive Postmodern University* (2002). He is now retired and envisages the creation of a Whiteheadian university, which would focus on the real needs of both the students and the world without being concerned about the divisions among academic disciplines. At the conference he organized the track on higher education.

MARK R. DIBBEN is Dean of the School of Business & Economics at the University of Tasmania. His research focuses on applying process thought to management, issues of trust, organization, human relations, and leadership. He was Executive Director of the International Process Network from 2008 to 2011 and remains on the board. He serves on the Editorial Board of *Process Studies* and is also a co-editor of the journal, *Philosophy of Management* . His book, *A Process Philosophy of Management,* is forthcoming from Process Century Press (2016). He organized the management track at the "Seizing an Alternative" conference.

VIJAY SATHE was a professor at the Harvard Business School for ten years prior to joining the Drucker School at Claremont Graduate University. He has taught in numerous executive education programs around the world, served as a consultant to corporations worldwide, and advised government agencies and not-for-profit organizations. His most recent books are *Corporate Entrepreneurship: Top Managers and New Business Creation,* and *Manage Your Career: 10 Keys to Survival and Success When Interviewing and On the Job Business.*

HOWARD VOGEL, Emeritus Professor at Hamline University School of Law, is known for not only teaching the principles of law, but also for helping students learn how to think seriously about their professional identity as lawyers. He works at the intersection of law, religion, and ethics in a pluralistic society. In 2003, he received the highest award given by the University, the John Wesley Trustee Award for outstanding commitment to leadership and service. Since retiring he continues to teach restorative justice in the Dispute Resolution Institute. He was lead organizer of the track of philosophy of law at the "Seizing an Alternative" conference.

ELLEN HODGSON BROWN is an American author, political candidate, attorney, public speaker, and advocate of alternative medicine and public banking. She is the founder and president of the Public Banking Institute and president of Third Millennium Press. She is author of twelve books, including *Web of Debt* and *The Public Bank Solution.* She has appeared on cable and network TV, radio, and internet podcasts, including a story on derivatives and debt on the Russian network RT, and the Thom Hartmann Show's "Conversations with Great Minds." At the conference on "Seizing an Alternative" she responded to Herman Daly.

MARK ANIELSKI is co-founder and Chief Well-being Officer of the Genuine Wealth Institute in Edmonton, Canada, with a mission of building flourishing communities of well-being by measuring what matters.. He is an ecological economist and served as the President of the Canadian Society for Ecological Economics from 2003-05. In 2007 he published *The Economics of Happiness: Building Genuine Wealth,* providing a roadmap for an economy aimed at well-being. (Chinese version, 2010.) His book won a gold medal in the Los Angeles Nautilus Book Awards and a bronze medal in the Axiom Book Awards in New York. At the "Seizing an Alternative" conference, he responded to Herman Daly.

REBECCA ANN PARKER is a United Methodist minister in dual fellowship with the Unitarian Universalist Association. Before assuming leadership of Starr King School in 1990, she spent 10 years as a parish minister in the Pacific Northwest and taught at the Northwest Theological Union in Seattle. Her doctoral studies focused on Alfred North Whitehead's theory of consciousness as a basis for a spirituality that integrates aesthetics and social engagement. Among her books are two co-authored with Rita Brock, including *Saving Paradise*, which showed that for a thousand years Christians focused more on paradise than crucifixion.

Section Five

CHRIS DANIELS has spent most of his adult life as an audio engineer and producer in the music business. In 1996 he earned his undergraduate degree from the University of Calgary in Religious Studies and Applied Ethics, with a joint degree in Religious Studies and Philosophy. Returning to school in 2006, Daniels did his Masters and PhD work at the University of Calgary, specializing in religious diversity and process philosophy. His PhD dissertation, titled "All My Relations: A Process-Indigenous Study in Comparative Ontology," investigates the close parallels between Whiteheadian process metaphysics and the relational worldviews and ways-of-knowing of Indigenous peoples. At the conference on "Seizing at Alternative" he gathered an especially interesting group of indigenous elders to share their wisdom.

TONI M. BOND LEONARD is a Ph.D. student in Religion, Ethics and Society at Claremont School of Theology (CST). She has been an activist in the women's movement for over twenty years and is one of the founding mothers of the reproductive justice movement, a framework that radically changed the reproductive health and rights movements, bringing the voices of marginalized women (women of color, young women, and poor women) to the center. She is the co-founder and former President/CEO of Black Women for Reproductive Justice. She is also a student of Ifá, the religion of her African ancestors, and Christianity, the religion of her mother and maternal and paternal grandmothers. She organized a group on African spirituality at the "Seizing an Alternative" conference.

ZHIHE WANG is Director of the Institute for Postmodern Development of China. He is also Professor of Philosophy and Director of the Center for Constructive Postmodern Studies at Harbin Institute of Technology. He earned his B.A. and M.A. in Philosophy from Peking University, and his PhD from Claremont Graduate University. Since 2002, together with his wife, Meijun Fan, he has established more than 20 institutes for constructive postmodern studies in Chinese universities. He has helped organize more than 70 international conferences on ecological civilization, sustainable urbanization, ecological agriculture, postmodern law, science and spirituality, education reform, social responsibility in business, land and social justice, and, management. He has arranged more than 300 lectures by non-Chinese scholars in China. He organized the track on the Enlightenment at the "Seizing an Alternative" conference.

MEIJUN FAN is professor of Humanities and Social Sciences at Harbin Institute of Technology, and program director of the Institute for Postmodern Development of China. She is editor-in-chief of *Cultural Communication,* a Chinese newspaper, and with husband Zhihe Wang a co-director of the China Project of the Center for Process Studies in Claremont. She completed a masters program at Peking University and doctoral studies at Beijing Normal University where she taught philosophy for many years. During a period when the Chinese government discouraged classical Chinese thought, she kept this alive through teaching Chinese traditional aesthetics and aesthetical education. She chaired a group on Eastern and Western aesthetics at the "Seizing an Alternative" conference.

SHERI LIAO is a Chinese environmental activist, journalist, and producer of documentaries, whose work is credited with leading the Chinese environmental movement. After graduating from Sun Yat-Sen University in 1986, she taught philosophy at the Chinese Academy of Social Sciences, where she became interested in environmental philosophy. She founded the non-governmental organization, Global Village of Beijing, making models for green neighborhoods and rural communities, and organizing public awareness campaigns regarding pollution, recycling, and reducing consumption. She is now focusing on developing ecological villages in contrast to industrial agriculture. Her effort to renew traditional Chinese values has recently gained favor in government circles. She has been awarded several international prizes, and gave a plenary speech at the "Seizing an Alternative" conference.

RITA SHERMA is the Swami Vivekananda Visiting Faculty for Hindu Studies at the University of Southern California. Her interests include Hindu Dharma, interreligious studies, and theory and method in the study of religion. She holds an MA in Religion and a PhD in Theology and Ethics from Claremont Graduate University. She is editor of the Hinduism volume of the *Encyclopedia of Indian Religions* and a founding co-editor of the *International Journal of Dharma Studies.* She is the Vice-President and Director of Programs of the Dharma Academy of North America, studying India's indigenous religions. She has co-chaired ten thematic DANAM conferences, and is the co-founder of the Hinduism Program Unit of the American Academy of Religion. She organized a Hindu track at the "Seizing an Alternative" conference.

LOURDES ARGUËLLES, Ph.D., LMFT is a Lopon (Senior Dharma Teacher) and a Ngakma (ordained lay tantric practitioner) in the Drikung Kagyu lineage of Tibetan Buddhism. She is also Professor Emerita of Education and Cultural Studies at Claremont Graduate University and a Senior Staff Therapist at the Clinebell Institute for Pastoral Counseling and Psychotherapy in Claremont, Caifornia. A former member of the Board of Directors of the Buddhist Peace Fellowship, she is now a member of the Advisory Board of Pando Populus. She is a student of interfaith encounters and research, with a special interest in the area of Buddhist/Catholic dialogue. She organized the Buddhist group at the "Seizing an Alternative" conference.

ANNE RIVERO, LCSW is a Ngakma (ordained lay tantric practitioner) in the Drikung Kagyu lineage of Tibetan Buddhism and a Camaldolese-Benedictine Oblate associated with the New Camaldoli Hermitage in Big Sur, California. She is a retired clinical (psychiatric) social worker who currently volunteers as a chaplain for the frail elderly in an assisted living facility. She is a student of interfaith encounters and research, with a special interest in the area of Buddhist/Catholic dialogue.

Joseph E. B. Lumbard did his doctoral studies at Yale University. He is now an Assistant Professor of Classical Islam at Brandeis University. He is a general editor for *The Study Quran,* an associate editor for the *Integrated Encyclopedia of the Quran,* and a former advisor for interfaith affairs to the Jordanian Royal Court. He has traveled the world to engage in interfaith dialogue. Lumbard is a leader in promoting Jewish/Islamic dialogue and has published over a dozen articles in the fields of Sufism, Quranic Studies, Islamic Philosophy and Interfaith Dialogue and in 2001he founded the Islamic Research Institute. He organized the track on Islam and the environment for the conference on "Seizing an Alternative."

Denys Zhadiaiev teaches Philosophy and Business Ethics in the Department of Philosophy and Pedagogy of State HEI, National Mining University, in Ukraine. In 2011 he defended his dissertation, "Whitehead's Process Metaphysics: Historico-Philosophical Analysis," at Oles' Honchar Dnipropetrovsk National University. He joined the International Whitehead Network and is currently translating Whitehead's *Aims of Education* into both Ukrainian and Russian. He is not a member of the Orthodox Church, but he thinks some of its teachings may contribute to ecological civilization.

William E. Lesher is a pastor of the Evangelical Lutheran Church in America. He was President of the Lutheran School of Theology at Chicago from 1979-97. He is also a past president of Pacific Lutheran Seminary in Berkeley, Ca. Earlier he was pastor of inner-city congregations in St. Louis and Chicago. He has been active in the Parliament of the World's Religions since its centennial gathering in Chicago in 1993. He served on the Council preparing for the Parliament in 1999 in Cape Town and was elected to the Board of Trustees. He chaired the Council for the Parliament, 2003-09, convening the fourth and fifth Parliaments in Barcelona (2004), and Melbourne 2009.

Section Six

Bonnie Tarwater is an eco-feminist Christian minister, social activist, visual and theater artist, playwright, musician, and dream worker. She was ordained a Unitarian Universalist and has served both UU and United Church of Christ churches. She now serving the Church of Mary Magdalene and is director of Art, Wisdom, the Earth, and Dreams (AWED), dedicated to encouraging awe for the sacredness of life. She received an MFA from the American Conservatory Theater and an MDiv from Claremont School of Theology.

VERN VISICK is an environmentalist, scholar, and ordained minister who remains active in retirement at Pilgrim Place. He did his graduate work in ethics at the University of Chicago Divinity School. He served as campus minister at the University of Wisconsin, and was Director of New College Madison, an "Experiment in Prophetic Ministry." He led the Agenda for a Prophetic Faith, highlighting the church's interest in ethical issues. In 1996 he received the Francis Asbury award for "creativity in campus ministry programming." He played a key role in planning and organizing the "Seizing an Alternative" conference and chaired the section on society.

FRANZ RIFFERT teaches education at the University of Salzburg. He is a psychotherapist who has studied Catholic theology, philosophy, psychology, and education there and in Eichstätt. He researches philosophy of science, anthropological aspects of education, interdisciplinary relations between philosophy, education, and psychology, as well as such educational topics as learning cycles, a module approach to self-evaluation of school development, and subconscious processes in problem solving. He gave a section plenary address at the conference on "Seizing an Alternative."

JOSEPH BRACKEN, SJ, is Emeritus Professor of Theology at Xavier University in Cincinnati, Ohio, United States. He received his PhD from the University of Freiburg in Germany in 1968 and taught at University of Saint Mary of the Lake Mundelein Seminary and at Marquette University in Milwaukee before becoming Chairman of the Theology Department at Xavier in 1982. As a Catholic theologian he has made major contributions to the development of process philosophy. He organized a discussion of Whitehead and Thomas at the "Seizing an Alternative" conference.

VESSELIN PETROV is Professor at the Bulgarian Academy of Sciences Institute for Philosophical Research. He has an MA in Mathematics from Sofia University and a PhD from the Bulgarian Academy of Sciences, Sofia. He is editor in chief of the international philosophical journal, *Balkan Journal of Philosophy*. He is a member of the Union of Scientists in Bulgaria and president of the Bulgarian Ontological Society and the Bulgarian Center for Process Studies. He is currently the Executive Director of the International Process Network.

MARIA-TERESA TEIXEIRA holds a PhD in contemporary philosophy from Faculdade de Letras da Universidade de Lisboa. She is a researcher at Universidade de Coimbra. She is the author of two books: *Being, Becoming and Perishing: Creativity in Whitehead's Philosophy"* and *Consciousness and Action: Bergson and Neuroscience."* She has translated Whitehead's *Process and Reality* into Portuguese. She is the Executive Director-Elect of the International Process Network.

Section Seven

PHILIP CLAYTON is a philosopher and theologian specializing in the range of issues that arise at the intersection between science and religion. Over the last several decades he has published and lectured extensively on all branches of this debate, including the history of modern philosophy, philosophy of science, comparative religions, and constructive theology. He is president of the Institute for Postmodern Development of China, and his book on *Organic Marxism* is considered a serious option there. At the "Seizing an Alternative" conference, he chaired the section on science and organized a track on Whitehead and Marx.